THE FORMATION
OF INTER-ORGANIZATIONAL NETWORKS

The Formation of Inter-Organizational Networks

Edited by

MARK EBERS

OXFORD
UNIVERSITY PRESS

OXFORD

UNIVERSITY PRESS

Great Clarendon Street, Oxford OX2 6DP

Oxford University Press is a department of the University of Oxford.
It furthers the University's objective of excellence in research, scholarship,
and education by publishing worldwide in

Oxford New York

Athens Auckland Bangkok Bogotá Buenos Aires Calcutta
Cape Town Chennai Dar es Salaam Delhi Florence Hong Kong Istanbul
Karachi Kuala Lumpur Madrid Melbourne Mexico City Mumbai
Nairobi Paris São Paulo Singapore Taipei Tokyo Toronto Warsaw
and associated companies in Berlin Ibadan

Oxford is a registered trade mark of Oxford University Press
in the UK and certain other countries

Published in the United States
by Oxford University Press Inc., New York

© the various contributors 1997

The moral rights of the author have been asserted
Database right Oxford University Press (maker)

First published 1997
(Reprinted new as paperback 1999)

British Library Cataloguing in Publication Data

Data available

Library of Congress Cataloging in Publication Data

ISBN 0–19–828948–0 (hbk.)
ISBN 0–19–829602–9 (pbk.)

1 3 5 7 9 10 8 6 4 2

Typeset by Best-set Typesetter Ltd., Hong Kong
Printed in Great Britain
on acid-free paper
by Biddles Ltd., Guildford & King's Lynn

PREFACE

In the present times of corporate downsizing and outsourcing, many managers and management theorists ask which tasks a firm should fulfil in-house and for which it should rely on the market. While internal task accomplishment gives management more control over their products and services and can produce competitive advantage through co-specialization of resources, it also comes at a cost: bureaucratization, high fixed costs, and thus inflexibility. By subcontracting tasks to outside firms, on the other hand, a firm may become leaner, reduce its fixed costs, and can gain in flexibility; yet again there can be a costly downside: dependence on third parties, problematic co-ordination and control, and potential loss of unique capabilities and thus of competitive advantage.

In recent years, a third solution has been widely perceived by both managers and management scholars as a promising organizational alternative: the networked firm. Rather than going it alone or subcontracting, networked firms collaborate, for example, with their suppliers and customers in product development, pursue technological innovation through setting up joint ventures with unrelated companies, forge strategic alliances with their competitors to develop new markets, or enter long-term accords for collaboration with a limited number of select suppliers or distributors. Network forms of organizing seem so attractive because they allegedly combine the benefits of internal organization with those of subcontracting, while avoiding the respective drawbacks. Based on the much publicized achievements of exemplary companies such as Benetton, Corning, Nike, Philips, and Toyota, network forms of organizing accordingly have been hailed for their increased responsiveness and flexibility, lower overhead costs, greater efficiency of operations, rapid and effective decision-making, as well as for their learning and innovation potential (Contractor and Lorange 1988; Jarillo 1993; Lorenzoni and Baden-Fuller 1995; Miles and Snow 1986; Ohmae 1989).

While research is only beginning to produce empirical data on these expected achievements (Alter and Hage 1993; Hamel 1991; McGee, Dowling, and Megginson 1995; Mosakowski 1991; Provan and Milward 1995), more and more firms join the networking wave. A 1994 survey among 373 leading US, Canadian, European, and Mexican companies, for example, found that about one-fifth of the companies surveyed reported the level of their various alliance activities to be high and to remain so in the foreseeable future. At the same time, more than one-third of the respondents stated that their alliance activities were important or very important for their core businesses (Hart and Garone 1994: 43).

This book is concerned with when, why, and how firms engage in inter-organizational networking, rather than rely on arm's-length market relations or in-house procurement. The book discusses these issues under the heading of the formation of inter-organizational networks. Formation denotes, according to Webster's dictionary, (1) the act of giving form or shape to something or of taking form (its shaping or emergence) and (2) the manner in which a thing is formed (its form or structure).

By focusing on the formation of inter-organizational networks, the book addresses two topical issues that complement earlier research and are of considerable relevance for both management theorists and practitioners. First, this volume highlights the processes by which inter-organizational networks emerge and take form. The book thus goes beyond the prevalent focus on the motivations for networking, such as greater flexibility, cost savings, or enhanced learning. Of course, these motivations are important for understanding why firms may engage in networking relationships with other firms. However, from both a practical and theoretical point of view, it also seems important to know the different elements and intermediate steps that are required in order to fulfil these motivations. Several papers in this volume accordingly analyse which kinds of processes lead to the formation of a viable network, and which kinds of considerations and actions translate particular motivations into specific networking structures.

Secondly, with regard to the forms of inter-organizational networking, the book applies a micro-level perspective. It thereby complements the network-level and institutional-level perspectives taken by some earlier research (Alter and Hage 1993; Burt 1992; Fichman and Goodman 1996; Grabher 1993; Whitley 1993). Specifically, as the introductory chapter will spell out, this book suggests that the formation of inter-organizational networks can be fruitfully examined by analysing three kinds of micro-level relationships that link organizations, namely resource flows, information flows, and mutual expectations that exist between actors. None of these micro-level ties is entirely new to the literature. Nevertheless, the book suggests that they can be fruitfully combined in comparative analyses in order to achieve a better understanding and explanation of the contingencies and the processes that lead to the formation of inter-organizational networks.

The three main chapters of the book each focus on one of these micro-level relationships impacting on the formation of inter-organizational networks. The introductory chapter presents a general framework for the remainder of the book, and introduces in greater detail the single contributions to this volume. It suffices to say here that the book brings together research from a variety of disciplines (economics, sociology, information systems, organization studies, marketing, business strategy), theories (transaction cost economics, entrepreneurship theory, learning theory, population ecology theory, resource dependence theory), methodologies (case studies, historical studies, block-modelling, survey research), countries (Germany,

Italy, the Netherlands, Sweden, UK, USA), and settings (small- and large-firm networks, mechanical industry, free-standing companies, research and development (R&D) networks, product development networks). The book therefore to some extent reflects the richness and variety of the research on, and the practice of, inter-organizational networking. However, the individual contributions to this volume are not as disparate as the above-mentioned differences may seem to suggest; rather, they share important linkages, relate to a common agenda and framework. Thereby, over and above its substantive argument, it is hoped that the book also corroborates the fruitfulness of interdisciplinary dialogue within network research. Moreover, it is hoped that the book thus shares important features with its object of enquiry, inter-organizational networks: namely that both are made up of heterogeneous, yet complementary, elements that can produce joint gains by developing intensive linkages.

Mark Ebers

REFERENCES

Alter, C., and Hage, J. 1993. *Organizations Working Together.* Newbury Park, Calif.: Sage.

Burt, R. S. 1992. *Structural Holes: The Social Structure of Competition.* Cambridge, Mass.: Harvard University Press.

Contractor, F. J., and Lorange, P. (eds.) 1988. *Cooperative Strategies in International Business.* Lexington, Mass.: Lexington Books.

Fichman, M., and Goodman, P. 1996. 'Customer-Supplier Ties in Interorganizational Relations'. *Research in Organizational Behavior.* 18: 285–329.

Grabher, G. (ed.) 1993. *The Embedded Firm: The Socio-Economics of Industrial Networks.* London: Routledge.

Hamel, G. 1991. 'Competition for Competence and Inter-Partner Learning within International Strategic Alliances'. *Strategic Management Journal.* 12: 83–103.

Hart, M., and Garone, S. J. (eds.) 1994. *Making International Strategic Alliances Work.* New York: The Conference Board.

Jarillo, J. C. 1993. *Strategic Networks: Creating the Borderless Organization.* Oxford: Butterworth-Heinemann.

Lorenzoni, G., and Baden-Fuller, C. 1995. 'Creating a Strategic Center to Manage a Web of Partners'. *California Management Review.* 37 (3): 146–63.

McGee, J. E., Dowling, M. J., and Megginson, W. L. 1995. 'Cooperative Strategy and New Venture Performance: The Role of Business Strategy and Management Experience'. *Strategic Management Journal.* 16: 565–80.

Miles, R. E., and Snow, C. C. 1986. 'Organizations: New Concepts for New Forms'. *California Management Review.* 28 (Spring): 62–73.

Mosakowski, E. M. 1991. 'Organizational Boundaries and Economic Performance: An Empirical Study of Entrepreneurial Computer Firms'. *Strategic Management Journal.* 12: 115–33.

Ohmae, K. 1989. 'The Global Logic of Strategic Alliances'. *Harvard Business Review*. 67 (March–April): 143–54.

Provan, K. G., and Milward, H. B. 1995. 'A Preliminary Theory of Interorganizational Network Effectiveness: A Comparative Study of Four Community Mental Health Systems'. *Administrative Science Quarterly*. 40: 1–33.

Whitley, R. D. 1993. *European Business Systems: Firms and Markets in their National Contexts*. London: Sage.

PREFACE TO PAPERBACK EDITION

Network forms of conducting business have now established a formidable presence in both organizational practice and research. We continue to see more and more firms engaging in alliances, contractual joint ventures, and other forms of inter-organizational relationships. While the individual organizational forms are not entirely new, the fast proliferation of collaborative ventures in many industries clearly constitutes a noteworthy phenomenon, and may perhaps herald a significant change in the ways that firms try to build and sustain competitive advantage (Child and Faulkner 1998; Doz and Hamel 1998; Lewin, Long, and Carroll 1998; Volberda 1998).

In the two years since this book was first published, an unusually large number of individual publications and journal Special Issues (*Academy of Management Journal* 1997; *International Studies of Management & Organization* 1998; *Organization Science* 1998; *Organization Studies* 1998; *Strategic Management Journal* 1999; *Research in the Sociology of Organizations* 1999) have appeared that follow and reflect the rise of inter-organizational collaboration, testifying to the perceived importance of the subject area. It would be beyond the scope of this Preface to outline and discuss systematically how this new research has enriched our understanding of inter-organizational relationships and networks. Instead, I shall merely highlight a number of themes that have emerged in the recent literature and relate them to key issues pursued in this book.

Viewing recent developments in the field of research on inter-organizational networks, it seems that the traditional dissociation of social network analysis, studies of (mainly bilateral) inter-organizational relationships from an organizational and/or strategy perspective, and research on industrial districts is slowly eroding. Scholars from all three research traditions have begun mutually to acknowledge their research, increasingly attend the same conferences, and have started to enrich their studies by employing other than their own traditions' methods and research foci (e.g. Araujo and Brito 1998; Paniccia 1998; Staber, Schaefer, and Sharma 1996; Stuart 1998; Tsai and Goshal 1998).

As a consequence, we are beginning to see more studies that acknowledge, and in fact investigate, how influence factors from different levels of analysis together shape the forms and outcomes of inter-organizational relationships and networks. Oliver and Liebeskind (1998) in their study of the biotechnology industry, for example, found that three kinds of network relations (namely, intra-organizational network relations among individual organization members, inter-organizational network relations among individuals from different organizations, and inter-organizational network relations among organizations) each played a different role in providing critical resources for collaborating firms. Relatedly, Zaheer, McEvily, and Perrone (1998) report that inter-personal and inter-organizational trust have different impacts on the costs of negotiation and the level of conflict in inter-firm relationships, as well as on firm performance. Osborn *et al.* (1998) shows that the formation of international alliances depends on an alliance's industry, governance form, and product/knowledge flows among the partners; moreover, among all three mentioned influence factors there exist two- and three-way interaction effects, suggesting a mutual embeddedness of these variables.

With respect to the substantive focus of research, of the three important influence factors on the formation of inter-organizational relationships and networks highlighted in this book, resource flows and activity links still seem to figure most prominently in research. Numerous studies confirm that the nature and scope of the resource linkages, as well as the resource endowment of networked organizations, importantly shape the design, results, and the evolution of inter-organizational relationships (e.g. Dussauge and Garrette 1998; Gulati 1998; Khanna 1998; Madhok and Tallman 1998; Provan and Sebastian 1998). In a recent meta-analysis of 158 articles on inter-organizational relationships and networks that were published between 1980 and 1996 by four major social-science journals, Oliver and Ebers (1998) indeed found that resource dependence over time clearly represents the most frequently used, and the most central, concept as well as theory within the field. Network position and network 'theory' came in as close seconds.

While comparatively less significant over time, the second theme emphasized in this book—trust in inter-organizational relationships and networks—has also continued to receive considerable scholarly attention in recent journal Special Issues and other publications (e.g. Carney 1998; Oliver 1997; Zaheer, McEvily, and Perrone 1998). Among the more recent monographs devoted to this theme, Kramer and Tyler's (1996) book on trust has now been complemented by one edited by Lane and Bachmann (1998) that gives greater prominence to non-US scholars and settings, as well as to the role of trust in inter-organizational relations.

Our understanding of how information flows in general, and catalysts in particular, shape the formation of inter-organizational relationships and networks has been further enhanced in at least two directions. Some studies have fruitfully viewed the formation and change of inter-organizational networks as a process of social construction of reality (e.g. Araujo and Brito 1998; Delmestri 1998; Hardy, Phillips, and Lawrence 1998; Sydow, van Well, and Windeler 1998). By taking this perspective, the authors in different ways have alerted us to the importance of the cognitive schemes that actors apply to their networking activities, the processes of communication that create, change, and unmake shared meanings among the collaborating parties, and the power struggles among actors that underlie these processes. A second strand of the pertinent literature has analysed information flows among collaborating organizations in terms of learning processes (e.g. Ariño and de la Torre 1998; Hennart, Roehl, and Zietlow 1999; Larsson *et al*. 1998). While the theme of learning has always featured prominently in the field of inter-organizational network research, this latest research goes beyond stating learning as a major motive for collaboration. Rather, it analyses in greater depth the processes by which firms acquire knowledge from their partners, and the obstacles and challenges that have to be overcome in order to reap the benefits of mutual learning.

In the Conclusion to this volume, Anna Grandori and I noted as two important issues for the future development of the field, the analysis of the (social) costs and the dynamics of inter-organizational relationships and networks. While the first of these issues has not received much attention so far, over the past two years we could witness a significant increase in the number of studies that focus on development processes within inter-organizational relationships (e.g. Araujo and Brito 1998; Ariño and de la Torre 1998; Dussauge and Garrette 1998; Ebers 1999; Hennart, Roehl, and Zietlow 1999; Jones *et al*. 1998; Kumar and Nti 1998). As a major driving force behind the dynamic development of inter-organizational relationships, this research identifies discrepancies between expected and realized processes as well as outcomes of collaboration, which in turn affect actors' evaluations of the relationship and their subsequent action. Basically, many of these studies thus view the dynamic development of inter-organizational relationships as a process of intra- and inter-organizational learning. In my view, the addition of a much-needed dynamic perspective to heretofore largely comparative static research designs, coupled with analyses of intra- and inter-organizational learning processes, represent the most noteworthy recent developments in the field.

Mark Ebers

REFERENCES

Araujo, L., and Brito, C. 1998. 'Agency and Constitutional Ordering in Networks: A Case Study of the Port Wine Industry'. *International Studies of Management & Organization*. 27(4): 22–46.

Ariño, A., and de la Torre, J. 1998. 'Learning from Failure: Towards an Evolutionary Model of Collaborative Ventures'. *Organization Science*. 9: 306–25.

Carney, M. 1998. 'The Competitiveness of Networked Production: The Role of Trust and Asset Specificity'. *Journal of Management Studies*. 35: 457–79.

Child, J., and Faulkner, D. 1998. *Strategies of Co-operation: Managing Alliances, Networks, and Joint Ventures*. Oxford: Oxford University Press.

Delmestri, G. 1998. 'Do all Roads Lead to Rome . . . or Berlin? The Evolution of Intra- and Inter-Organizational Routines in the Machine-Building Industry in Italy and Germany'. *Organization Studies.* 19: 639–65.

Doz, Y., and Hamel, G. 1998. *Alliance Advantage: The Art of Creating Value through Partnering.* Cambridge, MA: Harvard Business School Press.

Dussauge, P., and Garrette, B. 1998. 'Anticipating the Evolutions and Outcomes of Strategic Alliances between Rival Firms'. *International Studies of Management & Organization.* 27(4): 104–26.

Ebers, M. 1999. 'The Dynamics of Inter-Organizational Relationships'. *Research in the Sociology of Organizations.* 17 (forthcoming).

Gulati, R. 1998. 'Alliances and Networks'. *Strategic Management Journal.* 19: 293–317.

Hardy, C., Phillips, N., and Lawrence, T. 1998. 'Distinguishing Trust and Power in Interorganizational Relations: Forms and Facades of Trust'. In C. Lane, and R. Bachmann (eds.). *Trust Within and Between Organizations: Conceptual Issues and Empirical Applications.* 64–87. Oxford: Oxford University Press.

Hennart, J.-F., Roehl, T., and Zietlow, D. S. 1999. ' "Trojan Horse" or "Workhorse"? The Evolution of US–Japanese Joint Ventures in the United States'. *Strategic Management Journal.* 20: 15–29.

Jones, C., Hesterly, W. S., Fladmoe-Lindquist, K., and Borgatti, S. P. 1998. 'Professional Service Constellations: How Strategies and Capabilities Influence Collaborative Stability and Change'. *Organization Science.* 9: 396–410.

Khanna, T. 1998. 'The Scope of Alliances'. *Organization Science.* 9: 340–55.

Kramer, R. M., and Tyler, T. R. (eds.) 1996. *Trust in Organizations: Frontiers of Theory and Research.* Thousand Oaks, CA: Sage.

Kumar, R., and Nti, K. O. 1998. 'Differential Learning and Interaction in Alliance Dynamics: A Process and Outcome Discrepancy Model'. *Organization Science.* 9: 356–67.

Lane, C., and Bachmann, R. (eds.) 1998. *Trust Within and Between Organizations: Conceptual Issues and Empirical Applications.* Oxford: Oxford University Press.

Larsson, R., Bengtsson, L., Henriksson, K., and Sparks, J. 1998. 'The Interorganizational Learning Dilemma: Collective Knowledge Development in Strategic Alliances'. *Organization Science.* 9: 285–305.

Lewin, A. Y., Long, C. P., and Carroll, T. N. 1998. 'The Co-Evolution of New Organizational Forms'. Working Paper, Center for Research on New Organization Forms, Duke University, Durham (NC).

Madhok, A., and Tallman, S. B. 1998. 'Resources, Transactions and Rents: Managing Value through Interfirm Collaborative Relationships'. *Organization Science.* 9: 326–39.

Oliver, A. L. 1997. 'The Nexus of Organizations and Professions: Networking through Trust'. *Sociological Inquiry.* 67: 227–45.

Oliver, A. L., and Ebers, M. 1998. 'Networking Network Studies: An Analysis of Conceptual Configurations in the Study of Inter-Organizational Relationships'. *Organization Studies.* 19: 549–83.

Oliver, A. L., and Liebeskind, J. P. 1998. 'Three Levels of Networking for Sourcing Intellectual Capital in Biotechnology'. *International Studies of Management & Organization.* 27(4): 76–103.

Osborn, R., Hagedoorn, J., Denekamp, J. G., Duysters, G., and Baughn, C. C. 1998. 'Embedded Patterns of International Alliance Formation'. *Organization Studies*. 19: 617–38.

Paniccia, I. 1998. 'One, a Hundred, Thousands of Industrial Districts: Organizational Variety in Local Networks of Small and Medium-Sized Enterprises'. *Organization Studies*. 19: 667–99.

Provan, K. G., and Sebastian, J. G. 1998. 'Networks within Networks: Service Link Overlap, Organizational Cliques, and Network Effectiveness'. *Academy of Management Journal*. 41: 453–63.

Staber, U. H., Schaefer, N. V., and Sharma, B. (eds.) 1996. *Business Networks: Prospects for Regional Development*. Berlin and New York: de Gruyter.

Stuart, T. E. 1998. 'Network Positions and Propensities to Collaborate: An Investigation of Strategic Alliance Formation in a High-Technology Industry'. *Administrative Science Quarterly*. 43: 668–98.

Sydow, J., van Well, B., and Windeler, A. 1998: 'Networked Networks: Financial Services Networks in the Context of their Industry'. *International Studies of Management & Organization*. 27(4): 47–75.

Tsai, W., and Goshal, S. 1998. 'Social Capital and Value Creation: The Role of Intrafirm Networks'. *Academy of Management Journal*. 41: 464–76.

Volberda, H. W. 1998. *Building the Flexible Firm: How to Remain Competitive*. Oxford: Oxford University Press.

Zaheer, A., McEvily, B., and Perrone, V. 1998. 'Does Trust Matter? Exploring the Effects of Interorganizational and Interpersonal Trust on Performance'. *Organization Science*. 9: 141–59.

ACKNOWLEDGEMENTS

The research presented originates from a collaboration within a sub-programme on inter-organizational networks that I have the pleasure of co-ordinating. The papers assembled in this volume stem from the first workshop that I organized in Berlin for this sub-programme. The sub-programme is part of a larger programme entitled 'European Management and Organization in Transition (EMOT)', which is sponsored by the European Science Foundation (ESF). I take this opportunity to gratefully acknowledge the generous financial support by the ESF for the EMOT programme.

This book would not have been possible without the contributions of a number of people whose valuable support I greatly appreciate. Anna Grandori and Richard Whitley deserve much praise for initiating and skilfully directing the EMOT programme, which at the time was aptly administered by Glenn Morgan as research co-ordinator. My sincere thanks also go to Martin Hermesch, Frank Kullak, and Edeltraut Pöppe for helping organize the workshop from which the papers of this book originated. A number of reviewers provided thoughtful evaluations of manuscripts and constructive suggestions for revision, namely Howard E. Aldrich, Ronald S. Batenburg, Rudi K. Bresser, Gian Carlo Cainarca, James Crowley, Robert D. Galliers, Anna Grandori, Martin Hermesch, Kristian Kreiner, Bengt-Åke Lundvall, Martin Matzke, Andreas Mehlhorn, Niels Noorderhaven, Johannes M. Pennings, Torger Reve, John Scott, Steve Smithson, and Richard Whitley. I am most grateful for the helpful advice these scholars generously provided and for their gracious efforts to try and make this book a better product. At the same time, I wish to thank the authors for their responsiveness to the feedback they received on their papers. I extend my gratitude to David Musson of Oxford University Press for his gentle editorial support (and patience). Finally, I wish to warmly thank those last in the production chain: Rowanne Sayer for helping authors overcome language barriers by language-editing the manuscripts, Stefanie Heucke and Carmen Bosch for checking the typescripts, completing bibliographical information and bringing the manuscripts into the form required by the publisher, Monika Blank for cheerfully administering the project, and Hilary Walford and Leonie Hayler of OUP for courteously prodding me, for copy-editing the manuscripts, and preparing them for print.

Mark Ebers

CONTENTS

LIST OF FIGURES

LIST OF TABLES

LIST OF ABBREVIATIONS

AMD	Advanced Micro Devices
BT&D	British Telecom and DuPont
CAD	computer-aided design
CAM	computer-aided manufacture
CD	compact disc
CEO	chief executive officer
CIOR	co-operative inter-organizational relationships
CNC	computer numeric control
CONCOR	convergence of iterated correlations
DRAM	dynamic random access memory
EC	European Community
EDI	electronic data interchange
EMOT	European Management and Organization in Transition
ESF	European Science Foundation
FPME	fluid power machinery and equipment
FIAM	Fraunhofer-Institut für Angewandte Materialforschung
IOS	inter-organizational system
IS	information systems
LWF	Laboratorium für Werkstoff- und Fügetechnik at Paderborn University
MCC	Microelectronics and Computer Technology Corporation
NBF	new biotechnology firm
NPD	new product development
OEM	original equipment manufacturer
PPM	packing and packaging machinery
R&D	research and development
RAM	random access memory
SCA	sustained competitive advantage
SME	small and medium-sized enterprises
SRAM	static random access memory
VCR	video cassette recorder
VW	Volkswagen

LIST OF CONTRIBUTORS

LUIS ARAUJO	Lancaster University, UK
MARK CASSON	University of Reading, UK
HOWARD COX	South Bank University, London, UK
PAUL DE LAAT	University of Groningen, The Netherlands
ANNA DUBOIS	Chalmers University of Technology, Gothenburg, Sweden
GEOFF EASTON	Lancaster University, UK
MARK EBERS	Augsburg University, Germany
ALESSANDRO GRANDI	University of Bologna, Italy
ANNA GRANDORI	University of Modena, Italy
HÅKAN HÅKANSSON	Uppsala University, Sweden
CHRISTOPHER P. HOLLAND	University of Manchester, UK
ANDREA LIPPARINI	University of Bologna, Italy
†GEOFF LOCKETT	University of Leeds, UK
ALESSANDRO LOMI	University of Bologna, Italy
SUSANNE LÜTZ	Max-Plank-Institut für Gesellschaftsforschung, Cologne, Germany
PETER SMITH RING	Loyola Marymount University, Los Angeles, Calif., USA
MAURIZIO SOBRERO	University of Bologna, Italy

I

INTRODUCTION

1

Explaining Inter-Organizational Network Formation

MARK EBERS

In recent years, we have witnessed remarkable growth in various forms of co-operation among organizations. There has been a considerable increase in inter-organizational alliances during the 1980s, particularly in high-technology industries (Haagedoorn 1993; 1995; Hergert and Morris 1988; Mowery 1988). Within the US biotechnology industry, for example, firms without any formal co-operative ties to other firms have become increasingly rare, while the connectivity of firms within the industry has increased significantly (Powell *et al*. 1996). In the hospital systems software industry, inter-firm co-operation was unusual up until 1970, increased slightly in the 1970s, but showed significant growth in the 1980s and 1990s (Mitchell and Singh 1996). A similar pattern can be detected for the car industry. According to Helper (1991), beginning in the 1980s US car manufacturers have been reducing their degree of vertical integration and have increasingly relied on longer-term contracts with a limited number of tightly linked suppliers. Many European car companies also adopted this strategy at around the same time (Altmann and Sauer 1989; Morris and Imrie 1991; Turnbull *et al*. 1989). In other industries inter-organizational co-operation has been a more long-standing practice. In construction, for example, consortia and enduring sub-contracting relationships are well-entrenched forms of organizing large projects (Eccles 1981). In the US film industry, after World War II, the major studios progressively outsourced production of feature films while retaining finance and distribution (Robins 1993); therefore, for some time now, persistent patterns of contracting are related less to formal organizations such as the studios, but crystallize out of relatively stable networks of producers, directors, cinematographers, actors, and musicians (Faulkner and Anderson 1987). Regional industrial districts in the Italian textile and clothing (Brusco 1982; Lazerson 1988, 1993; Mariotti and Cainarca 1986), German metals (Grabher 1993*b*; Sabel 1989; Herrigel 1993), or US electronics industries (Saxenian 1994) represent other often-mentioned examples of long-standing patterns of co-operative inter-organizational relations, as do Japanese Keiretsu (Gerlach 1992) and Korean Chaebol (Steers *et al*. 1989).

In the following, we shall refer to these and other forms of inter-organizational co-operation (such as contractual joint ventures) as inter-organizational networking relationships. If more than two organizations are linked through such networking relationships, they constitute an inter-organizational network. At this point, it suffices to say that inter-organizational networking represents a particular form of organizing, or governing, exchange relationships among organizations. While networking can take different forms, all these forms are characterized by recurring exchange relationships among a limited number of organizations that retain residual control of their individual resources yet periodically jointly decide over their use. A more extensive characterization of inter-organizational networks will be offered later in this chapter.

Irrespective of their precise definition, the rise and extending scope in practice of co-operative inter-organizational relationships raises a number of questions for research. Why do firms (increasingly) engage in inter-organizational co-operation and when? With whom are firms likely to ally and why? How do firms organize and control their co-operation? Why and when do they choose a particular organizational form of co-operation? Which forms of network structure result? What are the outcomes and implications for the networked firms and for third parties?

A surging wave of publications has addressed these and other relevant questions (e.g. Alter and Hage 1993; Axelsson and Easton 1992; Burt 1992; Contractor and Lorange 1988; Grabher 1993*a*; Håkansson and Snehota 1995; Jarillo 1993; Nohria and Eccles 1992). It would be beyond the scope of this chapter to try to comprehensively discuss the results and achievements of this and other pertinent research (see Grandori and Soda 1995; Mizruchi and Galaskiewicz 1993; Powell 1990; Powell and Smith-Doerr 1994; Sydow 1992). Instead, I shall try and indicate where and how the present volume might complement and add to this body of literature.

This book focuses on the formation(s) of inter-organizational networks, that is, on the contingencies and processes that lead to the emergence of inter-organizational networking relationships and to particular forms of organizing these relationships. Therefore, in the first section of this chapter I shall present a summary of the results of some earlier approaches to the analysis of the formation(s) of inter-organizational networks.

Secondly, I shall introduce the conceptual framework that was used to organize the contributions to this volume. This conceptual framework can be conducive to understanding and explaining inter-organizational network formation. It takes as its vantage point three content dimensions of micro-level ties that link organizations within inter-organizational networking relationships, namely resource flows, information flows, and flows of mutual expectations. I shall try to demonstrate the potential fruitfulness of the conceptual framework in two ways. On the one hand, I argue, it provides a common conceptual ground for systematically distinguishing network forms of organizing from alternative institutional forms of governing economic exchange relations, namely the market and the firm. It therefore provides a basis for systematically analysing and comparing these institutional alternatives, for example in terms of their relative merits and shortcomings under different circumstances. On the other hand, I shall try to show that the proposed conceptual framework can be helpful for analysing important contingencies and processes of inter-organizational network formation. This volume places particular emphasis on three such contingencies and related processes, each exemplifying one of the three above-mentioned content dimensions of ties. Specifically, it highlights the roles that activity links, trust, and catalysts play for the formation(s) of inter-organizational networks. For each of these concepts I shall therefore spell out in general terms how it relates to the formation of inter-organizational networks.

Thirdly, I shall briefly introduce the individual contributions to this volume. This overview highlights how the individual papers relate to the proposed conceptual framework and contribute to the aims of the book. I leave it to the concluding chapter by Ebers and Grandori to present a summary of the general argument of the book and to outline some implications for organizational research and practice.

EXPLAINING THE EMERGENCE OF INTER-ORGANIZATIONAL NETWORKS

A rich literature has developed that examines when, where, why, and how organizations engage in inter-organizational networking. As in the field of organization studies as a whole, pertinent research has employed a number of different approaches and theories. These include industrial economics, organizational economics, industrial marketing and purchasing, organizational sociology, game theory, resource dependence theory, population ecology, institutional theory, and social network approaches. Each of these major theoretical strands of research has produced distinct explanations of inter-organizational network formation that partially overlap and partially compete (for summaries and reviews see Alter and Hage 1993; Auster 1994; Grandori and Soda 1995; Mizruchi and Galaskiewicz 1993; Sydow 1992). Rather than discussing these different approaches, in the following I shall summarize from this literature some of the more important factors that have been found to enable, trigger, and influence the formation of inter-organizational networking relationships. It should be noted at the outset, however, that we currently know comparatively more about the factors that account for the emergence of inter-organizational networks than about the factors that influence the organizational forms of networking relationships.

This is why this introductory chapter will give greater prominence to the first-mentioned issue, while the concluding chapter of this book, because among other topics it addresses implications for future research, will say a little more about the latter.

Research has tried to explain the formation of inter-organizational networks at three levels of analysis: the actor level, the level of pre-existing relations among actors, and the institutional level. At the actor level, research has mainly concentrated on discerning the motivations of corporate actors for forging networking relationships, whereas at the relational and institutional levels, scholars have sought to identify conditions that facilitate and constrain (different forms of) inter-organizational co-operation.

Motives

The motives for engaging in an inter-organizational networking relationship can be quite varied. Nevertheless, in the realm of business organizations they ultimately boil down to two main sets of motives.

On the one hand, through co-operation, organizations attempt to increase their revenue. Inter-organizational networking can be conducive to this end, because co-operating organizations can collude against common rivals or reduce competition by binding competitors as allies (Porter and Fuller 1986). Furthermore, through networking, organizations can access complementary resources and/or capabilities or can closely co-ordinate their use of resources; in this way, they hope to enhance their competitiveness, for example, in terms of improved products, better market access, or faster market entry, and thus to increase their revenues (Contractor and Lorange 1988; Harrigan 1985; Zajac and Olsen 1993).

On the other hand, inter-organizational co-operation can also be motivated by cost reduction. Cost savings may be the result of economies of scale and/or scope that can be achieved, for example, through joint research, marketing, or production (Contractor and Lorange 1988; Håkansson and Snehota 1995). Moreover, in specific circumstances organizations may establish networking relationships in order to economize on the governance costs of co-ordinating their activities (Hennart 1991; Thorelli 1986). For example, inter-organizational networking represents a cost-efficient way of gaining access to crucial know-how that can neither be made available internally nor be easily transferred by licensing (Badaracco 1991; Dyer 1996; Kreiner and Schultz 1993; Teece 1986). Relatedly, inter-organizational networking is seen as a fast, effective, and efficient way of learning and of short-circuiting the process of acquiring and appropriating skills (Dodgson 1993; Hamel 1991). Finally, risk reduction comes into play as a cost-related motivation for inter-organizational networking when organizations seek to spread financial or other risks, for example when shouldering (mostly large) innovations or other risky projects (Contractor and Lorange 1988; Mariti and Smiley 1983).

Drawing on an analysis and integration of the earlier literature, Oliver (1990) offered a slightly different summary of the main reasons why organizations establish inter-organizational relationships with one another. She proposed the following six predictive contingencies of inter-organizational relationship formation: (1) necessity, when organizations are mandated through law or regulation by higher authorities to establish relationships; (2) asymmetry that allows one party to exercise power or control over another one or its resources; (3) reciprocity, when through co-operation organizations can pursue common or mutually beneficial goals or interests; (4) efficiency, when through co-operation organizations can achieve higher input/output ratios; (5) stability, when through co-operation organizations can better forestall, forecast, or absorb uncertainty affecting their activities; and (6) legitimacy, when through co-operation organizations can establish or enhance their reputation, image, prestige, or congruence with prevailing norms.

Glaister and Buckley (1996) conducted one of the few studies that have compared the relative importance of different motivations for inter-organizational networking (see also Mariti and Smiley 1983). In their empirical study of ninety-four international equity and non-equity joint ventures involving British firms, Glaister and Buckley distilled five underlying factors from an original list of sixteen strategic motivations in a factor analysis. In diminishing order of explained variance, these key motivational factors for engaging in international joint ventures were technology development, market power, market development, resource specialization (loading on higher margins, scale economies, faster payback), and large project size (loading on the spreading of risks, low product diversification). The study further showed that the most important sets of motivating factors predominate irrespective of the contractual form of the alliance, relative partner size, primary geographical location, broad industry group of the alliance, and nationality of the non-British partner.

Although it is important to know what motivates organizational decision-makers to forge inter-organizational relationships, motives alone provide only a weak guide when trying to explain the emergence of inter-organizational networking relationships or their organizational form. This is because some of the above-mentioned motives *per se* could equally motivate organizational actors to vertically integrate or to outsource particular activities. For a more complete explanation, we therefore need to know in addition under which conditions, and why, each of the noted motivations will be prevalent; moreover, we also need to clarify under which conditions, and for what reasons, these motives will lead organizational actors to engage in inter-organizational networking, rather than in, say, hierarchical or market relationships; and finally, we need to elucidate the processes by

which particular motivations lead to the establishment of particular networking structures under these conditions. While the first of these questions
to my knowledge has not yet been addressed, the (perhaps more important) second question has received some attention in the literature, while
research is only beginning to tackle the third question. Let us look at the
issues in turn.

Contingencies

Research examining which conditions facilitate and constrain the formation of inter-organizational networking relationships has mostly been
conducted at the institutional and relational levels of analysis. Institutional-
level studies trace back the formation of inter-organizational networks to
particularities of the institutional environment, and its dominant social
institutions, characteristic of the society in which a network is formed.
Relational-level research tends to study how particularities of the various
links and interdependencies that exist among organizations, and/or among
individuals from different organizations, influence their inclination to
engage in inter-organizational networking. Institutional-level studies thus
base their explanations on attributes of the institutional system under
scrutiny, whereas relational-level research emphasizes as explanatory
factors the attributes that characterize the content of the linkages among
actors, be they individuals, groups, or organizations. While they represent
different levels of analysis, both these approaches to the analysis of inter-
organizational networking share the view that the social and economic
context within which organizations are embedded significantly influences
the formation of inter-organizational networks.

At the *institutional level*, research has pointed out how certain political,
legal, cultural, industry, and/or regional environmental conditions impact on
the likelihood of network formation. With regard to explaining the formation of business networks found in Japan and other East Asian countries,
scholars for example have emphasized the supporting influence of the role
of the state in industrial development, particularities of the financial, tax,
and corporate governance systems, and particular cultural norms prevailing in these societies (see e.g. Dore 1986; Gerlach 1992; Hamilton and
Biggart 1988; Whitley 1993*a*). Other studies have concentrated on the institutions that have come to prevail in different European countries, and their
characteristic variations, and have spelled out how these contribute to
explaining the particular business networks that can be found in these societies (Lane and Bachmann 1996; Scott 1987; Whitley 1993*b*). Research is
only beginning, though, to develop a theoretically systematic and more
general account of which societal institutions are of particular importance
for, and how they interact in, the social construction and reproduction of
'business systems' (Whitley and Kristensen 1995).

On a regional level, institutional conditions fostering the formation of inter-organizational networks have been investigated in analyses of regional and industrial districts. Here, one line of reasoning stresses that networking among firms is enabled and supported by regionally embedded institutions such as chambers of commerce, employers' unions, banks, science parks, universities, and training centres (Saxenian 1994). These institutions often act as informational brokers that support the exchange of information among firms, encourage and facilitate mutual learning, and can thus foster the responsiveness, adaptability, and innovativeness of networked firms (Herrigel 1995; Gemünden *et al.* 1992). Moreover, these institutions also often provide important resources, for example, capital or access to distribution channels and potential customers. Because of this institutional backing, networked firms enjoy competitive advantages over non-networked rivals.

According to another line of reasoning, inter-organizational networking is traced back to the spatial clustering of specialized resources and know-how in regional or industrial districts. This attribute of districts is held to be conducive to networking, because smaller, co-specialized firms can share and flexibly recombine their resources and capabilities. They can thus more easily learn from one another and be lighter on their feet than larger, more integrated competitors. Collectively, these firms are therefore said to be able to adapt more quickly to changes in demand, both quantitatively and qualitatively (Sabel 1989; Saxenian 1994). Since these advantages are particularly important in markets characterized by steep rates and costs of innovation, short product life cycles, and pressure to respond quickly to changing customer needs, inter-organizational networking seems particularly salient under such conditions (Axelsson and Easton 1992; Powell 1990; Powell *et al.* 1996; Teece 1992). A similar line of reasoning also features prominently in much of the strategic management literature that has been devoted to inter-organizational networking (Contractor and Lorange 1988; Hamel 1991; Jarillo 1993; McGee *et al.* 1995). However, in both fields there is still a dearth of comparative studies that could flesh out predictive contingencies of inter-organizational networking that are effective across industries, across industrial or regional districts respectively, as well as across different forms of networking.

A different line of argument in the literature on regional and industrial districts focuses on the *relational level* of analysis. It stresses how pre-existing social relations among the individuals in a region foster and support the development of more formal business networking relationships among organizations (Chapters 7 and 8, this volume; Eisenhardt and Schoonhoven 1996; Håkansson and Snehota 1989; Granovetter 1994; Herrigel 1995). The reasoning here is that family and friendship ties among local business people, common membership in local trade associations, sports clubs, and political institutions create and sustain social networks of mutual obligation, loyalty, and trust. In such cases, business relations are not only governed and monitored by formal contracting but also through these social ties. In business relations, social sanctioning therefore complements economic sanctioning. This makes it possible for actors who are members of the same social network to economize on more formal contractual safeguards when conducting business with one another. Moreover, network members through their social network can have better access to resources, for example, capital and political influence. Their intense social ties also permit and foster a freer and more reliable exchange of information among network members. This in turn encourages mutual learning and innovation.[1] For all these reasons, it is argued, inter-organizational networking relationships are more likely to be formed when actors can rely on dense and spatially constrained social networks.

A second strand of relational-level literature has explored the effects on the formation of networking relationships of organizations' positions in their industry. Central to this research is the thesis that *how* potential relationships are located within a given set of relations significantly influences *whether* they will be realized. Burt (1992) in particular has developed an impressive model that specifies how different positions within a web of relationships affect the opportunities of the incumbents of these positions. In their empirical studies, Kogut *et al.* (1992) as well as Gulati (1995) have shown, for example, that over time the number and density of earlier direct and indirect linkages among firms play an increasingly positive, and more important, role for their choice to co-operate than firm-specific attributes such as size and age. The scholars attribute this finding to the fact that a larger number of linkages provides firms with more and better information about one another; firms therefore have a greater understanding of each others' intentions and capabilities. The formation of new networking relationships is fostered, because these potential partners are thus in a better position to detect new opportunities for co-operation as well as to handle the risks that are associated with such relationships.

A different, and perhaps more widespread way of conceptualizing the positions of firms within the wider web of their inter-organizational linkages has been to focus on the interdependencies that exist among firms (Chapters 2 and 3, this volume; Håkansson and Snehota 1995; Oliver 1990). The general argument here is that firms will forge networking relations to govern their access to those resources and capabilities which in the actors' view will reduce their dependence or otherwise improve their competitive

---

[1] However, the literature on industrial and regional districts has also pointed out some longer-term disadvantages of inter-organizational networking under such conditions. Grabher (1993*b*) for example argues that intense social ties can also blind the members of a network in the sense that they lock them into a specific world-view. He shows for the German Ruhr district that such cognitive lock-in can lead to reduced responsiveness by networked firms to changing conditions and can thus sometimes forward their economic decline.

position. In their study reconstructing the network of strategic linkages in the global car industry, Nohria and Garcia-Pont (1991) were able indirectly to confirm this thesis. These scholars meaningfully partitioned the network of intra-industry linkages into several strategic blocks, and they found only a few differences in the set of strategic capabilities across blocks.

More direct evidence of the positive effects of organizational interdependence on the formation of networking relationships has been produced in the literature on interlocking directorates and joint ventures. Pertinent research for example showed that business organizations often use their boards to co-opt representatives of other organizations on which they perceive themselves to be dependent. In the case of financial dependence, measured for instance by the debt/equity ratio, representatives of financial institutions are likely to be invited to join; in the case of high downstream-market dependence, important customers may sit on the boards (for an overview see Pfeffer 1987; for recent empirical data on board interlocks in Germany and the UK and their predictors see Windolf and Beyer 1993). Within the joint venture literature, transaction cost theoretical arguments figure prominently. These stress quite generally the important role that investments in relationship-specific assets can play for the formation of joint ventures (for an overview see Kogut 1988). These factors have also been found to impact on the particular form of joint venture that is realized. Pisano (1989), for example, found that the presence of R&D in a collaboration, the wide scope of such collaboration, and small numbers of potential co-operation partners led organizations to engage in equity joint ventures, rather than contractual ones (see also Blodgett 1991; Osborn and Baughn 1990).

Others likewise argue that dependence on R&D resources and know-how is an important contingency of inter-organizational co-operation (Baughn and Osborn 1990; Chapter 6, this volume; Haagedorn 1993; Teece 1992). With respect to industries experiencing rapid technological change, authors claim that because advanced technological systems are not and cannot be created in splendid isolation, innovating organizations must form horizontal and vertical linkages to be successful. Teece (1992) highlights a number of operational and strategic interdependencies characteristic of innovative activities (e.g. the coupling of users and suppliers, coupling to competitors, connections among technologies) that are most appropriately organized by inter-organizational networking. According to Teece, the interdependencies that are crucial for successful innovation can be handled more effectively and efficiently by inter-organizational networking than by the price system of markets or the internal organization of firms. As compared to the price system, he argues, networking has advantages because it allows for close and concise co-ordination of investments, better avoids duplication of effort, and can overcome appropriability problems associated with technological spillovers; while compared to internal hierarchical organization, networking bears stronger incentives and provides quick and efficient feedback mechanisms.

With regard to resource dependencies in the areas of procurement and distribution, Reve (1992) reports on horizontal and vertical networks that were formed to overcome the dependence that individual organizations experienced in relation to their highly concentrated supplier and buyer markets. Relatedly, in their study of strategic alliances in the semiconductor industry, Eisenhardt and Schoonhoven (1996) find that a vulnerable strategic position (characterized by emergent markets, innovative technologies, or high competition) encourages firms to form strategic alliances.

Dyer (1996) in his study of supplier networks in the car industry explores specific investments as a source of mutual dependence among organizations. His research reveals that tightly integrated and spatially condensed production networks with high levels of co-specialized human resources outperform more loosely integrated production networks with low levels of inter-firm specialization. Alter and Hage (1993) extend the standard resource dependence argument by an organizational one about the effects of technology. They investigate empirically with regard to a sample of public agencies how the technology of task accomplishment (characterized e.g. by the tasks' scope, intensity, duration, and volume) influences the network structure and the co-ordination mechanisms that actors employ. These authors have thus conducted one of the few studies that have examined, compared, and tried to explain in some detail different forms of inter-organizational networking (other examples include Grandori and Soda 1995; Oliver 1990, 1991).

Although we have discussed them separately above, the three levels of analysis of actors, their relations, and their institutional embeddedness should not be viewed in isolation. Rather, between them there exist recursive influences which should be considered when analysing the formation of inter-organizational networks. Obviously actors' motives and strategies influence the networking relationships that emerge (for a vivid example see Chapter 9). And conversely, as Burt's (1992) research has suggested, particular structural features of networks create or constrain possibilities for action by individuals and organizations. Network relationships, through their institutionalization and outcomes, also have repercussions at the institutional level; for example, they change the industry structure, the resource allocation within a region, as well as the distribution of power and wealth (Kamann 1993; Osborn *et al.* 1993; Chapter 4, this volume; Perrow 1992). Finally, as pertinent research described above has outlined, institutional factors in turn involve incentives and restrictions which have an impact on the networking relationships that are emerging within a specific institutional context and on actors' behaviour (see e.g. Chapter 7). Therefore, a full account of the formation of inter-organizational networking relationships needs to consider all three levels of analysis and their interrelations.

Processes

Research hitherto has focused mainly on the motives and contingencies of inter-organizational networking and its structures. We know much less about how inter-organizational networking relationships are built, develop, and dissolve. That is, we know little about the intermediate processes, the steps and activities, that translate motives into particular network structures and about the contingencies that facilitate and constrain these processes. However, a few scholars have addressed these issues.

What are the main phases of network formation? Research has provided different answers, yet most suggest three, similar developmental phases. Larson (1992) in her case studies of high-growth entrepreneurial networking relations distinguishes a pre-networking stage in which the preconditions for establishing a relationship are set out; a second phase in which conditions to build a relationship are established; and a third phase in which the networking relationship solidifies. Gray (1987) identifies a problem-setting phase in which potential partners identify one another and mutually scrutinize possible joint interests; a direction-setting phase in which potential networking partners articulate their values and begin to develop a sense of common purpose; and a structuring phase in which the partners develop and build the structures that are intended to support their co-operative activities. In a similar vein, Snow and Thomas (1993) distinguish the phases of network formation, development, and testing.

These scholars then identify for each of the phases a characteristic set of contingencies that facilitate and constrain the full completion of each phase. In this way, they provide a more detailed account of the conditions of network formation. Larson (1992), for example, found that personal reputations, prior relations, and firm reputations were important preconditions that had to be fulfilled before partners began to contemplate establishing a networking relationship. According to her study, partners would only build a networking relationship when they perceived mutual economic advantage, had agreed on a trial period, and when one of the parties took the lead. For the relationship to work, operational and strategic integration were required as well as some social control. Though arguing on the basis of a similar phase distinction, Gray (1987) proposes a slightly different set of facilitative conditions for each phase. She strongly emphasizes the importance of interdependence among the actors, of shared perceptions of legitimacy, and shared power. Finally, Snow and Thomas (1993), drawing on case studies of three networks in the health care industry, examine the facilitative influence in the phases of network formation of three broker roles and their associated, phase-specific behaviours. These will be discussed in more detail in the next section of this paper. In addition, the longitudinal studies by Gulati (1995) and Powell *et al.* (1996) provide evidence that once network relations are established, experience with networking, mutual learning, and diversity of ties stimulate the formation of further network-ing relationships.

While the above-mentioned process studies outline sequential models of network development, Ring and Van de Ven (1994) propose a cyclical model. A further difference between their model and others is that it centres on the social-psychological processes as much as on the managerial issues of network formation. Specifically, Ring and Van de Ven (1994) suggest that networking involves an ongoing, repeated process of negotia-tion of mutual expectations, commitments for future action, and executions of commitments which is assessed in terms of equity and efficiency. Under-lying these cyclical phases are formal and informal processes of sense-making, understanding, committing, and enacting (for an extension of the argument see Chapter 5). On the basis of an elaboration of these processes and their effects under various conditions, the authors then develop specific propositions with regard to the development, forms, and dissolution of net-working relationships.

On the basis of in-depth case studies, Doz (1996) inductively developed a similar framework for analysing the evolution of co-operation in strategic alliances. His process model spells out how specific initial conditions (task definition, partners' routines, structure of the organizational interface, and actors' expectations) facilitate or hamper partner learning (about the envi-ronment, tasks, processes, skills, goals). The case studies suggested that more successful alliance projects realize a sequence of interactive cycles of learn-ing that allow for a re-evaluation of the project (in terms of efficiency, equity, and adaptability), which in turn leads to readjustments in the initial conditions of alliance partner co-operation. Conversely, less successful alliance projects were highly inertial, did not result in mutual learning, and failed periodically to readjust individual partner behaviours and the condi-tions of co-operation to changing circumstances.

When reviewing the impressive body of research on inter-organizational networking that has only been briefly and selectively described above, a number of impressions remain. Without anticipating Chapter 11, we can note the following. First, the surging wave of publications demonstrates that researchers have noticed and responded to the growing importance in prac-tice of inter-organizational networking.

Secondly, the literature is quite substantial yet fragmented and disjointed. It is fragmented among disciplines, theoretical bases, levels of analysis, and substantive foci of research. Though they contribute to the richness of the field, these differences not uncommonly also create communication barri-ers among scholars studying networks and network phenomena. As a con-sequence, Nohria (1992: 14) notes, 'we are nowhere near having a systematic framework or theory for predicting what kinds of ties matter under what kinds of circumstances in what ways'.

Thirdly, much of the research stems from a single institutional setting, relates to organizations from one or a few industries, and/or focuses on one or two forms of networking only. Comparative research that would allow us to systematically detect and explain similarities and differences in the antecedents and outcomes of formation of networks across institutional settings, industries, and organizational forms of networking is still rather rare. Therefore, although the literature has made valuable contributions to our understanding of inter-organizational networking, we still have some way to go before we can claim that we sufficiently understand when, where, why, and how organizations form which kinds of inter-organizational relationships and to what effect. Accordingly, I shall refrain from summarizing here the main factors that account for the formation of inter-organizational networking on the basis of the research outlined above.[2]

Fourthly, this state of affairs suggests that more research is needed that collects data at multiple levels of analysis, utilizes multiple methods, compares the formation of different kinds of inter-organizational relationships, compares formation across settings, and on this basis develops and tests predictions about the formation of inter-organizational networks and about the outcomes of inter-organizational networking (Oliver 1990; Aldrich and Whetten 1981). The following section proposes one of a number of ways in which we might begin to tackle this task.

A CONCEPTUALIZATION OF INTER-ORGANIZATIONAL NETWORKS

In both theory and practice, the notion of inter-organizational network is applied to a wide variety of relationships among organizations, for example, to joint ventures, strategic alliances, corporate interlocks, single-sourcing relationships, industrial districts, consortia, social networks, and others (cf. Borys and Jemison 1989; Grandori and Soda 1995; Oliver 1990; Powell 1990). This is possible because the notion of 'network' is sufficiently abstract. It can be employed to characterize any set of recurring ties (e.g. resource, friendship, informational ties) among a set of nodes (e.g. individuals, groups, organizations, information systems, and so on) (Fombrun 1982). Recurring buyer–supplier relations among a set of organizations in a market therefore qualify as a network phenomenon, as do the recurring

---

[2] This assessment is underscored by the fact that scholars who have singled out such main explanatory factors have reached different conclusions. For example, Oliver (1990) concludes from her review of the literature that three generalizable conditions facilitate inter-organizational relationship formation: resource scarcity, an intermediate level of industry concentration, and domain consensus among prospective networking partners. By contrast, Powell (1990) stresses as critical contingencies of network formation know-how-based activities, the demand for speed, and trust among actors. While these lists are not mutually exclusive and are both supported by pertinent research, we do need more comparative research before we are in a position to assess the relative importance of the different explanatory factors offered.

interactions among the members of a (network) firm (Miles and Snow 1986), and R&D alliances among divisions of different firms. As these uses show, because the notion of network is so general, its application to organizational analyses runs the risk of extending the notion indiscriminately until it ceases to have whatever analytical and theoretical power it might possess for organizational research (Aldrich and Whetten 1981; Nohria 1992; Salancik 1995). In order to be able usefully to exploit the network concept as an analytical and theoretical tool within the realm of organizational research, we therefore need at least two things: first, a more specific delineation of the term that allows us to distinguish it from and compare it with other forms of organizing; and secondly, a conceptualization of the term that allows us substantively to link it to questions of interest to organizational research.

Surely there exist different ways in which this could be achieved. Given the aims just noted, delineations and conceptualizations should and will differ according to the substantive questions a researcher intends to answer. The latter, in turn, will be focused by the theory that a researcher applies. Accordingly, we can for instance observe in the literature conceptualizations of inter-organizational networking that are fruitfully aligned to resource dependence theory (Alter and Hage 1993), institutionalist theory (Grabher 1993), the strategy literature (Jarillo 1993), internationalization theory (Buckley 1994), social network analysis (Burt 1992; Wasserman and Faust 1993), or to institutional economics (Hennart 1991).

Dimensions

Because of its basis in organization studies, this chapter takes as its vantage point for developing a delineation and conceptualization of inter-organizational networking a view widespread in the literature (cf. Grandori and Soda 1995; Powell and Smith-Doerr 1994), namely that inter-organizational networks represent one institutional form of co-ordinating, or governing, economic exchange relations among actors. It thus chooses to view networking as a particular organizational form that is worthy of study, rather than as a particular research perspective that examines how properties of their internal and external networks influence organizations (see Powell and Smith-Doerr 1994 for a comparison of these two perspectives). Traditionally, two other institutional forms of governance are often distinguished from network forms, namely the market and the firm. The exact delineation of these forms, as well as how to explain which of these institutional forms prevails under which circumstances and for what reasons, has been the focus of intense scholarly debate (see e.g. Aoki *et al.* 1990; Bradach and Eccles 1989; Hennart 1993; Pitelis 1993; Powell 1990; Ring and Van de Ven 1992; Simon 1991).

One important precondition for tackling these questions is to define some common dimensions on the basis of which the institutional forms can be compared. Otherwise commonalities and differences among the institutional forms cannot be identified; and comparative assessments of the forms would lack a common denominator. For the present purposes, five dimensions will be employed to characterize and delineate in an ideal-typical way the three institutions of markets, firms, and inter-organizational networks. The five dimensions underlying the conceptual framework include three dimensions that capture aspects of the content of the relationships among actors, that is, the nature of their micro-level ties, namely resource flows, mutual expectations, and information flows. The other two dimensions depict the institutional-level organizational forms through which actors co-ordinate their relations, that is, aspects of the governance structure, namely the distribution of property rights over resources and co-ordination mechanisms. The five dimensions are related in that variations in the three content dimensions of micro-level ties are held to be conducive to explaining variations in the governance structures through which actors choose to co-ordinate their economic exchange relations.[3] In the present framework, the three content dimensions of micro-level ties thus play a double role. On the one hand, they allow us descriptively to distinguish related properties of the relations among actors that are characteristic of the institutions of markets, firms, and inter-organizational networks. On the other hand, at the same time they direct our attention to such factors that influence and thus help to explain the institutional-level forms of governance.

The three content dimensions of micro-level ties represent core concepts from organization theory that have been found to be important predictors of organizational arrangements across a number of approaches (e.g. contingency theory, resource dependence theory, institutional economics, behavioural theory of the firm). Specifically, resource (inter)dependence and information flows are among the core dimensions in which organizational research has classically analysed the problem of co-ordination and its solutions (e.g. Alchian and Demsetz 1972; Galbraith 1973; Lawrence and Lorsch 1967; March and Simon 1958; Thompson 1967; Woodward 1965). Although it could and perhaps should be subsumed under the notion of information flows, mutual expectations was added as a third predictive content dimension. The reason is that in much of the current literature, particularly that on inter-organizational networking, people-related expectations such as opportunism, trust, and fairness figure prominently in their own right. They may thus warrant separate treatment from more classical information-related issues such as complexity and uncertainty. Moreover,

---

[3] It is obvious that neither the three micro-level ties, nor the thesis that these impact on governance structures are new to the literature. What might be a little more innovative is their combination, coupled with the attempt to utilize these dimensions for delineating different economic institutions of resource allocation, in order to spell out how the dimensions can be utilized in explanations of institutional choice.

in a similar way in the network literature too this dimension has been employed next to resource-related and informational dimensions to characterize inter-organizational relations (e.g. Aldrich and Whetten 1981; Van de Ven 1976).

The other two dimensions provide a conceptual basis for differentiating the institutional-level arrangements through which the economic activities of actors are co-ordinated. Two sets of governance mechanisms are used to characterize and distinguish the different forms: the distribution among actors of property rights over resources, and the co-ordination mechanisms that actors employ when allocating these resources. The property rights distribution has been extensively employed in the institutional economics literature for comparing and explaining the institutional choice between markets and firms (e.g. Alchian and Demsetz 1972; Barzel 1989; Fama and Jensen 1983). It has less frequently been applied to the analysis of inter-organizational networks. The property rights structure, which is often contractually fixed among actors, governs the behaviour of actors by establishing a specific distribution of rights (over resources and outcomes) and incentives. The second set of governance mechanisms, the co-ordination mechanisms, relates to the ways in which the (inter)dependencies that exist, or are to be established, between parties to an exchange are managed. These mechanisms are less frequently contractually fixed. They govern behaviour by establishing rules of conduct and by providing and structuring information that then guides behaviour. They too have been used in the organizational literature to characterize institutional forms of organizing economic exchange relations among actors (e.g. Grandori and Soda 1995; Hennart 1993; Simon 1991).

All five dimensions thus allow us to link analyses of inter-organizational networks to the main body of organizational research and on that basis to develop propositions with regard to why and how networking may be employed as an institutional solution for achieving co-ordination among organizations.

Markets, Firms, and Networks

In the following, I shall briefly characterize the three institutional forms of markets, firms, and networks along the five above-mentioned dimensions using an ideal-typical approach. The proposed conceptualization is ideal-typical in that it attempts to use the five dimensions for outlining generic features that characterize the three institutions. This seems appropriate because the three notions of 'market', 'firm', and 'network' are generic terms, as are the terms 'tree' or 'house'. Therefore, in the same way as trees or houses, markets, firms, and networks can take different forms. Although a palm tree differs considerably from an oak, as do a castle from a villa, an auction from long-term contracting, a barber's shop from a multinational enterprise, or a supplier network from a consortium, we may nevertheless for some purposes find it convenient and appropriate to subsume these different forms under the generic notion of tree, house, market, firm, or network respectively. Accordingly, the proposed framework does not assume that there is no variation in the actual forms that we subsume under each ideal-type. Rather, it intends to carve out the common denominators shared by the different forms.

The typification has three purposes. The first one is purely definitional: if one uses the notion of network and networking, and compares it to other forms of organizing economic exchange relations, one should define the terms, particularly when there exists considerable debate about their precise meaning. Specifically, the framework should identify the unique properties shared by all forms of networking that distinguish these forms from other forms of governance.

The second purpose is to propose the elements of a framework that might perhaps usefully inform our view of the formation of inter-organizational networks. In the literature there is some debate whether networks should be regarded as a hybrid form that in varying degree combines institutional features of both the market and the firm (Bradach and Eccles 1989; Sydow 1992; Hennart 1993) or as a distinct form with some unique characteristics (Håkansson and Snehota 1995; Powell 1990). The proposed framework in this debate adopts a somewhat different position. In a Weberian tradition, the framework uses the generic typification of inter-organizational networks as an analytical strategy, in order to direct attention to particular characteristics of networking and their contingencies. As Nohria (1992: 13) puts it: 'This rhetorical framing of network as form forces the analyst to attend to what it is that makes these new arrangements efficient, governable, and flexible compared with traditional modes of organizing.' However, it will become clear in the course of the argument that from an organizational point of view, the generic terms are perhaps less interesting than the underlying choice of governance mechanisms. From both a theoretical and practical point of view, it seems far more rewarding to examine and perhaps to be able to say why and how the particular content of their micro-level ties under specified conditions leads actors to choose a particular combination of governance mechanisms, rather than to be able to stick a label to this chosen combination marking it as being of the type of 'market', 'firm', or 'network'. Thus, paradoxically, the typification tries to pave the way for a move away from the discussion of types and towards a somewhat more fine-grained view of inter-organizational governance modes (as Ebers and Grandori elaborate in this volume). In this endeavour, the proposed framework attempts in its degree of differentiation to strike a balance between highly general accounts of networks *per se*, and extremely differentiated analyses of multiple forms of networking and their divergent antecedents. While the former tend to gloss over important differences in the forms and contingencies of networks, the latter beg the question of whether there exist sufficient commonalities among the different forms and their pertinent explanations such that they could be subsumed for research purposes under one general label.

The third purpose of the typification is to provide a conceptual framework that allows us to systematically relate the different contributions contained in this volume. Again, to this end a difficult balance had to be struck. The framework needs to be general enough to accommodate different theoretical approaches and research foci towards the analysis of inter-organizational networks. Yet it also needs to be specific enough to relate the various contributions, despite their differences, in a theoretically meaningful way.[4]

After these prolegomena, let us now take a closer look at the characteristics of the three institutional forms. Following Weber (1972: 382 ff.), we can succinctly state that *markets* institutionalize competition among actors for opportunities of exchange (see also Hodgson 1988). We can distinguish two characteristic phases of a market relationship that represent the core of the market phenomenon. It begins as a competition among a number of actors (potential buyers and sellers) who bargain over opportunities for exchange of resources (these can include informational resources). In this first, competitive phase, actors exchange information on the resource flows they would like to induce. In a second phase, a subset of these actors then realize their agreed bargain and engage in the exchange of resources.

Within the framework suggested in this book, market relationships thus can be characterized by comparatively limited flows of information (on prices, quantities, and qualities) that induce flows of resources (goods, services, money) between actors. Mutual expectations narrowly centre on the fulfilment of the agreed terms of exchange; the identity of the exchange partners hardly matters. Each actor has full control over his or her resources until the completion of the exchange transaction and individually bears the residual risk associated with the exchange. Relations between actors are confined to discrete acts of exchange between independently acting individuals or organizations: 'Sharp in by clear agreement; sharp out by clear performance' (MacNeil 1974: 378). Competition (for exchange opportunities) and bargaining (over conditions of exchange) are the characteristic co-

---

[4] It should be noted that this framework, which is reflected in the organization of the book, was not spelled out as a blueprint before the authors submitted their contributions. Rather, it emerged from the discussions at the Berlin EMOT workshop for which the chapters were originally prepared. It has hence evolved as an idiosyncratic *ex post* rationalization of some common viewpoints of the participants. As workshop organizer and subsequent editor of selected papers, I suggested to the authors the three concepts as well as the more general framework at the risk of imposing a greater unity of perspective than originally might have been reflected in the individual contributions. However, it seems to me that the three micro-level ties provide a helpful conceptual schema for organizing and relating the chapters of this book, and perhaps other pieces of research on inter-organizational networks.

ordination mechanisms among actors. Of course, this characterization does not cover all aspects of markets that have been noted in the huge literature on the concept. There is considerable variation in the characteristics of markets in history, across regions, industries, and theories (see Swedberg 1994). However, for the comparative exercise attempted here, the particular emphasis on content dimensions of economic exchange relationships and the dimensions characterizing the governance mode seems useful and sufficient.

Firms are characterized by the fact that members for an unspecified duration pool their (complementary) resources and establish a corporate actor with collective decision-making rules as well as rules for the allocation of income (or losses) from the joint activities and resources (Vanberg 1982). Members typically do not individually hold all rights over the resources that they bring to the firm. Rather, property rights over resources are diluted in that decision-management, decision-control, and residual risk bearing are either separated among the members of a firm or shared among a number of actors (Fama and Jensen 1983). Accordingly, in firms, we find a relatively higher degree, and a wider scope, of resource interdependence and of information exchange among actors than on markets. The relationships among actors therefore involve bilateral co-ordination of actors' activities, rather than unilateral co-ordination as on markets. Economic co-ordination within firms is based on the authority (to set up rules of behaviour and to make decisions binding for other members) that comes with the employment contract; in addition, the identification of members with their firm can provide some co-ordination (Simon 1991). As they expect to transact repeatedly, have a great deal of information about one another, and are a relatively small group, firm members anticipate and indeed develop longer-term social relationships. Their economic relationships thus become infused with social exchange, that is, with unspecified anticipated obligations and mutual expectations about conduct (Blau 1964).

Inter-organizational networks institutionalize recurring, partner-specific exchange relationships of finite duration (often based on goal accomplishment) or of unspecified duration among a limited number of actors. Actors individually retain residual control over their resources, yet periodically negotiate, sometimes even jointly decide on, their use. Inter-organizational networking relationships therefore differ from market relationships in that transactions among actors involve bilateral, rather than unilateral, co-ordination of plans and activities; they differ from firms in that the parties to an inter-organizational network do not establish a corporate actor but retain unilateral decision-control with regard to their resources and bear some residual risk.[5] Actors co-ordinate their resource allocation decisions

[5] In contrast to some other views, according to this definition equity joint ventures thus do not represent a network form of governance but should be regarded as firms.

in processes of negotiation. These can, but need not, result in formal contracts governing actor relations. In their negotiations over the allocation of their resources, actors exchange a wider range of information (e.g. on the resources' characteristics, production and use, on plans, or strategies) than in an ideal-typical market relation. Because inter-organizational networks establish recurring, partner-specific exchange relationships, actors, as in firms, develop contractually unspecified reciprocal obligations and mutual expectations about relation-specific activities (Bradach and Eccles 1989; Chapter 7, this volume; Ring and Van de Ven 1992).

Table 1.1 summarizes the ideal-typical characterization of the three institutional forms of governing economic exchange relations.

Comparative Assessment

The literature has extensively examined and discussed why and when the market or the firm are the governance structure of choice (see e.g. Hennart 1993; Jarillo 1993; Pitelis 1993; Reve 1990; Ring and Van de Ven 1992; Williamson 1985). It therefore suffices here to remark that particularities of the resource flows among actors as well as their state of information have figured prominently in pertinent explanations of these institutional forms. With regard to resource characteristics, the degree of asset specificity, the frequency of transactions, resource interdependence, the complementarity of resources, the ease of protecting one's rights over resources, and the minimum efficient scale of production, among others, have been identified as important predictors. With regard to information, complexity, uncertainty, and risk have been shown to impact on institutional choice in different ways, as have the expectations of opportunism, trust, and norms.

As the earlier brief outline of inter-organizational network research has revealed, and as indeed this book argues, the same or similar concepts also play a prominent role (in relational-level) explanations of the formation of inter-organizational networks. The three dimensions of resource flows, information flows, and mutual expectations therefore seem to represent important, yet not the only, dimensions that should be acknowledged when attempting to explain the prevalence of each of the three institutional forms of governance. In a nutshell, the general argument is that the three factors pose particular organizational challenges and opportunities that can best be met or exploited by institutionalizing a particular governance structure. Williamson (1985) especially has suggested a concise theory that attempts to outline and substantiate pertinent relationships. However, a number of other theories too have acknowledged the importance of the three noted dimensions, although they tend to conceptualize them in different ways. The three dimensions could thus perhaps function as bridging concepts among different theories that allow us to relate different research perspectives; at least for the present volume, they serve this purpose.

Table 1.1. Ideal-typical characterization of three economic institutions governing the allocation of resources among actors

Characteristics	Market	Inter-organizational network	Firm
Distribution of property rights over resources (residual claims and decision-making rights)	unilateral decision-management and decision-control with residual risk bearing by transaction partners	unilateral decision-control and residual risk bearing combined with periodical joint decision-making by transaction partners	separation of decision-management, decision-control, and residual risk bearing among transaction partners
Resource flows among actors	infrequent, discrete acts of exchange of resources	repeated partner-specific exchange of resources	resource pooling of co-specialized resources
Mutual expectations among actors with regard to relationship	narrow, confined to terms of contract	wider, including contractually unspecified reciprocal obligations and mutual expectations	wider, including contractually unspecified reciprocal obligations and mutual expectations
	short-term economic exchange relation	longer-term social relationship	longer-term social relationship
	finite duration	finite duration (based on goal accomplishment) or unspecified duration	unspecified duration
Information flows among actors	confined to terms of exchange (price, quantity, quality, delivery)	higher degree of information sharing with regard to a wider spectrum of information	higher degree of information sharing with regard to a wider spectrum of information
Main co-ordination mechanisms	bargaining and competition	negotiation and concurrence	authority and identification

Before I outline in a little more detail how a closer look at the three dimensions could perhaps help us better to understand the formation of inter-organizational networks, I should like to address one issue at a more general level: the seeming attractiveness of inter-organizational networking as a form of governance. Several comparative assessments of inter-organizational networking suggest that this organizational form can be superior to both the market and the firm, or at least may be considered a viable form of governance (e.g. Jarillo 1993; Miles and Snow 1986; Ohmae 1989; Powell 1990). The above typification provides some clues why these authors, and apparently quite a number of practitioners of inter-organizational networking, might have come to this conclusion. A comparison of the network form with the firm and market forms of governance reveals some comparative advantages of the former. One could argue that firms engaging in inter-organizational networking may enjoy comparative advantage over self-sufficient firms, because they can draw on specialized yet complementary partner contributions that extend the resource base and capabilities of the networked firms, and can entail production cost advantages. Networked firms may enjoy competitive advantage over firms that organize identical exchange relations in the form of market relations, because the recurring exchange relations, a high degree and wide scope of information sharing, reciprocal obligations, and periodic joint decision-making among the networked firms lead to improved inter-organizational co-ordination and control. Finally, networked firms may enjoy competitive advantage over firms that vertically integrate identical exchange relations, because the match between the distribution of influence over outcomes and the distribution of risks and rewards, which the property rights structure among networked firms realizes, creates stronger performance incentives and thus economizes on co-ordination costs.

Does the network form accordingly represent the best of both worlds of governance, that is, of markets and firms? Several cautionary notes clearly are in order. Whether or not networked firms enjoy comparative advantage *vis-à-vis* differently governed competitors depends on the circumstances, for example on characteristics of the resources that are exchanged and on informational aspects. The research described in this chapter has specified a number of such contingencies so that they need not be repeated here. Moreover, the above comparison of the different governance forms gives great prominence to potential comparative benefits of networking. What it neglects, and what we know much less about, are the specific costs and disadvantages that networking among firms entails. In the concluding section, we address this issue in somewhat more detail (see Chapter 11). Finally, there are many different ways in which one can organize a networking relationship. Clearly, the comparative advantages or disadvantages of networking also depend on the detailed organizational design of a relationship. Yet in this area much more work needs to be done before we can draw any general conclusions.

The next, and final, section now outlines how characteristics of the three noted micro-level ties can help us to understand and explain which institutional-level ties, namely different organizational forms of governing their economic exchange relations, organizations will form. At the same time, the following section briefly introduces the individual papers contained in this volume and their particular contribution to the present subject.

As the following heading indicates, this book neither claims to capture all the relevant reasons for and influences on the formation of inter-organizational networks, nor does it seek to offer a comprehensive treatment of the three dimensions of micro-level ties. Rather, it discusses in three separate chapters why and how activity links (an element of resource flows), trust (an element of mutual expectations), and catalysts (an element of information flows) impact on the formation of inter-organizational networks.

THE ROLES OF ACTIVITY LINKS, TRUST, AND CATALYSTS FOR EXPLAINING THE FORMATION OF INTER-ORGANIZATIONAL NETWORKS

Resource Flows and Activity Links

The main resource and activity-related argument for the formation of inter-organizational networks rests on the proposition that firms can achieve gains by co-ordinating in a network mode specific resource and activity links with other firms. A number of such gains have been identified in the literature. I have already summarized them in the above section discussing the motives for networking. It therefore suffices here to briefly remind readers of the general reasoning. Through networking, it is argued, firms can gain competitive advantage because they can gain access to desired resources and capabilities that are complementary to their own; they can thus in different ways enhance their abilities, share risks, gain market power, or realize economies of scale and scope.

It remains to be answered why and when these desired resource and activity links might best be managed through, and exploited by, specific forms of inter-organizational networking rather than in other governance structures. Inter-organizational networking provides advantages over internal development when firms lack relevant know-how, resources, or capabilities. As Nohria and Garcia-Pont (1991: 108) argue, this is because

strategic capabilities are the outcome of long-term strategic commitments by firms, and mobility barriers and isolating mechanisms make the imitation of desired strategic capabilities difficult. Linkages are a way of circumventing these barriers, and offer a more rapid means of repositioning than internal development. Also, linkages are often less costly and do not involve the irreversible commitment associated with internal development. (Porter and Fuller 1986)

Networking linkages are preferred to full integration when there exist barriers to integration. Such barriers for example could be significant bureaucratic diseconomies that would come with large firm size, or when there is demand for complex, integrated products or services that are beyond the scope of one company (Chapter 3). Another barrier to integration are legal constraints, such as competition policies or local content conditions in the case of foreign direct investment, that would prevent a merger or acquisition (Reve 1990). Moreover, widely differing minimum efficient scales of production within the value chain can be a further barrier to integration that would turn the scales in favour of the formation of an inter-organizational network (Jarillo 1993). In addition, finally, the formation of an inter-organizational network must be preferable to establishing market-mediated resource and activity links. This is the case, for example, when there is a lack of competition among suppliers or buyers, when firms have made significant dedicated investments, or when the exchange of non-codifiable knowledge is involved (Teece 1992).

To these considerations the chapters in Part II add the following. Dubois and Håkansson in their chapter propose a general model that allows them to describe and analyse the various relationships that exist between the members of a network. On the basis of this model and of a case study of a Swedish fork-lift producer, they then suggest that the relationships that evolve among the organizations of a network depend on the properties of the resources that are exchanged among the organizations, in particular on their potential for realizing cost reductions or differentiation benefits. The authors further argue that the choice of governance mode for a particular network relationship not only depends on the properties of the resources exchanged but also on the history of the relationship as well as on the nature and density of other linkages that the organizations might entertain.

While Dubois and Håkansson highlight the density of, and potential benefits to be gained from, inter-organizational resource flows as important antecedents for the formation of a networking relationship, Easton and Araujo show why and how the stability and predictability of resource flows between organizations influences the likelihood that a network relationship evolves. Easton and Araujo argue that because inter-organizational networks are well suited to mitigate and absorb market uncertainties, they are the governance mode of choice under conditions of heterogeneous demand over time. Specifically, these authors offer a comparative analysis of seven possible organizational responses to conditions of heterogeneous demand over time. They submit that the formation of inter-organizational networks can be understood as a result of transmission and configuration strategies for dealing with heterogeneous demand over time. The other organizational strategies they discuss in contrast are more likely to rely on market or intra-firm mechanisms. According to Easton and Araujo, firms turn to the transmission strategy when they find that within the confines of their own resource bases and administrative mechanisms they cannot achieve the flexibility required by their customers, but have to transmit specific tasks to their suppliers or other exchange partners. In this case, networks form as a result of continuous exchanges between firms who rely on each other for accessing the resources and capabilities they lack. The configuration strategy involves the creation of temporary network configurations to meet the heterogeneous demands of customers as they change over time. Pertinent examples include project-based networking relationships that are formed for large construction or film projects. Easton and Araujo note for both the transmission and the configuration strategy that core firms often act as catalysts for network formation—a theme that the papers in Part IV of this volume take up and discuss in greater detail.

In their empirical study of inter-firm relationships in the southern Italian mechanical industry, Lomi and Grandi identify network structures by means of block-modelling techniques. In particular, they explore the patterns of supply relationships, quality control agreements, technology transfer and equity relations that exist among the 106 manufacturing organizations within their sample. Their analysis reveals that, despite public policy incentives to locate large productions units of mainly large northern Italian firms in underdeveloped regions of the south, the northern 'transplants' are but little integrated in the regional economies and have only partially contributed to the industrial development of the regions. That is, while the financial incentives provided by the Italian government have led large northern Italian firms to produce in southern regions, counter to public policy intentions the large producers are only rarely linked to independent regional firms in terms of supply, technology transfer, or equity relations, and have not induced a flow of orders to local suppliers. The empirical analysis further shows that southern Italian firms too are only weakly integrated with one another. The dense horizontal links among firms which have been reported for northern and central Italian industrial districts within the mechanical industry thus seem to be largely absent in the south. One implication of this finding is that government incentives apparently are not always sufficient for inducing companies to form inter-organizational networks.

Furthermore, Lomi and Grandi report that the relatively few ties that do exist among the firms studied tend to be organized along the supply chain. Perhaps unsurprisingly, in their sample the supplier networks tend to take the form of hub–spoke structures, with large producers occupying central positions and small suppliers on the periphery. Like Easton and Araujo, Lomi and Grandi thus stress the catalytic role of relatively large core firms for inter-organizational network formation. Finally, Lomi and Grandi find that specific types of resource-based ties are more likely to give rise to network relationships than others. In particular, equity relations tend to entail other resource ties, for example, supplier or technology development relationships. In conclusion, like Dubois and Håkansson, Lomi and Grandi thus stress the significance for network formation of possible

interdependencies among the various resource flows that link organizations. Should this thesis hold, it implies that studies of networks should
extend their focus. Rather than centring on the properties of individual
transactions only, they should give greater prominence to the analysis of
possible transactional interdependencies.

Mutual Expectations: Trust

Flows of mutual expectations among the parties to an exchange influence
actors' perceptions of the opportunities and risks of co-operation and thus
significantly shape the formation of inter-organizational networks. Chapters
in Part III analyse in greater detail the role of trust in the processes that
lead to the formation of inter-organizational networks. The three chapters
show how and why trust develops as a consequence of particular enabling
conditions. Moreover, they illuminate how trust then facilitates the emergence of networking relationships.

The chapters postulate that when there exists trust between the transaction partners, the formation of network relationships is more likely as networks can then be a more effective means of economic co-ordination. In a
nutshell, the main argument linking trust with the formation of inter-
organizational networks is that under conditions of (particular kinds of)
trust, the parties to an exchange can achieve gains from improved co-ordination and control of their exchange relations and a more open as well as
a more reliable exchange of information. This in turn encourages the parties
to develop longer-term exchange relations with their trusted partners,
rather than infrequent, short-term relations as on markets. Through networking, they can thus in principle achieve the gains that result from
improved bilateral co-ordination, but can avoid the bureaucratic costs of
unified governance.

So far, in the literature, the concept of trust has often been employed in
a rather general way. Moreover, trust is often treated as a monolithic
concept. Scholars have thoroughly discussed the differences between trust
and related concepts such as risk and predictability, have overcome confu-
sions between trust and its antecedents and outcomes, and have specified
empirical referents for trust (Mayer *et al.* 1995). Nevertheless, the concept
of trust itself, with some notable exceptions (Williamson 1993; Zucker
1986), is hardly ever differentiated. Trust is mainly conceived as a uniform
concept theoretically; and in empirical studies trust is often operationalized
as a dichotomous variable that either exists among parties or does not exist.
In contrast, the papers in Part III point out that it is necessary to distinguish different kinds of trust as well as to acknowledge their respective
dynamics. The reason is that different kinds of trust and their dynamics have
different impacts on the relationships that evolve between actors.

In his chapter, Ring suggests that we distinguish two kinds of trust: fragile trust and resilient trust. He submits that the formation of inter-organizational networks rests on resilient trust, that is, on the predictability of the moral integrity and goodwill of prospective network members. Fragile trust, however, which is supported by contractual safeguards, is more likely to lead to arm's-length market relations according to Ring's analysis. In his chapter Ring explores possible antecedents of both kinds of trust as well as consequences for networking. For example, he submits that kinship or strong social ties will increase the likelihood that transaction partners will rely on resilient trust—a point that is also stressed in Chapter 7. In cross-border networks, however, according to Ring, resilient trust will be slow to develop so that reliance on fragile trust (and thus market relations) will predominate, *ceteris paribus*.

In his chapter Ring places particular emphasis on the formal and informal processes that lead to the development of fragile or resilient trust. Specifically, he proposes and characterizes as the primary processes by which economic actors learn to rely on fragile or resilient trust in networks, the formal processes of negotiation, transaction, and administration, and the informal processes of making sense, understanding, and committing. He then outlines some process-specific contingencies that influence whether a particular process will lead to the development of resilient rather than fragile trust among actors. These include, for example, the existence, perceived success and fairness of past transactions, as well as the type of learning that actors apply in their sense-making processes. Finally, Ring outlines how the conditions under which, and the way in which, the noted processes unfold have important implications for the formation of inter-organizational networks, for instance for the likelihood, lead time, and organizational forms of inter-organizational networking relationships.

The chapter by de Laat identifies and discusses a variety of institutional mechanisms which can ensure that network members develop expectations of reliability with regard to expected resource and information flows within R&D alliances. De Laat's chapter complements that of Ring in two ways. First, it identifies and discusses institutional mechanisms which safeguard fragile trust, for example, classical contracting, credible commitments, and reciprocity. Secondly, the chapter explores how these institutional mechanisms impact on the development of resilient trust. De Laat is particularly concerned with the dynamic consequences of relying on particular governance mechanisms. He thus addresses an important, yet heretofore under-researched issue. Specifically, de Laat argues that within R&D alliances reliance on classical contracting produces a spiral of rising distrust and encourages opportunism; whereas balanced and credible commitments foster mutual trust among actors and diminish opportunistic behaviour.

Casson and Cox concur with Ring and de Laat that a climate of trust that is sustained by moral (as opposed to material) sanctioning is the hallmark of inter-organizational networking. By contrast, the two main institutional alternatives to networking relations (the market and the firm) are characterized as low-trust mechanisms of co-ordinating economic activities. Casson and Cox submit that inter-organizational networking under specific conditions can be a more efficient institutional form of co-ordinating economic activities than the market or the firm. In particular, this is the case when members of transacting organizations belong to, or through trusted intermediaries have access to, the same social networks. Casson and Cox argue that social networks create an 'invisible infrastructure' of social bonds among actors, as exemplified by the social relations among the members of a family, a church, a particular school, club, university, professional association, trade union, or political party. These social bonds and the efficacy of associated moral sanctions according to Casson and Cox have positive efficiency effects, because they will lead actors to exchange more accurate and undistorted information. Investments in social networks and the institutions creating them will thus reduce the cost of networking relative to other forms of co-ordinating economic activities.

Casson and Cox in their chapter moreover outline how the formation of inter-organizational networks can be explained by the role intermediaries play with regard both to the formation of mutual expectations and to the flow of information between prospective network members. According to Casson and Cox, intermediaries can foster the formation of inter-organizational networks in at least two ways. First, under specific conditions intermediaries may engineer trust between prospective network members, that is, influence members' expectations. Secondly, intermediary actors may furthermore facilitate the formation of inter-organizational networks by channelling and synthesizing information flows between prospective network members. The authors substantiate that both measures can enhance the effectiveness of economic co-ordination between network organizations. Finally, Casson and Cox demonstrate the fruitfulness of their argument by analysing a particular historical form of inter-organizational (and international) networking in late Victorian Britain: the free-standing company.

The analysis by Casson and Cox of the role of intermediaries for the formation of inter-organizational networks is very much in line with the arguments presented by the chapters in Part IV of the book. It thus nicely bridges and integrates the chapters on mutual expectations and information flows.

Information Flows: Catalysts

While resource and activity links as well as trust are by now familiar themes in the organizational network literature, the issues that the chapters of Part IV address have so far received comparatively less attention (see however McEvily and Zaheer 1995; Snow and Thomas 1993). The papers illuminate how and why informational intermediaries, be they people or inter-organizational information systems, may facilitate and shape the formation of inter-organizational networks.

Informational intermediaries can influence the formation of inter-organizational networks in different ways. They can act as information brokers and thus allow firms to exploit informational synergies (e.g. better information flows, broader information access) that would otherwise go unnoticed or could only be realized at comparatively higher cost. Furthermore, as mutually trusted linchpins between social groups, human catalysts can bridge and help overcome informational asymmetries, establish a common set of expectations, and facilitate goal alignment. They can thus foster co-operation and exchange that otherwise would not occur. Finally, human catalysts can play an important role in conflict resolution among networking parties when they act as neutral arbitrators. In sum, the chapters argue that informational intermediaries can reduce communication costs, diminish uncertainties, and facilitate better co-ordination for network members.

In their empirical study of innovation and entrepreneurship in Italian small-firm networks, Lipparini and Sobrero analyse and compare empirically the roles played by entrepreneurs and professional management in fostering product innovation through external partnering. They hypothesize that entrepreneurs tend to rely more on external partnering for the development of innovations than do professional managers; furthermore, the authors propose that networks co-ordinated by entrepreneurs will achieve more radical and more complex innovations than when professional managers lead the participating firms. According to the authors, entrepreneurs should thus be the better catalysts for the formation of innovation networks. Lipparini and Sobrero substantiate the first of their hypotheses by outlining that entrepreneurs, as compared to managers, can have a more profound effect on the degree and extent of inter-firm development of innovation because, as a result of their individual and professional socialization processes, they can rely on stronger and older ties within their communities. These ties give them easier access to critical resources. Moreover, they reduce uncertainties about potential partners' abilities and interests, contribute to a better mutual understanding among the partners within a network, induce trust, and lead to more intense information sharing, all of which may foster the likelihood of innovation via external partnering. With regard to the second hypothesis, Lipparini and Sobrero propose that comparatively more radical and more complex innovations will result from entrepreneurial networks because entrepreneurs thrive on uncertainty and are inclined towards taking greater risks, while managers are portrayed as being more risk averse.

Lipparini and Sobrero's study shows that privileged access to, as well as effective management and exploitation of, information can play an important role for the formation of inter-organizational networks. Moreover, the study provides some evidence that personal or social group characteristics

of the catalysts involved might be of some importance for the differential
outcomes of inter-organizational networking. It thus urges us to acknowledge within network research the potential impact of divergent motivations,
partnering capabilities, and co-ordination skills of the individuals and social
groups that engage in inter-organizational networking. Indeed, the next
chapter—an intensive case study by Lütz of a research collaboration in
German industry—confirms the potential fruitfulness of such an approach.

Lütz studied the process in which a network of R&D personnel from
twenty participating organizations (chemical companies, steel companies,
car manufacturers, and research institutes) tried to develop new adhesion
technologies to be applied within the automotive industry. Her paper presents rich empirical detail on the processes of inter-organizational network
formation in general and on the role of catalysts in particular. In this case,
the research collaboration only materialized because research institutes
acted as information brokers and integrators among the relevant actors.
Without these catalysts the research collaboration most probably would not
have succeeded. Lütz analyses how the initially diverging interests and
expectations fuelled conflict, prejudices, secrecy, and distrust among the
project participants, quite generally impeded collaboration, and thus contributed to disappointing early project results. However, catalytic interventions by the research institutes contributed to changes in this unfavourable
situation, particularly with regard to the mutual expectations that the
parties held. The research institutes took on the role of catalyst, because
owing to the specific funding arrangements they were the only parties that
were interested in and thus committed to the success of the joint endeavour. Helped by specific circumstances, the research institutes induced
several changes in the participants' cognitive orientations towards one
another and the project as a whole. Lütz describes, for example, how the
parties were nudged into reducing their perceived status differences; reinterpreted their former competitive behaviour as 'sportsman-like' competition between equally qualified technical experts, rather than as competitive
struggles for future markets between the participating firms; and redefined
the situation from a zero-sum game to a positive-sum game in which all
parties could benefit from collaboration. These changes in cognitive orientation and mutual expectations paved the way for the project members to
develop a more open exchange of information, a give-and-take mentality,
a greater trust, and more intensive collaboration. The result was that
through these changes a more effective collaboration was possible, which
in turn eventually led to favourable project outcomes.

While Lipparini and Sobrero and Lütz focus on how human catalysts
through their management of information flows foster the formation of
inter-organizational networks, Holland and Lockett in their study analyse
the role of technology as a catalyst. Holland and Lockett try to determine
how inter-organizational information systems may influence the resource

relationships between networked organizations and thus the governance structures of inter-organizational networks. The authors argue that inter-organizational information systems enable their group of users to better exploit their competitive advantages *vis-à-vis* the members of competing groups. Specifically, organizations increasingly implement inter-organizational (information) systems (IOS) in order to manage their existing exchange relationships more efficiently and effectively. The general observation of Holland and Lockett is that through the introduction of inter-organizational information systems existing inter-organizational network relationships become more accentuated because the information flows between participating organizations can be handled more effectively and efficiently. Holland and Lockett therefore conclude that inter-organizational information systems stabilize existing inter-organizational network relationships. According to Holland and Lockett, the use of IOS, however, can also change the form of the inter-organizational networking relationships. The authors submit that this is because IOS tend to increase the specificity of partners' assets. They then predict and exemplify that, as a consequence, firms are likely to establish more hierarchical forms of governing their inter-organizational networking relationships.

CONCLUSION

The papers brought together in this volume give rich and detailed insights into issues that are pertinent to the formation of inter-organizational networks. The concluding Part V consists of a chapter by Ebers and Grandori that outlines some implications for organizational theory and practice that may be derived from the papers assembled in this volume. It returns to the issue of how to characterize and conceptualize inter-organizational networking relationships. Specifically, we call for and suggest a more fine-grained conceptualization and explanation of inter-organizational networking relationships. We then illuminate two important yet under-researched issues, namely the dynamics and possible costs of inter-organizational networking. Finally, we point out a number of implications for practice that may be derived from the research reported in this book.

In concluding this introductory chapter, it therefore suffices to stress but one aspect that in my view represents one of the more important messages of this book. The contributions contained between the covers of this volume are diverse in several respects, for example, with regard to their research focus, theory, methodology, level of analysis, and research setting. As a consequence, we cannot expect, of course, the same degree of comprehensiveness, coherence, and integration as in a monograph by a single author. However, the noted diversity also may be a strength of the book for several reasons. First, the book testifies to the general applicability of the network concept in that it shows the concept's relevance for a number of theories, disciplines, and empirical settings. Secondly, the collection presents a wide variety of empirical cases of networks in different settings and thus sensitizes us to the variety of contingencies and processes of network formation. Thirdly, despite their diversity, the contributions nevertheless speak to a common agenda that goes beyond their common interest in networks, and shed some light on similar phenomena, though from different angles.

In particular, it seems to me that the contributions all demonstrate, though in different ways, that researchers and practitioners might better understand the formation of inter-organizational networks, if they analyse the three kinds of micro-level ties that form the conceptual backbone of this book, namely resource flows, information flows, and mutual expectations among actors. The papers thus also demonstrate that there might be more common ground in our highly fragmented field than we sometimes assume or wish to admit. The book might therefore encourage us to be more alert to such common ground and common insights that span established boundaries. Over and above our motivation, this would require that we begin to be more open to engage in a dialogue between different disciplines and research perspectives and that we become more apt at finding common terms in which we can discuss issues of common interest. Accordingly, I hope that over and above its substantive contribution, in this sense too the book may provide a fruitful stepping-stone for further research.

REFERENCES

Alchian, A. A., and Demsetz, H. 1972. 'Production, Information Costs, and Economic Organization'. *American Economic Review*. 62: 777–95.

Aldrich, H., and Whetten, D. A. 1981. 'Organization-Sets, Action-Sets, and Networks: Making the Most of Simplicity'. In Nystrom, P. C., and Starbuck, W. H. (eds.). *Handbook of Organizational Design*. I: 385–408. Oxford: Oxford University Press.

Alter, C., and Hage, J. 1993. *Organizations Working Together*. Newbury Park, Calif.: Sage.

Altmann, N., and Sauer, D. (eds.) 1989. *Integrative Rationalisierung und Zulieferbetriebe*. Frankfurt am Main: Campus.

Aoki, M., Gustafsson, B., and Williamson, O. E. (eds.) 1990. *The Firm as a Nexus of Treatise*. London: Sage.

Auster, E. R. 1994. 'Macro and Strategic Perspectives on Interorganizational Linkages: A Comparative Analysis and Review with Suggestions for Reorientation'. *Advances in Strategic Management*. 10B: 3–40.

Axelsson, B., and Easton, G. (eds.) 1992. *Industrial Networks: A New View of Reality*. London: Routledge.

Badaracco, J. L. 1991. *The Knowledge Link: How Firms Compete through Strategic Alliances*. Boston, Mass.: Harvard Business School Press.

Barzel, Y. 1989. *Economic Analysis of Property Rights*. Cambridge: Cambridge University Press.

Baughn, C. C., and Osborn, R. N. 1990. 'The Role of Technology in the Formation and Form of Multinational Cooperative Arrangements'. *Journal of High Technology Management Research*. 1: 181–92.

Biemans, W. G. 1991. *Managing Innovation within Networks*. London: Routledge.

Blau, P. M. 1964. *Exchange and Power in Social Life*. New York: Wiley.

Blodgett, L. 1991. 'Partner Contributions as Predictors of Equity Share in International Joint Ventures'. *Journal of International Business Studies*. 1: 63–78.

Borys, B., and Jemison, D. 1989. 'Hybrid Arrangements as Strategic Alliances: Theoretical Issues in Organizational Combinations'. *Academy of Management Review*. 14: 234–49.

Bradach, J., and Eccles, R. 1989. 'Markets versus Hierarchies: From Ideal Types to Plural Forms'. *Annual Review of Sociology*. 15: 97–118.

Brusco, S. 1982. 'The Emilian Model: Productive Decentralisation and Social Integration'. *Cambridge Journal of Economics*. 6: 167–84.

Buckley, P. J. 1994. 'Introduction: Cooperative Forms of Transnational Corporation Activity'. In Buckley, P. J. (ed.). *Cooperative Forms of Transnational Corporation Activity*. 1–20. London: Routledge.

Burt, R. S. 1992. *Structural Holes: The Social Structure of Competition*. Cambridge, Mass.: Harvard University Press.

Contractor, F. J., and Lorange, P. (eds.) 1988. *Cooperative Strategies in International Business*. Lexington, Mass.: Lexington Books.

Dodgson, M. 1993. 'Learning, Trust, and Technological Collaboration'. *Human Relations*. 46: 77–95.

Dore, R. 1986. *Flexible Rigidities*. Stanford, Calif.: Stanford University Press.

Doz, Y. L. 1996. 'The Evolution of Cooperation in Strategic Alliances: Initial Conditions or Learning Processes?' *Strategic Management Journal*. 17: 55–83.

Dyer, J. H. 1996. 'Specialized Supplier Networks as a Source of Competitive Advantage: Evidence from the Auto Industry'. *Strategic Management Journal*. 17: 271–91.

Eccles, R. G. 1981. 'The Quasifirm in the Construction Industry'. *Journal of Economic Behavior and Organization*. 2: 335–57.

Eisenhardt, K. M., and Schoonhoven, C. B. 1996. 'Resource-Based View of Strategic Alliance Formation: Strategic and Social Effects in Entrepreneurial Firms'. *Organization Science*. 7: 136–50.

Fama, E. F., and Jensen, M. C. 1983. 'Separation of Ownership and Control'. *Journal of Law and Economics*. 26: 301–25.

Faulkner, R. R., and Anderson, A. 1987. 'Short-Term Projects and Emergent Careers: Evidence from Hollywood'. *American Journal of Sociology*. 92: 879–909.

Fombrun, C. J. 1982. 'Strategies for Network Research in Organizations'. *Academy of Management Review*. 7: 280–91.

Galbraith, J. R. 1973. *Designing Complex Organizations*. Reading, Mass.: Addison-Wesley.

Gemünden, H. G., Heydebreck, P., and Herden, R. 1992. 'Technological Interweavement: A Means of Achieving Innovation Success'. *R&D Management*. 22: 359–76.

Gerlach, M. L. 1992. *Alliance Capitalism*. Berkeley, Calif.: University of California Press.

Glaister, K. W., and Buckley, P. J. 1996. 'Strategic Motives for International Alliance Formation'. *Journal of Management Studies*. 33: 301–32.

Grabher, G. (ed.) 1993*a*. *The Embedded Firm*. London: Routledge.

——1993*b*. 'The Weakness of Strong Ties: The Lock-in of Regional Development in the Ruhr Area'. In Grabher 1993*a*: 255–77.

Grandori, A., and Soda, G. 1995. 'Inter-Firm Networks: Antecedents, Mechanisms, and Forms'. *Organization Studies*. 16: 183–214.

Granovetter, M. 1994. 'Business Groups'. In Smelser, N. J., and Swedberg, R. (eds.). *The Handbook of Economic Sociology*. 453–75. Princeton, NJ: Princeton University Press.

Gray, B. 1987. 'Conditions Facilitating Interorganizational Collaboration'. *Human Relations*. 38: 911–36.

Gulati, R. 1995. 'Social Structure and Alliance Formation Patterns: A Longitudinal Analysis'. *Administrative Science Quarterly*. 40: 619–52.

Haagedoorn, J. 1993. 'Strategic Technology Alliances and Modes of Cooperation in High-Technology Industries'. In Grabher 1993*a*: 116–38.

——1995. 'Strategic Technology Partnering During the 1980s: Trends, Networks, and Corporate Patterns in Non-Core Technologies'. *Research Policy*. 24: 207–31.

Håkansson, H. (ed.) 1982. *International Marketing and Purchasing of Industrial Goods—An Interaction Approach*. Chichester: Wiley.

——and Snehota, I. 1989. 'No Business is an Island: The Network Concept of Business Strategy'. *Scandinavian Journal of Management*. 15: 187–200.

————1995. *Business Networks*. London: Routledge.

Hamel, G. 1991. 'Competition for Competence and Inter-Partner Learning within International Strategic Alliances'. *Strategic Management Journal*. 12: 83–103.

Hamilton, G. G., and Biggart, N. W. 1988. 'Market, Culture, and Authority: A Comparative Analysis of Management and Organization in the Far East'. *American Journal of Sociology*. 94 (Supplement): S52–95.

Harrigan, K. R. 1985. *Strategies for Joint Ventures*. Lexington, Mass.: Lexington Books.

Helper, S. 1991. 'Strategy and Irreversibility in Supplier Relations: The Case of the U.S. Automobile Industry'. *Business History Review*. 65: 781–824.

Hennart, J. F. 1991. 'The Transaction Costs Theory of Joint Ventures'. *Management Science*. 37: 483–97.

——1993. 'Explaining the Swollen Middle: Why Most Transactions are a Mix of "Market" and "Hierarchy" '. *Organization Science*. 4: 529–47.

Hergert, M., and Morris, D. 1988. 'Trends in International Collaborative Agreements'. In Contractor and Lorange 1988: 99–109.

Herrigel, G. B. 1993. 'Power and the Redefinition of Industrial Districts: The Case of Baden-Württemberg'. In Grabher, G. 1993*a*: 227–52.

——1995. *Industrial Constructions: The Sources of German Industrial Power*. New York: Cambridge University Press.

Hodgson, G. M. 1988. *Economics and Institutions: A Manifesto for a Modern Institutional Economics*. Cambridge: Polity Press.

Jarillo, J. C. 1993. *Strategic Networks: Creating the Borderless Organization*. Oxford: Butterworth-Heinemann.

Kamann, D.-J. F. 1993. 'Barriers, Bottlenecks and Filters in Networks: Theory and Practice'. Paper presented at the European Science Foundation EMOT

Conference: 'Assessing Inter-Organizational Networks'. 3–4 February 1994, Jouy-en-Josas.

Kogut, B. 1988. 'Joint Ventures: Theoretical and Empirical Perspectives'. *Strategic Management Journal*. 9: 319–32.

——Shan, W., and Walker, G. 1992. 'The Make-or-Cooperate Decision in the Context of an Industry Network'. In Nohria and Eccles 1992: 348–65.

Kreiner, C., and Schultz, M. 1993. 'Informal Collaboration in R&D: The Formation of Networks Across Organizations'. *Organization Studies*. 14: 189–211.

Lane, C., and Bachmann, R. 1996. 'The Social Constitution of Trust: Supplier Relations in Britain and Germany'. *Organization Studies*. 17: 365–93.

Larson, A. 1992. 'Network Dyads in Entrepreneurial Settings: A Study of the Governance of Exchange Relationships'. *Administrative Science Quarterly*. 37: 76–104.

Lawrence, P. R., and Lorsch, J. W. 1967. *Organization and Environment*. Cambridge, Mass.: Harvard University Press.

Lazerson, M. H. 1988. 'Organizational Growth of Small Firms: An Outcome of Markets and Hierarchies'. *American Sociological Review*. 53: 330–42.

——1993. 'Factory or Putting-out? Knitting Networks in Modena'. In Grabher 1993a: 203–26.

McEvily, B., and Zaheer, A. 1995. 'The Moderating Effects of Mediators: Exploring the Role of Third Parties in Interorganizational Networks'. Paper presented at the European Science Foundation EMOT Conference: 'Industry Structure and Interorganizational Networks'. 1–2 December 1995, Geneva.

McGee, J. E., Dowling, M. J., and Megginson, W. L. 1995. 'Cooperative Strategy and New Venture Performance: The Role of Business Strategy and Management Experience'. *Strategic Management Journal*. 16: 565–80.

MacNeil, I. R. 1974. 'The Many Futures of Contract'. *Sourthern California Law Review*. 47: 691–816.

March, J. G., and Simon, H. A. 1958. *Organizations*. New York: Wiley.

Mariotti, S., and Cainarca, G. C. 1986. 'The Evolution of Transaction Governance in the Textile-Clothing Industry'. *Journal of Economic Behavior and Organization*. 7: 351–74.

Mariti, P., and Smiley, P. H. 1983. 'Co-operative Agreements and the Organization of Industry'. *The Journal of Industrial Economics*. 31: 437–51.

Mayer, R. C., Davis, J. H., and Schoorman, F. D. 1995. 'An Integrative Model of Organizational Trust'. *Academy of Management Review*. 20: 709–34.

Miles, R. E., and Snow, C. C. 1986. 'Network Organizations: New Concepts for New Forms'. *California Management Review*. 28: 62–75.

Mitchell, W., and Singh, K. 1996. 'Survival of Businesses Using Collaborative Relationships to Commercialize Complex Goods'. *Strategic Management Journal*. 17: 169–95.

Mizruchi, M. S., and Galaskiewicz, J. 1993. 'Networks of Interorganizational Relations'. *Sociological Methods and Research*. 22: 46–70.

Morris, J., and Imrie, R. 1991. *Transformation in the Buyer-Supplier Relationship*. London: Macmillan.

Mowery, D. C. (ed.) 1988. *International Collaborative Ventures in US-Manufacturing*. Cambridge, Mass.: Ballinger.

Nohria, N. 1992. 'Is a Network Perspective a Useful Way of Studying Organizations?' In Nohria and Eccles 1992: 1–22.

——and Eccles, R. G. (eds.) 1992. *Networks and Organizations: Structure, Form, and Action*. Boston, Mass.: Harvard Business School Press.

——and Garcia-Pont, C. 1991. 'Global Strategic Linkages and Industry Structure'. *Strategic Management Journal*. 12: 105–24.

Ohmae, K. 1989. 'The Global Logic of Strategic Alliances'. *Harvard Business Review*. 67 (March–April): 143–54.

Oliver, C. 1990. 'Determinants of Interorganizational Relationships: Integration and Future Directions'. *Academy of Management Review*. 15: 241–65.

——1991. 'Network Relations and Loss of Organizational Autonomy'. *Human Relations*. 44: 943–61.

Osborn, R. N., and Baughn, C. C. 1990. 'Forms of Interorganizational Governance for Multinational Alliances'. *Academy of Management Journal*. 33: 503–19.

——Denekamp, J. G., and Baughn, C. C. 1993. 'The Prevalence of Technology-Intensive Alliances'. Paper presented at the European Science Foundation EMOT Conference: 'Assessing Inter-Organizational Networks'. 3–4 February 1994, Jouy-en-Josas.

Perrow, C. 1992. 'Small Firm Networks'. In Nohria and Eccles 1992: 471–90.

Pfeffer, J. 1987. 'A Resource Dependence Perspective on Intercorporate Relations'. In Mizruchi, M. S., and Schwartz, M. (eds.). *Intercorporate Relations*: 25–55. New York: Cambridge University Press.

Pisano, G. P. 1989. 'Using Equity Participation to Support Exchange: Evidence from the Biotechnology Industry'. *Journal of Law, Economics, and Organization*. 5: 109–26.

Pitelis, C. (ed.) 1993. *Transaction Costs, Markets, and Hierarchies*. Oxford: Blackwell.

Porter, M. E., and Fuller, M. B. 1986. 'Coalitions and Global Strategy'. In Porter, M. E. (ed.). *Competition in Global Industries*: 315–44. Boston, Mass.: Harvard Business School Press.

Powell, W. W. 1990. 'Neither Market nor Hierarchy: Network Forms of Organization'. *Research in Organizational Behavior*. 12: 295–336.

——Koput, K. W., and Smith-Doerr, L. 1996. 'Interorganizational Collaboration and the Locus of Innovation: Networks of Learning in Biotechnology'. *Administrative Science Quarterly*. 41: 116–45.

——and Smith-Doerr, L. 1994. 'Networks and Economic Life'. In Smelser, N. J., and Swedberg, R. (eds.). *The Handbook of Economic Sociology*: 368–402. Princeton, NJ: Princeton University Press.

Reve, T. 1990. 'The Firm as a Nexus of Internal and External Contracts'. In Aoki *et al*. 1990: 133–61.

——1992. 'Horizontal and Vertical Alliances in Industrial Marketing Channels'. *Advances in Distribution Channel Research*. 1: 235–57.

Ring, P. S., and Van de Ven, A. H. 1992. 'Structuring Cooperative Relationships Between Organizations'. *Strategic Management Journal*. 13: 483–98.

————1994. 'Developmental Processes of Cooperative Interorganizational Relationships'. *Academy of Management Review*. 19: 90–118.

Robins, J. A. 1993. 'Organization as Strategy: Restructuring Production in the Film Industry'. *Strategic Management Journal*. 14: 103–18.

Sabel, C. F. 1989. 'Flexible Specialization and the Re-emergence of Regional

Economies'. In Hirst, P., and Zeitlin, J. (eds.). *Reversing Industrial Decline?* 17–71. Oxford: Berg.

Salancik, G. R. 1995. 'WANTED: A Good Network Theory of Organization'. *Administrative Science Quarterly*. 40: 345–9.

Saxenian, A. 1994. *Regional Advantage*. Cambridge, Mass.: Harvard University Press.

Scott, J. 1987. 'Intercorporate Structures in Western Europe: A Comparative Historical Analysis'. In Mizruchi, M. S., and Schwartz, M. (eds.). *Intercorporate Relations*. 208–32. New York: Cambridge University Press.

Simon, H. A. 1991. 'Organizations and Markets'. *Journal of Economic Perspectives*. 5: 25–44.

Snow, C. C., and Thomas, J. B. 1993. 'Building Networks: Broker Roles and Behaviours'. In Lorange, P., Chakravarthy, B., Roos, J., and Van de Ven, A. H. (eds.). *Implementing Strategic Processes: Change, Learning and Co-operation*. 217–38. Oxford: Blackwell.

Steers, R. M., Yoo, K. S., and Ungson, G. 1989. *The Chaebol: Korea's New Industrial Might*. New York: Harper and Row, Ballinger.

Swedberg, R. 1994. 'Markets as Social Structures'. In Smelser, N. J., and Swedberg, R. (eds.). *The Handbook of Economic Sociology*. 255–82. Princeton, NJ: Princeton University Press.

Sydow, J. 1992. *Strategische Netzwerke*. Wiesbaden: Gabler.

Teece, D. J. 1986. 'Profiting from Technological Innovation: Implications for Integration, Collaboration, Licensing and Public Policy'. *Research Policy*. 15: 785–805.

——1992. 'Competition, Cooperation, and Innovation: Organizational Arrangements for Regimes of Rapid Technological Progress'. *Journal of Economic Behavior and Organization*. 18: 1–25.

Thompson, J. D. 1967. *Organizations in Action*. New York: McGraw-Hill.

Thorelli, H. B. 1986. 'Networks: Between Markets and Hierarchies'. *Strategic Management Journal*. 7: 37–51.

Turnbull, P., Oliver, N., and Wilkinson, B. 1989. 'Recent Developments in the UK Automotive Industry: JIT/TQC and Information Systems'. *Technology Analysis and Strategic Management*. 1: 409–22.

Vanberg, V. 1982. *Markt und Organisation*. Tübingen: Mohr.

Van de Ven, A. H. 1976. 'On the Nature, Formation, and Maintenance of Relations among Organizations'. *Academy of Management Review*. 2: 24–36.

Wasserman, S., and Faust, K. 1993. *Social Network Analysis: Methods and Applications*. New York: Cambridge University Press.

Weber, M. 1972. *Wirtschaft und Gesellschaft*. 5th edn. Tübingen: Mohr.

Whitley, R. D. 1993a. *Business Systems in East Asia: Firms, Markets and Societies*. London: Sage.

——(ed.) 1993b. *European Business Systems: Firms and Markets in their National Contexts*. London: Sage.

——and Kristensen, P. H. (eds.) 1995. *The Changing European Firm*. London: Routledge.

Williamson, O. E. 1985. *The Economic Institutions of Capitalism*. Cambridge: Free Press.

——1993. 'Calculativeness, Trust, and Economic Organization'. *Journal of Law and Economics*. 36: 453–86.

Windolf, P., and Beyer, J. 1993. 'Cooperative Capitalism: Corporate Networks in Germany and Britain'. Paper presented at the European Science Foundation EMOT Conference: 'Assessing Inter-Organizational Networks'. 3–4 February 1994, Jouy-en-Josas.

Woodward, J. 1965. *Industrial Organization: Theory and Practice*. London: Oxford University Press.

Zajac, E. J. and Olsen, C. P. 1993. 'From Transaction Cost to Transactional Value Analysis: Implications for the Study of Interorganizational Strategies'. *Journal of Management Studies*. 30: 131–45.

Zucker, L. G. 1986. 'Production of Trust: Institutional Sources of Economic Structure 1840–1920'. *Research in Organizational Behavior*. 8: 53–111.

II

RESOURCE FLOWS:
The Role of Activity Links

2

Relationships as Activity Links

ANNA DUBOIS AND HÅKAN HÅKANSSON

SUMMARY

One of the key problems in industrial markets is that activities in related companies have to be co-ordinated, not just within each company but also between them. One of the main ways of handling the co-ordination is developing relationships with the business counterparts. Business relationships have been analysed as some kind of simple on-off switch: from an economic point of view, either there is a relationship or there is not. In this article we try to go one step further and describe, characterize, and exemplify the content of business relationships as a continuous variable. In particular, we focus on how the relationship can function in terms of linking activities. Linking has different directions and dimensions, and therefore has different effects on the companies involved. The effects are analysed in three different analytical dimensions: the control actors gain over one another, the utilization of resources, that is, economic effects, and the possibility for individual actors to actively take part in change processes.

INTRODUCTION

One of the key problems in industrial companies is that their activities have to be related to those of others. The market mechanism (price) is supposed to take care of the general resource allocation. However, there are also other relational needs and problems (noted by Richardson as early as 1972). Issues like speed, lead times, waste, and capital rationalizations, and applying 'solutions' such as just-in-time, total-quality-control, time-based management, and lean production, have all been focused on during the last decade. All these solutions include, in addition to advice on the design of internal operations, recommendations regarding closer connections with external counterparts, like suppliers and customers. These new 'solutions' point to an interesting empirical question about how companies combine their internal activities with those of customers and suppliers. They also point to the importance of analysing this 'relating' in theoretical terms.

Previously, relationships between companies, from an economic point of view, have been identified in the transaction cost paradigm as a form of governance between the pure forms market and hierarchy. In this context, a relationship is seen as a mechanism that can be used to govern the transaction between two companies in case of market failure. Thus, relationships in terms of trust are assumed to be a complementary mechanism to price (market governance) and authority (hierarchical governance). From an analytical point of view, the relationships have, in this context, been seen as a rather simple on-off switch—either there is a relationship or there is not.

Empirical results from studies of business relationships give us reason to question this way of analysing relationships, and to extend the analysis both to how relationships affect the way activities performed by different actors are co-ordinated as well as how they affect resource utilization. This theoretical issue is addressed in this article, along with the previously identified empirical question as to how activities performed in different companies are systematically related.

We begin by describing in the first two sections research results from earlier studies. One specific aspect is the linking of activities. In the third section, the content of this linking of activities is more thoroughly discussed and the section concludes with an identification of two important variables. In the fourth section, some empirical examples dealing with attempts made by a fork-lift company to outsource some sub-systems are described. In analysing the cases, effects in three different dimensions are identified: the content of the links affects (a) the control an actor will exercise in relation to others, (b) the efficiency in resource utilization, and (c) the ability to take part in the change process. The article concludes with a discussion of the importance of relationships when identifying the relevant boundary of the company.

CONTENT AND FUNCTION OF RELATIONSHIPS

Empirical studies of relationships have been made in Europe, the USA and Japan, especially in the last decade (e.g. Håkansson 1982; Turnbull and Valla 1986; Ford 1990; Biemans 1991; Axelsson and Easton 1992; Frazier *et al.* 1988; Anderson and Narus 1990; Saxenian 1991; Takeuchi and Nonaka 1986; Teramoto 1990; Nonaka 1991). The main observations regarding business relationships found in these studies can be summarized under three major headings. The first concerns the general features of relationships. These can be described as follows.

- *Continuity*: major relationships between companies often show striking continuity. Figures like ten to twelve years have been found in many of the above-mentioned studies.

- *Complexity*: complexity can be seen, for example, in terms of number and type of individuals involved in the relationships. Numbers like five to ten or more persons on each side representing different organizational and task units have often been found; frequently technicians from production and R&D are important participants.
- *Low degree of formalization*: formal agreements are generally not regarded as especially effective in dealing with the uncertainties in the process. Instead, informal mechanisms such as trust and confidence are pointed out as key attributes.
- *Symmetry in resources and initiative*: in business markets both sides have resources and capabilities and are active in the relationships.
- *Adaptations are frequently made between parties*: some kinds of adaptation made by one of the two parties are generally a prerequisite for maintaining or developing the relationship. The counterparts have to make adaptations in order to function better *vis-à-vis* one another. Technical adaptations are common, but the same goes for administrative and logistic adaptations. The adaptations tie the two parties together in a physical sense.
- *Both co-operation and conflicts are present*: relationships are, in general, co-operative by nature, although they always include inherent conflicts. A relationship does not mean that the conflict has been resolved once and for all. Conflicts might even be necessary in order to keep the relationship 'alive', but the existence of the co-operative element directs the conflicts towards constructive solutions.

In summary the studies have revealed that relationships between companies are much 'thicker' than is depicted by any market model.

A second major observation is the importance of single relationships, that is, the *concentration* ratio on both the buying and the selling side in industrial companies. In Håkansson (1989), 123 small and medium-sized companies or business units were studied. The ten largest customers accounted for an average of 72 per cent of the sales, and the ten largest suppliers for almost the same percentage (70 per cent) of the purchased products. The same type of ratios were found by Perrone (1990) and Cowley (1988).

One consequence of the concentration of the volumes on a few important counterparts is that a limited set of relationships have a dominating influence on many companies both from an economic and a technological point of view. The handling of these relationships and how they are related to internal characteristics of the company as well as to other relationships are thus often perceived as important parameters by the management.

A third observation, related to both the observations above, is the *connectedness* of relationships. Connections between relationships have been identified as an important influencing factor both in research studies and by managers when asked about reasons for the development of certain relationships. Different types of connections have been identified. One major connection, which we have studied intensively, is the technical connection (Håkansson 1987, 1989; Laage-Hellman 1989; Waluszewski 1989; Lundgren 1994). The technical content of different relationships is connected mainly in relation to two basic technological characteristics. First, any single product or item is always used in a certain technical environment, within a technical system, which means that it is interdependent on and interrelated to other items. Secondly, every production system is part of a larger system and is dependent on what is done 'before', 'alongside', and 'after' it. Together, these two types of interdependency give rise to great variation of connections between the relationships.

Other connections are built on administrative, social, or time dependencies, making the relationships form network patterns. These patterns are influenced and shaped by the development in individual relationships, and they also give these relationships a specific and structured context (Håkansson and Snehota 1989).

ANALYSING ECONOMIC EFFECTS OF RELATIONSHIPS WITHIN NETWORKS

These empirical observations have led to the development of a network model in which the economic consequences of relationships are the focus (Håkansson and Snehota 1995). Major factors that have to be considered when assessing the economic outcome of a relationship have been identified as the two dimensions forming the schema in Fig. 2.1. The vertical dimension indicates that three different types or aspects of content have been identified. First, the economic outcome is dependent on how a relationship links activities. In some relationships, the activities of one actor are closely linked to the activities of the counterpart. Through relationships between several actors, this linking might result in extensive activity chains. In turn, these chains become interwoven causing the single individual links, together, to form an activity pattern. Consequently, when analysing the economic consequences of the linking in a certain relationship, the effects on this activity pattern have to be included. In the same way, the economic outcome for a single company of a certain activity is highly dependent on how it connects this activity to other internal activities, as well as to activities in relationships with its most important counterparts.

Secondly, the economic effects of a relationship are dependent on its content in terms of technical or other co-operation. Such co-operation affects the resources on both sides, that is, it results in ties between the resources. From a resource point of view, co-operation can be seen as a systematic relating—finding complementarities, similarities, and combination possibilities—and can result in adaptations of the resources. Such adapta-

FUNCTION

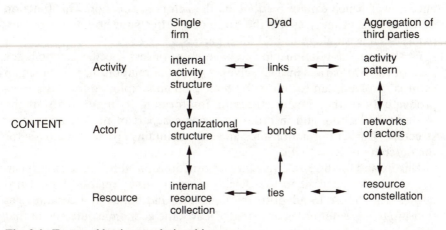

Fig. 2.1. Facets of business relationships
Source: Håkansson and Snehota 1995.

tions tie the resources of different actors together. Again, this tying will take place over several actors' resources and these ties in a single relationship become a brick in a larger structure, become part of a resource constellation. When assessing the economic effects of a resource tie in a single relationship, as well as the economic outcome of a single company's total resource collection, these interdependencies have to be considered.

Thirdly, the economic effects of a relationship depend on the content in terms of bonds between the actors (companies). The bonds are important for several reasons. One reason is to create security. To link activities or to tie resources is an uncertain business, as the outcome depends partly on a counterpart's willingness and ability to fulfil his or her part. Thus its success requires that the parties trust one another. Trust is built up over time and results in bonds. Another factor is the identity of each actor, which gives an actor certain 'attributes'. The actor is perceived as having certain attributes and thereby certain capabilities. This is partly influenced by the question of whom the actor is perceived as being related to. Thus, an identity always includes certain established 'bonds' which influence both potential counterparts as well as third parties' willingness to link activities or tie resources to that actor.

The second dimension (the horizontal dimension in Fig. 2.1) indicates that the economic effects of a relationship can be identified in relation to the function it has for three different 'subjects'. First, and most peculiar from a theoretical point of view, a relationship must have some functions for the dyad itself (the pair of actors). In order to be a 'real' relationship it must become a 'quasi-organization' in itself. In order to become a 'dyad' there must be opportunities to rationalize, to develop, and/or exercise influence/power which cannot be done by the actors in isolation. This function of the dyad is primary, as it is the cause of all effects for both the two companies seen as single units and third parties.

Furthermore, a relationship can have more or less specific functions for each of the two parties in themselves. Any of the relationships, in which an actor is involved, can (or must) be both used and exploited for shaping its productivity in the activity structure, for forming its innovativity in the resource collection, and in order to become a part of the organizational structure. The set of relationships an actor maintains provides the basis for the outcome of its activities.

Thirdly and finally, a relationship has functions for 'third' parties, as it can be used as an element in the development of other relationships. Third parties can choose to adapt to the links, ties, and bonds in a certain relationship to a greater or lesser extent. Clearly, the economic outcome of that relationship is dependent on the degree to which this takes place.

The framework developed indicates two critical theoretical conclusions. One is general: that the boundary of the firm, which is the boundary between hierarchical and market governance, is not as clear as is supposed in theory. The existence of relationships in terms of links, ties, and bonds blurs both the supposed control over the activities and resources inside the company and the supposed independence *vis-à-vis* activities and resources within other companies. The other conclusion is more specific, although even more important. The reason for distinguishing among links, ties, and bonds is that this blurring of the boundary is different for the activity, resource, and actor dimension. There might be bonds between two companies without any links or ties. There might be close links between two companies but no ties, and there might be ties but no links. This means that we have to break up the theoretically convenient assumption that companies combine and optimize activities and resources within their boundaries, and that the market mechanism takes care of the co-ordination between them.

This article focuses on the activity dimension. The aim is to show how relationships are used to link the activities performed by different companies and to try to give a first indication of important boundaries in relation to the activity structure. Resources and actors are also included, but only in order to characterize the activity linking. Activities are performed by actors, and resources are used and produced in the activities. However, this involvement of actors and resources elicits efficiency aspects of the linking, since it can be done either to reduce the use of resources or to create special values for a counterpart. Relationships examined as a tying of resources and as a mechanism to develop resources, are discussed in Håkansson (1993 and 1994).

LINKING OF ACTIVITIES

In order to analyse any single activity from an economic point of view, it has to be characterized in at least two respects: how the activity in itself is performed (as it determines both what is created and the resources consumed), and how the activity relates to other activities, that is, the interface between the activity and those other activities to which it is related. For example, a production activity such as a welding operation first has to be characterized in terms of what is welded, volumes and resources used, that is, use of equipment (e.g. a welding robot), consumption of man hours, consumption of electrodes, and so on. Secondly, it has to be characterized in terms of how it is related to other activities directly and indirectly, as long as there are some interdependencies among them, such as activities performed before, after, or in parallel. The value of what is created by the activity is dependent on how both these aspects are dealt with. Furthermore, the two aspects may be (and often are) negatively related to one another. If the activity is better designed in terms of use of less resources per unit (i.e. increasing the internal efficiency), this might result in problems regarding how the other activities relate to it (i.e. external efficiency might suffer). Another problem is that the need to relate the activity to other activities entails a dynamic element. As long as all of these activities are not perfectly adapted to all the others, there will be 'internal' reason to make adjustments which, in turn, give rise to new adjustments in other activities and so on. Furthermore, there might also be external changes affecting some activities, necessitating adaptation in some others.

Activities controlled by one actor are designed and related to one another through hierarchical governance, while activities performed by different actors can either be related to one another via a standardized market or through business relationships. As described in the previous section, activities within relationships can be directly related to one another. We call this 'linking'. The linking connects the performance of different actors' activities to one another. An example of how this can be done is given below.

The firm being examined in our example is a subcontractor manufacturing components for its four customers by performing five activities: (1) blending, (2) cutting, (3) drilling, (4) welding, and (5) milling, in different combinations (see Fig. 2.2). The first activity, blending, is a standard activity, that is, it is done in exactly the same way for all the customers. The cutting activity, which comes next in the row of activities, is performed for all customers with a high degree of similarity, since the same cutting equipment is used for all customers, albeit in different forms. Drilling is only done for two of the customers, and, as in the cutting activity, the same equipment can be used, although the different products to be produced for the two

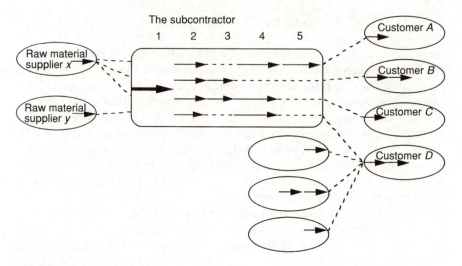

Fig. 2.2. Examples of activity links

customers require different placing and sizes of the holes drilled. The welding activity performed by the firm is directed towards three of the customers. Compared to the other activities, there is less similarity with reference to what is made for the customers. Although the same welding equipment can be used, different customer-specific fixtures are needed, and a special raw material used for customer D also requires a special electrode in the welding. The fifth activity, milling, is only done for customer A.

The subcontractor in this example manufactures components for its four customers which assemble these components with other components also purchased from suppliers (exemplified in Fig. 2.2 by customer D). Thus, the activities performed by the subcontractor have parallel connections to the activities of these other suppliers, as well as sequential connections to the assembling activities performed by its own customers. Furthermore, in using a special raw material for customer D, supplied by raw material supplier y, the subcontractor also, by his activities, indirectly links raw material supplier y with customer D.

The activities performed by the subcontractor in the example above can be analysed in three different but interrelated ways: (1) the individual activities (which can be included in several different activity chains), (2) the activity chains directed towards different actors, and (3) all activities performed within the frame of one actor, in this case the subcontractor.

First, the efficiency of the individual activities is dependent on the degree to which economies of scale may be captured. This, in turn, depends on the degree to which a certain activity can be performed in a uniform way, or by the same set of resource units. In our example, the subcontractor utilizes the highest share of scale effects for activity 1, and, to some extent, for activities 2, 3, and 4 also. The better the company can connect different customers' needs to one another, the more cost efficient it will be, from this point of view.

Secondly, the activity chains directed towards the different customers determine the uniqueness of what is produced for each customer and, in this way, influence the value created. In our example, all four customers obtain unique solutions from using this supplier, since the supplier is able to combine and adapt its activities in different ways for each of them. Thus, they may gain input that is adapted to their specific situation in terms of equipment, other inputs, or the special requirements of their customers. In this way, the linking gives the activities direction, as they can be combined with some activities and thereby 'exclude' others. One result is that we get linking in a series. The activities are linked into chains which stretch over several actors. There are both direct links—between actors with direct contact—and indirect links—as exemplified by supplier y, in Fig. 2.2, to customer D.

Thirdly, all activities performed in the frame of the subcontractor determine the overall efficiency or productivity of this actor. The internal efficiency is dependent on its ability to combine and to integrate different resource elements needed to perform the activities, as well as on its ability to create unique solutions with a high value for its customers.

The examples show that linking an activity means to design it in such a way that the output can be used as inputs for other activities or in combination with outputs from other activities. By directing the activity, that is, by development of a link, it is possible both to reduce costs and to increase revenues. By linking, different actors can take advantage of internal economies of scale and integration effects, even when they need to produce something individualized. They can take advantage of the fact that there are always similarities and complementarities in activities and resources, but that these (1) do not have to be the same for all, and (2) do not have to be constant over time, but that they (3) have to be combined. The existence of links opens up the possibility of making 'local' adjustments to different changes taking place in activities performed by different counterparts. Linking, thus, makes it possible to adapt single activities within an actor's activity structure to specific changes in the activities of a counterpart without changing the whole structure.

There may be different types of dependencies among the activities which will correspond to different types of links. Here, we will limit the discussion to three types: links based on time, administrative, and technical dependencies. Linking activities, from a time point of view, is a way to reduce all types of 'buffers'. Links are thus a means to synchronize the timing. The link is the use of the same 'clock'. Administrative links are developed to take care of difficulties in the co-ordination of activities. As both internal planning procedures (executing the hierarchy governance) and external exchanges (governed by the market or the relationship) demand information handling, links are procedures which integrate these different information flows. A third type regards technical dependencies. The technical links relate to the combination of outputs from different activities. In the previous example, the output of the subcontractor is used by the customers as components for their different end-products. Hence, there are technical dependencies among these components, since they are connected to one another in the end-products. Thus, if one of the customers makes a change in its end-product, this may have different direct and indirect impacts on the other parts. If it results in changes in one of the components supplied by the subcontractor in our example, this may have positive or negative impacts on the activities performed towards the other customers.

Consider, for instance, that customer A and customer C change their end-products, resulting in an adaptation of activity 4, undertaken by the subcontractor, which increases the similarity in the performance of the activity with reference to these two customers. A consequence may be that customer D, to which activity 4 is also directed, experiences negative effects, since the degree to which common resources may be shared becomes reduced *vis-à-vis* this actor. This illustrates how technical changes in individual activities may affect the performance of individual actors through direct and indirect links among their activities.

Another example of the effects of technical links is if raw material supplier x develops a better material which allows customer B to eliminate one activity, for example, a surface treatment activity. However, the subcontractor may, because of changing materials characteristics, experience difficulties in some of its machining activities. Naturally, this may, in turn, affect the other customers of the subcontractor.

The three types of links are sometimes closely related in one relationship, while in other cases only one type may prevail. Since they have different effects, variation in this respect must consequently be covered. Linking is, in conclusion, a tool for companies to take advantage of internal and external dependencies, and is employed to obtain economy in the performance of single activities, provided that each of these activities is dependent, in one way or another, on other activities performed by other actors. In order to identify the effects, the links have to be assessed in terms of direction and types.

OUTSOURCING OF THREE SUB-SYSTEMS BY A FORK-LIFT PRODUCER

To illustrate linking, we have chosen an example where some activities are subject to outsourcing, that is, some activities are moved from one actor to another. Although this is a rather simple and straightforward change, it can have different effects, illustrated by the following three examples regarding the outsourcing of three sub-systems by a fork-lift producer.

The fork-lift producer (henceforth referred to as SweFork) purchased all the components for its products, concentrating its production on assembling activities. The fork lifts were produced in a few basic models, largely adapted to customer-specific requirements. A new, smaller model was developed to cover a new market segment which was believed to demand more standardized products, manufactured in large volumes. As it turned out, however, the majority of these lifts were, to some extent, also adapted to individual customer requirements. Production considerations came into the development process early. The assembling activities were to be performed in two main steps: pre-assembly of component systems and final assembly (including various complementary activities, such as painting) into finished products. Pre-assembly was performed in general workstations with various types of equipment, such as fixtures and jigs, although the systems were quite heterogeneous in terms of assembly activities. Problems in connecting the different systems appeared, partly owing to the differences among them. Owing to these problems and the fact that capacity was generally under pressure during the late 1980s, consideration was given to whether or not the pre-assembly could be outsourced to some of the suppliers. Two main advantages were perceived. First, it would allow the company to concentrate on final assembly activities, in other words, to become more specialized. Secondly, efficiency could also be increased if the system suppliers were better suited to handle the different pre-assembly activities, and were thus able to perform them at lower costs.

System 1

The first system contains two parts. One of these is well defined with respect to its interface with other parts and components, making it easy to break out of the structure. This part is also relatively standardized and is thus not subject to individual adaptations. Outsourcing this part of the system meant that several people on the SweFork staff, occupied with developing this system, could be reassigned. The other part of the system is more difficult to handle separately, owing to specific end-customer requirements. Accordingly, sequential restraints became apparent, since the end-customer-specific components were not assembled last. For this reason, some alternative conditions would have to be fulfilled to make outsourcing possible: Either the connections between some of the components could be changed in order to make it possible to assemble the end-customer-specific components as the last step. This could then be done by either SweFork, if these components could be taken out of the system, or by the supplier, which would, however, increase the co-ordination needed between the firms; or an attempt could be made to standardize this part of the system.

In this case a previously unknown supplier was found, who specialized in producing more or less standardized systems of this kind. The volumes produced by this supplier were about ten times larger than SweFork's production. Economies of scale seemed to be utilized, as reflected in the prices given by the supplier.

However, another problem appeared. There was an important component in the second part of the system, in terms of technical function as well as in terms of value. This component was bought from a supplier with whom SweFork had had a long-lasting relationship, and from whom it bought a large variety of components. Although SweFork was a rather marginal customer for this very large supplier, SweFork always received assistance, not least technical assistance, which was considered as very important. One solution would be to let this supplier deliver the component to the system supplier. Another solution would be to let the system supplier use its own newly developed version of this major component. Neither of these alternatives was, however, perceived to be acceptable by the old component supplier. Furthermore, it was assumed that SweFork's main competitor was buying a similar system, with some minor adaptations, from the same supplier but without having any actual impact on the technical performance of the system.

In this situation there were apparent efficiency gains that could be taken advantage of, owing to economies of scale in outsourcing the first sub-system. The second sub-system raises questions regarding the specific adaptations to end-customers. One alternative was to eliminate these dependencies through standardization. This would, however, probably have a negative impact on the relationships between SweFork and its customers. If these are considered to be too high, the end-customer-specific adaptations have to be dealt with. The second alternative was to make adjustments in the second sub-system to facilitate the necessary co-ordination. Thus, the way different components are connected to one another becomes a matter of interest. These connections might be changed in order to achieve an interface between what is standardized and what is not, so that the specific components can be assembled last. Technical dependencies in the system can be changed to make another allocation of activities possible.

Another restraint in this case may be the competitive aspects, that is to say, negative effects of the connectedness between one relationship and others. In this case there were two such competitive relationships to be considered. The important component supplier from whom SweFork also buys many other components was one of them. If the situation was not handled properly, it could result in severe losses in the other purchases made from the component supplier, and these indirect effects could easily eliminate all positive direct effects achieved by outsourcing the system. The second com-

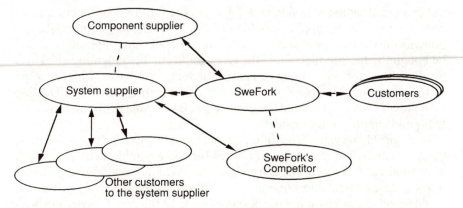

Fig. 2.3. Relationships to be considered in the outsourcing decision of system 1

petitive relationship, which needed to be considered, was the competitor of SweFork who was buying from the same system supplier. In order to judge whether or not this should be seen as a threat or as an opportunity (relating to potential cost savings in production and development), further analysis of this system's importance in terms of technical performance and also the company's own ability to develop and produce a better system, was needed. Therefore, the analysis of the consequences of outsourcing this system could not be made in isolation, but had to incorporate potential impacts on other important relationships (see Fig. 2.3).

System 2

The second system contained about forty components of various kinds, both standardized and SweFork specific. The system was divided into two parts which enabled assembly to be split into two steps: first separate assembly of the two parts, and then assembly of these two parts together with a few additional components. One question was whether the whole system could be outsourced to one and the same supplier, or whether it should be outsourced to two or even three different suppliers. One particular supplier of some of the specific components was chosen as a potential system supplier. Calculations made by SweFork and the supplier showed that the supplier could handle the first pre-assembly step, that is, mounting the two parts, at a lower cost. The second step, however, seemed to be less costly for SweFork to perform.

If we focus on the activities, outsourcing this part system can mainly be seen as moving the activities performed. The system supplier had, just like the customer, a general workshop in which different kinds of labour-intensive activities were performed. Most components in the system were

not produced by the supplier, and, owing to the different production technologies, the system supplier would not be able to take any additional components into its own production. Therefore, some of the components should
be bought by the supplier, while the rest should still be bought by SweFork.
SweFork's reason for staying in control of some purchases was that some
of the component suppliers were also used for other purchases. Dealing
with these purchases enabled SweFork to get favourable prices and to maintain good supplier relationships.

Some problems were brought up during the outsourcing discussions. One
of these concerned the estimated times for the assembly activities, which
were found to be inaccurate. Corrections needed after assembly consumed,
in some cases, about the same amount of time as the assembly itself. This
could be solved by changing the design of some of the components. Furthermore, problems with late discovery of faulty parts could not be resolved by
outsourcing the system. However, these problems were highlighted since
their effects became obvious potential sources of conflict. These problems
must thus be subject to actions if outsourcing were to be possible, since
problems of this kind could not as easily be concealed when they were no
longer handled within the framework of SweFork's own activities.

There seemed to be no apparent efficiency gains to be exploited in this
case, at least not on a short-term basis, owing to the fact that both firms
used general workshops with no direct scale benefits, because of the low
degree of similarity among the activities they performed. Furthermore, the
way the purchases were to be handled seemed to imply an increased need
for co-ordination if the system was to be assembled by the system supplier,
rather than keeping the activities in-house at SweFork.

However, there may be positive long-term effects of outsourcing this
system, such as the cost reduction potential the system supplier may exploit
by linking its own activities with those of other customers who have similar
needs in terms of the activities performed. This may, in a longer-term perspective, give rise to economies of scale to be utilized by the system supplier, which could not have been achieved by SweFork. Another long-term
effect may be that if SweFork succeeds in outsourcing all systems that were
previously assembled in the same general workstation, this resource unit
could be eliminated. However, during the process of change, this general
workstation will be less utilized the more systems are outsourced, and thus
become increasingly inefficient, given that it has some fixed costs.

Other potential gains from outsourcing this system are related to the
interface between the activities performed by the system supplier and those
performed by SweFork. The interface can itself force the companies to solve
some of the inefficiencies that were previously hidden within SweFork's
activity structure, because they would otherwise become sources of conflict
between the firms.

The reason why it seemed most efficient, from a cost point of view, to outsource the first part of the system but not the second, may be partly explained in terms of how the calculations were made. A traditional product accounting method was used, which meant that general overheads were apportioned to the direct costs of labour and purchased materials. Thus, even though the efficiency of a minor part of the structure could be increased by outsourcing, the overall cost structure, in combination with the accounting system, entailed cost estimates which favoured in-house production.

System 3

The system included only ten components but its value was about ten times higher than that of System 2. One major component included was bulky and heavy and was difficult to handle without special equipment. The supplier of this component turned out to have a workstation with feasible equipment for handling assembly of this kind of system. This made the supplier able to assemble the system in half the time it took SweFork. It also turned out that the supplier had already developed special carriers for this component to facilitate transportation in its own production. These carriers could also be used for external transports, as well as to make SweFork's internal materials handling more efficient. Additionally, the supplier was able to paint the system at its own facilities. The painting was previously done partly by SweFork and partly by other suppliers. Since the supplier bought larger volumes of paint, it was also able to achieve favourable prices, compared with SweFork. Moreover, the supplier offered to buy paint for SweFork for other purposes on its contract. The supplier could also, within the frame of its existing activities, produce a few other components included in the system. Moreover, the supplier was already purchasing some of the other components, in comparably large volumes, for other purposes.

Among its customers, the supplier had a few very large and powerful automotive companies on whom the supplier was heavily dependent. These customers were considered very demanding, not least concerning continuous cost reductions. The supplier was thus constantly trying to find new materials, production techniques, and designs in order to be able to obtain the cost reduction goals set by these customers. In order to be able to benefit from these improvements, SweFork had to be open to adjustments which might also affect other related parts to some extent.

Here, cost reductions could be accomplished by outsourcing the system to the particular supplier. Different advantages, mainly related to the performance of the three activities, could be obtained. First, system assembly could be more efficiently performed by the supplier, owing to economies of scale. These could be achieved since the resources used by the supplier were better adapted to this kind of assembly which, in turn, was explained by the assembly activities performed by the supplier (and directed to the supplier's other customers) having a high degree of similarity. Secondly, the painting of this system could be done more efficiently. By handing over all painting to this supplier, the need for co-ordination could be reduced as compared with the previous situation. Thirdly, the efficiency of purchasing could be improved if the large volume benefits this supplier had built up were taken advantage of (or even increased).

Another advantage of outsourcing the system to this supplier was related to the supplier's other customers, who forced the system supplier to increase its efficiency in different respects, mainly in relation to the production methods and the materials used. It is easy to see the positive effects of this, but it may also, in a longer-term perspective, force SweFork to make adaptations in order to be able to benefit from these changes. The technical dependencies between the system subject to outsourcing and other parts of the end-product may thus require analysis in order for SweFork to be able to view the consequences of these potential benefits.

An additional observation in this case is that there seemed to be several cost reduction potentials to be utilized without outsourcing the whole system to the supplier. These potentials could be exploited simply by co-ordinating some of the activities already performed by the two companies. For instance, the purchasing of some components could be co-ordinated in order that both companies could acquire advantages of scale. Furthermore, the use of the carriers already developed could be extended without necessitating any additional changes. However, to accomplish this type of effect, active participation on the part of the supplier is required, which, in turn, requires 'orientation' towards the particular customer. This might be impossible to achieve without outsourcing.

DISCUSSION OF THE CHANGES

Despite the fact that the three examples are similar as they all concern the same basic change, namely, outsourcing of a production activity to a supplier, they have quite different effects both in terms of how they change the control the buying company exercises over the activities and in their economic effects. In order to determine these effects in a more precise way, the changes have to be analysed in terms of linking activities.

When discussing control and economic effects of outsourcing, a good starting-point is given in Fig. 2.1. Outsourcing basically means some changes in the activity structure, i.e. new or changed activity links, and such changes might influence both resources and actors. The linking of activities influences the way actors are related to one another and it also affects the use of resources. When links are changed, both actors and resources are affected. Outsourcing, in all three examples, gives rise to different changes in the links and thus to different effects on the actors and the resources.

Control has to do with how the actors relate their activities to one another's and the economic results of how the resources are utilized. We begin the analysis in the actor dimension, that is to say, the effects on control, and then move to the resource dimension, that is, the design of the resource units needed to perform the activities.

Effects on the Control of Actors

All activities are performed by individual actors and are also controlled by actors. However, the existence of activity chains gives rise to a specific direction in each activity, towards other actors, which blurs up the control dimension. To give an activity a certain direction means to link it to a certain counterpart's activities. The direction can thereby imply that the counterpart is given some control over the design of the activity. This is obvious in the situation when one activity is directed towards only one other actor. From a design point of view, it can then be compared as similar to an internal activity of that counterpart. When it is directed towards a group of actors, each one is 'given' some design control, but at a much lower level than in the previous situation. The larger this group, the less control each actor has, that is, the direction becomes generalized. The discussion points to a need to differentiate between the control of the resources used to perform an activity and the control of how the activity is designed. The economic outcome of an activity can, in this way, be mutually controlled by two or more counterparts, that is, there is a 'link' between them.

Every activity is thus co-ordinated in two different ways, one towards other activities performed by the focal actor (degree of integration) and the other towards activities performed by other actors (degree of direction).[1] Consequently, a change of an activity, for example, outsourcing it, will have different effects on control, depending on (1) how the activity was previously directed towards external activities and (2) how well it was integrated with other internal activities.

Every actor can be seen as a node, or as a 'switchboard', where a certain number of activity chains have been knotted together. Every actor can thus be characterized both by how it is directing its activities and how the counterparts direct their activities towards the actor. We will here use the term orientation to capture this dimension. Any activity link has to be assessed within this context.

Moving an activity can, to summarize, have the following effects with regard to the control of actors:

(1) the direction of performed activities might change. This relates to activities within the focal company as well as different counterparts.

---

[1] Integration concerns combinations of activities and resources, while direction concerns activities alone.

When this change is of any magnitude it will affect the orientation of the existing companies;

(2) the outsourcing might also change the direction of activities performed by completely new actors. Such changes might lead to both redirections and reorientations in new dimensions.

The outsourcing in the three examples can now be assessed in this respect. In the first example a new actor is considered. However, using this actor would create problems in relation to one of the existing suppliers, who might withdraw its orientation. The giving of 'direction' is voluntary and always based on certain conditions.

In the second example the outsourcing of an activity will increase the direction of the supplier's activity towards the customer. This might increase the orientation of this supplier towards the customer in such a way that possible long-term positive effects open up. Furthermore, by becoming involved in these activities, the supplier might be able to mobilize other customers with similar needs (cause them to direct their activities). In turn, this might be positive from a resource utilization and development point of view. At the same time, however, it might direct the supplier's activity more towards other actors, which might be negative in the long run for SweFork.

In the third example, the supplier is trying to take advantage of the existence of already established links between the supplier and some demanding customers who are strongly forcing the supplier into continuous improvements. By directing its own activities towards the supplier, which also means towards these customers, SweFork will lose control of the design. Nevertheless, it can benefit in resource terms.

EFFECTS ON THE ACTIVATED STRUCTURE OF RESOURCE UNITS

In order to perform activities resources are needed. In order to perform a certain activity (for example, a production activity) some resources have to be related and fixed to one another. To perform an activity, a resource structure has to be crystallized. Consequently, a certain 'stiffness' is built into the system. For example, when a workstation is designed, some physical resources are combined with some human resources and the result, that is, a resource unit, is fixed both in a certain place and a certain form.

Resources have several important characteristics with respect to activities. One is that resources are always limited, which restricts the possibilities of performing activities. Furthermore, as resources have to be fixed in relation to one another in order to be used, at least in certain dimensions, they can only be used to perform certain activities. A third aspect is that they also become fixed to a geographical location which gives rise to certain co-ordination activities, for example, transports.

Any move of an activity has effects in terms of these three aspects. The effects of moving an activity can be:

(1) the resources needed for performing the activity may be better utilized because of the possibility of taking advantage of similarities with other activities;

(2) the resource units concerned might have to be changed—resources within the units may have to be added, eliminated, and/or changed;

(3) the co-ordination activities needed to utilize the set of resource units might have to be changed (increased or decreased).

All three aspects have cost effects and, when assessing a change, they must be considered. In our three examples of outsourcing, there are very clear effects of the first type in the first and third examples. In the first example the supplier can use a set of resource units producing ten times the volume produced within the earlier used set of resource units (within SweFork). Economies of scale can thus be exploited. In the third example, the supplier has a resource unit designed in such a way that it can perform the activity in half the time it took SweFork. Owing to specialization and greater volume, the resource utilization clearly increased after the change. However, this will not be the case in the second example, since the same type of resource unit was already used by SweFork. There is no reason to believe that the utilization of the resources will be changed because of such a move.

The second aspect above concerns effects on the resource units of changes in the activity links. There is no really good example of this in the three case descriptions. An obvious effect which is not covered regards the use of the internal resource elements which became less utilized owing to the outsourcing.

In order to use a set of resource units, there must be some co-ordination activities. In the third example, co-ordination activities related to painting could be eliminated if all painting activities were done in one resource unit of the system supplier. In the second example, the co-ordination with some other suppliers' resource units may increase as the system supplier will not be allowed to make their own purchases. Finally, in the first example, a necessary condition to outsource the second sub-system was that SweFork's customers' requirements (how to use the fork lift within their resource units) were co-ordinated with the use of the system supplier's resource unit.

Linking as a Dynamic Mechanism

The characteristics of activity links are very much a consequence of the linking process. Linking is generally done through small successive adaptations. It is done day by day, step by step, by several actors, relating several actors. Links emerge over time. The emerging process is a consequence of the impossibility of ever finding one totally optimal solution as there are so many dimensions and so many aspects to consider for so many different actors. Consequently, the state today is just a compromise, which will be followed by a new compromise tomorrow, and so on. The links developed by others give both opportunities and restriction to the individual company. In order to survive, in order to keep its position within the network, it has to more or less continuously, in a more or less conscious way, adjust its own links. Its previous counterparts will demand this process, and potential new ones often require it in order to be interested in taking part in exchange.

Linking has some interesting features from a dynamic point of view. First, it facilitates management by giving the actor some focal points. A link is a definition of a critical dimension in the interface with one or several counterparts.

Secondly, it gives a certain structure to the change process which facilitates learning. Change always includes learning (Lundvall 1988) and the linking process gives an opportunity to direct the learning about the design of its own activities in a way that is interesting for at least some of the counterparts. The positive effects of learning can in this way be increased—it becomes directly complementary to the previous knowledge of the counterparts, as well as to what they are learning. It constitutes the learning-overlapping—and gives it, at the same time, some common elements as there is a certain complementarity. The linking process contributes in this respect.

Thirdly, links in terms of mutual directions are also important from an investment point of view. Every change of activity has a double effect on investment. For one thing, investments are normally required to effect the change. New resources may be needed or old ones developed. Secondly, the changes make old investments obsolete. Both these effects can be seen as frictions, as factors defending the old structure. Consequently, it will always be risky to be involved in changes. Linking decreases these risks in two ways. First, linking is by definition a partial change, since an actor only adapts in some dimensions and towards specific counterparts. Consequently, the company can, in this way, reduce the risk and reach a level which is acceptable for it. Secondly, as linking is often mutual, it includes an ingredient of mobilization; an actor can, through its orientation, exert influence where its counterparts direct their activities. Risks can in this way be shared with the counterparts. Through the linking process, each actor knows that there are at least some other actors who are travelling the same road and that the journey will thus be safer.

The main argument is, in summary, that the linking process facilitates the individual company in handling the trauma involved in making changes. It helps to find out what is important (for itself as well as for main counterparts), what should and what can be learnt, and to reduce the uncertainties in investing in the future.

CONCLUSIONS

In the introduction we claimed there was a need to extend the way relationships are analysed from an economic point of view. In the analysis we have penetrated one specific aspect of the content—the inclusion of activity links—and its effects on control and efficiency. We have tried to describe linking as a way to incorporate a specific dimension in an activity. The links can be characterized in terms of different types (technical, administrative, time based, and so on) and different directions (which activities a specific activity is linked to). When evaluating a certain type of change—outsourcing of production activities—we have tried to demonstrate the need to bring in the links in order to measure the effects. Three types of effects have been covered.

First, the control different actors have in relation to one another is related to the existence, the distribution, and the direction of activity links. The degree of control seems to be positively related to the extent to which the company can induce others to link their activities in a specific way to the activities performed by that company, and negatively to the need for the company to link its activities to those performed by others. One problem is that in the latter case there are often positive outcomes as shown in the third system example.

Secondly, the economic outcome of the activities is dependent on the use of resources which is also influenced by the direction of different links. The economic effects seem to stem to a large extent from how the focal relationship can be connected to the other relationships of the suppliers. If there are no connections to other relationships, the outsourcing seems, as in the second example, to be nothing more than a formal move of an activity. Such a move has no effect on costs.

Thirdly, the linking process is a tool for companies to handle problems concerned with dynamics. Furthermore, we have also concluded that the control an actor has over the design of an activity does not have to follow the control of the resources used for performing the activity. Thus, activities and resources have to be analysed separately.

The existence of relationships makes it difficult to identify the appropriate analytical boundary of the firm. From an activity-link point of view, we can identify a boundary related to the control an actor has over the design of activities undertaken 'outside', which are hence directed to the firm in focus. Figure 2.4 shows the boundary delimiting activities undertaken outside, but linked to those performed within, a particular firm and those that are not linked.

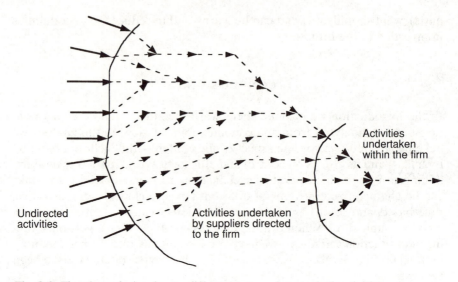

Activities
undertaken
within the firm

Undirected
activities

Activities undertaken
by suppliers directed
to the firm

Fig. 2.4. Firm boundaries due to different types of control of activities

In the examples given, the focus was on the supply side of SweFork. Out-sourcing the three systems can in principle be illustrated as a movement of the boundary separating activities which were linked to those carried out by SweFork and activities that were not linked.

REFERENCES

Anderson, J. C., and Narus, J. A. 1990. 'A Model of Distributor Firm and Manufac-
    turer Firm Working Partnerships'. *Journal of Marketing*. 54: 42–58.
Axelsson, B., and Easton, G. (eds.) 1992. *Industrial Networks: A New View of Reality*.
    London: Routledge.
Biemans, W. G. 1991. *Managing Innovation within Networks*. London: Routledge.
Cowley, P. R. 1988. 'Market Structure and Business Performance: An Evaluation of
    Buyer/Seller Power in the PIMS Database'. *Strategic Management Journal*. 9:
    271–8.
Ford, D. I. (ed.) 1990. 'Understanding Business Markets: Interaction, Relationships
    and Networks'. London: Academic Press.
Frazier, G. L., Spekman, R. E., and O'Neal, C. R. 1988. 'Just-in-time Exchange Rela-
    tionships in Industrial Markets'. *Journal of Marketing*. 52: 52–67.
Håkansson, H. (ed.) 1982. *International Marketing and Purchasing of Industrial
    Goods: An Interaction Approach*. Chichester: John Wiley and Sons.
——(ed.) 1987. *Industrial Technological Development: A Network Approach*.
    London: Croom Helm.

——1989. *Corporate Technological Behaviour: Cooperation and Networks*. London: Routledge.

——1993. 'Networks as a Mechanism to Develop Resources'. In Beije, P., Groenewegen, J., and Nuys, O. *et al.* (eds.). *Networking in Dutch Industries*. 207–23. Leven-Apeldorn: Garant.

——1994. 'Economics of Technological Relationships'. In Granstrand, O. (ed.). *Economics of Technology*. 253–70. Amsterdam: Elsevier.

——and Snehota, I. 1989. 'No Business is an Island: The Network Concept of Business Strategy'. *Scandinavian Journal of Management*. 5: 187–200.

————1995. *Developing Relationships in Business Networks*. London: Routledge.

Laage-Hellman, J. 1989. 'Technological Development in Industrial Networks'. Unpublished dissertation. Department of Business Administration, University of Uppsala. Sweden.

Lundgren, A. 1994. *Technological Innovation and Industrial Evolution—The Emergence of Industrial Networks*. London: Routledge.

Lundvall, B. Å. 1988. 'Innovation as an Interaction Process: From User-Producer Interaction to the National System of Innovation'. In Dosi, G., Freeman, C., Nelson, R., and Silverberg, G. (eds.). *Technical Change and Economic Theory*. 349–69. London: Pinters Publishers.

Nonaka, I. 1991. 'The Knowledge-Creating Company'. *Harvard Business Review*. 69: 96–104.

Perrone, V. 1990. *Strutture organizzative dimpresa: driteri e modelli di progrettazione*. Milano EGEA.

Richardson, G. B. 1972. 'The Organisation of Industry'. *The Economic Journal*. 82: 883–96.

Saxenian, A. 1991. 'The Origin and Dynamics of Production Networks in Silicon Valley'. *Research Policy*. 20: 423–37.

Takeuchi, H., and Nonaka, I. 1986. 'The New Product Development Game'. *Harvard Business Review*. 64: 137–46.

Teramoto, Y. 1990. *Network Power*. Tokyo: NTT Press.

Turnbull, P. W., and Valla, J.-P. (eds.) 1986. *Strategies for International Industrial Marketing*. London: Croom Helm.

Waluszewski, A. 1989. 'Framväxten av en ny mekanisk massateknik—en Utvecklingshistoria'. (The Emergence of a New Mechanical Pulp Technology—A Development Story.) Doctoral Dissertation, Department of Business Studies, Uppsala University.

Williamson, O. 1985. *The Economic Institution of Capitalism*. New York: The Free Press.

——1991. 'Comparative Economic Organization: The Analysis of Discrete Structural Alternatives'. *Administrative Science Quarterly*. 26: 269–96.

3

Inter-Firm Responses to Heterogeneity of Demand over Time

GEOFF EASTON AND LUIS ARAUJO

ABSTRACT

This chapter examines the effects of heterogeneity of demand over time on modes of economic co-ordination in organizational markets. Departing from a discussion of different sources of heterogeneity of demand, the objective of the chapter is set in terms of examining the intra- and inter-organizational effects of coping strategies or response modes to short-term heterogeneity of demand over time. This perspective is contrasted with traditional approaches to the discontinuity–flexibility debate as in the manufacturing flexibility and strategy, and organizational change literatures. The discussion of firms' responses to heterogeneity of demand over time is organized under a framework provided by the flow through nodes model of change in industrial networks. Six categories of response—selection, reflection, adaptation, absorption, transmission, and configuration—are discussed in turn and implications derived for modes of economic co-ordination. In particular, we argue that the transmission and configuration response modes are more likely to give rise to the formation of inter-organizational networks, whilst other response modes tend to rely on either intra-firm or market mechanisms to deal with heterogeneity of demand over time.

INTRODUCTION

The genesis of this chapter occurred as a result of attempts to understand the emergence of network structures and processes of certain unusual organizational markets. The word market is used in this context to mean the place where a nexus of exchanges occurs rather than as an aggregation of customers, which seems to be the frequently employed definition used by marketing academics. Lazonick (1991: 59–60) points out that the classical definition of market exchange only applies in so far as buyers and sellers have equal, unrestricted access to each others' resources. As soon as this condition is violated—for example, by the parties entering into a long-term supply contract—the conditions for market exchange disappear. Every necessary piece of information to consummate exchanges is contained in price-quantity functions and nothing else about the transacting parties matters (see Chapter 1).

The organizational markets we allude to above, while being diverse in and among themselves, have certain interesting features in common. They are, unfortunately, labelled in a number of different ways which helps to hide the commonalities. Project marketing describes the process of marketing one-off projects such as the design of large-scale software systems and construction projects and is defined in terms of the end-product. Systems selling is concerned with the processes by which some firms bundle a mixture of tangible and intangible offerings in order to meet customer requirements more closely and is largely defined in terms of the marketing and selling process. By contrast jobbing refers to a production technology which offers high degrees of flexibility allowing the production of a wide range of tailor-made products in, for example, the printing or engineering industries. Hollow corporations, pyramidal supply structures, New Industrial Districts, and supply constellations are all related developments which suggest attempts by firms to externalize some of the activities that they might previously have undertaken themselves (Harrisson 1994).

What these markets have in common, we argue, is that they may be thought to involve some of the ways firms respond to demand which is presented to them as heterogeneous over time. Demand heterogeneity refers to variety in the form rather than the quantity of such demand. We are not concerned here with how firms meet unpredictable sales volumes, though this is important, but how they respond to variety in individual customer(s) wants over time. The customers in this case are firms, though the impact of heterogeneity in final consumer demand clearly has a major influence on what happens at the inter-organizational level.

In the first section of the chapter, demand heterogeneity is defined, its forms described, and its sources speculated upon. In the second and principal section, organizational responses to demand heterogeneity are categorized and discussed. The crucial point of relevance is that many, if not all, of these responses involve other firms and often novel and under-researched modes of economic co-ordination. These modes have usually been classified under the network form of economic co-ordination although, as we will attempt to show, there is a huge variety of network forms of economic co-ordination. As in the rest of this book (see Chapter 1), we take inter-organizational networks to refer to modes of economic co-ordination characterized by dense and relatively stable patterns of economic exchange, embedded in concrete time-space and institutional contexts.

Firms may employ different ways to respond to demand heterogeneity over time and six broad categories of response mode are identified and described. They have been developed from the flow through nodes model, a part of the industrial networks paradigm (Easton and Lundgren 1992), and have been labelled selection, reflection, adaptation, absorption, transmission, and configuration. Our objective in using the flow-through-nodes model is to illustrate how some organizational responses are more relevant and suited to some demand heterogeneity situations than others. The aim is to formulate a framework that will allow us to explain the emergence, persistence, or temporary character of a number of intra- and inter-organizational network forms and processes (e.g. jobbing firms, project marketing consortia) prevalent in a number of organizational markets. The chapter concludes with some reflections on the contingencies of network formation for each of the response modes identified.

HETEROGENEITY IN DEMAND

Before discussing heterogeneity in demand as a cause of uncertainty and unpredictability in firms' environments, it is important to place its role in context. Heterogeneity in demand is not the only source of turbulence that firms are called upon to respond to. We know, for example, that technological, social, and political factors have an impact upon firms through a variety of different vectors. Such factors can themselves, in an indirect manner, create heterogeneity in demand. However, we would wish to avoid the rather generalized models of response to a faceless environment prevalent in the strategy literature and use an approach that accords the environment a 'face', that of the specific firms with which a focal firm has relationships (Axelsson 1992). We do so by confining ourselves to a consideration of how firms respond to customers' wants varying over time.

In addition, we would wish to confine our attention to ways in which firms respond to short-term rather than long-term changes in demand, that is to say fluctuations, albeit it of a major kind, rather than discontinuities or long-term secular trends. Easton and Rothschild (1987) used the term adaptation to refer to organizational responses to long-term changes in technology or markets as against flexibility which was the ability to handle routine heterogeneity. In a similar fashion Carlsson (1989) distinguishes between operational flexibility (short term), tactical flexibility (medium term) and strategic flexibility (long term). Many writers confuse flexibility and adaptation which is hardly surprising since the difference is one of degree rather than kind. We are interested in a firm's flexibility rather than the way it handles fundamental change processes, though it is clear that the two processes need not be unrelated.

Not all customers of a firm demand different products or services each time they place an order or make a purchase. It is possible to envisage a continuum at one end of which demand heterogeneity over time is negligible (e.g. standard roller bearings) and at the other end of which demand heterogeneity over time is extreme (e.g. construction projects). Clearly some firms will face markets with a mixture of different time heterogeneities which in itself will create interesting response issues. However, the key question is: What are the sources of demand heterogeneity? There are a number of possible explanations about which we can speculate.

The first of these starts with the identification of *different kinds of customers*. Some but not all of organizational demand is derived from final consumer demand. Individual consumers may vary their purchases over time for different reasons. One important rationale is variety-seeking behaviour. Any individual customer may deliberately wish to choose different products each time they purchase. The dictates of fashion provide another source of variability. Some kinds of consumer demand are infrequent, concentrated, and heterogeneous (e.g. new housing) as a result. Of course it could be argued that these individual demands are aggregated by the industrial system which seeks to meet them and in doing so smoothes out their time-based heterogeneity. However it is conceivable that the network could actually pass on the final customer variability in certain cases. This issue is central to the theme of this chapter and will be dealt with in more detail in the next section. The point to be made here is, however, that final customer heterogeneity in demand over time is, at the very least, a potential source of heterogeneity at the level of inter-organizational exchanges. Governments are a major, though diminishing, final customer for a particular wide-ranging set of products and services and the demand is concentrated enough to ensure that any heterogeneity in demand over time, which they might require, would be felt directly by those firms acting as government contractors and suppliers.

Not all organizational demand is derived. Firms require organizational goods which are not included in the manufactured product or service operation and which depend directly on perceived customer wants. Capital goods are an obvious example but the term also applies to more frequently bought and divisible products and services. Heterogeneity of demand over time for organizational goods may be due to the same sorts of reasons adduced for final customers.

A second source of demand heterogeneity over time may be attributed to supposed *trends in the behaviour of economic systems* at the current time. Chen *et al.* (1992) list six trends of this kind: increased product diversity, shorter product life cycles, increases in buyer concentration, focused manufacturing, manufacturing technology innovation, and unexpected competitors. In practice these trends are quite closely related and have an impact upon one another. The underlying causal argument appears to be that markets have become, in general, saturated. As a result markets have become more fragmented. Firms are required to produce more products in response, or even proactively, to accept that their products will be superseded more quickly and to devise strategies to facilitate the quick introduction of new products (Sanchez 1995). To cope with these market changes, firms are having to invest in new flexible manufacturing systems and/or focus their manufacturing activities, as well modify their product design strategies through, for example, the use of modular or easily upgraded components (Garud and Kumaraswamy 1995). An altogether different factor is the concentration of buying power. In the retail sector this springs from the aggregated consumer power that retailers can bring to bear upon manufacturers, and would seem to be a function of volume, therefore rewarding homogeneity rather than heterogeneity of demand. In practice this appears to depend crucially upon the relative scale for different kinds of product.

The important issue is how trends such as these are likely to affect customer demand heterogeneity over time. It can do so in two ways. Any long-term changes in patterns of customer demand will mean that customers will be requiring different things each time they buy, and these changes will have to be handled by the relevant industrial systems. In addition, if the cycles of productive and exchange activity are speeding up, then those activities which were heterogeneous but rare (e.g. new product launches, new factory layouts) remain heterogeneous but become frequent. This in turn converts those markets that used to be long cycle to shorter cycle, and short-term heterogeneity into the demands for associated products and services.

The final source of demand heterogeneity over time concerns *exchange relationships* and is central to the arguments put forward in the next section. Demand heterogeneity has two sources at the level of the individual firm. The first is when it is a function of the demand by individual organizational customers with whom the focal firm has established relationships. A good example of this situation is that of a jobbing printer. Many of these firms work for a limited range of regular customers (e.g. advertising agencies) but each job is likely to be different. The alternative situation is where the heterogeneity is a function of the customers a firm serves. There are no long-term relationships. Each customer, from a large and changing population of such customers, is different and may never be serviced again. An example of this kind of situation is the general management consultancy market. Which of these two sources, or what mixture, of heterogeneity is present will determine how a focal firm handles the problems that arise.

In industrial networks theory, network structures and processes are assumed to emerge and develop around the matching of heterogeneous resources and heterogeneous customer needs. Heterogeneity is also a feature of each exchange relationship (Håkansson and Johanson 1984). Heterogeneity in this context is, however, implicitly static and cross-sectional. Resources and customer needs differ in comparison with other resources and needs existing at that time. However, the power of the industrial network approach lies in its desire to characterize and capture change (Håkansson 1992). But change in this sense is concerned with change in the large rather than in the small. While the constant evolution and adaptations within networks is recognized (Håkansson and Johanson 1992), relatively little work has been done to model the day-by-day changes that networks manage. Some of these changes are brought about in response to changes in demand by customers. Thus examination of these processes offers a way of perceiving the micro mechanisms of network formation and processes, to which task we now turn our attention.

FIRMS' RESPONSES TO HETEROGENEITY OF DEMAND OVER TIME

Discontinuity and Flexibility

Heterogeneity of demand by customers over time creates certain discontinuities in the activities of the firms concerned. Each new project in project marketing, job for a jobbing firm, or system for a systems seller is different, sometimes marginally but often substantially. This heterogeneity appears to imply discontinuity of buyer–seller relationships and the denial of the possibility of stable exchange structures, though we shall argue that such is not universally the case. At its simplest it requires firms to respond to these varying demands in terms of a suitable product or service offering. Note that we have used the word respond rather than match. Matching is only one of the ways in which a firm can respond. The general characteristic that is required in this situation, if the firm is to continue to survive, is flexibility. However, this notion of flexibility is a wider one than that currently used in the manufacturing flexibility literature, which will be examined in more detail later (Chen *et al.* 1992; Gerwin 1993; Ettlie and Penner-Hahn 1994), but a narrower one than that used in the strategy and organizational change literature (Ghemawat 1991).

The generality of definition in the latter case leads to somewhat anodyne prescriptions. In the contingency and population ecology theories, for example, firms are advised to mirror and internalize at least some of the complexities of their environment in their structures and processes (McKelvey and Aldrich 1983; Mintzberg 1983). Failure to do this implies lowering the probability of survival in hostile environments (Hannan and Freeman 1989). However, both external environments and internal structures are assumed to be relatively stable over long periods of time, and it is often assumed that environmental change can be monitored and responded to in an incremental fashion. Addressing the broader strategic issue of flexibility seems to offer few insights into the problem that we are addressing in this chapter and so we turn to a previously developed model of organizational response to micro-level change in a network context.

Flow through Nodes Model

Easton and Lundgren (1992) developed a model of the possible responses by a firm, characterized as a network node, to an unspecified change presented to it through a network link. In this model, actors are regarded as nodes connected through flows of different materials (products, money, information, texts, and so on). Easton and Lundgren (1992) identified five broad kinds of responses to change—reflection, adaptation, absorption, transmission, and transformation—and suggested what implications these might have for network processes. Gerwin (1993) identified, in a later paper, four generic strategies that firms might adopt to deal with uncertainty, a rather broader characterization of environmental turbulence. Adaptation is equivalent to absorption in the Easton and Lundgren model. Redefinition is a combination of reflection and adaptation. Reduction combines transmission and transformation. Banking involves the notion of investment in flexibility for the future and lies outside the scope of Easton and Lundgren's short-term flexibility model. Overall, the Easton and Lundgren model is better articulated and is certainly more suited for handling network formation implications of responses to demand heterogeneity over time. The major adaptation of the model to handle heterogeneity in customer demand involves the modification of the notion of the initiating change that the nodal firm is assumed to respond to. Rather than an analysis involving a single change, the model now has to deal with a continuing plethora of changes. As a result, an additional category of response, selection, has been added. Also, we have dropped the category transformation in the original Easton and Lundgren model and replaced it with a category we have labelled configuration. For the purposes of the present discussion, we are more interested in understanding how nodal actors can enlist external capabilities to increase the flexibility of their responses to heterogeneity of demand over time rather than how they transform demands for change. Thus we have introduced the category, configuration, as distinct from transmission to account for rather extreme situations of heterogeneity of demand over time, when temporary network forms are assembled for the purposes of short-lived projects. The process of assemblage of these temporary structures is underpinned by what we have labelled as virtual networks, composed largely of information/interpersonal networks that can be mobilized relatively quickly around specific projects.

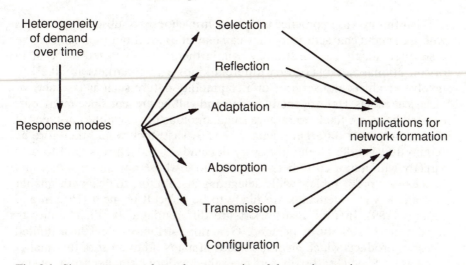

Fig. 3.1. Six response modes to heterogeneity of demand over time

The six different response modes are discussed below in an order which reflects a firm's attempts to first nullify, then assimilate, and finally pass on the impact of continuing variability in customer demand—or, put another way, reject, accept, or delegate the flexibility required to do so. Figure 3.1 sketches the structure of the following subsections. Demand heterogeneity over time generates unpredictability and uncertainty that is dealt with through a variety of coping strategies or response modes. Each response mode has implications for firms' strategies as well as wider implications at the level of inter-organizational relationships, as the problems posed by heterogeneity of demand over time can no longer be coped with inside hierarchies. Network forms of economic co-ordination may then arise as intended or unintended systemic and flexible responses to the unpredictability and uncertainty generated by heterogeneity of demand over time.

Selection

In an earlier section a distinction in terms of demand heterogeneity over time was made between that due to an existing stable portfolio of customers, each of which was heterogeneous with respect to demand, and that due to heterogeneity in demand across a heterogeneous population of customers with which stable exchange relationships do not exist. This 'disloyalty' may be a result of the transactional nature of the market, or because purchase frequency is so low that stable relationships are not sustainable. In these circumstances the nodal firm may decide to adapt a selective mode of response.

What this means in practice is that the firm chooses a subset of customers whose demand characteristics they can expect to meet but then ignores the rest. Interestingly such a strategy can, in theory, be expected to occur in organizational markets of very different kinds. These markets are likely to involve products and services of a commodity nature such as fasteners or electrical cables. Heterogeneity in demand will be present since many purchasing firms are likely to require small amounts of very different types of these products at different points in time. A vast stock would therefore be required to handle all the necessary demand. Manufacturers tend to deal directly with major customers—that is, those whose demand is larger and hence more predictable—while delegating distributors to deal with smaller customers whose demands are likely to be difficult to meet (Easton and Araujo 1989). In turn, distributors are differentiated by their ability to handle heterogeneity of demand. General distributors deal in a limited range of products which meet the needs of many if not most of the smaller purchasers. Specialist distributors meet the needs of a smaller group of customers whose demands are very heterogeneous, for whom the products concerned are important, and for which they are prepared to trade off other aspects of the offering, especially price. If this system seems to resemble that of consumer goods markets then that is entirely understandable. It possesses many of the same features. Indeed, what we are describing here in terms of selection could equally well be labelled targeting and segmentation. In the latter case, segments would be chosen on the grounds of their likely homogeneity in demand over time as well as at any one time.

The contrasting market is one where the inter-purchase period for any customer is long, the wants of any one customer over time heterogeneous, and the product or service complex and large scale. Such markets are often described as project markets. Although the problems may seem very different, the solution is rather similar, at least in principle. Where demand is as heterogeneous over time as it is in this case, the normal form of market making is through a bidding process. Since each project represents a major part of the capacity of a firm and since bidding is a complex and expensive process, a key decision is whether to bid for a particular contract or not. In effect the firm has to select which customers from amongst a population of possible customers it will attempt to capture. One of the key criteria in the selection will, or more accurately should, be the extent to which the project fits the current offering that the firm provides. That offering will, in itself, be rather flexible but nevertheless it remains open to the firm to ignore those projects where the fit is likely to be poor and to concentrate on those where it is likely to be good. Such a strategy relies on the occurrence of a sufficient number of compatible projects. It also contrasts with one where every project is pursued and the flexibility required to win and execute them is accessible by other means, some of which are described below. The latter strategy is best classified as high flexibility, high cost, and undifferentiated; the former low flexibility, low cost, and targeted. It is clear that neither is appropriate in all circumstances; they are merely different ways of dealing with a similar though not identical market situation.

It should be pointed out that the bid decision problem has a long history and remains topical (Rothkopf and Harstad 1994). Cova *et al.* (1993*a*), for example, distinguish between anticipatory and adaptive firm attitudes towards project marketing, the latter involving the development of project intelligence systems. Of course this is not the only way that firms involved in project marketing act flexibly and we shall return to this topic when discussing the configuration form of response to demand heterogeneity over time.

The network implications of this form of response to demand heterogeneity over time are relatively straightforward. The selection among customers by the nodal firm strongly suggests, in both cases, a lack of long-term stable relationships. Thus modes of economic co-ordination are, in theory, likely to be closer to markets than networks. There is little room for bilateral co-ordination of plans and activities since there is uncertainty about the possibility of future exchanges. However, it is difficult to imagine organizational markets totally without relationships, structure, or history. In practice some vestiges of a structure will be present though their impact upon firm behaviour may be slight.

Reflection

The reflective response means that the nodal actor refuses to accept the continuing changes requested by customers or implied by their behaviour. It reflects the changes back to the initiator. The customers do not get what they want. In particular, they wish for variety and do not get it. Where such variety is crucial, customers presumably adapt their own activities and absorb or control the sources of the variation where they can, or transmit it on to other actors in the network to whom they are connected. However, for this to be a viable form of response, customers must be unwilling or unable to buy from competitors. The ability of the firm to sustain exchange relationships in this context suggests an asymmetry in the power relationship between buyer and seller. There are a number of bases for supplier power which can help to explain such a situation.

The first of these is monopoly power. Customers may have no actual or perceived alternative. The monopoly may be legally enforceable, as in the case of patent protection, or simply be the result of a single firm creating strong barriers to imitation based on an idiosyncratic set of resources and skills (Easton and Araujo 1996). While monopoly is the extreme case, even where there is competition it is clear that some competitors by virtue of their access to key resources and ability to carry out key activities are very powerful *vis-à-vis* all or some of their customers. Such issues are discussed in the interaction approach under the heading of the atmosphere of a relationship (cf. Håkansson 1982).

However, in this case there is a more clear-cut issue to address. Why are customers prepared to give up their wish to change their requirements over time and accept something which, by implication, does not change? The answer must lie in the trade-offs that are central to any buying decision. In the limit, each customer would wish for a unique offering. In practice they cannot have this because the technological and economic system, of which the supplier is a part, cannot deliver. The customer must then decide what to trade off. In the reflective mode, the supplier can exert power by offering to provide important trade-offs in dimensions other than customization over time. The most obvious trade-off dimension is price. Customers may well be prepared to accept a standard offering, if the price is low enough and if they can adapt their own in-house operations and still make a profit. In a sense this is the rationale for Fordist modes of production and the rise of the modern business enterprise (Chandler 1990; Lazonick 1991). Economies of scale and experience curve effects are only viable if the offering is standardized and the volumes high. While customers may not be happy with this arrangement, they can accept its commercial logic.

There is no reason why reflection should not lead to relatively long-lived exchange relationships. The demand heterogeneity over time has either been suppressed or passed on to the customer or exported to other parts of the network (e.g. subcontractors). However, if the requirement for the demand heterogeneity remains and is a source of continuing stress to customers, then it is likely that the relationship will be both conflictual and unstable. In particular, the emergence of alternative modes of economic co-ordination which can offer something approaching responsiveness over time without too great penalties in other dimensions will be enough to break such relationships. Langlois and Robertson (1995) argue that in some extreme cases (where there are no significant economies of scale in assembling a final package of components), customers may prefer to assemble their own tailor-made packages by picking and choosing from an array of compatible components. In other words, they move to a situation of building their own modular systems, made up of a set of interchangeable and easily upgraded components, rather than accept pre-set packages. Langlois and Robertson (1995) focus on the cases of the consumer hi-fi stereo systems and the personal computer industry, but organizational markets offer a plethora of other examples (e.g. process control and instrumentation systems). The implications for network formation arising from this development are quite clear. One possible development is the formation of a network centred around one core producer, who largely defines standards of compatibility, with a set of satellite suppliers of compatible components and peripherals. This is akin to the configuration response mode, to be discussed later. The other possibility is the formation of a network of decentralized producers, where standards of compatibility are defined collectively.

Adaptation

Adaptation as a response strategy involves managing the changes between the organizations rather than either one taking the lion's share of the responsibility. It requires working with rather than against customers/suppliers. For such a strategy to be successful it would appear that a precondition of flexibility must exist for both supplier and customer. For the customer, the flexibility lies in the willingness to accept alternative solutions to their problems. In extreme cases the problem may be so ill specified that the supplier is involved not only in offering solutions but also in clarifying the problem in the first place. Therefore one element of adaptation, already mentioned for the reflective mode, is for the supplier to be close to the customer as, or even before, the process of specification and problem solving starts. This clearly relies on a good market-scanning system of some kind. However, the supplier must also be relatively flexible in its operation since no amount of problem definition can help if the solution set is outside its capabilities.

One form of response in this category is termed systems selling (Mattsson 1973; Page and Siemplenski 1983; Paliwoda and Bonaccorsi 1993). Firms involved in this strategy attempt to create a compromise between the benefits of extreme flexibility in terms of customer adaptation and the costs of maintaining a system where the economies of scale are largely absent. The systems in these cases can be regarded as a mixture of relatively standardized components (e.g. computer systems and peripherals), configurable components (e.g. software), and tailor-made elements (e.g. system specification and training). In systems selling, the resource base resides in the 'heterogeneous engineering' required to configure assorted components (the question of own manufacture or bought in is relatively secondary here) in tailor-made systems. In this case, contrary to the possibilities alluded to in the previous section, the supplier rather than the customer takes the responsibility for the heterogeneous engineering required to build a system out of assorted components. The knowledge base develops with both addition of skills and learning by doing (cumulative experience and standardization of solutions, build-up of larger modules).

Easton and Rothschild (1987) suggest that there are two other categories of products which have characteristics similar to that of the systems product. A configured product is one 'which initially has the potential for taking on a variety of forms but is permanently fixed in character either at the last stage of the production process or by the customer' (Easton and Rothschild 1987: 318). Examples include shelving systems and electronic instruments. Similarly, reconfigurable products are those which customers can themselves change as a result of changing requirements or needs—computers, robots, and any product to which accessories can be added. In both of these cases flexibility is built into the product so that both the supplier and the customer have, in theory, the ability to adapt.

In situations where more extreme forms of flexibility are required such as in projects or jobbing, firms find it difficult to make long-term strategic decisions about capacities and capabilities other than in a totally adaptive mode. They also find it difficult to make marketing decisions when what they are, in effect, offering are their very substantial capabilities. Issues of targeting and positioning become highly problematic. Ways of focusing the firm and its offering include pseudo-projects (Cova *et al.* 1993*a*), core offerings, or ghost products. The purpose is to crystallize the notions of what the firms can do in a way which is concrete in the eyes of potential customers. Each of these can be seen as a device for beginning the process of adaptation to the customer in a way which is more helpful than simply asking 'what would you like us to do?'.

There are at least two other mechanisms by which adaptation can be managed. The first is to use relationships with other customers. Firms, of course, learn how to adapt from their experiences with other customers (Håkansson and Snehota 1995). But it may also be possible to involve more than one customer in the process at a time. For example, if customers acted together in a group so as to help manage the problems of their demand heterogeneity over time, or if customers were chosen so as to draw upon different rather than the same capabilities (e.g. for seasonal products), they would behave in a complementary rather than competitive fashion. Joint ventures or horizontal co-ordination activities provide another vector for adaptation (Harrigan 1987). In this case the process is likely to be more permanent and systematized and the adaptations would help both parties to deal with heterogeneity over time in a routine way. Clearly such devices are limited to a few customers and may have other and less acceptable network effects on other exchange relationships.

Adaptation ought to be an important network process since it occurs in the 'space between organizations'. However, as described here, it is a relatively localized activity. It largely confines the changes to the individual relationship and has few direct network consequences, although clearly knowledge and experience are transferred and the customer grouping or joint venture activities represent an exception to the general statement. Adaptation can occur in the context of relatively stable long-term exchange relationships, but if the degree of demand heterogeneity is large it is difficult to see how adaptation can solve all the resulting problems. It is no coincidence that most of the examples discussed above are concerned with situations in which purchase frequency is low and where networks, when they form, are ephemeral in nature.

Absorption

The absorption response involves firms meeting the variation over time in customers' needs internally by means of their own resources. They seek neither to modify customers' demands nor to pass on the heterogeneity to other members of the network. In a word, they seek to cope with external demand heterogeneity through internal flexibility. Much has been written on organizational flexibility, so it is well to be reminded that in this instance we are concerned only with customers' demands, and therefore the equivalent product or service offering. However, it is not simply the product design or features that are important but all the other aspects of the augmented product, including delivery and quality as well as associated services. In addition, one should not equate flexibility in relation to product offerings with manufacturing flexibility alone. The systems in a firm which support the physical creation of those parts of the offering that require it are equally as important. Human resource management is responsible for the recruitment and training of a flexible workforce and the incentive and motivation context which ensures that they perform. Purchasing is responsible for ensuring that the components and materials bought are appropriate and there when required. Marketing is concerned with the accurate prediction and interpretation of customers' requirements, especially in the context of demand heterogeneity which varies over time. What we shall discuss below in relation to manufacturing systems applies equally well, though with different parameters, to the other sub-systems within the firm. Eccles and Crane (1988), for example, describe how investment banks organize themselves to cope with a significant heterogeneity of deals over time.

There is a large and expanding literature on manufacturing flexibility. Much of this appears to be driven by two factors. The first is the apparent demise of Fordist modes of production and the disintegration of the Chandlerian firm (Piore and Sabel 1984; Kenney and Florida 1993; Harrisson 1994). For reasons discussed earlier in this chapter, flexibility is held to be a necessary condition for the survival of firms in the future. Life is never quite so simple as this but academics have risen to the bait. The second factor is rather more solid and has to do with technology. Advances in microelectronics and mechatronics have created a potentially immense capacity for flexibility in many kinds of production processes. Like many such revolutionary technologies before it, flexible manufacturing, to use a generic term where it does not really apply, has progressed more slowly than its advance publicity suggested. Nevertheless, real progress has been made and cannot be ignored (Ettlie and Penner-Hahn 1994).

What we should not forget, however, is that flexible manufacturing systems have always existed, although they may not have been very efficient. Labour-intensive manufacturing using a skilled workforce has always had this capacity, as can be seen, for example, in the shipbuilding industry. In the automotive industry, craft production methods were used prior to the Fordist revolution and have persisted to the present in specialized niches (Womack *et al.* 1990). Indeed, it has often been argued that flexibility is a characteristic of craft modes of production, preceding the rise of Fordist mass production methods (Piore and Sabel 1984). What is evident is that there will always exist pressures to make manufacturing processes more efficient. Efficiency is defined in general in terms of maximizing on the basis of accepted goals and criteria which are, in manufacturing, likely to include such measures as high volume and low cost. Such criteria may actually conflict with the criteria for effectiveness where flexibility may well be a high priority. There is always likely to be a trade-off between efficiency and flexibility and in the manufacturing process at least the former is more likely to win.

But what is flexibility in this context? Easton and Rothschild (1987) defined it as the ability of a system to take on a variety of predetermined forms. Defining these forms has led many authors to offer different taxonomies of the dimensions of flexibility (Gerwin 1993). They have, in effect, attempted to answer the question: flexible in respect of what? Sayer and Walker (1992: 199), for example, distinguish between seven types of flexibility:

- flexibility in output volume;
- product flexibility;
- flexible employment;
- flexible working practices;
- flexible machinery;
- flexibility in restructuring;
- flexible organizational forms—for example, networks of specialist producers.

It is clear that such taxonomies, of which that listed above is a representative example, can be pitched in terms of different units of aggregation: organization, factory, productive process, machine. The problems, however, do not end there. The next step is to define measures for the dimensions and then estimate the range of possibilities over which the unit's flexibility can perform. But the mapping cannot be complete without knowing how flexibility in one dimension affects flexibility in another. The whole process is complex and difficult. Håkansson and Johanson (1992) rightly argue that the combination of resources and activities within a network actor can be achieved in an infinite number of ways. Nevertheless, limitations occur because some of these combinations, while technically feasible, are unacceptable economically, politically, or socially. Even more important, the cognitive complexity of the task described above is a very real constraint to anything like full realization of the technical flexible potential in an organization.

The classic example of firms which absorb demand heterogeneity over time are jobbing firms. On the whole the relative simplicity of the product and processes, many of which are highly labour intensive, allow such firms to deal with a vast variety of different kinds of demands often at short notice. Casual observation suggests that they can be involved in rather close exchange relationships, often with much larger organizations which generate a large volume of demands for different products over time, or else they have a much larger number of less close relationships where the heterogeneity between customers is conflated with the heterogeneity over time of each individual customer.

The network implications of absorbing nodal firms seem at first sight to be rather limited. Such nodes simply act as sinks for network change. Yet networks require such sinks if they are not to be infinitely reactive and volatile. What is of more practical interest is to examine the limits of flexibility. Clearly no firm can absorb all the changes that are demanded of it by customers. One response is to reflect; another is to transmit or transform. But what governs when and how a firm will change its response mode? Two scenarios can be identified, though clearly there will be many more. The first is where requirements for a particular kind of sub-process (e.g. seven colour printing) cannot be met technically, but where the process is becoming increasingly more in demand and there are obvious subcontractors or suppliers readily available. The second is where the cognitive complexity of meeting all demands placed upon the firm becomes too much to handle.

In Piore's (1992) terms, the hierarchical firm is a mode of economic co-ordination too rigid to handle the necessary balance between specialization and integration in the social division of labour. Network forms of economic co-ordination emerge that combine the ability of specialist firms to deepen their own specific competencies with relatively supple forms of horizontal co-ordination amongst them. There has been a great deal of recent interest in the so-called network form of organization (Powell 1990; Baker 1992; Snow and Thomas 1993). 'Unlike a bureaucracy, which is a fixed set of relationships for processing all problems, a network organization moulds itself to each problem' (Baker 1992: 399). Such organizations are analogous to internal markets where decisions are made at the periphery and resources are allocated on the basis of solving the immediate problems. The social networks are strong while the hierarchy is weak or non-existent. Clearly network organizations are not confined to managing only internal relationships and so are not just concerned with absorption. Nevertheless, the notion of an interpersonal organizational network within an inter-organizational network offers both a model of one kind of absorption mechanism as well as interesting opportunities for theoretical integration at a number of different levels.

Transmission

Transmission is the process whereby the nodal firm passes on the effects of the changes in demand over time to other actors to whom they are connected. By and large those actors will be their own suppliers, but they could be complementary suppliers, co-operating competitors, or suppliers' suppliers. The term transmission is used here in a somewhat broader sense than in Easton and Lundgren (1992). It implies that the process is one where the nature of the change may be modified or interpreted by the nodal firm either a great deal or hardly at all. In practice, some change in the demand is likely to take place in every situation. It is sufficient to merely recognize that the extent will vary from case to case. The transmission mode represents a break with other modes discussed above. The problems associated with unpredictability and variability in demand are transferred to the network of relationships the focal firm engages in. Firms may find that flexibility cannot be achieved within the narrow confines of their own resource bases and administrative mechanisms, but have to be reflected or else transmitted to their exchange partners. Networks form as a result of continuous exchanges between firms which rely on each other for accessing resources and capabilities they lack. The network provides firms with access to external capabilities much in the same way as Marshallian industrial districts or the geographically based networks in high-tech industries thrive on widely distributed capabilities and specialization of individual firms (Langlois and Richardson 1995: 124–32).

There are a number of phenomena, with associated literature, which are relevant to the process of transmission of demand changes. Most of the cases are concerned with how firms can or may respond to change. However, response to change is usually equivalent to adaptation and not flexibility in our terminology. Even so, there are important similarities and transfers of insight to be expected.

Many of the phenomena are to do with post-Fordism. They provide alternatives to the large-scale, big business, specialized production process, vertically integrated, Chandlerian firms that appear to have dominated Western economies for so long. In doing so they implicitly or explicitly argue that Fordism is dead (Piore and Sabel 1984). It is perhaps worthwhile to point out at the outset that such a characterization is probably overdrawn (see e.g. Sayer and Walker 1992: 196) and that one should beware of the polemics which attach to much of what is written on this subject.

Tom Peters has, for example, argued that firms should 'return to the core', 'stick to their knitting', and 'unbundle' (Peters 1988). A number of different arguments are conflated but the underlying rationale appears to be concerned with size and complexity. Large complex organizations cannot be understood and managed and therefore cannot change to meet new circumstances. The answer is to cut away anything that can be regarded as non-essential, particularly unrelated diversified activity, and reduce that which you can do better than the competition to a minimum. Firms are composed of a core of intrinsic and idiosyncratic capabilities and a set of ancillary capabilities that can be supplied internally more cheaply than they can be acquired through market transactions. But, as Langlois and Robertson (1995) emphasize, as time passes and other firms have the chance of learning, the temptation to outsource or discontinue activities, which rely on capabilities that have been replicated at a lower cost by other firms, may prove too strong. Accordingly the boundaries of the firm contract. Where the core is small, one is approaching a 'hollow corporation', for example, Amstrad. Such gross prescriptions should always be regarded with suspicion (Hendry 1995). Nevertheless, they are important because they have a certain logic and appeal and are being acted upon.

In the arguments concerning the demise or otherwise of Fordism and the move to flexible forms of industry structure, one countervailing example, much studied, is that of Japan. Since Japanese industry appears to have succeeded in mass production areas—notwithstanding the contrast between 'mass production' and 'lean production' outlined by Womack *et al.* (1990)—with many of its characteristics mirroring that ascribed to Fordism, it is a difficult counter-example to explain. De Meyer *et al.* (1989) reported that Japanese companies placed flexibility higher on their list of priorities than managers from Western companies, and suggested that, having controlled quality, they were now moving on to flexible response as their key strategic weapon. However, it is arguable that the Japanese industry has always had a higher degree of flexibility due to its structure (Fruin 1992; Gerlach 1992). There are, apparently, two sources of flexibility.

Dore (1986) coined the oxymoronic term 'flexible rigidity' to describe the Japanese industrial system. The rigid element comprised among other things obligated trade relationships between firms and inflexible employee relationships within. The flexibility occurs in the way in which the system then uses this stability as a platform upon which to change. Strong inter-firm relationships mean that the suppliers and customers are confident enough to undertake joint actions to cope with change in terms of adaptation or flexibility. The changes are largely transmitted to suppliers, though there is inevitably some absorption. An interesting sub-strategy differentiates between responses to flexibility and adaptation. In the longer term it could be argued that cosy relationships such as these inhibit innovation. Therefore Japanese manufacturers who make use of close ties encourage their suppliers to enter other markets. This not only makes them more independent and less likely to accept industry recipes, but also offers a route to new technologies. Van Kooij (1990) describes this as the antennae function of suppliers in Japanese industry which is an excellent example of the use of indirect network relationships.

A second source of flexibility has to do with the pyramidal structure of the supply network. While strong and relatively symmetrical relationships occur at the first level of these pyramids, at the lower levels of subcontracting and sub-subcontracting, the power relationships are much more one-sided. Larger numbers of small suppliers provide a cushion for the system as a whole along many dimensions, not the least of which is flexibility in response to product changes (Semlinger 1993). In this way, the manufacturers/assemblers appear to have the best of both worlds.

Sayer and Walker (1992) also argue that such a system is very much dependent upon the culture within which it is embedded. The mixture of rigidity and flexibility described here is quintessentially Japanese. It is doubtful whether it could be exported. 'One of the great dangers of theorising about the development of industrial capital is to assume that it derives simply from a dynamic purely endogenous to an industry, ignoring the influence of local conditions' (Sayer and Walker 1992: 222). This point is emphasized in a study by Lorenz (1989) comparing French and English subcontracting practices in regional engineering industries. The former were involved in much more subcontracting than the latter, and this was held to be a function of the different states of the markets in the two regions and the need to keep value added within the firm in the English companies.

One phenomenon which does not appear to be confined to one context is that which has been labelled New Industrial Districts. The new appellation arose because Marshall in the 1920s identified industrial areas (e.g. Sheffield and steel) where geographical concentration was a key aspect of an industry and called such areas industrial districts. With the rise of Fordism it was assumed that corporations were the vector for industrial production and, since their plants could be located anywhere, industrial districts would cease to play a role in industrialized economies. However, after the war there emerged in a number of different countries (the USA, Italy, Germany, France, and Japan) at different periods similar geographically concentrated industries, which were often, but not always, based upon new technology (see e.g. Storper and Harrison 1991). These New Industrial Districts appeared to represent a general phenomenon and one which is related to both size of firm and flexibility. However, as Sabel (1989), one of the key students of New Industrial Districts, makes clear, there are as many differences as similarities among these regions. Nevertheless, a general argument for the existence of industrial districts can be made and is rehearsed here because it touches upon the forces which may drive firms to transmit their heterogeneity in demand to other firms within geographically limited areas. In a sense, industrial districts can be regarded as geographical agglomerations of firms employing network-form modes of economic co-ordination.

A description of the classic New Industrial District is given by Capecchi (1989) and describes the industrial system in the Emilia-Romagna area in northern Italy from the 1950s to the 1970s. It comprised a large number of small, geographically concentrated firms, small batch producers with flexible and skilled workforces co-operating closely with their customers. The roles that individual firms took in the system were not clear cut and there was a mixture of competition and co-operation. Such systems were inherently flexible and met the needs of markets that were both fragmented and changing fast. Industrial districts provide an alternative to the major corporation trading on economies of scope instead of economies of scale and flexibility/innovation as against standardization and low costs. It should be noted that implicit in this view is the notion that, as in Japan, it is the system that provides the flexibility and not necessarily the individual firm (Sabel 1989; Imai 1992).

While this particular New Industrial District was successful up to the 1970s, it is meeting new problems in more recent times. Sabel (1989), for example, points out that large firms equipped with flexible manufacturing systems are offering small firms in the New Industrial Districts intense competition. It is also clear that the social and political contexts which supported the emergence of this form of industrial system have changed, and with them some of the underpinnings (Harrisson 1994). Still other commentators (Best 1990; Lazerson 1995) highlight that in industries where there are few throughput efficiencies and limited economies of scale as well as supportive institutional frameworks, decentralized networks of producers may be an effective mode of economic co-ordination to respond to volatility of demand and continuous changes in consumer tastes. The important issue from our point of view is whether and how such constellations of specialized firms transmit change to and from one another. This issue will be discussed below.

A different view of 'constellations of firms' (Lorenzoni and Ornati 1988) as a source of flexibility occurs if a lead firm, as key customer, is large in comparison to its ring of suppliers. Often quoted examples are Benetton and IKEA (Harrisson 1994). Semlinger (1993) analyses the situation facing small firms in this situation and concludes that their future looks bleak. He distinguishes between active versatility and passive pliability. The former appears to be a response to temporary market niches, presumably in situations where customer heterogeneity varies over time and space, and relies on the fleetness of foot of the small *vis-à-vis* the large company. The latter occurs where there are likely to be longer-term relationships between the large customer and small supplier as heterogeneity is lower or more predictable. In this case, the power of the customer leads to an absorption of heterogeneity by the supplier more or less under duress. Herrigel (1993) has examined the relationships between these two issues of New Industrial Districts and large/small firm relationships and concludes that a battle between the traditional (Fordist) forces and the non-traditional (transformers) has been joined, but that the battle lines are confused and no simple prediction of outcome is to be expected.

Finally, those who perceive networks as an organizational form, whatever the level of aggregation, seek to provide a more micro-level theoretically based view of transmission processes (cf. Nohria and Eccles 1992). Network organizations have already been mentioned as one, probably rather extreme, manifestation of this view of the world. However, to regard what goes on within and between organizations as not only linked but also as theoretically similar phenomena must be regarded as a potentially fruitful line of attack. Since transmission of change involves both kinds of process, it offers an important testing ground for this newly rediscovered perspective.

This short review of some of the literature which addresses the issue of flexibility through inter-firm relationships demonstrates the current interest in the topic as well as its inherent heterogeneity. We need to return to the theme of this section in order to develop the concept of transmission against such a rich background of possibilities. Firms choose to transmit heterogeneity and hence change, at least from a rationalist point of view, because they perceive that some other firm or firms can handle it better. A more interesting and tractable question is how do they do so. One issue which is raised by a study of the literature and which has key network implications is how the network itself is structured to absorb changes. Wherein does its flexibility lie? There are two extreme alternatives.

The first is that supplying firms are themselves rather generalist and act as absorbers. In this case they can have quite close long-term relationships with the transmitting firm and frequent exchanges occur. All that is happening here is that the nodal firm simply acts as a conduit and the heterogeneity is absorbed at one remove. Such firms are likely to be less well rewarded since they are not providing the key resource but only access to it, unless, as Semlinger points out, they are large enough or have some other source of network power.

The second alternative is where the nodal firm has a wider range of possible specialist suppliers which it deals with rather less frequently and manages heterogeneity through its choices. In this case much more is required of the transmitting firm since the network is wider, less stable, and the right choice of firms and combinations of firms for every particular order is a complex organizational task. One might label this transmission as channelling. In addition, the supplying firms depend on the commitment of the customer at some level. This seems to require some stability in the key areas of demand or some way of ensuring that firms achieve a flow of demand of whatever kind, if the market is not to be purely transactional in nature. The Modena knitwear industry provides a good example of how a degree of stability is engineered in the relationship between artisans and manufacturers (Lazerson 1995: 52 f.).

Such relationships mirror those in Japanese industry, where suppliers are encouraged to work across different industry sectors, spreading risk and transferring technological and other sorts of information to their ultimate advantage (Fruin 1992). However, it is not clear which mode describes the structure in the New Industrial Districts. In different places different authors stress the complementarity or similarity of the firms concerned. It is likely that, following Herrigel (1993) and Sayer and Walker (1992), it would depend upon the specific institutional context underlying economic exchange relationships in an industrial district.

Configuration

Configuration, as a response to demand heterogeneity over time, involves the creation of temporary network configurations to meet the heterogeneous demands of the customers as they change over time. In some cases an identifiable nodal firm actively manages the flexibility of the network, creating a strong core–ring differentiation (Storper and Harrisson 1991). In others the processes of configuration are themselves network rather than nodal firm centred. In some senses all nodal firms seek to configure the networks they are involved in—what Storper and Harrisson (1991) labelled as all-ring/no-core networks.

In the discussion of transmission above, two alternative response modes were distinguished. Where a nodal firm works with relatively few generalist absorbers, decisions to reconfigure are likely to be relatively rare and somewhat incremental. The core–ring system is thus relatively stable and the identity of the partners does not change. Where the nodal firm chooses among a wider number of specialist partners, the configuration may change from exchange to exchange episode, though the overall structure may well be rather stable. In other words, although the system as a whole remains stable, the identity of the ring firms may change over time. Configuration becomes more important, the greater the demand heterogeneity over time becomes. What might be regarded as the most extreme case is described below.

Projects are major industrial products/services that typically involve a number of firms as contractors, subcontractors, and suppliers. The demand for such projects represents the extreme case of heterogeneity over customer and over time. Each project will be different, large in relation to the capacity of the firms involved, and the next project of this general type will occur at an unpredictable interval. In project marketing, the demand from the current client may be interpreted by a lead firm, often called a project management firm, and this could be identified with the nodal firm as discussed in the cases of the other response modes described above. In interpreting demand (usually an invitation to tender), they transform that demand into the requirements for the project and identify the appropriate partner firms. This can occur before the project is bid or after, if the client organization is able to take some part in the early stages of project management to the extent of asking for bids for parts of the contract rather than the whole. An even more extreme form of configuration occurs where there is no lead organization but a consortium of firms jointly bidding for a contract or where there are several lead organizations. Here the demand is interpreted and configured by and through the different members of the consortium in negotiation.

The key question is not so much what the different configurations might be, though that is an important empirical issue, but how these configurations are formed when projects are intermittent and dependent on highly unpredictable and heterogeneous demand. One of the crucial mechanisms is what we have termed the virtual network. We argue that where discontinuity and uncertainty are high, firms form networks, based largely on interpersonal relations, which exist outside, and form the context for, the exchange networks, which are the visible evidence of economic activity (Cova *et al.* 1993*b*). They are virtual in the sense that the actors, for the most part, are not involved with one another in projects but merely have the potential to be. Projects provide the opportunity of mobilizing the virtual network and making it coalesce into a visible and temporary organization, which will evolve as the project unfolds. Eccles (1981) describes such temporary forms of organization in the construction industry as quasi-firms. Storper (1989), Baker and Faulkner (1991), and Robins (1993) describe similar decentralized production structures and the coalescing of temporary forms of project-based organizations in the film industry. Lipparini and Sobrero (see Chapter 8) relate a similar situation in the case of entrepreneurial firms involved in innovation activities. Entrepreneurs, relying on trust and reputation generated in prior relationships, are able to mobilize and configure a virtual network of latent relationships to serve their own product development needs.

Virtual networks are based upon history and perceptions. History, that is, previous experience of being members of the same network and having worked together, is crucial in establishing memberships of projects. Perceptions are important because the number of possible relationships in the network is very large and not all firms will have direct experience of all possible network members. As a result, reputation in the virtual network is vital.

Virtual networks, as with all other networks, have structure. One aspect of structure are the relatively formal ties of ownership or informal agreement. In the construction industry there exist sweetheart or evergreen relationships between clients and particular firms. Such agreements will be serviced by both actors despite the absence of a project to bind them together. Projects will often form with such links acting as the backbone. Not all actors in the virtual network are equivalent. Clearly firms have different capabilities both in terms of activities and capacities. Thus there will be firms seen as competitors and firms seen as complementary suppliers. As a result, additional structuring can be expected around local concentrations of ties in a network—or a net, in the language of industrial networks theory (Hägg and Johanson 1983)—which are both complementary and competitive within that network. However, the differences are by no means as straightforward as they first appear. The same firms, especially if they are very different in size, may well be both competitors and collaborators. In addition, the membership of a particular virtual network may be dangerous if that network does not win contracts. It pays firms to be involved with and respected by any number of nets (Hägg and Johanson 1983). Virtual nets are also structured hierarchically in some senses by virtue of the firms' relationship with potential clients. Thus a project management firm may be regarded as more powerful than a design consultancy. However, the design consultancy will, in its turn, have potential access to more projects than a project management firm. Conversely, the client may well be prepared to configure the project themselves and create an alternative hierarchy. A final structural determinant is the current pattern of projects that firms are involved in. It will usually be easier for a firm to work with firms which they are already involved with rather than to seek unknowns. There is a further crucial issue to do with the existing pattern of project involvement.

A related concept is that of the temporary actors. Temporary actors are the equivalent of the project which is defined in terms of activities and resources. Such temporary organizations may be formed from a virtual network or may involve firms which are either unknown to one another or else actually antagonistic. It is also a feature of such temporary organizations that they are in a state of continuous change. Projects involve a sequence of different kinds of activities which, in turn, require different actors joining and leaving the project as cycles of activities start or finish. For example, in a construction project the design house may never interface with the commissioning consultants. There will, however, be a core of actors which will remain throughout the project, though here again roles can and do change. When the project ends, what remains of the temporary organization ends and the actors, or subsets thereof, move on to new projects and new positions in the virtual network.

SUMMARY AND CONCLUSIONS

This chapter has examined the concept of organizational responses to demand heterogeneity over time using a flow through nodes model. The perspective taken was to look at the micro episodes of change as they affect the daily lives of network actors, rather than concentrate on discontinuous, long-term, or macro-level changes. An amended version of the flow through nodes model (Easton and Lundgren 1992) provided us with a framework to discuss different organizational responses to demand heterogeneity over time and their network formation implications. These responses were categorized under six categories and each one discussed in turn.

We concluded that the transmission and configuration modes of response are more likely to induce the formation of inter-organizational networks, as firms attempt to enlist and mobilize external capabilities in their quest to find flexible responses to heterogeneity of demand over time. The other four response modes—selection, reflection, adaptation, and absorption—rely largely on intra-firm or market-based mechanisms as a coping strategy. However, even when discussing some of these response modes, we are inevitably drawn into attempting to predict inter-organizational implications of particular organizational response modes. For example, in the absorption response mode, internal limits to flexibility may push firms to rely on external relationships (e.g. specialized subcontractors) to help absorb part of the heterogeneity of demand.

Overall the model proved to be a powerful theoretical device, allowing us to bring together and integrate a host of issues that are usually addressed in rather separate and often divergent ways—for example, subcontracting practices, manufacturing flexibility, project marketing. By focusing on how demand heterogeneity over time and supply responses, at the organizational and network level, interact, we were able to discuss and relate a number of much neglected cases in organizational markets (e.g. jobbing firms), as well as join, albeit marginally, some key debates (e.g. flexible specialization and post-Fordist modes of production). This contribution should not, however, be seen in the light of any ambition to formulate a grand and all-encompassing theory of organizational markets, but as a realistic attempt to categorize and explain a number of cases of organizational and network responses to demand heterogeneity over time.

However, by using the flow through nodes framework as a device to categorize different response modes, we do not wish to suggest that firms use only one type of response to demand heterogeneity over time. On the contrary, we believe that all firms use a mixture of different response modes, some of which may coexist for the same firm at any one time and across firms in a population of firms facing the same set of circumstances. Luetz (Chapter 9) presents, albeit in a different context, a very good example of how different organizations chose different response modes to a publicly sponsored research collaboration initiative and how those response modes evolved over time. Also, by separating out the effects of heterogeneity over time from the effects of heterogeneity over customers, we were able to conclude under what circumstances the two types of heterogeneity create both similar and different organizational responses and network effects.

Our objective in using the flow through nodes model was to illustrate how some organizational responses were more relevant and suited to some demand heterogeneity situations rather than others. The evaluation of this end-product should be seen in terms of the objectives we set out in the introductory section: to formulate a framework that would allow us to explain the emergence, persistence, or instability of a number of organizational and network forms and processes prevalent in a number of organizational markets. By choosing to tackle this problem from the angle of organizational and network responses to demand heterogeneity over time, we have unashamedly taken a rationalist, economics-type approach. We are, however, well aware that social and institutional contexts play a key role in explaining organizational responses to demand heterogeneity over time, as documented for example in Glasmeier's (1991) study of the Swiss watch industry or in the Saxenian (1994) study of production networks in Silicon Valley and Route 128.

Our approach also evaded the equally important issues of short-term flexibility versus long-term adaptation which we alluded to at the beginning of this chapter. In a sense, this was provoked by a reaction to current trends in the literature to concentrate solely on long-term adaptation to faceless environments, whilst ignoring how these patterns of adaptation emerge out of the daily decisions by firms on how to cope with the conflicting demands of a full-faced environment. The task of linking these two levels of analysis, as well as providing a more coherent taxonomy of heterogeneity of demand and corresponding organizational responses, and of network implications, remains a challenge for the future.

REFERENCES

Axelsson, B. 1992. 'Corporate Strategy Models and Networks: Diverging Perspectives'. In Axelsson, B., and Easton, G. (eds.). *Industrial Networks: A New View of Reality*: 184–204. London: Routledge.

Baker, W. E. 1992. 'The Network Organisation in Theory and Practice'. In Nohria and Eccles 1992: 397–429.

——and Faulkner, R. R. 1991. 'Role as Resource in the Hollywood Film Industry'. *American Journal of Sociology*. 97: 279–309.

Best, M. H. 1990. *The New Competition: Institutions for Industrial Restructuring*. Cambridge: Polity Press.

Capecchi, V. 1989. 'A History of Flexible Specialisation and Industrial Districts in Emilia-Romagna'. In Pyke, F., Becattini, G., and Sengenberger, W. (eds.). *Industrial Districts and Inter-Firm Cooperation in Italy*. 20–36. International Institute for Labour Studies, Geneva.

Carlsson, B. 1989. 'Flexibility and the Theory of the Firm'. *International Journal of Industrial Organization*. 7: 179–203.

Chandler, A. D. 1990. *Scale and Scope: The Dynamics of Industrial Capitalism*. London: Harvard University Press.

Chen, I. J., Calantone, R. J., and Chung, C.-H. 1992. 'The Marketing-Manufacturing Interface and Flexibility'. *Omega*. 20: 431–43.

Cova, B., Mazet, F., and Salle, R. 1993a. 'Towards Flexible Anticipation: The Challenge of Project Marketing'. In Baker, M. J. (ed.). *Perspectives on Marketing Management.* iii: 375–400. Chichester: John Wiley and Sons.

——and Muet, F. 1993b. 'Intelligence Gathering Networks: The Case of Contracting Firms'. Paper presented at the 9th IMP Conference, University of Bath, September.

De Meyer, A., Nakane, J., Miller, J. G., and Ferdows, K. 1989. 'Flexibility: The Next Competitive Battle'. *Strategic Management Journal.* 10: 135–44.

Dore, R. 1986. *Flexible Rigidities: Industrial Policy and Structural Adjustment in the Japanese Economy, 1970–1980.* London: Athlone.

Easton, G., and Araujo, L. 1989. 'The Network Approach: An Articulation'. In Hallen, L., and Johanson, J. (eds.). *Advances in International Marketing: Networks of Relationships in International Industrial Marketing.* iii: 97–119. Greenwich: JAI Press.

——1996. 'Characterising Organisational Competence: Combining Resource-Based and Industrial Network Approaches'. In Sanchez, R., Heene, A., and Thomas, H. (eds.). *Dynamics of Competence-Based Competition: Theory and Practice in the New Strategic Management.* New York: Pergamon Press.

——and Lundgren, A. 1992. 'Changes in Industrial Networks as Flow through Nodes'. In Axelsson, B., and Easton, G. (eds.). *Industrial Networks: A New View of Reality.* 89–104. London: Routledge.

——and Rothschild, R. 1987. 'The Influence of Product and Production Flexibility on Marketing Strategy'. In Pettigrew, A. (ed.). *The Management of Strategic Change.* 300–26. Oxford: Basil Blackwell.

Eccles, R. G. 1981. 'The Quasi-Firm in the Construction Industry'. *Journal of Economic Behavior and Organization.* 2: 335–57.

——and Crane, D. B. 1988. *Doing Deals: Investment Banks at Work.* Boston, Mass.: Harvard Business School Press.

Ettlie, J. E., and Penner-Hahn, J. D. 1994. 'Flexibility Ratios and Manufacturing Strategy'. *Management Science.* 40: 1444–54.

Fruin, W. M. 1992. *The Japanese Enterprise System: Competitive Strategies and Cooperative Structures.* Oxford: Clarendon Press.

Garud, R., and Kumaraswamy, A. 1995. 'Technological and Organizational Designs for Realizing Economies of Substitution'. *Strategic Management Journal.* 16: 93–109.

Gerlach, M. L. 1992. *Alliance Capitalism: The Social Organization of Japanese Business.* Berkeley, Calif.: University of California Press.

Gerwin, D. 1993. 'Manufacturing Flexibility: A Strategic Perspective'. *Management Science.* 39: 395–410.

Ghemawat, P. 1991. *Commitment: The Dynamic of Strategy.* New York: Free Press.

Glasmeier, A. 1991. 'Technological Discontinuities and Flexible Production Networks: The Case of Switzerland and the World Watch Industry'. *Research Policy.* 20: 469–85.

Hägg, I., and Johanson, J. 1983. *Firms in Networks.* Stockholm: Business and Social Research Institute.

Håkansson, H. (ed.) 1982. *International Marketing and Purchasing of Industrial Goods.* Chichester: John Wiley and Sons.

——1992. 'Evolution Processes in Industrial Networks'. In Axelsson, B., and

Easton, G. (eds.). *Industrial Networks: A New View of Reality*. 128–43. London: Routledge.

——and Johanson, J. 1984. 'Heterogeneity in Industrial Markets and Implications for Marketing'. In Hägg, I., and Wiedersheim-Paul, F. (eds.). *Between Market and Hierarchy*. Uppsala: Foeretagsekonomiska Institutionen.

————1992. 'A Model of Industrial Networks'. In Axelsson, B., and Easton, G. (eds.). *Industrial Networks: A New View of Reality*. 28–34. London: Routledge.

——and Snehota, I. (eds.) 1995. *Developing Relationships in Business Networks*. London: Routledge.

Hannan, M. T., and Freeman, J. H. 1989. *Organizational Ecology*. Cambridge, Mass.: Harvard University Press.

Harrigan, K. R. 1987. 'Joint Ventures: A Mechanism for Creating Strategic Change'. In Pettigrew, A. (ed.). *The Management of Strategic Change*. 195–230. Oxford: Basil Blackwell.

Harrisson, B. 1994. *Lean and Mean: The Changing Landscape of Corporate Power in the Age of Flexibility*. New York: Basic Books.

Hendry, J. 1995. 'Culture, Community and Networks: The Hidden Cost of Outsourcing'. *European Management Journal*. 13: 193–200.

Herrigel, G. B. 1993. 'Power and the Redefinition of Industrial Districts: The Case of Baden-Württemberg'. In Grabher, G. (ed.). *The Embedded Firm: On the Socioeconomics of Industrial Networks*. 227–51. London: Routledge.

Imai, K. 1992. 'Japan's Corporate Networks'. In Kumon, S., and Rosovsky, H. (eds.). *The Political Economy of Japan (Vol. 3): Cultural and Social Dynamics*. 198–230. Stanford, Calif.: Stanford University Press.

Kenney, M., and Florida, R. 1993. *Beyond Mass Production: The Japanese System and its Transfer to the US*. New York: Oxford University Press.

Langlois, R. N., and Robertson, P. L. 1995. *Firms, Markets and Economic Change: A Dynamic Theory of Business Institutions*. London: Routledge.

Lazerson, M. 1995. 'A New Phoenix? Modern Putting-Out in the Modena Knitwear Industry'. *Administrative Science Quarterly*. 40: 34–59.

Lazonick, W. 1991. *Business Organization and the Myth of the Market Economy*. Cambridge: Cambridge University Press.

Lorenz, E. H. 1989. 'The Search for Flexibility: Subcontracting Networks in British and French Engineering'. In Hirst, P., and Zeitlin, J. (eds.). *Reversing Industrial Decline? Industrial Structure and Policy in Britain and Her Competitors*. 122–32. Oxford: Berg.

Lorenzoni, G., and Ornati, O. A. 1988. 'Constellations of Firms and New Ventures'. *Journal of Business Venturing*. 3: 41–57.

McKelvey, R., and Aldrich, H. 1983. 'Populations, Natural Selection, and Applied Organizational Science'. *Administrative Science Quarterly*. 28: 101–28.

Mattsson, L.-G. 1973. 'Systems Selling as a Strategy on Industrial Markets'. *Industrial Marketing Management*. 3: 107–20.

Mintzberg, H. 1983. *Structure in Fives: Designing Effective Organizations*. Englewood Cliffs, NJ: Prentice-Hall.

Nohria, N., and Eccles, R. G. (eds.) 1992. *Networks and Organisations: Structure, Form and Action*. Boston, Mass.: Harvard Business School Press.

Page, A. L., and Siemplenski, M. 1983. 'Product Systems Marketing'. *Industrial Marketing Management*. 12: 89–99.

Paliwoda, S. J., and Bonaccorsi, A. J. 1993. 'Systems Selling in the Aircraft Industry'. *Industrial Marketing Management*. 22: 155–60.

Peters, T. J. 1988. *Thriving on Chaos: Handbook for a Management Revolution*. London: Macmillan.

Piore, M. J. 1992. 'Fragments of a Cognitive Theory of Technological Change and Organizational Structure'. In Nohria and Eccles 1992: 430–44.

——and Sabel, C. F. 1984. *The Second Industrial Divide: Possibilities for Prosperity*. New York: Basic Books.

Powell, W. W. 1990. 'Neither Market Nor Hierarchy: Network Forms of Organization'. In Staw, B. (ed.). *Research in Organizational Behavior*. 12: 295–336. Greenwich: JAI Press.

Robins, J. A. 1993. 'Organization as Strategy: Restructuring Production in the Film Industry'. *Strategic Management Journal*. 14: 103–18.

Rothkopf, M. H., and Harstad, R. M. 1994. 'Modelling Competitive Bidding: A Critical Essay'. *Management Science*. 40: 364–84.

Sabel, C. F. 1989. 'Flexible Specialisation and the Re-Emergence of Regional Economies'. In Hirst, P., and Zeitlin, J. (eds.). *Reversing Industrial Decline? Industrial Structure and Policy in Britain and Her Competitors*. 17–70. Oxford: Berg.

Sanchez, R. 1995. 'Strategic Flexibility in Product Competition'. *Strategic Management Journal*. 16: 135–59.

Saxenian, A. L. 1994. *Regional Advantage: Culture and Competition in Silicon Valley and Route 128*. Cambridge, Mass.: Harvard University Press.

Sayer, A., and Walker, R. 1992. *The New Social Economy: Reworking the Division of Labour*. Oxford: Basil Blackwell.

Semlinger, K. 1993. 'Small Firms and Outsourcing as Flexibility Reservoirs of Large Firms'. In Grabher, G. (ed.). *The Embedded Firm: On the Socioeconomics of Industrial Networks*. 161–78. London: Routledge.

Snow, C. C., and Thomas, J. B. 1993. 'Building Networks: Broker Roles and Behaviours'. In Lorange, P., Chakravarty, B., Roos, J., and Van de Ven, A. (eds.). *Implementing Strategic Processes: Change, Learning and Co-operation*. 215–38. Oxford: Basil Blackwell.

Storper, M. 1989. 'The Transition to Flexible Specialization in the United States Film Industry: External Economies, the Division of Labour and the Crossing of Industrial Divides'. *Cambridge Journal of Economics*. 13: 273–305.

——and Harrison, B. 1991. 'Flexibility, Hierarchy and Regional Development: The Changing Structure of Industrial Production Systems and their Forms of Governance in the 1990s'. *Research Policy*. 20: 407–22.

Van Kooij, E. 1990. *Technology Transfer in the Japanese Electronics Industry: Analysis of Interorganizational Networks Supporting Small and Medium-sized Enterprises*. Zoetermeer: Department of Manufacturing Industry, Economic Research Institute for Small and Medium Sized Businesses.

Womack, J. P., Jones, D. T., and Roos, D. 1990. *The Machine That Changed The World*. New York: Rawson Associates.

4

The Network Structure of Inter-Firm Relationships in the Southern Italian Mechanical Industry

ALESSANDRO LOMI AND ALESSANDRO GRANDI

ABSTRACT

Inter-firm relationships in the southern Italian mechanical industry are considered in terms of four different structures of interaction generated by supply relationships, quality control agreements, technology transfer, and equity relations. Network-analytic techniques are used to explore patterns of community structure emerging from the system of intercorporate connections among 106 organizations.

INTRODUCTION

The study of organizations has moved beyond focusing on single organizations to an examination of how populations of organizations relate to their environments (Aldrich 1979). In this perspective, the population—rather than the individual organization—is taken as the basic unit of analysis, and adaptation is seen as a collective response to the problem of interdependence at the population and community levels (Hawley 1986; Hannan and Freeman 1989). This perspective is in sharp contrast with earlier research traditions on organizational environments which promulgated a firm-centred perspective by focusing on the relationship between individual organizations and their immediate environment (Lawrence and Lorsch 1967).

Earlier approaches to the study of the relationship between organizations and their environments tended to ignore the links among organizations not tied to the focal firm. This has been the crucial weakness of such studies as the structure of an organizational community is defined in terms of

This work has been partially supported by a research grant from the Italian National Research Council (CNR).

emergent inter-organizational networks, where centrality of any given actor is a hypothesis to be tested rather than an assumption to be maintained.

Secondly, members of an organizational population are typically connected by overlapping patterns of exchange which give rise to multiple dependencies. These are likely to result in complex relational structures that may not be easily discernible from the point of view of any single actor. This presents firm-centred theories with a problem because conventional bounded rationality arguments apply. Focal or 'central' organizations may not be aware of the complex relational structure of their environment, but may still be constrained by it.

Thirdly, earlier contingency approaches share a preference with more recent ecological theories of organizations for abstract definitions of environment. Organizational environments are typically construed in terms of abundance, patterns of availability, and the degree of criticality of (one or a few) key resources (Barley and Freeman 1991). Terms such as scarcity, turbulence, uncertainty, and the like assume meaning only in concrete social and economic contexts (Barley 1986; DiMaggio 1986) and environmental constraints are embedded in the institutional environment (Aldrich 1979). Understanding the implications of environments for organizational structure, strategy, and performance cannot be based on assumptions about atomistic actors uprooted from their institutional context but requires a careful analysis of networks in which organizational action is embedded (Granovetter 1985).

In this paper, we try to redress these shortcomings in the study of the relationship between organizations and their environments by concentrating explicitly on the structure of the institutional environment defined in terms of concrete patterns of inter-organizational linkages or, in other words, in terms of multiple relational networks among members of an inter-organizational community. Specifically, we define the organizational community under investigation as a 'set of organizations that have some functional interest in common' (Knoke and Rogers 1979). An obvious problem with this approach is defining the boundaries of the organizational community or 'interorganizational field' (DiMaggio 1986). Membership in an inter-organizational community is not limited to organizations directly involved in a specific functional activity but also includes organizations providing all sorts of ancillary services that are related only indirectly to the main functional interest.

The basic theoretical proposition underlying the present study is that organizational populations adapt to their environment through the evolution of institutional mechanisms for managing interdependence. Individual organizations try to relax their inherent 'bureaucratic constraints' by establishing network-like connections with other organizations in their environment. In either case, the result is an emergent system of inter-organizational relations which gives shape to the structure of organizational communities.

A network of organizations is always—at least to some degree—an artificial construct created by the investigator, that is, it exists independently of the awareness of the (individual or collective) actors participating in the network. In this sense the relevant question is not whether inter-organizational networks 'really exist', but rather: how can network concepts be useful to analyses of inter-organizational relations? This paper provides a first tentative answer to this theoretical question in the context of a specific empirical study of 106 organizations involved in the construction of means of transportation in southern Italy.

Specifically, intercorporate relationships in the southern Italian mechanical industry are considered in terms of four different structures of interaction: supply relationships, quality control agreements, technology transfer, and equity relations. The study represents one of the first attempts to apply modern network analysis techniques to understand the crucial link between economic policy and the structure of organizational communities, a link often ignored by policy-makers and organizational theorists alike. Although the analysis described below is at an exploratory stage, a few relatively unambiguous conclusions have emerged. First, financial incentives to private groups to locate large production units in under-developed areas have not contributed significantly to the development of a local industrial structure. Secondly, the inter-organizational community investigated is organized mainly along vertical lines with few horizontal linkages and a low degree of integration. Thirdly, the emergent inter-organizational role structure underlines the prominence of one or a few corporate groups with centralized supply strategies.

Following this general introduction, the next section provides some background on the organization of production in the Italian mechanical industry. The third section describes the sample and the methods used to analyse the data, and the fourth section presents the empirical results. A discussion concludes the paper by outlining the implications of the study and directions for future research.

INTER-ORGANIZATIONAL RELATIONS IN A DUAL ECONOMY

The Italian industrial system is characterized by a clear structural dualism resulting in dramatic economic and social differences between north and south. Industrialization in northern and central regions followed a distinct development path leading to the coexistence of very large and small to medium-sized firms operating mainly in traditional and mature economic sectors. This peculiar industrial organization, characterized by the existence of multiple networks of interaction and exchange among heterogeneous organizational forms, is deeply rooted in the social structure of central and northern Italian regions. Patterns of inter-organizational mutualism of this kind are often observable in industrial districts where a large number of small craft-like organizations contribute competencies, flexibilities, and specialized skills that can be exploited by a few large companies in exchange for organizational structures, financial leverage, and access to international markets.

A different picture emerges when we look at the economic development of southern Italian regions where industrial development has been lagging behind. This 'relative backwardness' has been responsible for Italy's characteristic uneven and incomplete economic development. During the last forty years the creation of large production units in capital-intensive industries by state-owned/controlled holding companies and by large private industrial groups (with public financial support) has been the state's major means of intervention in the southern Italian economy. The original policy objective was to develop a local industrial base both directly—by providing adequate incentives for the construction of new large-scale production plants—as well as indirectly—by stimulating entrepreneurship and helping the creation and diffusion of technical competencies and professional skills.

In terms of its original objectives this industrial policy has been only partially successful. While political intervention in industry generated direct employment through the creation of large manufacturing units, this economic policy failed to activate the process of development and growth of local industrial forces that policy-makers hoped for.

Organizational analysis of the mechanical industry in southern Italy may help to clarify the reasons for this partial policy failure. Owing to its relative weight in the economy and its technological complexity, understanding the organizational dynamics of the mechanical industry is crucial for an understanding of Italian industrial structure and performance. Historically, industrial development in Italy depended on the growth of the mechanical industry. Today, activities related to mechanical production account for 36.4 per cent of the value added by the whole manufacturing sector and 35 per cent of total Italian exports. Italy ranks third in the world in terms of trade surplus in the mechanical industry, after Japan and Germany (ISTAT 1991).

Mechanical production in Italy tends to be highly specialized on a regional basis. Mass production of cars and automotive parts is mostly concentrated in Piedmont and Lombardy, whereas the manufacture of automated machine tools and packaging machinery is concentrated in Emilia-Romagna. The major objective of public economic policy was to recreate these successful regional patterns of industrial organization in the south. Why did it not succeed? Understanding the processes that activate industrial development and entrepreneurship in economically disadvantaged regions would have important policy and practical implications as well as great theoretical value.

This paper reports the preliminary results of a study designed to analyse the structure of inter-firm relations in a particular set of activities within the mechanical industry in southern Italy referred to as 'construction of means of transportation' in Italian economic statistics. These activities include the production of locomotives and railway carriages, cars, trucks, earth movers, and motor vehicle components, and aircraft and related components. We selected these production activities for study because (i) they illustrate the organizational consequences of industrial dualism, (ii) they account for a large share of employment and value added in the economy of southern Italy, and (iii) they are currently targets of large-scale incentive policies designed by central and local governments to facilitate the localization of production units and the creation of new firms in the south.

The mechanical industry is characterized worldwide by a rather clear division of labour among firms. High levels of inter-organizational division of labour and the consequent need for intercorporate co-ordination should result in a high interdependence and integration among the different activities and organizations along the production chain. In fact, empirical studies of mechanical industries in different countries have consistently documented the existence of central firms orchestrating a network of suppliers of sub-systems and components (Lorenzoni 1979; Imai *et al.* 1985). If this is the case, the assessment of the structure and performance of any firm along the production chain requires an explicit focus on the concrete relationships through which that company is linked to others. As elaborated several times above, the methodological consequence of this theoretical focus is that the network structure of the relevant inter-organizational community becomes the prominent object of investigation.

Similarly, implementation (and assessment) of economic policies aimed at developing an industrial structure in disadvantaged regions (or economies) will have to take explicit account of the relational structure of the industry. In this sense we expect the present work to have relevant implications for policy design and evaluation and, ultimately, for the formulation of corporate strategy.

DATA AND METHODS

Data

After interviews with managers, executives, industry association officials, and industry experts, our understanding of the structure of the motor vehicles and transportation sector in the southern Italian mechanical industry suggested that the inter-organizational division of labour is organized into three distinct quasi-hierarchical levels. The first level is occupied by large national and international companies (more precisely, by their subsidiary production units) involved in manufacturing cars, trucks, scrapers and caterpillars, trains and aircraft. These large companies can be labelled 'core organizations' in the sense that they manufacture and sell a final product, and occupy the 'centre' of the industry. Size, activity, and function make these organizations prominent and powerful corporate actors within the industry and the national economy. The second level is comprised of small and medium-sized manufacturers of mechanical parts and components that are supplied to the core organizations and eventually assembled into the final product (e.g. a car). Often organizations at the second level are local branches of national companies that also maintain supply relationships with the core companies at other production sites. As one would expect, the third level includes very small local machine shops supplying specialized parts or services to second-level organizations.

We started our research on the network structure of the inter-organizational community of organizations operating in the transportation and motor vehicles sector of the southern Italian mechanical industry by using the 11 core organizations in our sample as name generators to start a snowball sampling scheme. A questionnaire was designed and submitted to the managers responsible for supply and inventory in the 11 core organizations. In the questionnaire, managers were asked to produce the names of their organization's 20 most important suppliers of mechanical materials, parts, and components operating in southern Italy. For each organization cited as a supplier, the questionnaire elicited data on the value of the supply relationships reported (absolute and in terms of incidence within the total value of supplies), on the existence of relationships deriving from quality control agreements (formal and informal), on technology transfer (formal and informal), and on equity arrangements (direct and indirect). Supply and inventory managers in each of the 11 core organizations were also shown a list containing the names of the other 10 core organizations at the first level and asked to identify the existence of the same kinds of relationships, that is (i) supply; (ii) quality control agreements; (iii) technology transfer; and (iv) equity.

The sample included 11 first-level core companies, jointly accounting for 35,712 employees, approximately 60 per cent of the total employment in the transportation and motor vehicles industry in southern Italy. The 11 first-level producers jointly identified 161 second-level suppliers, 33 of which appeared in more than one network. Of the 161 organizations listed, 15 were no longer operational by the time the data was collected, 7 were not involved in activities related to the production of mechanical parts and components, 11 returned unreliable (or clearly false) questionnaires, and 33 refused to participate in the study. This left us with a total of 95 second-level suppliers. The 11 core organizations with their 95 second-level suppliers jointly account for 46,498 employees, corresponding to approximately 77 per cent of the total employment in the southern Italian transportation and motor vehicle industry.

The same snowball procedure was repeated at the second level. The 95 organizations cited by the original name generators were contacted and asked about the relations among themselves. Organizations at the second level were also asked to produce a list of their 10 most important suppliers of mechanical parts and components operating in the southern regions. The questionnaire was designed to identify the presence/absence of inter-organizational relationships in the four networks specified above. To date, the 95 organizations at the second level have produced a list of 425 supplier organizations which represent part of the third (and last) level of the inter-organizational network. The data on this third level has not been analysed in the present study.

This observation scheme has generated four adjacency matrices of size 106 by 106 (one for each network), which were analysed to produce the results reported in the empirical part of the paper. The first matrix contains information on the supply relations between each pair of organizations in the sample. In this matrix, the generic entry a_{ij} contains a direct measure of the relation between actors i and j, that is, the monetary value of the goods and services supplied by the jth organization to the ith organization. The remaining three matrices are binary matrices recording the presence or absence of (i) joint involvement in programmes for quality control and improvement, (ii) relations of technology transfer, and (iii) equity relations among every possible organizational dyad in the sample.

The matrix containing information on the value of supply relations was binarized and left asymmetric to maintain the inherent directionality of buyer–supplier relations. The remaining three networks were symmetrized by the union rule for analytical convenience (the entry $a_{ij}^{(s)}$ in the symmetrized matrix $A^{(s)}$ is equal to $\max(a_{ij}, a_{ji})$ where a_{ij} and a_{ji} are generic entries in the raw data matrix A).

Block-Models of Inter-Organizational Networks

Research on inter-organizational networks requires some technique for partitioning relational data into distinct groups of actors that are similarly embedded in networks of relations (Faust and Wasserman 1992). To identify the structure of the inter-organizational community under investigation, we first partition the overall inter-organizational network into a system of jointly occupied positions (or equivalence classes), and then reconstruct the relational structure among these positions.

One of the major objectives of a positional analysis of this kind is to simplify the information contained in the network data. This simplification consists of a representation of the network in terms of the positions occupied by structurally equivalent actors (image matrix) and a statement of how these positions are related to each other (density table). An image matrix is a summary of the relational ties between and among positions so that each tie is coded as either present or absent between each pair of positions. Ideally, submatrices in the image matrix are either filled with zeros (called 'zero-blocks') or ones (called 'bonds'). An image matrix, along with the description of which actors are assigned to which positions, is called a block-model. In the analysis reported below, we use average density across all networks (=0.016) to define the cut-off value in the density table, above which an entry in the corresponding image matrix is defined as a bond. A density table is a matrix that has positions (rather than individual actors) as its rows and columns, and the values in the matrix are the proportions of relations that are sent from actors in row position to actors in column position.

In a block-model, actors are assigned to positions, and network relations are presented among positions—defined in terms of structurally equivalent sets of actors—rather than among individual actors. The equivalence definition specifies the conditions under which actors in a network will be assigned to equivalence classes (or positions). Among the many possible definitions of equivalence available in the technical literature we decided to adopt the notion of structural equivalence to explore the network structure of the inter-organizational community under investigation.[1] According to this notion, organizations in an inter-organizational network are structurally equivalent if they have identical relations to (and from) all other organizations in the network. In order to be relevant to the analysis of empirical inter-organizational fields, the word 'identical' in the formal definition of structural equivalence needs to be substituted by the word 'similar'. In this study we use correlation to implement this weaker structural equivalence construct and estimate the profile similarity of relational patterns across actors. Specifically, we use the CONCOR (convergence of iterated correlations) algorithm to identify subsets of structurally equivalent actors in the inter-organizational network. The formal behaviour of CONCOR, a hierarchical clustering algorithm commonly used in modern network analysis, is analysed in Breiger *et al.* (1975); some of its mathematical properties are described in Schwartz (1977).

The block-modelling analysis presented in the following section proceeds in two steps: first, the CONCOR algorithm is used to identify positions as collections of organizations which are 'similar' in their relations with others. Secondly, the emergent inter-organizational structure is modelled as systems of relations among positions. A third step, assessing and testing the adequacy of alternative block-model representations, goes beyond the exploratory nature of the present work.

---

[1] Structural equivalence in social networks can be formally defined as follows. Let S be a set and $\{R_i\}$ $(i = 1, 2, \ldots, m)$ be a set of binary relations defined on S. Units $a, b \in$ S are structurally equivalent if $\forall\, c \in$ S and $\forall\, R_i$, $aR_ic \Leftrightarrow bR_ic$, $cR_ia \Leftrightarrow cR_ib$.

RESULTS

We start by investigating the degree of integration of the organizational community, possibly the most important element of community structure. We do this by analysing the distribution of linkage relations across the four networks. In the network of supply relations—which seems to be the most compact of the four—approximately 93 per cent of all pairs are mutually reachable in four steps or fewer, and 5.39 per cent of all actors are directly connected. The supply network has a relational density of approximately 3 per cent.

In the network of quality control agreements (relational density 1.7 per cent), 60.74 per cent (6,760) of all the theoretically possible connections are absent and only 23 per cent of all pairs are mutually reachable in four steps or fewer, while 3.63 per cent of all pairs are reachable in seven steps. In the network of technology transfer agreements (relational density 1.1 per cent), 82.93 per cent (9,230) of all the theoretically possible links are absent indicating the relative rarity of technology transfer relationships. Only 1 per cent of all relations in this network are direct. Finally, 99 per cent (11,024) of all possible relations in the equity network (relational density 0.6 per cent) are absent, with only 0.56 per cent of the organizations in the sample connected by direct equity relations. Figure 4.1 summarizes the discussion so far, reporting on the horizontal axis the shortest path distances among all pairs of actors and on the vertical axis the percentage (or relative frequency) of all relations.

An important element of functional differentiation in the inter-organizational community concerns the involvement, visibility, or intensity of exchange activity, and its directionality. Actors with a high centrality score are visible in their networks and occupy a distinct relational role.

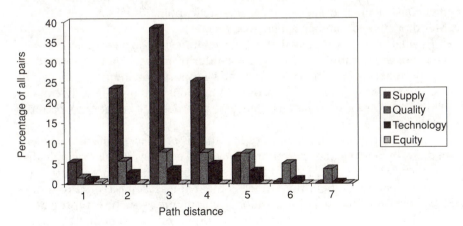

Fig. 4.1. Distribution of path distances in four networks

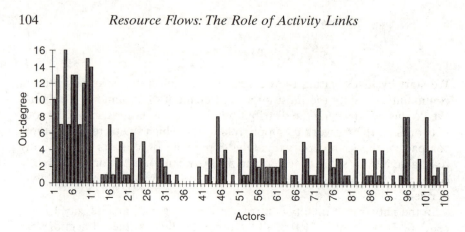

Fig. 4.2. Supply relations sent

Directionality in buyer–supplier relations requires that both in-degrees—number of links received—and out-degrees—numbers of links sent—be computed for each individual actor. Figure 4.2 reports a plot of out-degrees for each individual actor in the supply network.

By looking at Fig. 4.2 it is clear that community members can be partitioned into a sending and a receiving subgroup. This was largely expected on the basis of our understanding of the hierarchical and functional structure of the inter-organizational community according to which a restricted number of 'core' organizations rely extensively on a 'periphery' of much smaller second-level organizations for the supply of intermediate parts and mechanical components. This is reflected in a significantly higher number of relations sent by the first eleven organizations in Fig. 4.2, with a leading position assumed by the production units of Fiat Auto (numbers 4, 6, 7, and 10), and a lower relational intensity for the two organizations involved in the constructions of aeroplanes and helicopters (number 3, Elicotteri Meridionali, and number 8, Fiat Avio).

In what sense can we say that the eleven large first-level production units are 'core organizations'? How do they differ from organizations located on the 'periphery' of the motor vehicle and transportation industry? To answer these questions we identify sets of organizations that are similarly embedded in networks of relations (blocks), and describe relational patterns among such blocks.

We sought empirical regularities in patterns of inter-organizational associations by rearranging (permuting) rows and columns of the original adjacency matrices to reveal zero-blocks (submatrices, all of whose entries are zero) and bonds (submatrices which contain at least some 1's). Zero-blocks are 'holes' in the inter-organizational community structure representing the absence of relational activity—or organization—among the actors in the block. Bonds indicate at least some degree of cohesiveness among

Table 4.1. Image matrices

	Supply				Quality				Technology				Equity			
	A	B	C	D	A	B	C	D	A	B	C	D	A	B	C	D
A	1	0	0	0	1	0	0	0	1	0	0	0	0	0	0	0
B	0	1	0	1	0	1	0	0	0	0	0	0	0	0	0	0
C	1	1	1	1	0	0	1	1	0	0	1	0	0	0	1	0
D	0	1	1	1	0	0	1	0	0	0	0	0	0	0	0	0

structurally equivalent actors occupying the same (or similar) network position.

After some experimentation with the data, we decided that the inter-organizational community can be adequately represented by a four-block system. In this inter-organizational system each block represents a position jointly occupied by structurally equivalent organizations, that is, by organizations that have a similar pattern of connections with the other members of the inter-organizational community.

The final representation of this permutation is summarized by a block-model in the form of a series of image matrices (one for each network) which illustrate the positional structure of the inter-organizational community. The image matrices in Table 4.1 report a one every time the block density was found to be greater than the average density across all networks (0.016), and zero otherwise.

The community role structure emerging from the image matrix of the supply network in Table 4.1 illustrates the prominence of the position corresponding to block C containing all the Fiat units in the sample which constitute a sociometric clique in the equity network. Each block is characterized by the presence of one or more core organizations and a number of second-level suppliers. A closer look at the composition of each block shows that block A includes two core organizations in the aircraft industry (Alenia and Elicotteri Meridionali), and sixteen other organizations. Blocks B and D contain just one core organization each (Ansaldo Trasporti and Omeca), both manufacturing railway carriages and locomotives, and thirty-eight (block B) and seventeen (block D) second-level organizations, respectively. Block C contains all the Fiat Group's production units: four units manufacturing and assembling car engines and bodies, two units assembling trucks and commercial vehicles and one unit operating in the aircraft industry. Twenty-four second-level organizations complete block C.

A first indication of community structure differentiation emerges by looking at employment concentration in the blocks. Block C differs markedly from the other blocks. It is by far the largest block in terms of employees (and revenues generated by its member organizations)

Table 4.2. Density tables in four networks

Supply					Quality Control				
Block	A	B	C	D	Block	A	B	C	D
A	0.09	0.01	0.01	0.00	A	0.09	0.00	0.01	0.00
B	0.01	0.03	0.00	0.02	B	0.00	0.02	0.00	0.01
C	0.02	0.02	0.08	0.05	C	0.01	0.00	0.08	0.02
D	0.01	0.06	0.04	0.03	D	0.00	0.01	0.02	0.00

Technology Transfer					Equity				
Block	A	B	C	D	Block	A	B	C	D
A	0.09	0.00	0.01	0.01	A	0.01	0.00	0.00	0.00
B	0.00	0.00	0.00	0.00	B	0.00	0.00	0.00	0.00
C	0.01	0.00	0.06	0.01	C	0.00	0.00	0.05	0.01
D	0.01	0.00	0.01	0.00	D	0.00	0.00	0.01	0.00

representing about 65 per cent (85 per cent in terms of revenues) of the total sample. The seven core organizations of block C jointly account for approximately 91 per cent of total employment in the block. In block A the two core companies jointly account for 66 per cent of the employment in the block, with Alenia alone accounting for 52 per cent. In blocks B and D employment is less concentrated, with the core organizations accounting for 38 per cent and 18 per cent of employment in the respective blocks.

Assigning actors to positions and determining the patterns of zero-blocks and bonds is only part of the construction of a block-model. A second important part in a block-modelling exercise consists in the evaluation of connections among blocks of structural equivalent actors. The main interest in evaluating patterns of relationships among the blocks derived is in discerning the underlying patterns of intercorporate co-ordination and their influence out of which community role structure emerges. Below we report the density tables for the supply, quality control, technology transfer, and equity networks (Table 4.2).

Finally, the density matrices for all networks were averaged to yield a mean density table whose cells record the average density of relations within and among positions (Table 4.3).

Cell values range from 0 to 1 with greater values indicating a stronger relationship between the members of jointly occupied network positions (equivalence classes). While positions A and C are characterized by stronger relational ties within their position, smaller organizations in positions B and D seem to entertain relatively more frequent cross-positional relationships. All Fiat units occupy the position corresponding to block C

Table 4.3. Average density table (all networks)

Block	1	2	3	4
1	0.07	0.00	0.01	0.00
2	0.00	0.01	0.00	0.01
3	0.01	0.01	0.07	0.02
4	0.01	0.02	0.02	0.01

and their pattern of relations strongly influence intra-block characteristics. Taking a closer look at the relational structure of block B reveals that equity and quality relations play a prominent role at the intra-block level, whereas supply links cut more easily across block boundaries. In the supply network, position C clearly dominates all other positions.

DISCUSSION AND CONCLUSIONS

We started by identifying a number of shortcomings in traditional approaches to the study of the relation between organizations and their environments. We then reviewed the problems of industrial economic policy in southern Italy and concentrated on the mechanical industry to illustrate some of the organizational problems left unsolved by state intervention in the economy. Following the indications which have emerged from recent trends in the organizational theory literature, we treated the organizations in our sample as members of an inter-organizational community defined on the basis of a common functional interest. We analysed data on intercorporate relations among 106 organizations in four networks to explore patterns of community structure. We now conclude by discussing a few selected points emerging from the analysis of the data.

The structure of the inter-organizational community investigated is extremely loose. The analysis revealed low values of relational density in all the four networks investigated. The supply network presents a slightly higher level of integration among the members of the community, followed by the quality control network. Looking at the most integrated supply network it emerges that the dominant pattern of inter-organizational relations is articulated along the vertical dimension of the production chain. This result was partly expected due to the structure of the research design, but it does signal the lack of intermediary inter-organizational structures and the rarity of horizontal linkages. This further evidence of the lack of integration in the inter-organizational community studied may be interpreted as a lack of investment in relational structures by the core units and/or the impossibility for second-tier firms to diversify their markets and clients, because of technological or marketing limitations.

The positional analysis suggests the existence of a core–periphery pattern in southern Italy's mechanical industry, with few organizations representing the community's 'inner circle', in terms of prominence and influence on the whole community, and the rest of the organizations occupying the periphery. A list of specific attributes may be easily associated with organizations in different structural positions within the community. Core organizations are larger in terms of sales, purchases, and employees, they are closer to final product markets, and so on. At the periphery we find much smaller units and, interestingly enough, units that show a higher average percentage of mechanical purchases in the south as a fraction of total mechanical purchases. This can be interpreted as further evidence that smaller local units are more integrated in the regional industrial texture, while the large production units 'transplanted' into the area never developed a genuinely local supplier network. The proportion of mechanical purchases from suppliers located in the south compared with the total amount of mechanical purchases is much lower than the average for all core units.

Block-modelling analysis shows weak relational activity both among actors belonging to different blocks and among actors belonging to the same block. The extremely low inter-block relational intensity represents further evidence of the weak integration in the inter-organizational community.

The study is at an exploratory stage and the results are still preliminary. Future elaboration will require analysis of the full sample and a new—and more thorough—exploration of the industry role structure. For this, formal assessment of the adequacy of alternative block-models will have to be performed. However, the current results may have a number of implications for the design and evaluation of future and past industrial policies. First of all, incentives for large industrial groups to locate production units in the south have not induced the expected flow of orders to local suppliers of mechanical parts and components. In general, large core units are not satisfactorily integrated into the local industrial structure. Secondly, inter-organizational relations are strictly along the vertical production chain, converging towards the core organizations, leaving local firms on the periphery of the community. Finally, there is some evidence that supply and supply-related policies (quality control and technology transfer agreements) are conceived at the headquarters level and rarely involve local suppliers. Such policies tend to rely on suppliers based in the north which serve all the group's production units, regardless of location. These centralized corporate policies leave very few opportunities for learning, innovation, or growth at a local mechanical firm level.

The main contribution of this paper has been to propose a theoretically inspired framework to study inter-organizational relationships in dual economies. We found the idea of inter-organizational community useful in understanding the consequences of economic policy in the southern Italian mechanical industry. We were encouraged to adopt an explicit organizational framework by the fact that the primary means of state intervention in the industry were—in fact—organizational. The methodology applied to the analysis of the relational data collected was consistent with the theoretical position of the study on the relevance of concrete patterns of intercorporate co-ordination in which organizational actors are embedded.

REFERENCES

Aldrich, H. 1979. *Organizations and Environments*. Englewood Cliffs, NJ: Prentice Hall.

Barley, S. 1986. 'Technology as an Occasion for Structuring'. *Administrative Science Quarterly*. 31: 77–101.

——and Freeman, L. 1991. 'Niche and Networks: The Evolution of Organisational Fields in the Biotechnology Industry'. Working paper, Cornell University.

Borgatti, S. P., Everett, M. G., and Freeman, L. C. 1992. *UCINET IV Version 1.00*. Columbia: Analytic Technologies.

Breiger, R., Boorman, S., and Arabie, P. 1975. 'An Algorithm for Clustering Relational Data with Applications to Social Network Analysis and Comparison with Multidimensional Scaling'. *Journal of Mathematical Psychology*. 12: 328–83.

DiMaggio, P. 1986. 'Structural Analysis of Organisational Fields'. *Research in Organizational Behavior*. 8: 335–70.

Faust, K., and Wasserman, S. 1992. 'Blockmodels: Interpretation and Evaluation'. *Social Networks*. 4: 5–61.

Granovetter, M. 1985. 'Economic Action and Social Structure: A Theory of Embeddedness'. *American Journal of Sociology*. 91: 481–510.

Hannan, M., and Freeman, J. 1989. *Organizational Ecology*. Cambridge, Mass.: Harvard University Press.

Hawley, A. 1986. *Human Ecology: A Theoretical Essay*. Chicago: University of Chicago Press.

Imai, K., Nonaka, I., and Takeuchi, B. 1985. 'Managing the New Product Development Process: How Japanese Firms Learn and Unlearn'. In Clark, R. B., Hayes, R. M., and Lorenz, C. (eds.). *The Uneasy Alliance*. 337–75. Cambridge, Mass.: Harvard Business School Press.

ISTAT 1991. *Conti economici delle imprese pubbliche con 20 addetti e oltre. 1983–87*. Roma: ISTAT.

Knoke, D., and Rogers, D. 1979. 'A Blockmodel Analysis of Interorganizational Networks'. *Sociology and Social Research*. 64: 28–52.

Lawrence, P., and Lorsch, J. 1967. *Organization and Environment*. Homewood, Ill.: Irwin.

Lorenzoni G. 1979. 'Una tipologia di produzione in conto terzi nel settore metalmeccanico'. In Varaldo, R. (ed.). *Ristrutturazioni industriali e rapporti fra imprese. Ricerche economico-tecniche sul decentramento produttivo*. Milano: Angeli.

Schwartz, J. 1977. 'An Examination of CONCOR and Related Methods for Blocking Sociometric Data'. In Heise, D. (ed.). *Sociological Methodology*. 255–82. San Francisco: Jossey Bass.

Zavatta R. 1993. *Il posizionamento competitivo dell'industria meccanica meridionale*. Internal research report, Economisti Associati—LOGICA.

III

MUTUAL EXPECTATIONS:
The Role of Trust

5

Processes Facilitating Reliance on Trust in Inter-Organizational Networks

PETER SMITH RING

INTRODUCTION

From a review of the organization and strategic management literatures of the past five years, two conclusions can be drawn. First, for managers who want to achieve sustained competitive advantage (SCA) for their firms, capitalizing on, and leveraging, firm-specific resources is a necessary, but not a sufficient, condition (see e.g. Amit and Schoemaker 1993; Barney 1991; Lado and Wilson 1995; Mahoney and Pandian 1992; Prahalad and Hamel 1990). Secondly, in attempting to achieve SCA, many of these same managers now see co-operation between organizations as a useful means to gain access to critical resources beyond the boundaries of their own firms (see e.g. Gulati 1995; Håkansson and Snehota 1995; Nohria and Eccles 1993; Parkhe 1991; Powell 1990; Ring and Van de Ven 1992).

In the *Strategic Management Journal*, for example, over two dozen articles specifically dealing with either resources or with collaborations have appeared since 1990; in the *Journal of Marketing*, fifteen articles dealing with collaboration were published during the same time span. A very recent special issue of the *Academy of Management Journal* was devoted to the topic of collaboration, and many of our colleagues in the academy are undoubtedly responding to a call for papers for a special issue of *Organization Science* on strategic alliances and networks. In the *Wall Street Journal*, the leading daily business newspaper in the USA, Knecht (1994) reports that global strategic alliances reached record numbers in 1993.

As they seek the resources that they believe they will need in order to achieve their strategic intent (Hamel and Prahalad 1989), managers of business firms are using a much richer variety of what my colleague Andrew Van de Ven and I have described as co-operative inter-organizational relationships (CIORs). Generally, these co-operative exchanges of resources have been conducted either through discrete market transactions (e.g. cross-licensing of technology) or within hierarchical arrangements such as joint ventures (Friar and Horwitch 1985; Hennart 1988; Kogut 1988; Powell 1987; Teece 1986).

The CIORs investigated in research on these new governance forms (see Borys and Jemison 1989) have been described in terms such as strategic alliances (e.g. James 1985), partnerships (e.g. Perlmutter and Heenan 1986), coalitions (e.g. Porter and Fuller 1986), research consortia (Ouchi and Kremen-Bolton 1988), networks (Jarillo 1988; the chapters in this volume and the wide variety of research cited in them), and clans (e.g. Alvesson and Lindkvist 1993). These CIORs appear to be very different from traditional supplier relationships, marketing joint ventures, or technology licensing arrangements.

These new forms of co-operation frequently involve exchanges of idiosyncratic resources; that is, the resources are specifically designed to be used in connection with a single transaction. Received theory from transaction cost economists (see Coase 1937; Williamson 1985, 1975) predicts that the firms employing CIORs to exchange idiosyncratic assets should be using hierarchical arrangements. This apparent divergence from theory by practitioners is a primary cause of intense scholarly interest in collaboration. For example, Casson and Cox (Chapter 7) make a compelling case for networks as an efficient institutional solution to the problem of co-ordination (even when idiosyncratic assets are involved).

Aside from providing rich description about CIORs, however, it is my impression that the research has yet to lead to a discussion of the processes by which these alternative forms of CIORs emerge. This is especially so in the case of networks where, as the research presented in this volume confirms, much of the focus has been on antecedents of networks, their structure, and their relationship to economic performance (Chapter 9 provides an outstanding exception to this general statement about processes).

Accompanying this dramatic increase in interest in CIORs, we also find renewed interest in the role that trust plays in governing economic exchanges. Smith *et al.* (1995: 15) note that 'the study of trust and its impact on cooperative relationships at all levels may be a particularly fruitful area of future research'. To date, much of the literature has focused on the role that trust plays in CIORs, its impact on the costs of transacting, and on performance. Again, we have less understanding of the processes that can create trust, or are employed by parties relying on trust in governing economic exchange. In this chapter, I seek to begin a discussion of the issues related to the processes that permit economic actors to develop and rely on trust in network settings.

Following arguments outlined by Ring and Van de Ven (1992) on the role of trust between economic actors in co-operative relationships, I offer propositions dealing with issues that arise from reliance on trust in network settings. Informal processes of sense-making, understanding, and committing (Ring and Rands 1989; Ring and Van de Ven 1994) are proposed as the primary processes by which economic actors learn to rely on trust in networks.

CHARACTERISTICS OF NETWORKS

Let me state at the outset that I am of the opinion that the term 'network' should be used as a research concept.[1] If it is used otherwise, it must be carefully defined. In relatively simple terms, the concept of network for me implies co-operative efforts among business firms, governmental bodies or organizations, persons, or other entities that are interconnected in various ways. These connections permit them to be seen clearly apart from the environment in which they are embedded. There are a number of elements that appear to distinguish networks from other CIORs.

More so than in other forms of collaborations designed to facilitate economic exchanges, networks are also infused with social exchange. Blau (1964: 93) argues that 'social exchange differs in many important ways from strictly economic exchange'. He concludes that a 'critical distinction is that social exchange entails unspecified obligations'. This contrasts with basic economic transactions which are built on the foundation of 'a formal contract that stipulates the exact quantities to be exchanged'. The need for specificity differs sharply from 'the principle that one person does another a favor, and while there is a general expectation of some future return, its exact nature is definitely not stipulated in advance', that characterizes the governance of social exchange. In addition to obligations being unspecified, Murakami and Rohlen (1992: 74–5) have argued that social exchange implies a limited number of partners in the relationship: the fewer the numbers, the better the communication and co-ordination; the greater the stability of membership over time; and the more focused the resources for maintenance. In their view, social exchange also entails a normal degree of uncertainty. These views are similar to those reached by the Nobel laureate Douglass North (1990: 12), who argues that co-operation among economic actors is more likely to exist when the economic actors (a) repeatedly transact, (b) have a great deal of information about the other economic actors with whom they transact, and (c) are relatively small in number. These are certainly important characteristics of a network.

Kumon (1992: 118) provides further insight into the elements of a network. He observes that networks are

[1] I am indebted to Professor Howard Aldrich for providing me with a very persuasive argument on this point in his comments on an earlier draft of this chapter.

organized under the premise that information rights are legitimately established in some form or other and at the same time partially restricted within themselves. The main reason actors join a network is to share useful information/knowledge with other members, to achieve better mutual understanding; and to develop a firm base for mutual trust that may eventually lead to collaboration to achieve the actors' individual as well as collective goals.

This suggests two additional characteristics of a network: complicated norms regarding *information* exchange and *exchange* based on trust. Gerlach's (1992: 3) definition of intercorporate alliances suggests another key characteristic of a network: institutionalized relationships among firms based on localized networks of dense transaction.[2]

Lazerson's (1988: 333–4) study of Italian firms provides additional support for including these kinds of elements and characteristics in descriptions of networks. The firms he studied reflected a 'dense web of market relations, often marked by long-established reciprocal relations and inter-family connections'. These networks were clustered in compact geographic regions, were spatially divided, but co-operated to enjoy scale economies. Relationships between the firms were highly flexible, with frequent exchanges that facilitated and accelerated communication and the exchange of information. And as Teubal *et al.* (1991) have observed, two of the frequently observed characteristics in conceptual definitions of networks are recurring transactions and long-term, stable relationships.

The ways in which networks have been conceptualized in these studies suggest that the following elements will be necessary conditions for the emergence of a network. Networks reflect *relationships* which are relatively stable, involving long-established reciprocal relations that frequently entail unspecified *obligations*. Network relationships are *spatially* constrained, frequently operating in environments that are naturally bounded, or artificially created, by kinship, political, or cultural considerations, or by geographic boundaries. This localized nature of network relationships often leads to *transactions* which are dense. Dense transactions are, as Gerlach (1992: 4–5) observed, multiplex and extended; that is, the small group of firms that make up a network transact with each other quite frequently, for a variety of reasons (economic and social), over relatively long periods of time.

The results of the research on networks suggests that dense transactions are not at arm's-length, nor are they discrete. The evidence also suggests that transactions which take place within a network, for example, are likely to entail interwoven, recurring exchanges, among a number of economic actors, of financial, human, and 'social' capital (Coleman 1988). In addition, even when a transaction between economic actors in a network is dyadic

---

[2] Although Gerlach uses the term intercorporate alliance, it seems clear from the larger corpus of his work that he is studying network phenomena. I suspect his use of the term 'inter-organisational alliances' reflects his own concern about how the concept of network should be used in research dealing with co-operative activities by organizations.

in nature, that transaction remains embedded within the control systems governing the network, and these control systems are likely to serve as further constraints on the actions of the economic actors.

The actions of economic actors in a network are also constrained because their identity and the history of their prior relationships with each other are likely to be much more important in network transactions than in other modes of exchange. In terms derived from Macneil (1980, 1978, 1974), exchange within a network is relational rather than transactional. Relational exchange according to Macneil (1980: 13; emphasis added) is defined by personal relations that include 'the whole person, are unlimited in scope, are unique, and are nontransferable. *Communications* in such relations are extensive and informal as well as or instead of formal. Communication is not limited to linguistics but involves all the senses.' Thus, the relationships that exist between economic actors in a network are long term in nature and the rights and obligations of the members of the network, as they exist at any point in time, will be diffused and difficult to specify.

Lastly, because networks are infused with 'symbolic signification' (Gerlach 1992), they may persist without the necessity of 'formal legal arrangements or contracts' (Gerlach 1992: 5) or other formal *governance* mechanisms. For example, Lazerson (1988: 340) found that among the small firms he studied in Modena the longer and more continuous exchange relations were between economic actors, the less likely was the need to formalize them legally. In Table 5.1, these elements and characteristics of networks are summarized.

TRUST

Pervasive evidence from numerous disciplines supports the inclusion of trust as a critical factor in investigations of economic exchange.[3] A review of this literature suggests that trust plays two roles in facilitating economic exchange. First, through norms and sanctions trust may act as a substitute for the formal control systems that are frequently relied upon in governing economic exchanges.[4] Secondly, there is evidence that trust is an enabling

[3] The role of trust has been extensively investigated by a variety of scholars in fields such as organization and management (Bhide and Stevenson 1992; Bromiley and Cummings 1995; Butler 1991; McAllister 1995; Sitkin and Roth 1993; Ring and Van de Ven 1992); marketing (Anderson and Weitz 1989; Moorman *et al*. 1992); sociology (Barber 1983; Fox 1974; Gambetta 1988; Kollock 1992; Luhmann 1979; Shapiro 1987; Zucker 1986); economics (Frank 1988); philosophy (Baier 1986); and psychology (Johnson-George and Swap 1982; Rotter 1980, 1971).

[4] A discussion of this first role of trust is beyond the scope of this chapter. Norms might be developed about factors such as: timely performance, dealing with uncertainty, coping with interventions by third parties, reciprocity, equity, and other similar issues. The kinds of sanctions that would be employed in dealing with breaches of trust are likely to depend upon factors such as: the type of trust (e.g. interpersonal, institutional), the nature of the relationships between parties (e.g. purely economic, economic and social, economic and kinship, etc.),

Table 5.1. Elements and characteristics of networks

Elements	Illustrative Characteristics
Membership	Small in numbers Kinship-based at times Flexible, yet stable
Relationships	Long-term Unlimited—whole person Unique—non-transferable Localized
Obligations	Unspecified Reciprocal
Basis for exchange	Trust
Communication	Extensive Informal and formal Uses all senses Unlimited
Information rights	Well-established Partially restricted Partially shared Complicated norms
Transactions	Social and economic Frequent Dense and multiplex Recurring
Governance	More symbolic Less formalized Fewer safeguards
Spatial	Compact

condition which facilitates the formation of ongoing networks governing economic exchanges. One outcome of my analysis of this literature on trust is the conclusion that a single conceptualization of trust does not fulfil these two functions. Rather, it appears that different kinds of trust are at work in each case. In the discussion that follows, I pursue this supposition in greater detail.

Trust Defined

Interestingly, in spite of a substantial body of evidence (cited in n. 3), most economists, and many management researchers, operate from the assump-

the duration of those relationships. Sanctions might include refusal to do business with the party again, active efforts to publicly redefine the reputation of the party who breached trust, ostracism, and so on, in addition to resorting to sanctions provided by institutional guarantors, such as fines, damages, specific performance, and so on.

tion that economic actors will act in ways that maximize their own utility (even if at the expense of others' utilities). This kind of behaviour would seem to preclude extensive reliance on trust, other than: 'I trust that this person with whom I am considering a transaction will not spend a lot of time looking out for *my* interests!'

In economic theories of transacting that have dominated many recent investigations of inter-firm co-operation, such as the Williamson (1975, 1985, 1993) school, a further assumption is made that flies in the face of this evidence about the important role that trust appears to play in economic exchange. Many so-called transaction cost economists assume that, at times, the self-interested behaviour by economic actors can be strategic; that is, they will act opportunistically. Williamson describes this as self-interest-seeking with guile.

These assumptions do not absolutely preclude economists from recognizing that contrary behaviour might be possible, or desirable. Williamson (1985: 62–3), for example, somewhat begrudgingly acknowledges the utility of trust in transactions. He observes that '[o]ther things being equal, idiosyncratic exchange relations that feature personal trust will survive greater stress and will display greater adaptability'. None the less, trust does not play a major role in explanations of the actions of economic actors offered by most economists, or many other researchers relying on these economic models.[5]

Consistent with a view that assumes self-interested behaviour by economic actors, Baker (1984) has argued that, standing alone, trust is not a sufficient condition for the effective social control of business behaviour. Thus, even when it is recognized as part of economic life, trust is often viewed as a weak mechanism for controlling the opportunistic tendencies of economic actors. This view of the weak role of trust as a control mechanism may be the result of a failure to adequately distinguish between different types of trust.[6]

In developing my arguments, I rely primarily on the findings of researchers who have explored the role of trust in the management of business organizations. In this literature, two very different definitions of trust emerge (Ring and Van de Ven 1992). In the first definition, economic actors express confidence in the predictability of their expectations (Zucker 1986). In this definition, trust is frequently equated with the concept of risk, or the

---

[5] Robert Frank (1988), in *Passions Within Reason*, provides a seminal exception.

[6] It is also probable that the lack of rigorous empirical research on the role of trust in economic exchange is a key factor. For example, I have found no research that reports on how or why economic actors say they rely on trust in different types of transactions (e.g. dealing with different types of suppliers, domestic versus foreign competitors, people in or out of the same industry, etc.). Until we have these kinds of data, discussions such as that found in this chapter dealing with what trust means, or when it is relied upon, remain at best speculative. The same must be said for the question of whether the kinds of trust I am describing operate at both organizational and interpersonal levels.

probability that future outcomes associated with the transaction will be as predicted by the parties. Frequently, the risk that the economic actors are assumed to face is a consequence of the threat of opportunistic behaviour (embedded in the behavioural assumptions relied upon by researchers working with these economics-based frameworks).

I describe the kind of trust that exists under these circumstances as 'fragile', permitting economic actors to deal with each other, but only in guarded ways. In such circumstances, I would expect to find that the parties to a transaction are also relying on formal means (e.g. contractual) for governing their relationship. When the parties rely on this kind of trust, I would also expect to find that they have hedged their bets with the kinds of endogenous safeguards that economists frequently describe (hostages, bonds, insurance, and so on), or as a last resort depend on the kinds of institutional guarantors that Commons (1924) describes: courts, mediators, arbitrators.

What outcomes can this 'fragile' trust produce? Along with Blau (1964), I believe that fragile trust provides a foundation for developing stability in social and economic relationships.[7] As we have seen, stability is an important characteristic of network relationships, so that reliance on fragile trust may help parties lay the groundwork for creating a network.

Luhmann (1979) has asserted that a function of trust is to reduce complexity in social worlds. I argue that reliance on fragile trust can help the parties to simplify their economic relationships. By relying on fragile trust, for example, they may not need as many endogenous safeguards in order to undertake the frequent exchange of idiosyncratic assets, or they may not have to over-specify terms and conditions in a contract. In network contexts, fragile trust, once again, may help to create a foundation for simplifying governance; it does not, however, explain the informal means of governing that have been described in much of the literature on networks.

By describing this kind of trust as fragile, I imply that there may be other kinds of trust. Is there a basis for this? The literature reveals that trust is described as having different conceptual characteristics. Barber (1983: 9), for example, has defined trust in terms of the expectations that social actors (including economic actors) hold about one another. The expectations include beliefs that those with whom we transact will maintain a 'persistence and fulfillment of the natural and the moral social orders' to govern in a society or societies. Barber also asserts that parties expect 'technically competent role performance from those involved . . . in social relationships and systems', and that 'partners in interaction will carry out their fiduciary obligations and responsibilities, that is, their duties in certain situations to place other's interests before their own'. Barber (1983: 100–101) argues

---

[7] Certainly a desire for stability (in addition to higher quality, lower costs, or greater responsiveness) is one of the key motivating factors behind the increased reliance on a limited number of suppliers that we have witnessed of late, especially in the automotive industry.

that in so far as business is concerned, the public is supposed to typically define trust as meeting technical competence, not meeting a fiduciary responsibility.

It seems to me that Barber is describing more than one kind of trust. For example, his first set of expectations seems to be quite different, conceptually, from the other two. The second and third sets of expectations described by Barber relate to the expectations that our predictions about an individual's capabilities will stand up to the test of time, or that they will produce the results they promise to produce. I argue that these expectations reflect the existence of fragile trust; if the expectations are not met, continued reliance on trust by economic actors is likely to break down or be discarded altogether. Trust in the 'persistence and fulfillment of the natural and the moral social orders', on the other hand, seems to take on a very different character.

The discussion by transaction cost economists of a risk-based view of trust that can be secured by impersonal, third-party institutions (including guarantees, insurance mechanisms, hostages, law, or organizational hierarchy) seems consistent with what I describe as fragile trust. These third party guarantors are presumed to be needed, as we have seen, because of the assumption that trust by itself is not a sufficient means of controlling opportunistic behaviour by economic actors. This fragile trust, however, does serve as 'a sort of ever-ready lubricant that permits voluntary participation in production and exchange' (Dasgupta 1988: 49). Once again, however, it does not seem to explain the kinds of reliance on trust described in the research on networks.

Of course this view of fragile trust is based on an assumption that economic actors are, first and foremost, utility maximizers of their own preferences. It is also based on the assumption that if expectations regarding outcomes are not met, the state will intervene in support of an aggrieved party. The intervention of the state, however, frequently entails significant costs for all concerned. These costs place strains on the resources of the network and they seem inconsistent with the espoused motivations of many who create or join networks. They may be borne by those transacting or by many who are not directly parties to the transaction, such as taxpayers or other third parties who bear the costs of maintaining the institutional guarantors provided by the state (Commons 1924).[8]

As I have indicated, there is a second definition of trust frequently used by management scholars, sociologists, and philosophers. This definition appears to be quite different from what I have described as fragile trust. In this second definition, the confidence of economic actors rests, not in the predictability of outcomes, but in the predictability of the goodwill of others (Ring and Van de Ven 1992). This view of trust, similar in scope to that

---

[8] And as the residents of Orange County, California are discovering, the 'state' is not always a reliable supplier of such services.

offered by Baier (1986), emphasizes that trust is faith in the moral integrity or goodwill of others on whom economic actors depend for the realization of collective and individual goals as they deal with future, unpredictable issues. It describes a set of expectations that A will act in a manner that reflects 'persistence and fulfillment of the natural and the moral social orders' (Barber 1983: 9) in her relations with B. I describe this kind of trust as 'resilient' trust. By resilient I mean that this kind of trust survives the occasional transaction in which the expectations of economic actors regarding a specific economic exchange and the outcomes of that exchange do not fully converge. This resilient trust will also survive the occasional fall from grace of A in the eyes of economic actor B. It is this kind of trust, I believe, that leads to, and helps explain the stable, long-term relationships characteristic of networks. Reliance on resilient trust, I believe, also explains why many networks employ more symbolic and less formalized types of governance. In subsequent sections of this chapter, I will have more to say about both fragile and resilient trust, the processes that facilitate their development, and how resilient trust and the processes that are employed to foster it can lead to the formation of networks.

Reliance on Trust in Economic Exchange

Arrow (1973: 24) points out that 'there is an element of trust in every transaction' and that the level of trust varies with transacting parties. Needless to say, this condition applies to most modern business transactions. I believe, however, that Arrow is describing fragile trust. For example, reliance on fragile trust might be necessary even in cases of simultaneous exchange of non-idiosyncratic assets (e.g. money for fruit at roadside stands).[9] In these kinds of cases it may not be possible for the parties to determine at the time of the exchange whether the objects of exchange deliver or perform as expected over an extended period of time. But the parties trust that the objects will deliver or perform as expected. If they do not, the aggrieved parties are not likely to do business with the offending parties in the future.

In assessing when economic actors might rely upon trust, I believe that we can gain insight by considering the following example. In our personal lives the things that we are most likely to place in the care of a person whom we trust are those things that we value most.[10] Thus, two questions will have to be asked and answered by economic actors seeking to rely on trust in

[9] In many roadside stands in the San Joaquin Valley of Central California, the owners simply put the fruit out and trust in the good nature of those who stop to pay for the unattended goods they take.

[10] The things that organizations tend to value most are the kinds of things that provide a basis for sustained competitive advantage. In many instances these are likely to be idiosyncratic to that organization, i.e. tacit knowledge. Transaction cost economists predict that when idiosyncratic assets are frequently exchanged under conditions of uncertainty it is safe to assume that economic actors will engage in opportunistic behaviour.

inter-organizational networks: 'Who do we trust?' 'What do we trust them with?'

In considering who to trust, economic actors must consider factors derived from the behaviours of other economic actors. Jennings (1971) identified four attributes of trust on the basis of interviews with executives: loyalty, accessibility, availability, and predictability. Loyalty generally meant that actor A would keep a promise not to harm actor B. This kind of behaviour seems consistent with what I have described as implicit in resilient trust. Accessibility indicated an openness by one party to ideas presented by others. Availability indicated that when economic actor A needed to see economic actor B, the latter would be physically available to A. Predictability described behaviour related to decision-making: that an actor was consistent in her decisions, thus relieving others of a level of uncertainty. These three characteristics of trust seem to be more consistent with what has been described as fragile trust. They certainly are things that would lubricate economic exchanges, and they are essential elements in most good business dealings.

Gabarro (1978) conducted interviews similar to those undertaken by Jennings. Upon analysing responses of corporate presidents concerning their relationships with their vice-presidents, he identified nine factors which he associated with trust. These included people skills (interpersonal competence); discretion (the ability to maintain confidences); integrity (honesty); openness (freely expressing ideas); motives (intentions); task knowledge and skills (functional competence); judgement in decision-making; business sense (what makes a business work); and consistency of behaviour.

The first five factors identified by Gabarro, in my view, seem to relate more closely to conditions that give rise to resilient trust, while the remaining four more closely relate to fragile trust. Deep levels of trust are not likely to emerge unless the individuals involved display interpersonal competence. These kinds of skills seem essential to developing 'whole person' communication skills. The same seems to be the case for openness; unlimited relations, for example, are inconsistent with holding back things about yourself from those on whom you wish to rely in trusting ways. Loyalty and discretion would appear to be essential in sustaining moral integrity in dealings with others. The same is likely to hold true with regard to one's motives and intentions (e.g. the intention to fully share information).

Clearly, perceptions of the factors identified by Jennings and Gabarro may be based on prior relationships. They may also emerge from perceptions derived in the course of developing a relationship. These factors overlap conceptually in some instances, and this may be a source of problems in operationalizing them. There are, however, a number of factors that are quite distinct. Although it is manifestly an empirical question, I argue that the differences reflect differences between fragile and resilient trust. In Table 5.2, I summarize the foregoing discussion of my views on the kind

Table 5.2. Factors associated with reliance on trust

Fragile Trust	Resilient Trust
Business sense	Integrity
Consistency of behaviour	Loyalty
Availability	Discretion
Predictability	Motives
Accessibility	Interpersonal competence
Functional competence	Openness
Judgement	

Sources: Gabarro (1978); Jennings (1971).

of trust to which each of these various factors relate. As they seek answers to the question of who to trust, I argue that economic actors will consider these kinds of attributes. By considering these kinds of attributes, they will reach conclusions about the extent to which they are willing to trust each other in those cases in which the question of reliance on the trustworthiness of a party is an open one. This will help them to determine the extent to which they can rely on trust in dealing with other economic actors. It also suggests the following general propositions:

> *Proposition 1*a: Economic actors may rely on more than one kind of trust in the course of conducting economic exchange.
>
> *Proposition 1*b: The type of trust relied upon by economic actors will, in part, be a function of the nature of specific attributes of their past and current relationship.

How the parties answer the question of what to trust to the care of other economic actors is likely to be a function of a number of factors. What kind of property, assets, or resources will be exchanged? What is the nature of the relationship between the parties (e.g. are they competitors)? How long have they known each other? In addition to answering these questions, they will also have to decide whether they can trust each other and whether they are willing to rely on trust in governing their relationship.

Take, for example, two firms that stand in a buyer–supplier relationship, but have no prior dealings with each other. The buyer, a packaging equipment manufacturer, knows that the supplier firm provides the same kinds of components the equipment manufacturer currently uses to many of its competitors. The equipment manufacturer has developed new technology which will provide it with significant competitive advantages, but it needs to reveal that technology to the supplier so that the supplier can provide the necessary components.

A priori, we can expect to find that some degree of fragile trust exists between the parties. That level of fragile trust might enable the buyer firm to reveal to the supplier firm that it has developed this new technology and is seeking a supplier to provide the necessary component parts.

This is the kind of trust that lubricates economic exchange. If the supplier could not trust a buyer, it could only turn its technological breakthrough into operating machinery by making the parts itself, or by buying from a components manufacturer it hoped was capable of making the parts. (Remember, in the absence of fragile trust, it could not tell the acquisition target why it was interested in making the acquisition.) Whether the buyer is willing to rely exclusively on this fragile trust might be revealed in a decision not to require the supplier to sign a non-disclosure agreement.[11]

In contrast, what kind of trust explains a buyer immediately sharing the new technology with the supplier? What kind of trust explains the buyer firm simply asking the supplier firm to come in and work with it in developing the component parts? What kind of trust explains significant transfers of information related to the technology between the buyer and the supplier firm? What kind of trust would explain the absence of non-disclosure agreements? The absence of contracts? The absence of fears that if the supplier firm says it cannot do the job that the existence of, or details about, the new technology will leak out among its competitors? Such circumstances suggest that something other than fragile trust is at work: I would describe it as resilient trust that is associated with loyalty, openness, integrity, discretion, and interpersonal competence.

As Easton (1992: 8) has observed, the depth of a relationship can be measured by (1) the degree of mutual orientation among the parties; (2) the dependence one has (or perceives one has) on the other; (3) the bonds of various kinds and strengths that exist between the parties; and (4) the investments each has made in the relationship. Håkansson (1992) citing Hammarkvist *et al.* 1982, provides five examples of bonds, easily operationalized, that may exist in a relationship, or facilitate its creation: technical, time-related, knowledge-related, social, and economic/legal. I would expect that the deeper these bonds are, the more likely it is that resilient trust will exist between the parties to an exchange.

Although there is substantial anecdotal evidence that economic actors do rely on what I describe as resilient trust, there is also a theoretical basis for assuming that a resilient type of trust can exist between economic actors. This assertion regarding the existence of resilient trust is based on a premise that economic actors are moral persons.[12] Michalos (1990) describes two principles regarded by most moral philosophers as the fundamental basis

---

[11] And at the very least, the buyer would have to trust the supplier *not* to breach the confidentiality agreement.

[12] There appears to be nothing in the assumptions of neoclassical economics that precludes a rational economic actor from being a moral person. The assumptions of transaction cost economics, on the other hand, would appear to have this rational economic actor frequently engage in immoral behaviour.

of morality. The two principles are the *principle of beneficence* and the *no-harm principle*.

Acting in accordance with the principle of beneficence, economic actors ought to ensure that their actions impartially improve the human condition. Thus, our buyer firm should expect the supplier firm, in whom the buyer firm has vested trust by revealing the existence of a new technology, to act not only on its own behalf, but also in ways that would benefit other parties likely to be affected by its action (the buyer firm, its employees, owners, and so on). The need to rely on such a principle in explaining the development of a network seems likely to be greater in cases involving previously anonymous economic actors than, for example, parties to an exchange who enjoy a kinship relationship. According to the no-harm principle, the supplier firm, in whom the buyer firm has vested trust, would not harm the buyer firm, nor those things (the existence of, and details about, the new technology) that the buyer has entrusted to the care of the supplier firm.

How is it that our hypothetical buyer firm might come to rely on trust in dealing with its supplier firm? In describing the differences between reliance on fragile and resilient trust, I have attempted to demonstrate that there are different kinds of trust, and that reliance on them produces different economic consequences. Thus, I propose the following:

> *Proposition 2*a: Fragile trust is sufficient, but not necessary, for economic exchange, *ceteris paribus*.
>
> *Proposition 2*b: Resilient trust is a necessary and sufficient condition for economic exchange in a network.

It appears that reliance on trust by economic actors evolves for a number of reasons. First, reliance on fragile trust may be based on norms of equity as defined in exchange theory: the extent to which economic actor A judges that economic actor B will fulfil her commitments (Ring and Van de Ven 1994; Van de Ven and Walker 1984). Economic actors engaged in co-operative efforts appear to desire three things. First, they seek reciprocity: economic actor A is obligated to give economic actor B something in return for something received (Gouldner 1959). If A feels *morally* obligated to reciprocate, then resilient trust may be at work. Secondly, economic actors who are co-operating demand fair rates of exchange between utilitarian costs and benefits (Blau 1964). Finally, as noted above, economic actors seek fairness: those who co-operate expect, at some unspecified time in the future, to eventually receive benefits that are proportional to their investments (Homans 1961).

Reliance on fragile trust in a network may also stem from more direct, utilitarian roots. For example, King (1988: 480) has argued that as a result of an increasingly complex economy it is harder to spell out mutual responsibilities and obligations, either through contract or hierarchy. As time spans for action become compressed, legal action becomes more expensive. Thus, 'conditions of trust are . . . becoming increasingly crucial to competing—and cooperating—in today's business environment'. Moreover, there are many non-legal sanctions which make it expedient for individuals and organizations to fulfil commitments (Macaulay 1963). The prospect of repeat business discourages attempts to seek a narrow, short-term advantage. Thus, reliance on fragile trust is more likely when economic actors have earned a reputation in the market for following norms of equity as defined above.

Murakami and Rohlen (1992: 70–3) have argued that, over time, purely economic exchange can take on the greater complexity characteristic of social exchange. They assert that minimal levels of trust are required even in pure economic exchange (including barter). More specifically, they have observed that establishing trust takes time; that a 'track record' is one usual measure of trust; that trust is enhanced by actions that occur over and above the strict observance of norms, rules, and contracts; and that building up trust implies an investment in the time dimension of relationships. Many of these conditions are clearly present in networks, as reflected in Table 5.1. Thus it appears that network governance can give rise to trust, where it did not predate the creation of a network. Although Murakami and Rohlen appear to be describing a single kind of trust, I argue that what they have described is, in fact, a transformation of fragile into resilient trust. It is in the process of this transformation that a network truly emerges.

What I have described as resilient trust is more likely to precede the creation of a network when the economic actors enjoy either kinship ties, or are both geographically and culturally localized. Alvesson and Lindkvist (1993) observed in their investigation of numerous case studies of co-operation that blood-kinship and social-integrative clans evolved out of national or local 'cultures'. In these kinds of clans, long, serial memories, the social needs of belonging, or family relationships were more critical than equity in exchange. In an investigation of small business firms in the Modena area of Italy, long-established reciprocal relations and inter-family connections were important elements in the emergence of networks (Lazerson 1988). Lincoln *et al.* (1992) found many of the least formal, but most dense, networks which they studied in Japan to be associated with bonds that evolved from strong social relationships, such as school cliques (gakubatsu), regional loyalties, and family lineages. These conditions appear likely to create resilient trust. Thus, I propose that:

> *Proposition 3*: In networks in which norms and values stem from kinship or strong social ties, resilient trust will be relied upon more frequently than fragile trust, *ceteris paribus*.

Hertz (1992: 110), among others, has observed that 'the basis for trust [in networks] seems to be that the actors have certain important values and norms in common'. Since he was looking at a single setting, he did not have to consider what might occur if a group of economic actors, located in a region that straddled the borders of two different nation states (or regions of a nation state), attempted to establish reliance on trust on the basis of (presumably) uncommon norms and values, business sense, or judgement. None the less, I argue that reliance on a different kind of trust is likely under such circumstances because values and norms are likely to differ (creating problems of defining integrity), because kinship may be absent and/or national pride may intervene (creating problems of loyalty), and, finally, because language may hinder communication (creating problems for inter-personal competence). More specifically, I argue that:

> *Proposition 4*a: In networks that cross national borders, *ceteris paribus*, reliance on fragile trust will develop more rapidly than reliance on resilient trust.
>
> *Proposition 4*b: In networks that cross national borders, *ceteris paribus*, reliance on resilient trust will be slow to develop.

In postulating that economic actors will rely more on fragile trust in net-works that transcend national borders, I have assumed that this is due to barriers hindering effective direct communication.[13] While sufficient when acting in reliance on fragile trust in a business relationship, a *reputation* for trustworthiness is not sufficient when reliance is placed on resilient trust. If they are to rely on resilient trust, economic actors will have to experience equity in exchange first hand. They must come to know those with whom they transact (if kinship is absent). Reliance on resilient trust by economic actors can be expected only when the economic actors have successfully completed transactions in the past and they perceive one another as com-plying with norms such as equity and reciprocity. The more frequently eco-nomic actors successfully transact (i.e. they achieve both efficient and equitable outcomes), the more likely it is that economic actors will come to rely on resilient trust in subsequent transactions. As levels of resilient trust increase, even greater reliance may be placed on this kind of trust by an economic actor.

PROCESSES LEADING TO RELIANCE ON TRUST IN NETWORKS

Up to this point in the chapter, the existence of trust in a network has been taken as given. I have discussed a number of elements associated with the existence of trust, such as kinship ties and face-to-face contract in exchange. I have only hinted at the processes by which trust emerges and I now turn my attention to a central thesis of this chapter: where trust does not already exist, it may emerge from formal and informal processes of transacting.

---

[13] Recall that I have argued that resilient trust is more likely to arise where economic actors can engage in frequent, direct communications of the 'whole person' type (Macneil 1980).

Where trust does exist, those same processes provide opportunities for economic actors to deepen the levels of trust that exist between them, or to destroy it.

In postulating that economic actors can rely on something other than fragile trust in their dealings, I have assumed that fragile trust exists a priori (Arrow 1973). Economic actors can rely on fragile trust in dealing with each other unless there are good reasons to do otherwise. A well-established reputation for recurring opportunistic behaviour by a components manufacturer is one reason why buyer firms might be reluctant to even do business with the supplier, let alone rely on fragile trust.

While a 'good' reputation may be sufficient to permit reliance on fragile trust, reliance on a reputation for trustworthiness presupposes that the buyer is able to identify the supplier's reputation prior to establishing any contact with the supplier. This may not always be possible in a global economy, but is possible in a network context.

Even when it is possible to identify a reputation indirectly, however, our buyer might want to verify the reputation first hand. It will be much easier to do this in a network than in other forms of CIORs. As I have noted in Table 5.1, among the characteristics of a network are localized transactions and extensive communication. These characteristics should make it easier for economic actors to decide whether they will be able to rely on trust in dealing with each other. The sharing of information that is also characteristic of a network, and the nature of obligations that arise between members of a network, also imply that if the parties have transacted with each other on a recurring basis in the past, and met their obligations, then any reliance on trust is likely to be based on the kind of trust that I have described as resilient trust.

Formal Processes

Commons (1950) has argued that transacting involves a dynamic process made up of three temporally distinct phases: negotiation, transaction, and administration. These formal processes provide a basis for exploring the extent to which economic actors can, or will, rely on trust in intra-network exchanges. The three phases described by Commons often overlap, and frequently recycle. None the less, it is analytically useful to distinguish among the phases. This permits us to examine the interpersonal and social-psychological processes that tend to predominate in each phase of the formal processes of transacting. The distinction helps us sort out the timing of a willingness to rely on trust during the various stages of the formal processes of exchange. These same formal processes may also permit economic actors to develop reliance on resilient trust where once only fragile trust existed between them.

The more *formal* processes of negotiation, transaction, and administration (Commons 1924) associated with most business transactions are also accompanied by *informal* processes of sense-making, understanding, and committing (Ring and Rands 1989; Ring and Van de Ven 1994). The informal processes that take place in each of these formal stages of putting together a business deal provide opportunities for economic actors to directly experience the observance of norms such as equity or reciprocity.

The formal stages of negotiation and transaction provide the parties with opportunities for exploring the kinds of obligations that they expect from each other, while the formal stage of administration permits them to observe how they honour those obligations. Negotiation stages also require that decisions be made about information rights: what will be shared and what will be restricted.

The formal processes facilitate recurrent, extensive communications which permit the parties to use all their senses. As a transaction's importance to an economic actor increases, it is probable that the processes of sense-making, understanding, and committing required in negotiation and transaction phases will be sufficiently complex and time-consuming to provide the economic actors with an opportunity to determine if reliance on more than fragile trust is appropriate. Prompt reliance on resilient trust by economic actors seems likely only when the economic actors have successfully completed transactions in the past and perceive one another as complying with norms such as equity and reciprocity. The more frequently economic actors successfully transact (i.e. achieve both efficient and equitable outcomes), the more likely it is that economic actors will come to rely on resilient trust in subsequent transactions. As levels of resilient trust increase, even greater reliance may be placed on that trust by an economic actor.

In the context of network forms of economic exchange, the negotiation phase of the formal process of transacting is highlighted by the revelation of strategies and choice behaviours of economic actors. During negotiation, they initially approach, or avoid, potential participants in a network. This kind of process was foreshadowed in my earlier discussion of the packaging equipment manufacturer seeking component suppliers for a new technology.

The processes by which the economic actors find other network participants will be a function of factors such as their prior relationships, the technical reputations of the firms, their presence in a global market-place, or their advertising activities. Where kinship or other dense forms of ties exist, selection processes in network contexts will be, relatively speaking, routine. If the economic actor can contribute to achieving the objectives of the network, and is trustworthy, participation is highly probable. Where less dense ties provide the basis for the network, the economic actors will argue, persuade, and haggle over the appropriateness and interdependence of their individual and collective goals and objectives for the network. These

formal processes may be conducted impersonally through written communications, personally via telephone or more directly in face-to-face meetings, or through combinations of these media. Where the parties have not
had extensive economic or social relationships in the past, the informal
processes that occur during the formal process of negotiation are likely to
be more time-consuming. The parties will initially be exploring their respective business sense, functional competence, predictability, and judgement.
Careful attention will be paid to whether they are available to each other,
accessible, and act in consistent ways. In short, parties forming a network
will, in negotiation phases, determine the extent to which they can rely on
fragile trust.

During the process of negotiation, economic actors will also tackle the
questions: 'Who do we trust?' and 'What do we trust them with?' Answers
to these questions in newly emerging networks are likely to be tentative,
and final decisions will be postponed until they reach transaction stages. As
previously discussed, however, if resilient trust already exists, or ripens
during negotiation processes, then economic actors are more likely to
share information, even of a proprietary nature. As the amount of relevant
information shared between economic actors increases during the negotiation phase of transacting, the probability that they will advance to transaction and agreement phases increases.

Issues related to norms and sanctions that will govern the conduct of
members of the network may also be raised during the negotiation phase
of transacting. These norms may predate the creation of a network, or their
development may be essential to its creation. The types of norms that may
be relied upon may also depend upon the density of relationships among
the economic actors who comprise the network.

In the negotiation phase, economic actors may also need to decide
whether they will be willing to rely exclusively on trust in governing their
transactions. I do not expect that economic actors will make a conscious
effort to distinguish between what I have described as fragile and resilient
trust. But it does seem likely that if they have had extensive dealings with
each other in the past, if they have relied on trust in these deals, and if the
expectations of the parties generally have been met, then they are more
likely to rely on trust in governing their current transaction than if these
conditions were not present. In addition, the existence of these kinds of conditions may permit the same parties to rely on trust to govern a deal that
is riskier than those they have pursued in the past. The negotiation phase
provides the parties with an opportunity to determine whether they can all
agree that these kinds of conditions do exist. Negotiation processes also
permit the parties to determine whether prior breaches of trust were serious
enough to warrant reconsideration of continued reliance on trust to govern
the current transaction.

In short, analysis of the process of negotiation, and of its outcomes, provides an insight into whether the parties are relying on fragile or resilient trust. If progress towards developing a network fails to emerge as a result of the process of negotiation, it seems likely that resilient trust does not exist between the parties. The general characteristics of a network, as described in Table 5.1, are of such a nature that it seems unlikely that fragile trust could govern the conduct of the members of the network. And if the network predates the current transaction, and the negotiation stage is simply designed to determine if the network will be employed in governing the transaction, then it seems likely that if resilient trust existed between the parties, one outcome of the negotiation stage would be a quick decision to use the network to govern the transaction.

Even in this kind of case, however, the negotiation could be protracted. The parties might easily agree that they can rely on trust in dealing with each other in a very risky situation, but they might have to take some time to determine whether they are capable of performing the necessary tasks associated with the transaction (that is, revisiting the question of functional competence), or they might need to take time to determine who among them ought to perform which tasks.

In subsequent intra-network transactions, the negotiation phase will be employed to determine the nature of continuing expectations and obligations of the economic actors, as well as the extent to which they need to rely upon any contingent safeguards derived from the previously agreed norms and sanctions. I would argue that this is further evidence that the parties are relying on what I have described as resilient trust. This is a level of trust that does more than lubricate economic exchange. This level of trust transforms the fundamental nature of the exchange. Thus, I propose:

> *Proposition 5*: Over time, formalized safeguards, in network contexts, can be expected to give way to greater reliance on trust, and less formalized safeguards to give way to more symbolic safeguards.

Issues surrounding the kinds of information that members of the network will be expected to share with each other, and the conditions surrounding the sharing of information, will be a major concern in the negotiation phase. Where resilient trust exists, information will be more readily shared. The existence of norms of reciprocity in a network enhances the likelihood of the sharing of information. Kinship and related ties that exist in networks provide a basis for the sharing of information that can be described as tacit know-how (Winter 1987). As this kind of information can be the basis for co-operatively sustained advantage (Ring 1996), transaction cost economists argue that it is not likely to be voluntarily exchanged, except within hierarchies. Resilient trust mitigates opportunism. Based on the foregoing discussion, I argue that:

> *Proposition 6*: Reliance on resilient trust by economic actors will enhance their sharing of information during negotiation phases of intra-network transactions, *ceteris paribus*.

Proposition 7: A network will not emerge from negotiation phases, *ceteris paribus*, unless resilient trust exists between the parties.

During the transaction process, the wills of the parties meet by finalizing the terms of their network relationships, or by finalizing how they will govern a particular transaction within the network. In all likelihood, the economic actors will reach agreement on the rules for making rules (Hart 1961), obligations, expectations, norms, and sanctions. When economic actors can rely on resilient trust in their network transactions, the agreements reached by this process of give and take may take the form of psychological or implicit contracts. Research suggests that because networks are infused with 'symbolic signification' they may not be governed by 'formal legal arrangements or contracts' (Gerlach 1992: 5). As Lazerson (1988: 340) found, the longer and more continuous exchange relations were between economic actors, the less likely was the need to formalize them legally. Hertz (1992: 109) reached a similar result: 'Trust will influence the degree of formal-legal ties chosen when integration occurs'. Thus, I conclude that:

Proposition 8: Reliance on resilient trust in networks reduces the frequency of formal legal agreements as products of transaction processes, *ceteris paribus*.

Finally, the formal administrative processes of transacting involve the relatively well-understood ways by which economic exchange creates value: that is, the transformation of inputs into outputs whose value is greater than their combined production and transaction costs. In short, administrative processes cause the network to become operational. In this phase of the formal process of transacting, the members of the network pursue their individual and collective goals, transacting with each other and with economic actors outside the network. As the network persists over time, the intra-network transactions become more multiplex and extended. With the successful exchange of various forms of tangible assets and codified know-how assets (Teece 1986), the members of newly formed networks can increase their willingness to rely on resilient trust during this phase, and begin to engage in recurring exchanges of tacit know-how or so-called invisible assets (Itami 1987).

Other inevitable results of the formal administrative process are conflict, misunderstanding, and changing expectations. These may result in new rounds of negotiation and transaction; or they can lead to termination of the network. In the absence of a continued ability to rely on resilient trust, the probability that a network will dissolve is increased.

I have suggested that these formal stages of transacting are accompanied by informal processes. These informal processes are present in each phase of the formal process of transacting. In addition to facilitating the formal processes, I argue that the informal processes described below provide the means by which economic actors in a network can initially develop fragile trust among one another, transform that fragile trust into resilient trust, and use both forms of trust in controlling their behaviour within the network.[14]

Informal Processes

In the course of creating a network (or any other collaborative effort), economic actors employ a host of interpersonal processes that, ultimately, motivate and direct their actions in relation to other members of the network. For example, Turner (1987: 16) argues that the motivation theory implicit in most of the theory of economic exchange is that individuals seek co-operative relationships to maximize gratifications, or utilities, and to avoid deprivations, or punishments. This utilitarian theory of motivation can be used to explain transactional exchange. However, it sidesteps basic issues of how economic actors order values, how they decide on alternative lines of behaviour, or how the temporal duration of a relationship influences the cognitive processes and behavioural options of economic actors. These issues are clearly of paramount importance in the development of networks and the relational exchange that characterizes transacting within them.

In an extensive review of the social-psychological literature on motivation, Turner (1987) identifies three fundamental forces that motivate human thought and action: needs for identity, facticity, and inclusion. If, as Turner (1987) suggests, these three forces are important in explaining motivation in general, then they are essential ingredients in understanding the development of networks.

These traits manifest themselves in three forms of social-psychological processes: sense-making, understanding, and committing (Ring and Rands 1989). These processes reflect an ethno-methodological approach to the institutionalization (i.e. generational uniformity, maintenance, or resistance to change or cultural understandings) of individual efforts, culminating in a co-operative inter-organizational relationship (Zucker 1977).

Sense-making is an enactment process (Weick 1979) in which network participants come to appreciate the potential for transacting with others in the network by reshaping or clarifying their own identity. By projecting themselves onto their own environment, economic actors develop a self-referential appreciation of their own identity which, in turn, permits them to act in relation to their environment (Morgan 1986: 243). Psychologically, sense-making derives from the need among individual economic actors to have a sense of self-identity in relation to others (Kumon 1992; Turner 1987). To achieve this, economic actors must reinterpret the reality of their surrounding environment to make sense of the economic exchanges they are contemplating in the network (Neale and Northcraft 1991).

---

[14] In reality, economic actors who learn to rely on trust in dealing with each other in the network, are also likely to discover its advantages in dealing with economic actors outside the network as well.

Sense-making is likely to involve exploration of relationships, obligations, information rights, transactions, and governance, and the kinds of characteristics associated with these elements that are illustrated in Table 5.1. Sense-making is also likely to centre on issues related to functional competence, judgement, business sense, and motives, and other factors of the types outlined in Table 5.2.

In general, the sense of identity is a general orientation to situations, and helps maintain the esteem and consistency of one's self-conceptions in relation to others. Sense-making processes are also designed to permit individual economic actors in a network to view their own preferences in relation to those of all other economic actors in the network. These sense-making processes are designed to make important acts related to the network objective so that they can be repeated by others (Zucker 1977).

The processes of sense-making, as I have just described them, are learning processes. In the context of an analysis of networks, the learning that occurs during sense-making processes is conditioned by the type of network under consideration. For example, where a small network is based on kinship ties, sense-making processes, in relative terms, will be somewhat truncated. And what will need to be learned and how it is likely to have to be learned should be different from other kinds of networks. For example, a larger network made up of autonomous economic actors from different cultures, nation states, and industries is likely to be associated with intense sense-making. Much more will have to be learned, and different kinds of learning styles seem likely. This is because, if they are seeking to answer the question 'Should we rely on trust in dealing with each other?', the parties, I argue, will have to learn about all of the factors outlined in Table 5.2. In contrast, in a small, kinship-based network, issues such as integrity, loyalty, openness, and others which I have described as relating to resilient trust are not likely to require much sense-making at all.

As a learning process, sense-making may occur in (at least) two very different ways: separate and connected knowing (Belenky *et al.* 1986; Elbow 1973). Each of these ways of knowing is important in terms of the outcomes of sense-making processes as building blocks for reliance on trust in transacting within a network. In general, connected knowing seems best suited to sense-making that is focused on the actors in a transaction, their interpersonal competence, loyalty, integrity, motives, discretion, and openness. On the other hand, separate knowing is more likely to facilitate sense-making directed at the transaction itself and the business sense, availability, predictability, judgement, functional competence, and so on, of the parties.

Connected knowing is subjective and occurs through personalized exchanges. It is based on direct, personal experience. It requires a capacity for empathy. In combination, these characteristics of connected knowing enable economic actors who employ it to develop an understanding of themselves in relation to others. Thus, processes of sense-making that rely on connected knowing permit economic actors to become 'connected' to others' ideas, values, and objectives. This facilitates a willingness to believe in, and trust, others (Elbow 1973).

In contrast, separate knowing is impersonal. The 'self' of the economic actor is viewed autonomously from others. Rather than relying on first-hand, personal experience, sense-making by economic actors that involves separate ways of knowing will rely on authority. 'Laws' govern actions, not people. Objectivity is valued, the self is suppressed. Ideas and concepts (Kumon 1992) are challenged. Sense-making processes are designed to find loopholes in rules, norms, and sanctions, to find flaws in the reasoning of other economic actors. Economic actors using separate knowing reveal a doubting mind, rather than the believing and trusting mind of the connected knower. In separate ways of knowing, reason overrides the role of emotion inherent in connected ways of knowing.

This discussion suggests that in sense-making processes the ways of knowing employed by economic actors may affect the form of trust that can be developed between members of a network. Specifically, I argue that:

> *Proposition 9*a: When sense-making involves connected ways of knowing, the processes are more likely to produce resilient than fragile trust, *ceteris paribus*.
> *Proposition 9*b: When sense-making only involves separate ways of knowing, the processes are likely to produce only fragile trust, *ceteris paribus*.

Understanding is an informal process by which economic actors socially construct and agree to the terms of their relationship. Understanding is also a process that produces learning.

In Zucker's (1977) terms, understanding processes make acts exterior—subjective understanding is reconstructed as inter-subjective, permitting acts to be seen as a part of the external world. Achieving these kinds of objectives would seem to require connected learning.

Processes of understanding emerge from the need of individuals to construct a common external factual order in their environment. The parties seek 'facticity' in their relationship (Turner 1987). Interaction is constrained by the need among economic actors seeking to create a network to feel that they share a common understanding of an obdurate world (e.g. they both agree on the kinds of norms, the observance of which would define integrity). As Neale and Northcraft (1991) indicate, parties do more than just process (perhaps incorrectly) information about the context of an exchange. They perceive that context, and react to their perceptions in ways that validate or enact (Weick 1979) those perceptions. Thus, it is negotiators' cognitions which 'contextualize negotiations' (Neale and Northcraft 1991). When the contexts for which the parties seek facticity involve both the deal they are contemplating and the nature of the relationship which they are contemplating, then it seems likely that they will have to engage in both kinds of learning, connected and separate.

Communication among economic actors produces this shared interpretation. It often emerges gradually and incrementally, especially if separate learning is being used to explore relationships. The process of understanding will also take time if the parties employ different learning styles. By the same token, if understanding processes are to lead to reliance on resilient trust, they must involve economic actors in ways that 'include whole person relations, relatively deep and extensive communication by a variety of modes, and significant elements of non-economic personal satisfaction' (Macneil 1974: 723, footnotes omitted). Connected knowing should produce these kinds of results. However, this may not always be possible.

In cases in which understanding processes involve economic actors with different ways of knowing, facticity or other products of understanding processes (e.g. overlapping cognitive maps or organizational learning) may not be achieved or may be expensive (e.g. time-consuming). The problem confronting economic actors in such a case is that they have to cope with the fact that their different ways of knowing will, initially, create severe communication barriers. If these different ways of knowing are cultural in nature, the barriers may be insurmountable. Kumon (1992: 123) argues that the 'Japanese, like Mediterraneans, are "high context" communicators' (Hall 1976); that is, a premise of their communication process is the pre-accumulation of a large amount of commonly shared knowledge and information concerning the topic of communication and those with whom they communicate. This implies that a relatively small amount of new information is required for effective communication and networking. If these are merely individual traits, the problem may be overcome with time. Thus, I propose that:

> *Proposition 10*a: Processes of understanding are more likely to fail, *ceteris paribus*, when economic actors attempting to create a network come from different cultural backgrounds.
> *Proposition 10*b: Processes of understanding are more likely to fail, *ceteris paribus*, when economic actors attempting to create a network employ different ways of knowing.
> *Proposition 10*c: Processes of understanding are more likely to lead to resilient trust, *ceteris paribus*, when all the economic actors in the network employ connected ways of knowing.

Committing is an informal process that involves the establishing of psychological contracts (Argyris 1960; Levinson *et al.* 1962) between economic actors. Psychological contracts, as opposed to legal contracts, consist of unwritten and largely unverbalized sets of expectations and assumptions, held by economic actors about each other's prerogatives and obligations.

These expectations of what each party will give to and receive from the network vary in their degree of explicitness; the parties are often only marginally aware of their exact nature (Kotter 1973). Expectations address areas such as norms, work roles, the nature of the work itself, social relationships, or security needs. Individual economic actors' expectations are shaped by past experiences (many of which may predate the contemplated network), personal values, professional specialization, and the level of hierarchical organization (Nicholson and Johns 1985).

Following the previous discussion of network dynamics, where the network was based on kinship ties, or on collaboration 'between firms based on localized networks of dense transactions and a stable framework for exchange' (Gerlach 1992), it seems more likely that economic actors may not even need to engage in sense-making or understanding processes. Moreover, it is probable that committing processes which occur under the kinds of conditions I have just described will create an environment in which resilient trust becomes the basis for transactions. Where these kinds of conditions are absent, however, then the form of trust, if any, on which economic actors rely in networks is likely to be less a product of committing processes, than of sense-making and understanding processes.

These sense-making, understanding, and committing processes frequently can take far longer to develop than commonly thought. They are a cumulative product of numerous interactions through which trust in the goodwill of others may emerge. As I have indicated, the starting-points of economic actors can vary in the degrees to which they are acquainted and have had prior interactions with each other, and thereby had opportunities to come to know and understand the self in relation to the other. If, in these prior acquaintances, sense-making and understanding processes led to the creation of high levels of trust between the parties, they might be able to make commitments and begin rapidly to execute a network. Thus, networks among parties who have had prior economic relationships or social friendship ties tend to develop far more quickly than among organizations which have not previously experienced reciprocal sense-making, understanding, or commitment processes. More specifically, I propose that:

Proposition 11: The time required to create a network, or to consider new economic actors as members of the network, is a function of the informal processes that are employed by the parties.

CONCLUSIONS

Networks have always existed as a form of governance structure for transactions between economic actors. Accepting the assertions of transaction cost economists, this means that networks have efficiency properties (see Chapter 7). In this chapter, I have argued that one of these properties is trust and have suggested that there are two distinct forms of trust associated with economic exchange. I have described formal and informal processes that can lead to the emergence of, and reliance on, these two forms of trust, and discussed some of the benefits that I believe can be derived from reliance on trust in transacting.

My assertion that two distinct forms of trust exist in transacting requires more rigorous analysis. Until very recently, the literature on the role of trust in economic exchange has been silent on different kinds of trust, and distinguished only between trust as an individual attribute, as a behaviour, a situational feature, and as an institutional arrangement (Sitkin and Roth 1993).[15] It seems unlikely that a monolithic concept of trust can be employed equally well in each of these contexts, and especially in the last two. Moreover, measures of trust used in investigations of economic exchange have largely been based on investigations of social-psychological exchange. Butler (1991) has made an effort to test the adequacy of these measures and to develop a more robust instrument. Further work is required, however.

The model of emergent interpersonal transaction processes developed by Ring and Rands (1989) was based on a limited number of longitudinal case studies of transacting. Although these transactions involved actors from different sectors of the economy, they did not cross national boundaries. And, although they involved a number of interdependent transactions, the economic actors that Ring and Rands studied were not members of a network. Thus, the question of whether the processes of transacting in a network are similar to those on which my arguments have been based is an empirical question that requires further investigation. Regrettably, the extant literature on networks provides very little insight into the processes associated with their formation, or on the transactions that take place within them. Whereas the bargaining literature provides us with valuable insights into processes employed in dyadic exchange, the question is whether these insights apply as well to the multi-party, multiplex exchanges of a network.

I have proposed that the type of learning that characterizes sense-making processes will be instrumental in the kind of trust that emerges in economic exchanges. The model of learning proposed, however, is somewhat controversial. Derived from the work of feminists, it asserts that traditional models of learning have a strong gender bias (see e.g. Astin and Leland 1991; Gilligan 1982; Helgesen 1990; Kanter 1977; Rosener 1990; Tannen 1990). None the less, the behaviour implications of this approach to learning are entirely consistent with the needs of economic actors in networks. Thus, this approach appears to offer a worthy avenue for further investigations of learning within networks.

[15] As I have already indicated, *if* more than one form of trust exists between individuals, then we also need to explore whether in situational or institutional contexts different kinds of trust can be identified.

At the beginning of this chapter, I noted that I took the existence of networks as given and that I was not concerned about their type or their particular governance forms. Despite these disclaimers, the forms of governance employed in networks matter and we do need to know more about relationships between these different forms of governance and the formal and informal processes employed by the economic actors in the creation of the network. It is likely, for example, that the culture in which a network is embedded (Granovetter 1985) will be a major factor in determining structure and processes. In a similar vein, we need to investigate the relationship between these transaction processes and processes associated with the generation and distribution of knowledge. In short, the research agenda for those interested in enhancing our knowledge of the structure, but especially the processes, of networks is quite full. I hope that my own views on these issues will contribute in some small way towards our collective objective of enhancing our understanding of the emergence, forms, structures, management, development processes, or outcomes of inter-organizational networks.

REFERENCES

Alchian, A. A., and Demsetz, H. 1972. 'Production, Information Costs, and Economic Organization'. *American Economic Review*. 62: 727–95.

Aldrich, H., and Whetten D. A. 1981. 'Organizational Sets, Action Sets, and Networks: Making the Most of Simplicity'. In Nystrom, P., and Starbuck, W. (eds.). *Handbook of Organizational Design*. 385–408. London: Oxford University Press.

Alvesson, M., and Lindkvist, L. 1993. 'Transaction Costs, Clans, and Corporate Culture'. *Journal of Management Studies*. 30: 427–52.

Amit, R., and Schoemaker, P. J. H. 1993. 'Strategic Assets and Organizational Rent'. *Strategic Management Journal*. 14: 33–46.

Anderson, E., and Weitz, B. 1989. 'Determinants of Continuity in Conventional Industrial Channel Dyads'. *Marketing Science*. 8: 310–23.

Argyris, C. 1960. *Understanding Organizational Behavior*. Homewood: Ill.: Dorsey Press.

Arrow, K. 1973. *Information and Economic Behavior*. Stockholm: Federation of Swedish Industries.

Astin, H. S., and Leland, C. 1991. *Women of Influence, Women of Vision*. 2nd edn. Homewood, Ill.: Irwin.

Axelsson, B., and Easton, G. (eds.) 1992. *Industrial Networks: A New View of Reality*. New York: Routledge.

Baier, A. 1986. 'Trust and Antitrust'. *Ethics*. 96: 231–60.

Baker, W. E. 1984. 'The Social Structure of a National Securities Market'. *American Journal of Sociology*. 79: 774–811.

Barber, B. 1983. *The Logic and Limits of Trust*. New Brunswick, NJ: Rutgers University.

Barney, J. B. 1991. 'Firm Resources and Sustained Competitive Advantage'. *Journal of Management*. 17: 99–120.

Belenky, M. F., Clinchy, B. M., Goldberger, N. R., and Tarule, J. M. (eds.) 1986. *Women's Ways of Knowing, the Development of Self, Voice, and Mind*. New York: Basic Books.

Bhide, A., and Stevenson, H. 1992. 'Trust, Uncertainty, and Profits'. *Journal of Socio-Economics*. 21: 91–208.

Blau, P. M. 1964. *Exchange and Power in Social Life*. New York: John Wiley and Sons.

Bok, S. 1979. *Lying: Moral Choice in Public and Private Life*. New York: Random House.

Borys, B., and Jemison, D. 1989. 'Hybrid Arrangements as Strategic Alliances: Theoretical Issues in Organizational Combinations'. *Academy of Management Review*. 14: 234–49.

Bromiley, P., and Cummings, L. L. 1995. 'Transaction Costs in Organizations with Trust'. In Bies, Robert J., Lewicki, R. J., and Shepphard, Blair L. (eds.). *Research on Negotiations in Organizations*. Greenwich, Conn.: JAI Press.

Browning, L. D., Beyer, J. M., and Shelter, J. C. 1995. 'Building Cooperation in a Competitive Industry: SEMATECH and the Semiconductor Industry'. *The Academy of Management Journal*. 38: 113–51.

Butler, J. K. 1991. 'Toward Understanding and Measuring Conditions of Trust: Evolution of a Conditions of Trust Inventory'. *Journal of Management*. 17: 643–63.

Coase, R. 1937. 'The Nature of the Firm'. *Economica*. 4. Reprinted in Stigler, G. J., and Boulding, K. E. (eds.) 1952. *Readings in Price Theory*. Homewood, Ill.: Irwin.

Coleman, J. S. 1988. 'Social Capital in the Creation of Human Capital'. *American Journal of Sociology*. (Special supplement) 94: 95–S120.

Commons, J. R. 1924. *Institutional Economics*. New York: Macmillan.

——1950. *The Economics of Collective Action*. Madison: University of Wisconsin Press.

Dasgupta, P. 1988. 'Trust as a Commodity'. In Gambetta, D. (ed.). *Trust: Making and Breaking Cooperative Relations*. 49–72. London: Basil Blackwell.

Dwyer, F. R., and Lagace, R. 1986. 'On the Nature and Role of Buyer-Seller Trust'. *AMA Educator's Proceedings*: 40–5.

Easton, G. 1992. 'Industrial Networks: A Review'. In Axelsson and Easton 1992: 3–27. New York: Routledge.

Elbow, P. 1973. *Writing Without Teachers*. London: Oxford University Press.

Fox, A. 1974. *Beyond Contract: Work, Power and Trust Relations*. London: Faber and Faber.

Frank, R. H. 1988. *Passions Within Reason: The Strategic Role of the Emotions*. New York: W. W. Norton and Company.

Friar, J., and Horwitch, M. 1985. 'The Emergence of Technology Strategy: A New Dimension of Strategic Management'. *Technology in Society*. 7: 143–78.

Gabarro, J. J. (1978). 'The Development of Trust Influence and Expectations'. In Athos, A. G., and Gabarro, J. J. (eds.). *Interpersonal Behavior: Communication and Understanding in Relationships*. 230–303. Englewood-Cliffs, NJ: Prentice-Hall.

Gambetta, D. (ed.) 1988. *Trust: Making and Breaking Cooperative Relations*. London: Basil Blackwell.

Gerlach, M. L. 1992. *Alliance Capitalism: The Social Organization of Japanese Business*. Berkeley, Calif.: The University of California Press.

Gilligan, C. 1982. *In a Different Voice*. Cambridge, Mass.: Harvard University Press.

Gouldner, A. 1959. 'Reciprocity and Autonomy in Functional Theory'. In Gross, L. (ed.). *Symposium on Sociological Theory*. 241–70. New York: Harper and Row.

Granovetter, M. 1985. 'Economic Action and Social Structure: The Problem of Embeddedness'. *American Journal of Sociology*. 78: 481–510.

Gulati, R. 1995. 'Does Familiarity Breed Trust? The Implications of Repeated Ties for Contractual Choices in Alliances'. *Academy of Management Journal*. 38: 85–112.

Håkansson, H. 1989. *Corporate Technological Behavior: Co-Operation and Networks*. New York: Routledge.

——1992. 'Evolution Processes in Industrial Networks'. In Axelsson and Easton 1992: 128–43. New York: Routledge.

——and Snehota, I. (eds.) 1995. *Developing Relationships in Networks*. London: Routledge.

Hall, E. T. 1976. *Beyond Culture*. Garden City, NJ: Anchor Press.

Hamel, G., and Prahalad, C. K. 1989. 'Strategic Intent'. *Harvard Business Review*. 67: 63–76.

Hammarkvist, K. O., Håkansson, H., and Mattsson, L. G. 1982. *Marknadsföring for Konkurrenskraft*. Malmö: Liber.

Hart, H. L. A. 1961. *The Concept of Law*. Oxford: Clarendon Press.

Helgesen, S. 1990. *The Female Advantage*. New York: Doubleday.

Hennart, J. F. 1988. 'A Transaction Costs Theory of Equity Joint Ventures'. *Strategic Management Journal*. 9: 93–104.

Hertz, S. 1992. 'Towards More Integrated Industrial Systems'. In Axelsson and Easton 1992: 105–28. New York: Routledge.

Homans, G. 1961. *Social Behavior: Its Elementary Forms*. New York: Harcourt.

Itami, H. 1987. *Mobilizing Invisible Assets*. Boston, Mass.: Harvard University Press.

James, B. G. 1985. 'Alliance, the New Strategic Focus'. *Long Range Planning*. 18: 76–81.

Jarillo, J. C. 1988. 'On Strategic Networks'. *Strategic Management Journal*. 9: 31–41.

Jennings, E. E. 1971. *Routes to the Executive Suite*. New York: McGraw-Hill.

Johnson-George, C., and Swap, W. C. 1982. 'Measurement of Specific Interpersonal Trust: Construction and Validation of a Scale to Assess Trust in a Specific Other'. *Journal of Personality and Social Psychology*. 43: 1306–17.

Kanter, R. M. 1977. *Men and Women of the Corporation*. New York: Basic Books.

King, J. B. (1988). 'Prisoner's Paradoxes'. *Journal of Business Ethics*. 7: 475–87.

Knecht, B. 1994. 'Crossborder Deals Jumped Last Year to Record Levels'. *Wall Street Journal*. 25 January.

Kogut, B. 1988. 'Joint Ventures: Theoretical and Empirical Perspectives'. *Strategic Management Journal*. 9: 319–32.

Kollock, P. 1992. 'The Emergence of Markets and Networks: An Experimental Study of Uncertainty, Commitment, and Trust'. A Paper presented at the Fourth Annual International Conference of the Society of the Advancement of Socio-Economics, Irvine, Calif.

Kotter, J. P. 1973. 'The Psychological Contract: Managing the Joining up Process'. *California Management Review*. 15: 91–9.

Kumon, S. 1992. 'Japan as a Network Society'. In Kumon, S., and Rosovsky, H. (eds.). *The Political Economy of Japan*. iii: 109–42. Stanford, Calif.: Stanford University Press.

Lado, A. A., and Wilson, M. C. 1995. 'Human Resource Systems and Sustained Competitive Advantage: A Competency-Based Perspective'. *Academy of Management Review*. 19: 699–727.

Larzelere, R. E., and Huston, T. L. 1980. 'The Dyadic Trust Scale: Toward Understanding Interpersonal Trust in Close Relationships'. *Journal of Marriage and the Family*. 8: 595–604.

Lazerson, M. H. 1988. 'Organizational Growth of Small Firms: An Outcome of Markets and Hierarchies'. *American Sociological Review*. 53: 330–42.

Levinson, H., Price, C. R., Munden, H. J., and Solley, C. M. 1962. *Men, Management, and Mental Health*. Cambridge, Mass.: Harvard University Press.

Lincoln, J. R., Gerlach, M. L., and Takahashi, P. 1992. 'Keiretsu Networks in the Japanese Economy: A Dyad Analysis of Intercorporate Ties'. *American Sociological Review*. 57: 561–85.

Luhmann, N. 1979. *Trust and Power*. Chichester: John Wiley and Sons.

McAllister, D. J. 1995. 'Affect- and Cognition-Based Trust as Foundations for Interpersonal Cooperation in Organizations'. *Academy of Management Journal*. 38: 24–59.

Macaulay, S. 1963. 'Non-Contractual Relations in Business'. *American Sociological Review*. 28: 55–70.

McGrath, J. E. 1984. *Groups: Interaction and Performance*. Englewood Cliffs, NJ: Prentice-Hall.

Macneil, I. R. 1974. 'The Many Futures of Contract'. *Southern California Law Review*. 47: 691–816.

——1978. 'Contracts: Adjustments of Long-Term Relations under Classical, Neoclassical, and Relational Contract Law'. *Northwestern University Law Review*. 72: 854–905.

——1980. *The New Social Contract*. New Haven, Conn.: Yale University Press.

Mahoney, J., and Pandian, J. R. 1992. 'The Resource Based View within the Conversation of Strategic Management'. *Strategic Management Journal*. 13: 363–80.

Michalos, A. C. 1990. 'The Impact of Trust on Business, International Security and the Quality of Life'. *Journal of Business Ethics*. 9: 619–37.

Moorman, C., Zaltman, G., and Deshpande, R. 1992. 'Relationships between Providers and Users of Market Research: The Dynamics of Trust within and between Organizations'. *Journal of Marketing Research*. 29: 314–28.

Morgan, G. 1986. *Images of Organization*. Beverley Hills, Calif.: Sage.

Murakami, Y., and Rohlen, T. P. 1992. 'Social-Exchange Aspects of the Japanese Political Economy: Culture, Efficiency, and Change'. In Kumon, S., and Rosovsky, H. (eds.). *The Political Economy of Japan*. iii: 63–105. Stanford, Calif.: Stanford University Press.

Neale, M. A., and Northcraft, G. B. 1991. 'Behavioral Negotiation Theory: A Framework for Conceptualizing Dyadic Bargaining'. In Cummings, L. L., and Staw, B. M. (eds.). *Research in Organization Behavior*. 13: 147–90.

Nicholson, N., and Johns, G. 1985. 'The Absence Culture and the Psychological

Contract—Who's in Control of Absence?' *Academy of Management Review*. 10: 397–407.

Nohria, N., and Eccles, R. (eds.) 1993. *Networks and Organizations*. New York: The Free Press.

North, D. 1990. *Institutions, Institutional Change, and Economic Performance*. Cambridge: Cambridge University Press.

Ouchi, W. G., and Kremen-Bolton, M. 1988. 'The Logic of Joint Research and Development'. *California Management Review*. 30: 9–33.

Parkhe, A. 1991. 'Messy Research, Methodological Predispositions, and Theory Development in International Joint Ventures'. *Academy of Management Review*. 18: 227–68.

Perlmutter, H. V., and Heenan, D. 1986. 'Thinking Ahead'. *Harvard Business Review*. 64: 136–52.

Porter, M. E., and Fuller, M. B. 1986. 'Coalitions and Global Strategies'. In Porter, M. E. (ed.). *Competition in Global Industries*. 315–43. Cambridge, Mass.: The Harvard University Press.

Powell, W. W. 1987. 'Hybrid Organizational Arrangements'. *California Management Review*. 30: 67–87.

——1990. 'Neither Market nor Hierarchy: Network Forms of Organization'. In Cummings, L. L., and Staw, B. M. (eds.). *Research in Organizational Behavior*. 12: 295–336. Greenwich, Conn.: JAI Press.

Prahalad, C. K., and Hamel, G. 1990. 'The Core Competence of the Firm'. *Harvard Business Review*. 68: 79–91.

Ring, P. S. 1992. 'Cooperating on Tacit Know-How Assets'. Proceedings, First Annual Meeting of International Federation of Scholarly Associations of Management, Tokyo, Japan, 6–10 September 1992.

——1996. 'Networked Organization: A Resource Based Perspective'. *Acta Universitatis Upsaliensis, Studia Oeconomiae Negotiorum*. 39. Stockholm: Almqvist & Wiksell International.

——and Rands, G. 1989. 'Sensemaking, Understanding, and Committing: Emergent Transaction Processes in the Evolution of 3M's Microgravity Research Program'. In Van de Ven, A. H., Angle, H., and Poole, M. S. (eds.). *Research on the Management of Innovation: The Minnesota Studies*. 337–66. New York: Ballinger/Harper Row.

——and Van de Ven, A. H. 1992. 'Structuring Cooperative Relationships between Organizations'. *Strategic Management Journal*. 13: 483–98.

————1994. 'Developmental Processes of Cooperative Interorganizational Relationships'. *Academy of Management Review*. 19: 90–118.

Rosener, J. 1990. 'Way Women Lead'. *Harvard Business Review*. 68: 119–25.

Rotter, J. B. 1971. 'A New Scale for the Measurement of Interpersonal Trust'. *Journal of Personality*. 35: 651–65.

——1980. 'Interpersonal Trust, Trustworthiness, and Gullibility'. *American Psychologist*. 35: 1–7.

Schofield, N. 1985. 'Anarchy, Altruism and Cooperation: A Review'. *Social Choice and Welfare*. 2: 207–19.

Scott, W. R. 1987. 'The Adolescence of Institutional Theory'. *Administrative Science Quarterly*. 32: 493–511.

Shapiro, S. P. 1987. 'The Social Control of Interpersonal Trust'. *American Journal of Sociology.* 93: 623–58.

Sitkin, S., and Roth, N. L. 1993. 'Explaining the Limited Effectiveness of Legalistic Remedies for Trust/Distrust'. *Organization Science.* 4: 367–92.

Smith, K. G., Carroll, S. J., and Ashford, S. J. 1995. 'Intra- and Interorganizational Cooperation: Toward a Research Agenda'. *Academy of Management Journal.* 38: 7–23.

Tannen, D. 1990. *You just Don't Understand: Women and Men in Conversation.* New York: Ballantine Books.

Taylor, M. 1987. *The Possibility of Cooperation.* Cambridge: Cambridge University Press.

Teece, D. J. 1986. 'Profiting from Technological Innovation: Implications for Integration, Collaboration, Licensing and Public Policy'. *Research Policy.* 15: 285–305.

Teubal, M., Yinnon, T., and Zuzcovitch, E. 1991. 'Networks and Market Creation'. *Research Policy.* 20: 381–92.

Turner, J. H. 1987. 'Toward a Sociological Theory of Motivation'. *American Sociological Review.* 52: 15–27.

Van de Ven, A. H., and Walker, G. 1984. 'The Dynamics of Interorganizational Coordination'. *Administrative Science Quarterly.* 29: 598–621.

Weick, K. 1979. *The Social Psychology of Organizing.* Reading, Mass.: Addison-Wesley.

White, J. A. 1992. 'The Role of Individual Characteristics and Structures of Social Knowledge in Ethical Reasoning Using an Experiential Learning Framework'. Unpublished doctoral dissertation. Cleveland, Oh.: Case Western Reserve University.

Williamson, O. 1975. *Markets and Hierarchies.* Cambridge: Free Press.

——1985. *The Economic Institutions of Capitalism.* Cambridge: Free Press.

——1991. 'Comparative Economic Organization'. *Administrative Science Quarterly.* 36: 269–96.

——1993. 'Calculativeness, Trust, and Economic Organization'. *Journal of Law and Economics.* 36: 453–86.

Winter, S. 1987. 'Knowledge and Competence as Strategic Assets'. In Teece, D. E. (ed.). *The Competitive Challenge.* 159–84. Cambridge, Mass.: Ballinger.

Zucker, L. G. 1977. 'The Role of Institutionalization in Cultural Persistence'. *American Sociological Review.* 42: 726–43.

——1986. 'Production of Trust: Institutional Sources of Economic Structure'. In Staw, B. M., and Cummings, L. L. (eds.). *Research in Organizational Behavior.* 8: 53–112.

6

Research and Development Alliances: *Ensuring Trust by Mutual Commitments*

PAUL DE LAAT

Firms increasingly form alliances with external partners that involve co-operation in the sphere of research and development (R&D). Glossing over the intricate details, available statistics about European firms yield roughly the following picture. About 40 per cent of the companies performing some R&D nowadays co-operate with partners external to the firm. As is to be expected, the percentage is higher for large companies than for small and medium-sized companies (Kleinknecht and Reynen 1992; Dutch statistics). About one-tenth of the total R&D budget is destined for external co-operation (7 per cent for large companies, 16 per cent for small and medium-sized companies). These external funds concern co-operation with other companies as well as with research organizations and universities, in a two-to-one ratio (Riedle 1989; German statistics). Moreover, these alliances are not only national ones, but regularly cross borders. If larger firms are considered, it is not unusual to be involved in tens of alliances at the same time, many of which are with the same partners (Hagedoorn and Schakenraad 1990, 1992; Freeman 1991). Philips, Siemens, and Olivetti even manage hundreds of alliances simultaneously.

Although in practice they often overlap, various forms of R&D co-operation can be distinguished: joint ventures, research corporations, joint R&D, technology exchange, minority investment motivated by technological considerations, customer–supplier relations, and one-directional technology transfer (licensing and second-sourcing). All of these have grown rapidly in the last two decades (Hagedoorn and Schakenraad 1990; Freeman 1991). The amount of mutual interaction between partners that is

I would like to thank Boris Blumberg, Mark Ebers, Niels Noorderhaven, and two anonymous reviewers for their helpful comments on earlier versions of this chapter. More generally, the PIONIER programme 'Management of Matches', Faculty of Social Sciences, University of Utrecht (see Raub and Weesie 1991), has been a valuable source of inspiration in writing this chapter.

needed may differ considerably. Some forms, like technology exchange and technology transfer, often resemble a market transaction, where not much actual interaction is required. With other forms, like joint ventures, research associations, and joint R&D (for short: *R&D alliances*), the opposite applies: they involve an intense and ongoing co-operative relationship between partners. It is on the problems of mutual co-operation in these R&D alliances that attention will be focused in this chapter.

Let it be emphasized, to avoid confusion, that the joint ventures considered in this chapter have two special features. First, R&D activities are involved alongside production and marketing activities. Secondly, not only one, but all of the partners contribute to these R&D activities in the venture; the word co-operation has to be taken literally. In the terminology of Chakravarthy and Lorange (1991: Chapter 7): only type 3 alliances are considered.

The study of these new partnering phenomena shows a peculiar one-sidedness. Attention is almost exclusively focused on the question: what motivates the upsurge of these R&D alliances? Why do competitors feel the need to temporarily freeze competition? The evidence is not always consistent, but one of the most elaborate studies in the field lists as main motives the search for expansion and new markets, technological complementarity, and reduction of the innovation time span (Hagedoorn and Schakenraad 1990).

At the same time, however, little attention is paid to the question of how these alliances form and evolve over time. There is ample reason to consider these questions, as all the evidence available (mostly concerning joint ventures in general) indicates that these processes are fraught with risks. Data from McKinsey indicate that only about 15 per cent of negotiations between prospective partners lead to a formal agreement. Once started, only 30 per cent of the alliances thrive in the long term; the others fall short of expectations or are discarded (Alster 1986; Levine and Byrne 1986). Another study by Coopers & Lybrand and Yankelovitch, Skelly & White has the same tenor: only 12 out of 38 joint ventures studied (i.e. 32 per cent) met or exceeded partners' expectations (cited in Lewis 1990: 295). Moreover, only about 30 per cent of the 92 US-based joint ventures studied by Kogut (1989) were a long-term success; the others were either acquired by one of the partners or a third party (40 per cent) or simply dissolved (30 per cent). Slightly higher rates of success have also been reported, however. Harrigan (1988) found that 45 per cent of a sample of 895 strategic alliances were mutually assessed to be successful by their sponsors. Likewise, a summary of the results on stability of joint ventures, discussed in Kogut (1988*a*), provides instability percentages of between 30 per cent and 50 per cent.

Note that most of these studies are concerned with joint ventures *in general*. They may be assumed to be relevant for our purposes, however, as joint ventures increasingly seem to include technological co-operation.

While in 1976 only 7 per cent of US international joint ventures included R&D activity, in 1987 this figure had risen to 23 per cent (Hladik 1988; Hladik and Linden 1989). More generally, at least 30 per cent of recent co-operative agreements are estimated to involve joint R&D (cf. the overview in Dodgson 1993: 17–20; Mowery 1989).

Why would R&D alliances be so difficult to forge and sustain over time? On the one hand, technological, production, and marketing factors have to be taken into account (primary uncertainty of a 'state-contingent' kind: Williamson 1985: 57). Failure on these counts is not improbable: partners' technologies prove difficult to combine, marketing efforts fail, production is too costly, one partner decides to quit a certain market or abandon a field of technology, and so on (Alster 1986; Levine and Byrne 1986).

On the other hand, these difficulties are aggravated by a structural characteristic inherent in such alliances: each partner faces the temptation to engage in *opportunism*. Williamson (1985: 58–9) refers to this threat as secondary uncertainty of a 'behavioral' kind. Opportunism is to mean that a partner knowingly engages in self-seeking behaviour which is contrary to reaching the common goal. In terms of Buckley and Casson (1988) partners may cheat weakly (meeting minimal obligations only) or even strongly (actively engaging in acts that damage the alliance). Such opportunism is tempting, as it allows the cheat to gain even more from the transaction than prolonged co-operation would allow. It is all the more feasible, as the number of partners to an alliance increases. However, opportunism may easily backfire. The greater the number of partners that start cheating, the more the transaction yields substantially lower returns for all than prolonged co-operation would do. Moreover, duped partners may simply leave the alliance (an exit option, it should be noted, that is not available in the conventional prisoner's dilemma). Thus, opportunism may be self-defeating.

It is this problem of opportunism within R&D alliances which will be central to this chapter. The issue will be developed through a number of steps. The first task will be to examine what forms of opportunism actually take place within R&D alliances. Next, two general approaches for actors to create safeguards against opportunism are distinguished: classical contracting on the one hand, and creating credible commitments on the other. It is investigated how these instruments are actually applied to R&D alliances. In conclusion, the dynamic consequences of relying upon such guarantees are discussed; the concept of trust is central to this reasoning. As a whole, this chapter aims to explore whether a focus on creating credible commitments, as a form of private ordering, enhances our understanding of the dynamic of R&D alliances. Throughout, if empirical conclusions are drawn, these are the outcome of a search of the recent literature on R&D alliances. Let me stress, to avoid misunderstanding, that I did *not* conduct an empirical investigation of my own; for my exploratory purposes it sufficed to rely on existing data and analyses.

As can be seen from the above, the chapter focuses on structural features of R&D alliances, and their implications. My approach is a game-theoretic one. Aspects of process are only touched upon in passing, particularly in the section on the dynamics of trust. For a more explicit focus on process, such as recently advocated by Zajac and Olsen (1993), the reader is referred to Chapters 5 and 9.

OPPORTUNISM

What specific opportunistic hazards are generated whenever R&D is externalized in the form of alliances instead of being performed internally? An investigation of recent literature on R&D alliances yielded a number of complaints about opportunistic behaviour. First, consider the specialist contributions to R&D which partners are expected to commit to the alliance. These cannot be specified fully, but only in monetary terms. This gives a clear incentive to economize by delegating to the alliance second-rate personnel only. Such hedging is a frequent source of complaint within the US research corporations MCC (Microelectronics and Computer Technology Corporation) and Sematech (Semiconductor Manufacturing Technology) (Kanter 1989: 168). As a result, some US R&D consortia are forced to recruit from outside (Souder and Nassar 1990). In a similar vein, Pucik (1988) reports that the Japanese partner to a US-Japan joint venture adopted a consistent policy of delegating only second-rank employees.

Moreover, alliances need a lot of top management attention from their partners. In joint R&D, typically a collective board is created, in which all partners participate, to supervise the collaboration; sometimes special programme committees are also added (Niosi 1993). In research corporations, the governing body is a board of directors, consisting of top managers from participating companies and the chief executive officer (CEO) of the corporation. Moreover, partners have to devote top management manpower to the various programme committees (Peck 1986). Joint ventures, being separate entities as well, are likewise managed by a CEO and a board of directors. It is also not uncommon to insert an extra executive committee in between, consisting of top managers from all parents, which meets more regularly than the board. Here, standard matters may be dealt with, while only the most important decisions are referred to the board for approval (Lewis 1990: Chapter 12).

Parent companies may be tempted to economize on such top management attention for alliances once created. According to the study by Coopers & Lybrand *et al.* cited above, 'undermanagement' of joint ventures is common practice. Top management devotes its time most exclusively to creating a joint venture, developing a business plan, and drafting the legal documents required. Only 9 per cent of their time goes to setting up and running management systems for the alliances (Levine and Byrne 1986;

Alster 1986; Kanter 1989: 167). Note that this phenomenon may start out of sheer carelessness. However, once attendant problems come into the open, continued failure by top management to pay attention to them amounts to opportunism.

A further complication is the transfer of proprietary technological, production, and/or marketing knowledge to other parties in the alliance. This information can be misused opportunistically. Obviously, partners that have acquired proprietary information may leak and/or sell this to third parties not included in the alliance. In practice, though, the main concern seems to be that after a partner has transferred information, the other(s) use it directly against that partner to intensify competition. In order to see what this 'boomerang' hazard amounts to, joint ventures, research corporations, and joint R&D will be considered one by one.

An R&D joint venture not only performs R&D in mutual co-operation, it also produces and sells the products that are generated from it. In this case, the danger of opportunistic abuse looms large. After the joint venture has been operating for some time, any one partner may have appropriated enough technological, or, for that matter, production or marketing knowledge, to be able to go it alone. The disloyal partner starts out-competing the commonly owned joint venture. Allegiances of this kind have in particular been mounted against Japanese companies that entered into alliances with US companies (Teece 1986). Note that the same process might be set in motion by outsourcing or second-sourcing components. Thus, for example, by outsourcing microwave oven production to Samsung of South Korea, General Electric finally created a powerful competitor on the US market (Lei and Slocum 1992). Likewise, Matsushita would have ousted its former customer RCA from the American VCR market (Lewis 1990: 55). As regards second-sourcing, Intel's agreement with AMD concerning microprocessors ultimately established AMD as an independent competitor, producing 80×86 clone processors.

We consider joint R&D and research corporations next. In contrast to joint ventures, their only purpose is to generate technological results, available to all partners. After that, members' ways part; independently of each other, they will try to incorporate these results into new products and penetrate the market. Dangers of opportunistic abuse mainly exist, I would argue, in a situation of 'competitive R&D collaboration': partners involved aim to incorporate the prospective innovation into the same kind of products to be launched on the same markets. That is, competition between them is intended and inevitable. Motives for such an R&D collaboration might involve establishment of a common standard, or reaching the market before other competitors. In this situation, a partner in an alliance mainly faces the danger that another partner will use unfair market practices to force his way.

A case in point is the joint R&D agreement between Philips and Sony to develop common standards for compact disc (CD) players. Co-operation was explicitly confined to a period of eight months. After that, fierce competition on the consumers' market took over. No means were eschewed: both sides accused each other of unfair trading. Sony (and other Japanese companies) were charged with engaging in dumping practices, whereupon Philips (and other European companies) successfully pressed for EU levies upon CD players imported from Japan.

The situation may be less threatening than this, however. The common results may be destined to be incorporated into clearly differentiated products; or respective markets are clearly different. If one or both of these conditions applies—such R&D co-operation might be labelled 'non-competitive'—the hazards of abuse of knowledge are greatly reduced. Take for instance the co-operation between Philips and Siemens in the mid-1980s to develop integrated circuits. Philips focused on SRAMs, while Siemens's interest was in the development and production of DRAMs. These memory chips were to serve different applications in different markets: SRAMs were to be used in telecommunication equipment for the professional market, while DRAMs would upgrade electronic products for consumers. Another case in point is Bellcore (Bell Communications Research), the R&D consortium of the seven Bell telephone companies. These serve distinct areas, and may not even compete with each other. In both cases technological disclosure posed no competitive threat at all. Nevertheless, the danger of opportunism still lurks in the background. Their original position notwithstanding, partners may *unexpectedly* use the technology acquired for different purposes, and turn into competitors nevertheless. Moreover, unfair trading practices may be employed to penetrate markets.

A final hazard of R&D alliances is outright theft of knowledge. In every alliance, some information is knowingly and purposely shared. Problems begin as soon as partners try to gain more than the letter and the spirit of the agreement allow for. Partnering turns into prying. In general, joint ventures involving R&D are more risky than joint R&D or research corporations, as, in the former case, not only technological knowledge but also production and marketing information are put at risk. Theft of knowledge, of course, only serves to aggravate the problem of misuse of knowledge pointed out above.

Opportunism in R&D alliances, it may be concluded, may take on many forms: economizing on technical experts' and top management attention, misusing acquired information to engage in unexpected and/or unfair competition, and stealing valuable information from partners.

The chances of these forms actually happening will of course vary according to the specifics of an alliance. Consider features such as partner characteristics (e.g. size and age), alliance characteristics (such as number of partners, stage of R&D, similarity or complementarity of partners' R&D contributions), and environmental characteristics (e.g. number of other R&D suppliers in the product area involved and speed of technological change). How are the different forms of opportunism to be linked with these characteristics?

Some relations are rather straightforward (cf. Blumberg 1993). Take the kind of opportunism where effort is purposely reduced. This seems more likely to happen if more partners are involved, R&D is more basic, and partners contribute in a complementary fashion to the alliance. The reason is simple: 'soldiering' becomes less visible. Next consider opportunistic abuse and theft of information. This would seem more likely to take place if partners are larger (as larger firms have more opportunities for abuse at their disposal than smaller firms), more partners are involved (as more potential villains are around), and R&D contributions are of a similar kind (as it is easier to appreciate and hence to appropriate other partners' knowledge).

Also, the relationship between opportunism, of whatever kind, and the number of other R&D suppliers in the product area involved seems clear. If this number is high, switching to another partner is feasible in case the alliance breaks down, be it at a cost. If, however, the number becomes smaller (say three or less), exit becomes a less likely option. This checks the chances for opportunism to occur.

With regard to many other relationships, however, it seems to me that the picture is not quite clear. Take for example the stage of R&D involved. One could argue that opportunistic abuse of acquired information is more likely in applied R&D stages as application opportunities become more apparent. On the other hand, time is money, so abuse should take place as early as possible, depending on the kind of know-how already possessed by the opportunistic firm. Thus, any clear correlation seems non-existent here.

Moreover, empirical enquiry into this matter will be hard, as it has to face a subtle obstacle. If any dangers of opportunism lurk in the background, partners to an alliance will more often than not resort to safeguards; these will be discussed extensively later on. Such guarantees would precisely *eliminate* all clear correlations between characteristics of an alliance and opportunistic hazards, if any existed at all. For a useful discussion of the whole matter see Blumberg (1993). In what follows, I will take the dangers of opportunism as given, without bothering too much about what specific alliance features are involved.

Assuming, then, that each party to an R&D alliance in some measure faces the threat to fall victim to opportunism from his allies, how do parties proceed to limit these chances? What instruments are brought into play to constrain opportunism and make co-operation the more likely outcome? Of course, the problem of potential theft may be largely resolved by reducing opportunities for it to a minimum. In Hamel's terms: limiting the 'transparency' of one's organization is the key here. This can be done in a number of ways (Hamel *et al.* 1989; Hamel 1991). If work has to be done together, choose a site of work in a third location. That offers more protection than working together at one's own location. Moreover, personnel should beware of too much collegiality, and be instructed precisely as to which information they may share, and which they may not. Also, one or more individuals should act as gatekeepers. Only through these, may partners have access to people and facilities.

Measures such as these do reduce opportunities for opportunistic behaviour, but do not solve the problem as such. To deal with opportunism head-on, parties have to consciously regulate their relationships. Two general approaches may usefully be distinguished: classical contracting on the one hand, and building credible commitments on the other (cf. Schelling 1960; Macneil 1978; Galanter 1981; Williamson 1985; Raub and Weesie 1991).

TWO APPROACHES

On the one hand, parties to a transaction may resort to classical contracting (Macneil 1978; Williamson 1985): an explicit contract is drafted which aims to specify in detail all the rights and obligations of parties regarding the transaction, in all possible contingencies. Penalty clauses to be applied if a partner defaults, can be included. If contractual terms are not met, parties may have recourse to the courts (litigation). With classical contracting, parties essentially coerce each other to behave according to specifications. Owing to the central role of the courts in this approach, it is also frequently referred to as 'court ordering'.

As numerous commentators have stipulated, for long-term contracts in general under conditions of uncertainty this classical approach has its limitations. Apart from the costs involved, the ideal of complete and adequate specification of all transactional elements is elusive. Nobody can foresee in advance all eventualities that might happen. Those that can be foreseen, moreover, may require adaptations which can only be properly assessed at the time they actually happen. So contracts are necessarily incomplete. Moreover, whenever clear default takes place, litigation, apart from being costly, is not bound to be successful.

These objections of course apply even more when R&D co-operation is at stake (cf. e.g. Saxenian 1991). Outcomes of R&D can hardly be well defined in advance. There is also a more subtle drawback (Teece 1988). Drafting a well-specified R&D contract requires considerable disclosure of proprietary information at the pre-contract stage. This implies that one is already exposed to the risk of opportunistic abuse, even before a prospective contract has been signed.

Once it was recognized that long-term transactions under conditions of uncertainty cannot fruitfully be based on completely specified contracts and necessarily involve ongoing mutual adjustment, attention shifted to a search for other means to prevent opportunistic abuse. A variety of classical contracting is so-called 'neoclassical contracting': parties agree on the use of arbitrators instead of the courts to settle future disputes (Macneil 1978; Williamson 1985). This enhances flexibility in dealing with changing circumstances.

A more radical departure from this tradition has addressed the attendant problems of co-operation from another angle. Is it possible for parties to offer concrete and tangible guarantees, which clearly signal that they mean faithfully to carry out the agreement? In other words, how can parties build credible commitments towards each other? By incurring such commitments, parties voluntarily alter the stakes involved in the transaction. In game-theoretical terms: before transactions start, parties unequivocally change the mutual pay-off structure. If transactions take time to be completed, stakes can also be changed *en route*. Here, opportunistic behaviour punishes itself automatically; recourse to the courts or arbitrators to try and enforce continued co-operation is not necessary. Therefore, the chances for continued co-operation may be assumed to increase.

Note that in the context of co-operation two kinds of commitments may be distinguished. On the one hand, these may be 'self-directed': a partner commits something, which ties *himself* to the transaction. Classic examples involve the provision of pledges and hostages. On the other hand, commitments may be 'other-directed': a party makes commitments, that tie *other* partners to the transaction involved. Think, for example, of how firms can tie employees by offering an internal ladder of promotion, a firm-specific pension, and payment in stock options, to be exercised at a later date.

This approach of creating commitment is inextricably linked with the work of Thomas Schelling, who, in 1960, wrote his classic *The Strategy of Conflict*. Moreover, other scholars after him have carved closely related conceptions. Ian Macneil (1978), in his treatment of contract law, refers to 'relational contracting' (as opposed to '(neo)classical contracting'). Marc Galanter (1981), in his discussion of legal centralism, highlights the pivotal role of 'private ordering' (as opposed to 'court ordering'), that takes place in the shadow of the law. There are, of course, differences between these approaches, but they are all similar in spirit.

Both classical contracting and forging commitments, I contend, can be useful for governing transactions in general, and R&D transactions in particular. By arguing thus, it should be noted, I deviate from Williamson's (1985) scheme. To each kind of transaction he assigns one (and only one) 'efficient' governance regime. That is, he uses the scheme to highlight differences *between* types of transactions (inter-transactional differences) (cf. Williamson 1985: 79, fig. 3.2). While this is perfectly legitimate, I would maintain that this scheme can also be used to highlight different ways of handling one and the same kind of transaction (intra-transactional differences). Both instruments of governance may be applied to it. The range of possible applications, of course, depends strongly on the kind of transaction under consideration. The less frequently a transaction occurs, and the less specific the necessary investments are, the more instruments of classical contracting come to the fore; whilst, on the other hand, the more a transaction is recurrent and investments are transaction-specific, the more commitment devices are appropriate. With these qualifications in mind, I now turn to the specific analysis of R&D alliances.

GOVERNANCE OF R&D ALLIANCES

To what extent is the first approach, classical contracting, used in R&D alliances? A perusal of the literature revealed only a few sources to answer this question (Onida and Malerba 1989; Lewis 1990: Chapters 4 and 7; Niosi and Bergeron 1992; Niosi 1993). It would seem that contractual arrangements of this kind typically cover the following issues.

First of all, budgeting rules are established. Budgets may be accorded on a fixed-price basis, specifying a total budget only; if this is spent, the project stops. Cost-plus contracts are also used, which specify detailed goals to be reached rather than levels of expenditure. In addition, budgeting can be phased and made conditional upon specified technological or commercial results to be reached *en route*. Only if these minimum performance standards are realized, will co-operation continue. Obviously, in the case of a joint venture such a contract has to be more extended than in joint R&D or research corporations: it not only covers R&D co-operation, but also common production and marketing.

Next, property rights are contracted. In the case of joint R&D, three arrangements are common. Partners may agree to joint ownership of all results from the co-operation. Alternatively, each partner may remain the owner of his own R&D results, which are then made available to other partners. Finally, if there is a lead company in the collaboration, it may simply require the right to appropriate all results. To protect these results, secrecy is mostly deemed the best protection; only rarely (e.g. in biotechnology) patents are taken (Niosi and Bergeron 1992; Niosi 1993). If a separate corporate identity is created (research corporations and R&D joint ventures), results, patented or not, accrue to the corporation rather than to the partners. However, these have the right to obtain the results or take licences.

Supplementing these property arrangements, a pledge of secrecy may be required to prevent proprietary information—especially if not patented—from leaking to other competitors. Finally, it should be mentioned that transaction partners sometimes sign an agreement not to use the innovation to penetrate each other's markets, at least if antitrust regulations allow this.

These are the instruments of classical contracting as applied to R&D alliances, as far as I could detect from available sources. Also, it would seem, arbitrators are widely used, at least in the USA (neoclassical contracting). So much for the first approach to governance. It is time now to turn to the second approach. What instruments—if any—for forging credible commitment are used to govern R&D alliances? Have corporate equivalents of pledges, hostages, and bonds been invented in the context of R&D alliances, and if so, how are they used for governance purposes?

To answer this question, I carried out a search of the available literature. No publication was found which treated this question explicitly; answers could only be obtained by looking through publications written for other purposes, and reinterpreting them. In the end, I managed to piece together the following set of instruments, which are currently in use to effectively tie partners to R&D alliances.

Some kinds of commitment are inextricably bound up with the prospective transaction itself. To begin with, partners may of course have to invest in R&D equipment, R&D buildings, production facilities, and the like. Also, R&D specialists may have to be hired for the occasion. If, and only if, such investments are in some measure specifically tied to the transaction concerned and cannot readily be put to alternative use—which is often the case—will these not be wholly salvageable in the event of a breakdown of co-operation. In this way, partners gradually commit themselves to honour the agreements of the alliance.

Moreover, in a competitive situation where every month counts, investment in production facilities may have to be started even before the underlying R&D efforts have yielded results. This phenomenon may be called 'advance commitment' and is common, for example, in biotechnology. When US 'new biotechnology firms' (NBFs) collaborate with larger firms to commercialize their know-how, the bigger partner will often have to invest in production before the R&D cycle is completed (Pisano *et al.* 1988). A further case in point is Philips's investment in (wholly owned) trial production facilities to produce SRAMs. Construction of the plant had already started while its R&D collaboration with Siemens had just begun. The same applies to its partner Siemens: it also invested in trial production (of DRAMs) in advance. By doing so, each partner effectively tied itself to loyal co-operation with the other. In both of these cases, of course, advance investments are not wholly transaction-specific: other, albeit not too many, partners might be found to complete the transaction. But that would take time, costly in itself, and money.

Another bonding device in co-operative R&D efforts has to do with the fact that usually some sharing of proprietary knowledge is involved. As a result, stakes in the co-operation have been exchanged which cannot be retrieved if co-operation breaks down. Examples abound. The Philips–Sony joint R&D agreement to develop joint standards for the CD player implied that Philips had to share all technical information regarding electronics, optics, lasers, and plastics, while Sony had to be open about its digital encoding knowledge (Nayak and Ketteringham 1993: 305). The alliance between Philips and Siemens to develop state of the art megachips involved mutual exchange of all relevant knowledge about SRAMs and DRAMs.

Moreover, adequate timing of transaction-specific investment of knowledge may yield extra incentives for co-operation. A technique which may be labelled 'phased commitment' is widely used: a partner promises to share ever more knowledge as the alliance unfolds in the future. Note that such promises initially tie the receiving partner(s). Once a partner has carried out his promises, however, the tables are turned: he ends up being tied more firmly to the transaction himself. Notice, also, that phased commitment seems far superior to fully committing oneself at the beginning: it spreads incentives to indulge in opportunism more evenly between alliance partners. Some examples of phased commitment are the following.

In 1986, Motorola's expertise on HCMOS microprocessors and Toshiba's knowledge of RAMs were exchanged for each other. Moreover, these products were to be produced by a jointly owned plant in Japan. However, Motorola for the time being held back its vital knowledge on 32-bit microprocessors. Only by helping to establish sufficient access to the Japanese market, could Toshiba gain access to this knowledge (Link and Tassey 1989: 193–7). Next consider British Telecom and Du Pont, which went one step further. In 1986 they formed the BT&D joint venture, which involves R&D, production, and marketing of optoelectronic components. In order to strengthen their venture, both partners promised that if their own parallel R&D produced results, all of these would be commercialized exclusively by BT&D. Royalties are in any case due to the original inventing firm (Dodgson 1993: 104). As a final example of phased commitment we take a look at US NBFs. In their collaboration with established firms to commercialize their know-how, they usually grant their bigger partners the right to all future technical improvements of the initial product. This is an effective bond, as in general important improvements take place over the life cycle of such products (Pisano *et al.* 1988).

Sceptics will object that promises are only promises. Can agreements of this kind be *enforced* at all? This is indeed a problem. To lend more weight to these promises, one could envisage the following solutions. If some knowledge is held back for the moment (cf. the Motorola–Toshiba alliance), it could in written form be deposited with a notary, who would receive pertinent instructions for the next few years. If knowledge involved has to be produced yet (cf. BT&D, NBFs), arbitration could be agreed upon beforehand. Whether, in the instances cited above, guarantees of the kind have actually been employed in order to bolster credibility, is unknown to me.

It should be pointed out that, as regards the two kinds of transaction-specific investments just analysed—acquiring dedicated assets and sharing knowledge—not only their timing is variable. The absolute *amount* of them may also vary considerably. Because of this element of choice, partners to an R&D alliance have some grip on how much they are actually committing themselves. The point is best explained by referring to a distinction coined by Mangematin (1996). In co-operative R&D, he observes, one can choose either a more modular approach or a more systemic approach. In the modular approach, partners develop a product consisting of interconnected modules. Each partner takes care of one (or more) modules. In this case, of course, commitments are absolutely minimal. In the systemic approach, the product to be developed cannot be subdivided into parts; it forms an integrated whole. As a consequence, partners have to work together in one common laboratory. In this arrangement, I would argue, mutual commitment is much stronger. R&D assets employed, physical as well as human, are much more transaction-specific. Also, tight interconnectedness demands more sharing of knowledge between partners.

Whatever approach is chosen, partners still continue to conduct their own parallel research in-house. This home base is not only a competitor for first-rate personnel, it is also easy to fall back on in case co-operation breaks down. A strong form of commitment, therefore, is to agree to limit or even eliminate one's own independent research during the time of the alliance. This move is a variation on the familiar tactic of burning your bridges behind you. It is doubtful though, that such a drastic step will often be taken. The only incidence I have come across, is the close co-operation regarding R&D and production of VCR recorders between Philips and Grundig. Both firms simply fused their respective departments into one. This move, of course, had much to do with the fact that close ties already existed: Philips owned 31.6 per cent equity in Grundig (with an option to increase this percentage up to 50.5 per cent), had a major say in its policy, and was accountable for its losses.

Other kinds of commitment that I detected in the literature on R&D alliances are not directly linked to the logistics of the transaction as such, but are, as it were, specially crafted for the occasion. An intriguing scheme is employed in the MCC research corporation (Peck 1986). This involves special provisions to ensure that financial entry investments and (part of) the ensuing royalties cannot be recuperated after exiting from the transaction.

First, membership of MCC is contingent upon buying a share in it. However, this share is *non-transferable*, making it effectively a sunk cost. This 'entry fee', it should be noted, was set comfortably low at $150,000 when MCC started in 1983, to reflect the initial risks involved. In the years after, it continued to increase as MCC became more firmly established (up to $1 m. in 1986). Incidentally, such entry fees seem to be common practice in US R&D consortia in general (Souder and Nassar 1990).

Next, the licence system at MCC should be considered. Upon payment, member companies subscribe to specific technology programmes of their choosing. Whenever such a programme produces licensable technologies, companies participating in the programme receive exclusive licence rights for a period of three years. Then, after this period, licensing is granted to a larger clientele: to other MCC shareholders not included in the particular programme, and to non-MCC members. In all cases, royalties are due. These royalties are, for the most part, distributed to the programme participants in question. One aspect of this distribution is instructive for our purposes. Twenty-seven per cent licence income is awarded to programme participants in equal shares as so-called 'technology credits'. These can only be used *inside* MCC, as payment for participation on other MCC technology programmes. On exiting MCC, a company forfeits its technology credits.

Equity may serve bonding purposes in a more general fashion too. Governance forms that involve equity (joint venture, research corporation), as compared to those relying on a simple agreement only (joint R&D), have in-built commitment mechanisms (cf. Hennart 1988; Kogut 1988a; Osborn and Baughn 1990). Equity is held by all parties concerned. In this way a common interest is created which aligns partners' individual interests. Moreover, a new quasi-independent authority is installed, which oversees and controls the actions of parties involved in the transactions. Joint ventures and research corporations operate, therefore, as a quasi-hierarchy. As a result tendencies for opportunism are attenuated.

Also, prospective partners may not so much invest in the transaction itself, as in each other: cross-shareholdings (Lewis 1990: Chapter 8). By taking a stake in other parties, opportunistic action regarding the alliance will backfire by reducing the value of one's own equity. The percentage obtained is critical. On the one hand, it should reflect concern in the partner's well-being, and so not be too low. On the other hand, it must signal that control over the other is not intended, and therefore not be too large either. The golden mean should be chosen. What counts as such seems to be culture-bound: 25 per cent in the USA, only 5 per cent in Japan.

Taking direct equity can be practised by all concerned, or by just one firm. In the latter case, it usually concerns an alliance between a large and a small firm. The larger party takes equity in the smaller party, enabling the latter to finance his part of the deal. A well-known example is the AT&T–Olivetti joint venture of 1983, where AT&T agreed to take a minority share of 25 per cent in Olivetti, with an option to raise this up to 40 per cent. More recently, in 1990, Glaxo teamed up with Biochem of Canada, to form an R&D and marketing joint venture. Glaxo, a hundred times bigger, took a 10 per cent equity interest in Biochem, with an option to expand this to 20 per cent.

As such share-taking stresses a long-term perspective, it would seem that it is most appropriate for long-term joint ventures. Available statistics indicate that joint ventures in general are increasingly cemented by cross-shareholdings (Corzine 1991: 22). By implication, this could be valid for joint ventures involving R&D as well. Co-operation, limited to R&D

proper, is a short-term endeavour; therefore, taking direct equity seems less appropriate (cf. e.g. the data in Niosi 1993).

Commitments may also be used to protect partners from post-transactional calamities. At stake here is the prospect that a partner to the alliance unfairly runs off with the jointly developed product. To prevent this, commitment techniques have also been invented. Take, for example, AMD (Advanced Micro Devices) in its dealings with Sony to jointly develop SRAMs. Both were to produce and market them separately. AMD feared it would be exposed to the threat of Sony freezing AMD out of the market by more efficient production techniques or plain dumping. It therefore required Sony to buy part of future AMD chips production for an adequate price (Levine and Byrne 1986). Sony signed a contractual price guarantee. Thus it made its commitment credible, as price clauses in the electronics industry are effectively enforceable (Shepard 1987).

Until now, an R&D alliance has been treated as an isolated transaction. If we broaden our view, two final bonding schemes appear. First, next to the R&D alliance being considered, partners may engage in *other* collaborative deals at the same time—of whatever kind. Such bundling of agreements is a common enough practice, especially in R&D alliances concerning information technologies (Hagedoorn and Schakenraad 1990, 1992). This bundling implies that cheating in any one of them endangers the whole string of mutual ties. The results of Kogut (1989) show that this might be an effective check on opportunism: joint ventures (mostly involving R&D) between partners who co-operated otherwise as well (especially through other joint ventures or licence contracts) were more stable than stand-alone joint ventures.

Secondly, it is not unusual for governments or supra-national bodies like the EU to be involved in fostering alliances by forwarding subsidies. If so, a check on opportunism is created: partners to an alliance effectively stand to forfeit considerable sums of money (typically up to 50 per cent of expenses) if co-operation breaks down. This fact alone would imply that, on average, subsidized alliances will be more stable than non-subsidized ones.

Finally, a remark about commitments in general is in order. These can sometimes be contracted explicitly to enhance credibility. Most of the examples referred to above actually involved explicit contracting. Therefore, the distinction between classical contracting, on the one hand, and incurring credible commitments, on the other, should not be confused with the presence or absence of contractual provisions. Such provisions can be used in *both* approaches. The essential difference between the two, let it be repeated, is that with classical contracting, partners pin each other down to a precisely detailed performance, while in the case of the commitment approach, partners provide tangible, waterproof guarantees that commit them to faithfully executing the agreement.

EXCURSUS: REPUTATION

All of these provisions to curb opportunism can become quite elaborate. Sometimes, however, there is no need for them at all. The record of companies in dealing with others in the past—their reputation for short—can also do the job. Macaulay (1963) long ago alerted us to the fact that many market transactions are stabilized by a good reputation alone. The mechanism is simple enough (Dasgupta 1988; Raub and Weesie 1991). Whenever a reputable company indulges in opportunism, its partner(s) may retaliate by publicly announcing the abuse of faith. As a result, the former's reputation is severely damaged, and its prospect of future dealings with other companies is endangered. The damaged partner(s) may also retaliate more subtly: using the threat of public exposure to coerce the company in question to co-operate. Stated otherwise, the partner of repute forwards his high reputation as security. Upon defection, it risks forfeiting it.

For intercorporate transactions in general, and R&D alliances in particular, many questions remain to be answered. How is information on corporate behaviour transmitted: through persons, public sources, specialized agencies? How accurate can this transmission be? To what extent are reputations actually being considered when corporate actors gauge their transactions?

For R&D alliances, only scattered references could be found in the literature which suggest some tentative answers. Reputation does count when alliances are formed. When Corning Glass Works contemplates a joint venture, it uses third party information about a potential ally's conduct as partner to alliances in the past (Lewis 1990: 221). In establishing a reputation, associating with reputable companies may help considerably. Cipher and Microsoft both gained instant reputations by associating with IBM (although, it should be noted, this involved customer–supplier relationships) (Teece 1986). Reputation in general may be complemented by personal reputations. Sony had a high reputation for superior quality and marketing. Moreover, Sony's top executive, Morita, was considered to become 'obsessive', once he was convinced of the potential of a new product. Both circumstances together evoked enough trust for Philips to engage in the joint development of CD standards with Sony (Nayak and Ketteringham 1993: 304; more generally, cf. Lawton Smith *et al.* 1991).

Finally, companies do care about their reputation. In 1982, Hitachi was caught trying to steal industrial secrets from IBM. Instead of exposing Hitachi, IBM chose to use this piece of information to ensure continuing trading relations with Hitachi and access to the Japanese market (Helm and Cowan 1985). Then, in 1986, Hitachi was refused a licence to manufacture Motorola's 32-bit microprocessor. Did Motorola, by any chance, refuse on account of Hitachi's bad reputation? The answer is unknown.

Note, incidentally, that the literature referred to above fails to distinguish between two kinds of reputation: reputation for excellence in technology, production, and/or marketing on the one hand, and reputation for (dis)honest behaviour on the other. In future research these should not be mingled any more, but carefully distinguished.

This mechanism of 'control by reputation' notwithstanding, whenever prospective (or actual) partners to an R&D alliance purposely and explicitly want to reduce mutual fears of opportunistic abuse, two kinds of governance instruments predominate: classical contracting and building credible commitments. It is the use of these instruments which normally holds the key to the success or failure of such alliances. Existing literature assumes, mostly implicitly, that these can be used indiscriminately; both will produce the same kind of stabilizing effects. In the remainder of this chapter this assumption will be challenged. The dynamics of the two approaches differ greatly. The following tentative hypotheses will be developed: R&D alliances will be the more stable (a) the more commitment devices are used instead of classical contracting provisions, and (b) the more the commitments involved create a mutual balance between partners.

TRUST AND DISTRUST

In order to develop these hypotheses, the concept of trust is essential. It has been amply elaborated upon by authors like Deutsch (1962), Blau (1964), Zand (1972), and Fox (1974); these will loosely be referred to as the 'Deutsch tradition'. More recently, Gambetta (1988*b*) edited a volume on trust, with useful contributions by Dasgupta (1988), Gambetta (1988*a*), and Lorenz (1988). For a recent overview of the literature on trust, see Sitkin and Roth (1993), and Ring (Chapter 5, this volume). In what follows I will mainly rely on the Deutsch tradition.

This tradition focuses on problems of co-operation where mutual *vulnerability* exists, that is, where opportunistic abuse cannot be excluded. Trusting behaviour, then, consists in actions that increase one's vulnerability to the other; distrusting behaviour consists of actions that try to decrease vulnerability by controlling the other's behaviour. From these core assumptions, one can deduce the following model of interaction for partners to an exchange (cf. Zand 1972; Fox 1974: Chapter 2). In it, I have also incorporated the element of investments in a relationship, as these are often required if a relation is to flourish (Blau 1964: 98–9).

The model reads as follows. Partners who trust each other will feel no need to control each other. Instead, they will co-operate loyally, commit themselves to the relationship whenever necessary, communicate openly, and accept each other's influence. Loyalty in this context is to mean that partners not only meet standards of quantity and quality as agreed upon; they also go beyond these and spontaneously contribute in an innovative fashion whenever this seems necessary to reach the common goal. With mutual distrust, partners behave quite differently. First and foremost, they will attempt to control each other's behaviour. In addition to this, they will contribute at most what they are obliged to do, evade commitment, communicate with each other only as much as strategic considerations allow, and barely be receptive to each other's views.

Studies in the Deutsch tradition, moreover, confirm the notion that both trusting and distrusting behaviour are mutually reinforcing (cf. Zand 1972; Fox 1974: Chapter 2; Sitkin and Roth 1993). The more B perceives A as behaving trustfully towards him, the easier it is for B to trust A and reciprocate in the same fashion. Trust therefore tends to evoke trust, creating an upward spiral. The same goes for distrust. If B perceives A as behaving as if A distrusts him, the more B will be inclined to infer that he likewise cannot trust A, and reciprocate accordingly with distrusting behaviour. Consequently, distrust tends to evoke distrust, generating a downward spiral.

Blau (1964: Chapter 4) argues along similar lines. He distinguishes between economic and social exchange, which correspond closely to the conditions of low and high trust respectively. If distrust prevails, partners to an exchange will structure their relation along the lines of *economic* exchange. The prototype of this kind of exchange is a formal contract, stipulating in advance the exact quantities to be exchanged. If trust prevails, the exchange will take on the characteristics of *social* exchange. In it, one person does another a favour. Such favours create obligations to reciprocate in the future, but these are left unspecified and diffuse. One has to trust the other to discharge them. Notice that as mutual trust in social exchange spirals upwards, the association acquires some intrinsic significance. Mutual behaviour is no longer solely dictated by self-interest, but also by a sense of morality. In terms of Ring (Chapter 5): alongside fragile trust, some amount of resilient trust develops.

This model of trust and its dynamics is very versatile. It has been aptly used by Fox (1974) to analyse work role patterns in hierarchical organizations. More recently, I have applied this model in a study of matrix structures in R&D organizations (de Laat 1990). It is also, I would argue, a useful model to analyse the approaches to governance in (R&D) alliances, as distinguished above.

Whenever parties engage in a transaction, in which they expose themselves to potential opportunism, they will make an estimate of the chances that their partners will conform to obligations or violate these. That is, each partner asks himself how much he can trust the other(s). If trust is high enough, so that the expected outcome of the transaction is positive, all is well. But often trust is much lower; trust is lacking. In this case, partners may seize upon the governance instruments of classical contracting and/or creating credible commitments, hoping to overcome the problem of lack of trust. To what extent are these hopes justified?

Consider classical contracting first. It aims to specify all possible details of the prospective transaction, in order to minimize harmful actions from the others. The ideal, although unattainable, is complete restraint. Because of this emphasis on control, the whole approach can easily be characterized as betraying low trust in other partners involved. Consequently, such instruments tend to provoke a spiral of rising mutual distrust. Partners set out to increasingly specify each others' contributions. Contract execution, moreover, is seriously hampered. While communicating badly and barely accepting each others' views, parties are tempted to shirk their obligations to the transaction. What happens is clearly counter-productive: classical contracting runs the danger of provoking opportunism instead of curtailing it.

Of course, this potentially disturbing effect of classical contracting should not be overstated. Some contractual provisions make perfect sense to business partners; no unwanted control seems to be implied. When R&D partners specify some budget rules, deadlines, and property rights, this certainly establishes a minimal level of trust. Specifying both less and more than this, however, has its pitfalls. On the one hand, leaving out such provisions is not to be recommended. Not requiring any provisions of this kind may be interpreted by other partners as showing too much trust, as naïvety—a naïvety which stands to be exploited. Not granting any such provisions to others requiring them, is likely to arouse suspicion. On the other hand, specifications should not be overdone. If a business plan expands from a few pages to a manual, to be taken to the letter, then the risk looms large that this will be perceived as an act of control, and that spiralling distrust will creep in.

Consider, next, the approach of building credible commitments. Partners voluntarily provide tangible investments which contribute to the prospering of the co-operation. Such steps signal that they want it to become a success. This approach, therefore, clearly expresses high trust in the other(s). The consequences are straightforward: such strategic moves tend to create a spiral of rising trust. While communicating openly about and accepting each others' views on the matter in hand, partners loyally discharge their obligations, and are inclined to invest increasingly in the co-operative effort if required. Thus, the commitment approach not only effectively eliminates opportunistic dangers, its effects are much broader: it also tends to foster high quality co-operation. A real team spirit emerges. Such alliances will be optimally equipped to cope with external uncertainty and to adapt to changing circumstances over time.

Notice that this hypothesis of an upward spiral also implies that trust will assume moral overtones (cf. the paragraph above on social exchange). Parties come to feel moral obligations to one another. Phrased in Ring's terms (Chapter 5): forwarding safeguards initiates a process of rising trust, in the course of which fragile trust transforms into resilient trust.

As in the case of classical contracting, one should not overstate the case. Some investments in an R&D alliance seem to be indicated to establish a minimum of trust, such as sharing know-how and investing in mutual facilities. Reluctance to invest anything at all seems actually self-defeating: it shows a considerable lack of trust, jeopardizing the alliance at the outset. It is only when more extended commitments are made (such as commitment in advance, a systemic approach, entry fees, cross-shareholdings), that the spiral of rising trust is set in motion.

These arguments taken together suggest that in the process of designing and implementing regulatory mechanisms, the instruments of classical contracting and credible commitments cannot be interchanged indiscriminately to produce the same kind of protection against opportunism. On the contrary, both instruments, if used to the full, tend to produce *opposite* effects. Whenever undue stress is laid upon classical contracting, the chances for opportunism increase. An emphasis on credible commitments, however, tends to stabilize, and, in fact, optimize transactions.

Little evidence can be adduced as yet to support these speculations about R&D alliances. Some consultants tend to endorse them. Lewis (1990: 93) asserts that 'too much planning implies a lack of trust, which can hurt relationships'. Ohmae (1989) gives the same advice: 'Make sure you tie up a tight legal contract . . . Once signed, however, the contract should be put away. If you refer to it, something is wrong with the relationship.' Likewise, the vice-chairman of Corning, a firm that engages in a multitude of joint ventures, comments: 'Too much stress on contingencies and on termination provisions is a stress on the wrong elements. The essence of a joint venture is mutual trust between the parents. Too much time spent worrying about failure can cause failure' (Lewis 1990: 128, 143).

Scientific evidence is more mixed. Surveying four international joint ventures, Lyles (1987) found that firms stipulated all possible future events in contracts. Although helpful at times, at other times these contracts were deemed outdated and focused on the wrong set of issues; moreover, some partner firms saw it as a sign of mistrust to have to specify everything. Souder and Nassar's (1990) findings also partly contradict, partly confirm my allegations. On the one hand, a high degree of effectiveness of R&D consortia was correlated with the establishment of a strong and finely detailed charter before a consortium was initiated. On the other hand, in R&D consortia which were rated as the most effective of all, at least a minimum of pre-competitive knowledge was shared between partners.

RECIPROCITY

It is not enough that partners emphasize credible commitments. Attention must also focus on the problem of mutual 'fine-tuning' of such commitments. The concept of reciprocity in social relations can usefully be introduced here. It has been argued that as a general principle, reciprocation of goods, services, and favours has a stabilizing and nourishing effect on social relations (cf. Gouldner 1960; Fox 1974: Chapter 2). For our problem this suggests that credible commitments as a whole, if they are to effectively support social relations, should also be mutually balanced.

Why would such a balance be mandatory? Consider the situation where one partner to an alliance offers some kind of credible commitment, which in the longer run is not adequately reciprocated. In doing so, he has effectively manoeuvred himself into dependency. This dependency is potentially disruptive. For one thing, it could be abused in an opportunist way by other partners. For another, it could provoke defensive moves by the dependent partner to prevent this happening by constraining the others (classical contracting). This is not unlikely to set the spiral of distrust in motion. Therefore, as a general rule, it would seem that to promote enduring co-operation, credible commitments by partners should balance each other. Such an arrangement creates bilateral dependency, which effectively ties partners to each other.

One could object, that creating such a balance is not necessary, as one-sided commitments produce bilateral dependency *automatically*. Williamson (1985: 61–3) argues along these lines, calling this the 'fundamental transformation'. Normally, I would contend, this argument does *not* obtain for R&D alliances. Take the case of one-sided transaction-specific investments by A. Through these sunk costs, A is effectively committed to the alliance. B, however, is not. B might very well try to blackmail A, threatening to leave if demands are not met. Why? Because B can start partnering anew, almost without any loss, and try to lure another partner, with expertise in the same area of R&D, into the deal. In the final analysis, B threatening to leave is credible, while A threatening to do so is not. Bilateral dependency, I would argue, will only result if one-sided investments by A unfold over a longer time. Then, because time is usually at a premium, B's option of changing partners gradually vanishes. Correspondingly, B's threatening capacity diminishes, and his dependency on A increases.

What does such a balance concretely amount to for R&D alliances? One may, of course, match commitments of the same kind. Compare some of the R&D alliances mentioned above. The alliance between Philips and Sony to develop CD standards involved a roughly equivalent disclosure of proprietary knowledge. The same goes for the Philips–Siemens alliance focusing on RAMs. Moreover, each party invested equally in building its own special laboratory and trial plant. One may, however, just as well try to match commitments of different kinds; disclosure of proprietary knowledge is balanced, say, by a transaction-specific investment in production facilities. Notice, also, that if partners have a number of alliances between them, supporting commitments only have to match in an overall sense for all alliances together.

The process of actually creating such a balance, though, is a tricky process.

The one who commits himself first, risks being exploited by the other. Therefore each is tempted to wait for the other to move first—effectively risking ruining the relationship for lack of trust. On account of this first-mover disadvantage, partners should proceed slowly and commit themselves only bit by bit.

While commitments increase, moreover, the recipe of a mutual balance should not be taken too literally. Commitments from partners cannot always coincide in order to produce an exact balance all the time. A small biotechnology firm may have to develop a partner-specific technology early on, to be reciprocated later by the larger partner's investment in production facilities. Some variable margin of commitment between partners is unavoidable. However, this will not matter as long as partners' mutual commitments stay *close enough* to a balance in order not to create a sizeable dependency.

Until now, it has tacitly been assumed that partners to an R&D alliance co-operate *on equal terms*. That is, if technological, production, marketing, and financial strength regarding the alliance are taken into account, partners are equal (i.e. mutual strengths are equal), or, at least, equivalent (i.e. mutual strengths compensate for each other). If partners match, then indeed balancing commitments amounts to matching them: equal (or equivalent) commitments should be made by both sides.

In many cases, however, co-operating partners will not be on equal terms. They are simply no match. The weaker party is then exposed to opportunistic abuse by the stronger party. A technologically superior party may quickly out-learn the inferior one, which is reason enough to exit from the transaction. Superior market and/or financial strength is an invitation to run with the jointly developed results and engage in unfair competition. Inequality also has a more subtle effect: the effective 'rate of exchange' between partners' commitments is affected. Financial inequality, for example, affects the constraint value of monetary transaction-specific investments. If each partner invests the same amount of money, the richer one will feel less restrained and therefore less likely to abstain from opportunism. In economic parlance: wealth effects intrude. Similarly, fair sharing of technological secrets in an alliance represents a disproportionate tie for a technologically 'junior' partner.

Thus, if partners are not on equal terms, simply matching commitments will no longer do. Creating and maintaining a balance becomes much harder. Several possibilities seem to offer themselves. First, one might try to create a set of mutual commitments, which do not so much match, as allow for the mutual inequalities that matter to the alliance concerned to be compensated. The weaker party requires a one-sided commitment from the stronger party as an extra protection to balance the relationship. I might here refer back to some examples mentioned above. Financially, AT&T was much better off than its partner Olivetti in their joint venture. Therefore it took a minority share in Olivetti, which not only provided Olivetti with cash to carry out its part of the deal, but also proved AT&T's allegiance to the common joint venture. The same goes for the Glaxo–Biochem venture. AMD, in partnering Sony, feared that its much bigger partner would run with the jointly developed SRAMs. Therefore, it insisted on Sony committing itself to the guaranteed purchase of part of AMD's SRAM production.

As a second possibility, partners may enter into another mutual alliance, where vulnerability is reversed: the party which is weaker in the first alliance is the stronger one in the second alliance (Buckley and Casson 1988). By combining alliances, dependencies cancel out. Unfortunately, empirical evidence to substantiate this possible mechanism is lacking. Both mechanisms, of course, can also be used together. Parties engage in a bundle of alliances; by a proper spread over mutual strengths and weaknesses, and some compensatory commitments where necessary, an overall balance is created.

Finally, one may simply give up all hopes of reaching a balance, and try out a hierarchical arrangement. The stronger partner provides the major part of contributions and investments, and establishes himself as the dominant party. Compare two-party joint ventures, in which fifty–fifty shares are not taken, but, for example, a seventy–thirty arrangement is chosen. For such an arrangement to be stable, however, it would seem that two conditions must be satisfied. The weaker party must legitimize domination by the stronger party, while the latter, on his part, must resist the temptation to take advantage of the weaker party. These rules are not always respected. R&D alliances between big and small firms are a case in point. It seems that in the UK certain large firms specialize in drawing innocent small firms into an R&D alliance, and then opportunistically use the occasion to behave in a 'predatory manner' (Dickson *et al.* 1991; Lawton Smith *et al.* 1991). Corning's experience is also instructive. It only forms joint ventures with partners of roughly equal size, as it is convinced that size disparities spell trouble: 'We would have problems with a company that is much smaller than we are (they may feel defensive or even offensive) or with a company that is much larger (they might get condescending)' (a retired vice-chairman of Corning, cited in Kanter 1989: 173).

In the paragraphs above it has been argued that finding the right balance of commitments seems much less complicated between equal partners than between unequal ones. This is not to imply that the former kind of alliances are also more stable; the process of actually *creating*—and keeping—such a balance might well be more difficult between equals. Kogut's (1988*b*) results show no difference in stability, whether joint ventures were formed between firms of equal size or between firms that differed significantly in size. Moreover, as regards collaboration between technological equals in the aircraft industry, it seems to be marred by the reluctance of technological leaders to transfer key capabilities. As a result, those ventures even appear to be less stable than ventures between technological leaders and followers (Mowery 1989).

Many ramifications of this approach remain to be explored. For one thing, reaching a balance presents more puzzles than discussed above. If the same kind of commitments are to be matched, what level is mutually required? If different kinds are to be matched, what is the 'rate of exchange'? Moreover, inter-cultural differences between firms will have to be considered. If these obtain, stabilizing alliances is beset with even more problems. For example, if partners put a different emphasis on classical contracting, this spells trouble. Another case in point are Japanese firms. They consider trust to be highest when they actually yield power in an alliance (Hamel 1991). Their Western partners can hardly be expected to subscribe to this proposition.

CONCLUSIONS

It has been shown, first, that opportunism within R&D alliances is a problem indeed. Instances of economizing on much needed specialists' or managers' contributions and of misusing and stealing knowledge from partners have been reported in the literature. Next, two general approaches for actors to create safeguards against opportunism have been distinguished: classical contracting on the one hand, and creating credible commitments on the other. There has been an exploration of how both kinds of instruments are actually applied to R&D alliances. In particular, the second, more novel approach has been treated at length. Contrary to what might be expected, enforceable commitments can indeed be created. It turns out that a whole array of transactional elements can be used for this purpose: physical and human assets, knowledge, equity, and, of course, money. Note how the meaning of transaction specificity gets transformed in the process: originally conceived as an incentive to opportunistic behaviour, it has now turned into a guarantee against it.

Thereupon, the concept of trust has been introduced, to assess the dynamic consequences of relying upon such guarantees. Drawing upon exchange theory, the hypothesis has been put forward that in R&D alliances classical contracting tends to produce a spiral of rising distrust; instead of being curbed, opportunism is encouraged. Creating credible commitments, on the other hand, tends to produce a spiral of rising trust, which effectively eliminates risks of opportunistic abuse. Notice that in the process the exchange also gets imbued with moral significance; loyal co-operation ensues. Finally, a case has been made for closely balancing such commitments between partners; only then, are these effectively tied to each other. If partners to an alliance co-operate on equal terms, this amounts to matching commitments. If, however, inequality obtains between partners, creating a balance is more difficult; it might be easiest to let the stronger party take the lead.

On the whole, the focus on enforceable commitments as transactional guarantees has been a fruitful one. Along the way, many allegations and speculations have been put forward. The section on reciprocity, in particular, contains several controversial arguments. To put all of these to the test, more empirical evidence should urgently be amassed.

REFERENCES

Alster, N. 1986. 'Dealbusters: Why Partnerships Fail'. *Electronic Business*. 1 April: 70–5.

Blau, P. M. 1964. *Exchange and Power in Social Life*. New York: John Wiley and Sons.

Blumberg, B. F. 1993. 'The Management of R&D Alliances'. ISCORE paper no. 9. Faculty of Social Sciences, University of Utrecht.

Buckley, P. J., and Casson, M. 1988. 'A Theory of Cooperation in International Business'. In Contractor and Lorange 1988: 31–53.

Chakravarthy, B. S., and Lorange, P. 1991. *Managing the Strategy Process: A Framework for a Multibusiness Firm*. Englewood Cliffs, NJ: Prentice Hall.

Contractor, F. J., and Lorange, P. (eds.) 1988. *Cooperative Strategies in International Business*. Lexington, Mass.: Lexington Books.

Corzine, R. 1991. 'Acquisition Alternatives'. *Dealwatch, the KPMG Report on International Business Transactions*. 2: 21–7.

Dasgupta, P. 1988. 'Trust as a Commodity'. In Gambetta 1988b: 49–72.

De Laat, P. B. 1990. *Een Kwestie van Vertrouwen: Sociale Effecten van de Invoering van Matrixstructuren in R&D-Organisaties*. Groningen: Wolters-Noordhoff.

Deutsch, M. 1962. 'Cooperation and Trust: Some Theoretical Notes'. In Jones, M. R. (ed.). *Nebraska Symposium on Motivation*. 275–319. Lincoln, Nebr.: University of Nebraska Press.

Dickson, K., Lawton Smith, H., and Smith, S. L. 1991. 'Bridge over Troubled Waters? Problems and Opportunities in Interfirm Research Collaboration'. *Technology Analysis and Strategic Management*. 3: 143–56.

Dodgson, M. 1993. *Technological Collaboration in Industry: Strategy, Policy and Internationalization in Innovation*. London: Routledge.

Fox, A. 1974. *Beyond Contract: Work, Power and Trust Relations*. London: Faber and Faber.

Freeman, C. 1991. 'Networks of Innovators: A Synthesis of Research Issues'. *Research Policy*. 20: 499–514.

Galanter, M. 1981. 'Justice in Many Rooms: Courts, Private Ordering, and Indigenous Law'. *Journal of Legal Pluralism*. 19: 1–47.

Gambetta, D. 1988a. 'Can We Trust Trust?' In Gambetta 1988b: 213–37.

——1988*b* (ed.) *Trust: Making and Breaking Cooperative Relations*. Oxford and New York: Basil Blackwell.

Gouldner, A. W. 1960. 'The Norm of Reciprocity: A Preliminary Statement'. *American Sociological Review*. 25 (2): 161–78.

Hagedoorn, J., and Schakenraad, J. 1990. 'Inter-Firm Partnerships and Co-operative Strategies in Core Technologies'. In Freeman, C., and Soete, L. (eds.). *New Explorations in the Economics of Technical Change*. 1–37. London: Pinter.

—— —— 1992. 'Leading Companies and Networks of Strategic Alliances in Information Technologies'. *Research Policy*. 21: 163–90.

Hamel, G. 1991. 'Competition for Competence and Inter-Partner Learning within International Strategic Alliances'. *Strategic Management Journal*. 12 (S): 83–103.

——Doz, Y. L., and Prahalad, C. K. 1989. 'Collaborate with Your Competitors—and Win'. *Harvard Business Review*. 67 (1): 133–9.

Harrigan, K. R. 1988. 'Strategic Alliances and Partner Asymmetries'. In Contractor and Lorange 1988: 205–26.

Helm, L., and Cowan, A. L. 1985. 'IBM Wins the Key to Japan's High-Tech Labs'. *Business Week*. 19 August: 48.

Hennart, J.-F. 1988. 'A Transaction Costs Theory of Equity Joint Ventures'. *Strategic Management Journal*. 9: 361–74.

Hladik, K. J. 1988. 'R&D and International Joint Ventures'. In Contractor and Lorange 1988: 187–203.

——and Linden, L. H. 1989. 'Is an International Joint Venture in R&D for You?' *Research-Technology Management*. 32 (4): 11–13.

Kanter, R. M. 1989. *When Giants Learn to Dance: Mastering the Challenges of Strategy, Management, and Careers in the 1990s*. New York: Simon and Schuster.

Kleinknecht, A., and Reynen, J. O. N. 1992. 'Why Do Firms Cooperate on R&D? An Empirical Study'. *Research Policy*. 21: 347–60.

Kogut, B. 1988*a*. 'Joint Ventures: Theoretical and Empirical Perspectives'. *Strategic Management Journal*. 9: 319–32.

——1988*b*. 'A Study of the Life Cycle of Joint Ventures'. In Contractor and Lorange 1988: 169–85.

——1989. 'The Stability of Joint Ventures: Reciprocity and Competitive Rivalry'. *The Journal of Industrial Economics*. 38: 183–98.

Lawton Smith, H., Dickson, K., and Smith, S. L. 1991. ' "There Are Two Sides to Every Story": Innovation and Collaboration within Networks of Large and Small Firms'. *Research Policy*. 20: 457–68.

Lei, D., and Slocum Jr., J. W. 1992. 'Global Strategy, Competence-Building and Strategic Alliances'. *California Management Review*. 35: 81–97.

Levine, J. B., and Byrne, J. A. 1986. 'Corporate Odd Couples: Beware the Wrong Partner'. *Business Week*. 21 July: 98–103.

Lewis, J. D. 1990. *Partnerships for Profit: Structuring and Managing Strategic Alliances*. New York: Free Press.

Link, A., and Tassey, G. 1989. *Cooperative Research and Development: The Industry-University-Government Relationship*. Boston: Kluwer Academic Publishers.

Lorenz, E. H. 1988. 'Neither Friends nor Strangers: Informal Networks of Subcontracting in French Industry'. In Gambetta 1988*b*: 194–210.

Lyles, M. A. 1987. 'Common Mistakes of Joint Venture Experienced Firms'. *Columbia Journal of World Business*. 22 (2): 79–85.

Macaulay, S. 1963. 'Non-Contractual Relations in Business: A Preliminary Study'. *American Sociological Review.* 28: 55–67.

Macneil, I. R. 1978. 'Contracts: Adjustment of Long-Term Economic Relations under Classical, Neoclassical, and Relational Contract Law'. *Northwestern University Law Review.* 72: 854–905.

Mangematin, V. 1996. 'The Simultaneous Shaping of Organization and Technology within Cooperative Agreements'. In Coombs, R., Richards, A., Saviotti, P., and Walsh, V. (eds.). *Technological Collaboration: The Dynamics of Cooperation in Industrial Innovation.* 119–41. Cheltenham: Edward Elgar.

Mowery, D. C. 1989. 'Collaborative Ventures between U.S. and Foreign Manufacturing Firms'. *Research Policy.* 18: 19–32.

Nayak, P. R., and Ketteringham, J. M. 1993. *Breakthroughs!* New and expanded edition. Didcot: Mercury.

Niosi, J. 1993. 'Strategic Partnerships in Canadian Advanced Materials'. *R&D Management.* 23: 17–27.

—— and Bergeron, M. 1992. 'Technical Alliances in the Canadian Electronics Industry: An Empirical Analysis'. *Technovation.* 12: 309–22.

Ohmae, K. 1989. 'The Global Logic of Strategic Alliances'. *Harvard Business Review.* 67 (2): 143–54.

Onida, F., and Malerba, F. 1989. 'R&D Cooperation between Industry, Universities and Research Organizations in Europe'. *Technovation.* 9: 131–95.

Osborn, R. N., and Baughn, C. C. 1990. 'Forms of Interorganizational Governance for Multinational Alliances'. *Academy of Management Journal.* 33: 503–19.

Peck, M. J. 1986. 'Joint R&D: The Case of Microelectronics and Computer Technology Corporation'. *Research Policy.* 15: 219–31.

Pisano, G. P., Shan, W., and Teece, D. J. 1988. 'Joint Ventures and Collaboration in the Biotechnology Industry'. In Mowery, D. (ed.). *International Collaborative Ventures in U.S. Manufacturing.* 183–222. Cambridge, Mass.: Ballinger.

Pucik, V. 1988. 'Strategic Alliances with the Japanese: Implications for Human Resource Management'. In Contractor and Lorange 1988: 487–98.

Raub, W., and Weesie, J. 1991. 'The Management of Matches: Decentralized Mechanisms for Cooperative Relations with Applications to Organizations and Households'. ISCORE paper no. 1. Faculty of Social Sciences, University of Utrecht.

Riedle, K. 1989. 'Demand for R&D Activities and the Trade Off between In-House and External Research: A Viewpoint from Industry with Reference to Large Companies and Small- and Medium-Sized Enterprises'. *Technovation.* 9: 213–25.

Saxenian, A. 1991. 'The Origins and Dynamics of Production Networks in Silicon Valley'. *Research Policy.* 20: 423–37.

Schelling, T. C. 1960. *The Strategy of Conflict.* Cambridge, Mass.: Harvard University Press.

Shepard, A. 1987. 'Licensing to Enhance Demand for New Technologies'. *RAND Journal of Economics.* 18: 360–8.

Sitkin, S. B., and Roth, N. L. 1993. 'Explaining the Limited Effectiveness of Legalistic "Remedies" for Trust/Distrust'. *Organization Science.* 4: 367–92.

Souder, W. E., and Nassar, S. 1990. 'Managing R&D Consortia for Success'. *Research/Technology Management.* 33 (September–October): 44–50.

Teece, D. J. 1986. 'Profiting from Technological Innovation: Implications for Integration, Collaboration, Licensing and Public Policy'. *Research Policy.* 15: 285–305.

—— 1988. 'Technological Change and the Nature of the Firm'. In Dosi, G., Freeman, C., Nelson, R., Silverberg, G., and Soete, L. (eds.). *Technical Change and Economic Theory*. 256–81. London: Pinter.

Williamson, O. E. 1985. *The Economic Institutions of Capitalism: Firms, Markets, Relational Contracting*. London and New York: Macmillan.

Zajac, E. J., and Olsen, C. P. 1993. 'From Transaction Cost to Transactional Value Analysis: Implications for the Study of Interorganizational Strategies'. *Journal of Management Studies*. 30: 131–45.

Zand, D. E. 1972. 'Trust and Managerial Problem-Solving'. *Administrative Science Quarterly*. 17: 229–39.

7

An Economic Model of Inter-Firm Networks

MARK CASSON AND HOWARD COX

INTRODUCTION

Advocates of networking often commend networks as being more fair and more democratic than alternative organizational forms. This chapter uses the principles of economic theory to show that they are often more efficient too. It examines the conditions under which a network can be expected to emerge as an efficient institutional solution to a co-ordination problem. This means embedding the analysis of inter-firm networks within a more general economic theory of institutional choice. Implementing such an approach makes it necessary to identify the main alternatives to the network and to explain why, under certain conditions, these alternatives are inferior to the network itself. Identifying these conditions allows us to provide an explanation for why international business networks, which linked together an array of independent firms, developed out of Britain in the nineteenth century.

The chapter proceeds as follows. To begin with, the economic logic of a network linkage is explored, the importance of information flows is recognized, and the role of trust is identified as a key element in allowing for the transmission of reliable information. It is shown that trust can be based either on the rule of law or on moral imperatives. The importance of the distinction between warranted and unwarranted trust is emphasized. The concept of intermediation is then introduced. Intermediation is shown to be of considerable importance in facilitating economic co-ordination across a variety of institutional settings.

An analytical model is then presented to demonstrate the way in which various institutional frameworks deal with the problems of organizing economic transactions. The model identifies the role of an intermediator as a channel of communication and explains the circumstances under which inter-firm networks will emerge as an efficient response to the issue of co-ordination. Finally, the chapter turns to consider the actual operation of a particular form of inter-firm networking arrangements, centred on nineteenth-century Britain, which allowed for the co-ordination of a wide variety of international economic transactions. It identifies the social under-pinnings of these networks, illustrating the important role played by inter-mediators based mainly in the City of London.

CO-ORDINATION AND COMMUNICATION

Networks mean different things to different people. A simple definition of a network is a set of linkages which either directly or indirectly connect every member of a group to every other member of the group. But what is the basic unit from which such groups are formed? And what exactly qualifies as a linkage?

When examining inter-firm networks it may seem obvious to take the firm as the basic unit of analysis, and to study how networks are constructed by linking firms together. But it is actually more useful to focus on indi-vidual plants instead. Following conventional economic usage, the concept of a plant includes not only factory buildings and machinery, but also ware-houses, shops, and any location-specific operation that adds value to the flow of a product. The reason for focusing on the plant level is that the multi-plant firm is an alternative to a network operated by independent single-plant firms. The rationale of a network hinges on why a set of separate firms linked together is superior to a single integrated firm, and this can only be understood by going right down to the plant level (Casson 1992).

However, because of their complexity, inter-plant networks are difficult to describe in literal terms. Complications must be avoided by bold simpli-fications which abstract from inessential characteristics. The difficulty is to know what is essential and what is not. This chapter tackles the issue by using a schematic diagram to summarize the physical flows of resources (goods, services, and so on) between the plants.

The physical configuration of resource flows is dictated mainly by tech-nology. Technology determines what inputs are required in what propor-tions to generate a given output, and whether or not this transformation affords economies of scale. Geography is important too. The location of raw materials and energy inputs relative to final demand governs transport requirements. Geography also determines the main modal options that are available for freight traffic and, together with transport technology, deter-mines how far consignments need to be consolidated and fed into trunk systems before reaching their destination (Casson 1990: Chapter 2).

The study of networks as an organizational mechanism, however, is con-cerned mainly with the contractual aspects, rather than with the physical aspects of these flows. Contractual arrangements are dictated by co-ordination requirements rather than by technology. Decisions taken about the different flows need to be co-ordinated in order to optimize the performance of the network. In the context of this paper, the relevant performance criterion is the value added by network operations as a whole. Co-ordination involves intensive information flows which must occur prior to the flow of resources. At any instant of time the current flow of resources is the result of past co-ordination, whilst the current flow of information relates to future flows of resources. The only information flows that are concerned with current resource flows are those which involve checking that plans are being fulfilled, and rectifying errors when they are not.

In analysing networks it is thus the flow of information needed to coordinate the flow of resources, and not the flow of resources itself, that is crucial. Successful co-ordination depends on intelligible and reliable information flow. Intelligibility requires a common language, compatible communications equipment, and so on, while reliability requires the information exchanged to be accurate and reasonably robust. Because the environment is in a constant state of flux, knowledge must be continually updated if current decisions are to take full account of changes that have just occurred.

Sources of relevant information are widely distributed. Certain people have access to some information before others do, according to where they are based. One reason for this is that information is often generated as a by-product of another activity—thus the production engineer who rectifies faults has privileged information about the kind of design improvements in capital equipment that might be made; the sales assistant may detect a pattern in 'lost sales' which suggests an addition to the product line, and so on.

Such individual items of information are usually of little value unless they are synthesized. It may be impossible to produce the new line which customers want unless design improvements are made in production equipment, for example. Thus information on demand and supply must be combined in order to realize value from them. In economic analysis this is the conventional role of the price mechanism, and such information will be communicated in the form of changing relative prices.

For the price mechanism to work, however, the distribution of ownership must be appropriate to the co-ordination problem concerned. An inappropriate structure will not motivate the honest sharing of information. For example, rival owners may have an incentive to distort information in order to exploit market power. Thus where the owner of an upstream plant and the owner of a downstream plant are locked into a bilateral monopoly, the synthesis of information that is required for the efficient co-ordination of the resource flow may be impaired by mutual misrepresentation in the negotiation of the price. This would not occur if the plants concerned were both under the ownership of a single firm. Thus where price distortion is a serious problem, internalization of the linkage within a firm, that is, common ownership, may be the best solution to the co-ordination problem.

In addition to the issue of the distribution of ownership, the question of security of property rights must also be considered. This means not only that property rights must be well defined, but also that the exchange of rights involved in a contract must be safe. Ownership becomes particularly vulnerable when it changes hands. One approach is simply to restructure the ownership of the plants, as above, so that the product does not change ownership in the course of its flow. This eliminates the incentive to default and is essentially the internalization strategy, in which co-ordination by an integrated firm replaces co-ordination by the market.

The alternative to internalization is to leave ownership unchanged but to design powerful incentives to prevent deception and default. This can be done in two ways. One approach is simply to strengthen the law, to make conventional markets work better. The other is to invoke moral incentives which generate reliable information flows without recourse either to the law or to internalization. Morality can create a climate of interpersonal trust, and it is this climate of trust, it is suggested here, which is the hallmark of the network solution.

Thus in answer to the question raised at the outset, concerning the nature of a network linkage, it may be said that a network linkage is one which relies on a trust between the parties sustained by moral incentives. Thus short-term contracting qualifies as a network phenomenon if the two parties expect to remain loyal to each other, and neither attempts to exploit the other's loyalty by driving too hard a bargain with them. Informal contracts of all kinds, based on a handshake rather than a written agreement, also qualify as network arrangements.

The network may therefore be characterized as a high-trust co-ordination mechanism linking independent owners. In Table 7.1, the two main alternatives to the network, the market and the firm, are characterized as a low-trust mechanism involving independent owners and a mechanism based on integrated ownership, respectively.[1]

---

[1] An interesting point here is that the firm itself can apparently occur in both high-trust and low-trust variants. This is highlighted in Table 7.1, where the contrast in the top line between the market and the network is mirrored in the bottom line by the distinction between the high-trust and low-trust firm. This distinction can be related to a number of distinctions which have been made by other writers. In early twentieth-century Britain, for example, it was common to distinguish between paternalistic (high-trust) and bureaucratic (low-trust) organizations—not just amongst firms, but in public services and government too. McGregor's differentiation of theory X and Y in managerial leadership highlights a similar phenomenon, as does the familiar distinction between US-type and Japanese-type firms (Ouchi 1981; Aoki 1988). This illustrates the important point, which will not be pursued further here, that networks can be found within firms as well as between them. It raises the interesting possibility that firms with high-trust corporate cultures, which network internally, may also be better at networking externally, because the strategies governing internal and external relations are then alike. Conversely, firms that have low-trust corporate cultures may have difficulty participating in inter-firm networks as the principles of networking are not well understood (see the discussion of US-Japanese joint ventures in Casson 1992).

Table 7.1. A simple typology of co-ordinating
mechanisms

Ownership	Interpersonal trust	
	Low	High
Distributed	Market	Network
Consolidated	Low-trust firm	High-trust firm

THE CONCEPT OF TRUST

Several different concepts of trust can be found in the sociological literature. There is, for example, the well-known distinction between calculative
trust and non-calculative trust. There is also the distinction between
resilient trust and fragile trust employed by Ring (see Chapter 5). The
concept of trust employed in this chapter is related to both non-calculative
trust and to resilient trust, but is not completely coincident with either of
them.

Following Casson (1991), this chapter takes an economic approach to
trust, which means that it analyses trust in terms of rational action. Everything is therefore calculative in this context. Unlike most other economic
models, however, this model explicitly recognizes affective as well as material rewards. Affective rewards are morally framed; people reward themselves affectively for doing what they believe to be right and punish
themselves affectively for doing what they believe to be wrong. Morality
therefore provides an incentive structure quite distinct from the material
dimension. In this context calculative trust, as described by sociologists, may
be categorized as trust underpinned by material incentives (e.g. pecuniary
sanctions and rewards), while non-calculative trust is trust underpinned by
moral incentives. It is therefore preferable to distinguish between material
trust and moral trust rather than to invoke a distinction based upon
calculation.

Moral trust is resilient in the sense that it is able to survive occasional
unanticipated outcomes and other setbacks. The strength of moral trust lies
in its social endogeneity. Material trust, on the other hand, is fragile because
it depends for its support on an enforcement system which is exogenous to
the parties engaged in trade. Here, unanticipated outcomes which cannot
be speedily resolved by an effective legal system will quickly undermine
material trust. However, if the law is equipped with effective policing and
a sufficiently punitive set of sanctions, then under these conditions it may
engender stronger trust than moral incentives can. Which is the stronger,
moral or material trust, depends upon which mechanism society has made
the greater investment in.

Reduced to its basics, trust involves a belief that the other person will be honest. Trust is warranted when this belief is true. Trust, whether warranted or not, is vital to any transaction. There is no point in attempting to negotiate a deal with someone who is never likely to fulfil their side of it. Since it takes two to make a deal, mutual trust is required. A deal, once negotiated, will only go through as planned, however, when each party validates the other party's trust in them. Successful transactions therefore depend on warranted trust, and warranted trust must be mutual. For this condition to be met, each party must not only believe the other to be trustworthy, but must also be trustworthy themselves. A social equilibrium then prevails because each party's beliefs about the other are validated, and so there is no reason for them to change their beliefs in the future. If this condition is not satisfied, a trading equilibrium cannot be sustained. This highlights a distinction between warranted and unwarranted trust, which has received insufficient attention in the literature.

The thrust of this chapter can now be stated in the following way: the basic relation upon which networks are built is a relation of mutual warranted moral trust. The situation is illustrated in Table 7.2.

The two main alternative mechanisms, based on material and moral incentives, are indicated by the two columns, whilst the distinction between warranted and unwarranted trust is indicated by the two rows. Each type of mechanism is associated with a distinctive kind of investment: an investment in monitoring and the enforcement of sanctions in the case of the material mechanism, and investment in an 'invisible infrastructure' of social bonds in the case of the moral mechanism. The first is exemplified by the legal system, and by the internal discipline of the hierarchical firm, whilst the second is exemplified by bonding between members of a business élite, or between members of a cohesive management team within a firm.

Table 7.2. A classification of trust

			MECHANISM	
	INVESTMENT		*Material*	*Moral*
		Type of:	Monitoring and sanctions	Moral rhetoric and social bonding
		Level of:		
STATUS	*Unwarranted*	Too little	Defective property rights	Untrustworthy relations
	Warranted	Adequate	Law-based trust	Interpersonal trust

No investment of any kind will generate no trust at all. Too little investment will generate unwarranted trust—those inclined towards an optimistic
view of other people will find themselves the victims of cheating. Once their
trust in other people is betrayed, rational calculation will suggest that it is
better for them not to attempt to trade at all. Too little investment in a legal
system generates a problem of defective property rights, as shown in the
top left-hand quadrant of Table 7.2, whilst too little investment in a social
system leads to untrustworthy social relations, as indicated in the top right
quadrant of Table 7.2. It is only adequate investment in monitoring and
sanctions that creates a viable system of law, as indicated in the bottom left
quadrant, whilst only adequate investment in social infrastructure generates the high-trust relation shown in the bottom right quadrant of Table 7.2.
It is this latter high-trust relation which is the model for the network relation described in this chapter.

THE ROLE OF INTERMEDIATION

One of the obstacles to using moral incentives in support of business transactions is that these mechanisms tend to work best in small, stable, compact
groups. Table 7.3 summarizes the main kinds of group in which such socialization can occur.

Table 7.3. Social groups that support business networks

Institution	Specific economic functions		Affiliation strategy
	Technical training	Moral education	
Family	Passes on tacit business skills useful for self-employment	Provides basic moral teaching	Marry in
	Inheritance system develops useful concentration of business capital	Inculcates respect for age and experience (ambivalent effect)	Become an adopted protégé
Church	Reading of scriptures improves literacy	Ligitimates morality	Conversion
		Encourages concept of personal accountability to ancestors, God, etc. as well as to peers Perpetuates tradition (ambivalent effect)	

Table 7.3. *continued*

Institution	Specific economic functions		Affiliation strategy
	Technical training	Moral education	
School, university, qualification	Develops analytical decision-making skills	Inculcates loyalty (in both pupils and alumni)	Study to gain entry (where appropriate)
		Emphasizes achievement through hard work	
		Values ability and competence	
Military service	Teaches tactical and engineering skills	Teaches discipline, respect for authority, and how to cope with risky situations	Conscription or volunteering
Trade unions, professional associations, etc.		Promote craftsmanship and professional standards	Gain appropriate work experience
		Values solidarity (ambivalent effect)	
Clubs (sporting, charitable, hobbies, etc.)	Self-improvement through friendly competition	Value of teamwork (in team sports)	Attain sufficient proficiency, respectability, etc. (where appropriate)
	Develops management skills by participating in collective decision-making, etc.	Value of caring (in charitable activities— ambivalent effect)	
Political party	Make contacts linking public and private sectors	Cynical morality— 'the end justifies the means', etc. (negative effect)	Very easy to join
	Acquire 'charismatic leadership' skills by standing as candidate		

It also compares the kind of training in technical skills and moral values that the different groups provide. With some types of group multiple affiliation is possible, but not with others. Thus while a person may switch by conversion from one religion to another, they cannot credibly adhere to two different religions at the same time; by changing affiliation they distance themselves from the group to which they originally belonged. On the other hand, a person can quite credibly belong to two different local clubs or societies, and may indeed perform a valuable service in brokering between what might otherwise be two non-overlapping social groups.

Multiple affiliation is important in the development of business networks by entrepreneurs. The wider the range of an individual's affiliations, the greater will be his or her personal network of trusted contacts. This applies particularly to people with varied work experience and leisure interests ('playing hard' may be just as strategically important as working hard where the 'networked' entrepreneur is concerned). There is, of course, a trade-off between breadth and depth of attachments: people who change jobs frequently, or spread their leisure time thinly across several societies, are unlikely to become as strongly bonded to their colleagues as those who maintain steady allegiance to a small number of social groups. So far as business networking is concerned, however, a wide range of relatively superficial attachments can always be strengthened by subsequent social contact in the course of business negotiations.

In order for a social network to support a business network it is necessary for the members of the social network to be in place where the business operations require them. The economic logic of the business network will normally dictate where members of the social network need to be placed, rather than the other way round. If a social network is to fulfil a business role, its members therefore need to display a degree of mobility. The mobility required to operate an international network is, of course, much greater than that required for, say, a purely local one. It may be questioned whether a social network can really be effective over long distances, because opportunities for face-to-face contact will be very limited. The answer is that many of the social networks used for business purposes came into existence when people who were once together disperse. The school and the local community, for example, effect emotional bonding before a person's business career begins. The emotional intensity of togetherness amongst young people may be sufficient to bind them together for a considerable time after they have left school. Once they have revitalized their association for business purposes, the limited contact experienced in the normal course of business dealings may then be sufficient to keep the bond intact indefinitely.

One way of interpreting the role of the social groups illustrated in Table 7.3 is to say that they provide a mechanism through which their members may establish high-trust interpersonal relations. There may be cases, however, where members of different groups may stand to benefit from forming high-trust business links based on moral trust. In these cases an intermediator, in the form of a reputable individual who holds multiple affiliation, may be a way of extending the role of trust beyond the immediate group members.

Intermediation of this kind can take a variety of forms. In order to sustain trade, for example, the intermediator may buy a good from a seller and resell it to a buyer. This can build a chain of trust between the buyer and the seller where no direct trust exists between them. The buyer does not trust the seller to supply high quality goods. The buyer trusts the intermediator, however, because of the intermediator's reputation, whilst the intermediator has sanctions over the seller that the buyer does not. Trade can therefore proceed because quality assurance is provided by the intervention of the intermediator in the trade.

Intermediation is important in other ways as well. It was noted at the outset that successful co-ordination normally depends upon a synthesis of information. This process of synthesis often benefits from intermediation. The intermediator specializes in the task of combining information from diverse sources. This reduces the overall cost of co-ordination. Having effected a synthesis, the intermediator can then feed back to the appropriate parts of the system the particular information needed to ensure harmonization. Intermediation is a very general method of improving co-ordination. Unlike internalization, discussed earlier, which is concerned specifically with the replacement of a market by a firm, intermediation is relevant to all three modes of co-ordination—the firm, the market, and the network.

SCHEMATIC REPRESENTATION OF NETWORKS

This section extends the simple scheme for the representation of business systems used in Casson (1992) to examine strategic issues connected with networks. It begins by considering the problems which may arise in using the price mechanism to co-ordinate business transactions. It then considers the way in which the alternative mechanisms of the firm (formal internalization) and the network are able to perform the co-ordinating role. Using this framework, the chapter then illustrates why the network approach was especially appropriate for the co-ordination of Britain's international business networks in the nineteenth century.

The starting-point for the analysis of co-ordination mechanisms, as suggested above, is at the plant level where the basic linkage is that of product flow. The left-hand side of Fig. 7.1 illustrates a system comprising four plants.

A plant is indicated by a square, and is identified by a number. The flow

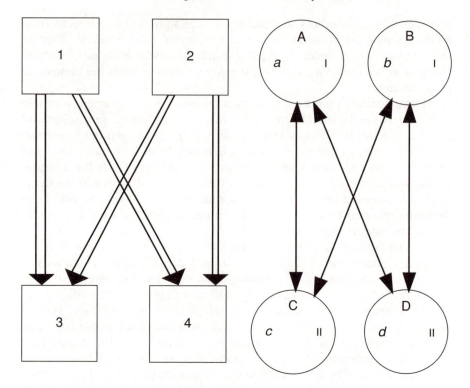

Fig. 7.1. Resource flows and information flows

of a product between the plants is shown by a double line, with the direction of flow indicated by an arrow. The figure shows two upstream plants, 1 and 2, located in Britain, which supply intermediate products to two downstream plants, 3 and 4, located abroad. The upstream plants may in turn receive raw materials from other plants at an earlier stage of the sequence. Likewise, the downstream plants will either supply a further stage of production, or sell to final consumers instead. These other flows are not illustrated because they are not part of the system being analysed. Since almost any system can be thought of as being part of a larger system, the use of artificial boundaries to limit the field of analysis in this way is usually unavoidable.[2]

Thus, in Fig. 7.1 the downstream plants 3 and 4 receive complementary inputs from the upstream plants 1 and 2. Each downstream plant may be a mining concern, for example, procuring two inputs from specialized pro-

---

[2] It is assumed that there is normally a flow of money payments in the opposite direction whenever the plants involved are owned by different firms (or, in the case of joint ventures, by a different consortium of firms). Equally, it is assumed that notional payments are only involved if the plants are owned by the same firms (or the same consortium of firms).

ducer good manufacturers. The first input is produced in plant 1; its supplies to plants 3 and 4 are substitutes for each other. The second input is produced in plant 2; its supplies to 3 and 4 are also substitutes for each other. When the plants are independently owned, this pattern of complementarity and substitution creates two markets, one for each input. The role of the network is to operate these markets more efficiently than ordinary impersonal mechanisms would do.

Each downstream firm has the job of seeing that the inputs are combined in suitable proportions, and of bidding for these inputs to their upstream suppliers. In turn, the upstream firms must decide how much of their product to supply to each of their downstream customers. If all the plants had a single common owner, then the co-ordination of product flow would be an internal affair. Whether internal or external, however, the co-ordination process involves a two-way information flow which must be completed before the products can be delivered.

Information flows connected with co-ordination are indicated by a single line. An arrow at either end of the line indicates that the flow is two-way. Information, however, flows between people; for this reason, people are distinguished from plants by the use of a circle rather than a square. A crucial feature of the scheme set out in this paper is that information flows used for co-ordination are represented on a separate diagram. They are not superimposed on the representation of the product flows. Thus, in Fig. 7.1 the information flows are represented on the right-hand side of the diagram. The figure illustrates four individuals each linked to two of the others by a two-way information flow.

Not only does separation make the diagrams more intelligible to the eye; it also facilitates a full recognition of the fact that information flows between people rather than the plants themselves. The information flows mainly to and from people who make decisions. These people are, in turn, often motivated to make good decisions by having ownership of a particular plant. But the relationship between individuals and plants is certainly not one to one in general. For example, the person who makes day-to-day decisions about a plant may be a manager employed for this purpose by the owner of the firm. Thus it is positively misleading in many instances to draw information flows as if they go from plant to plant, rather than from one person to another.

Individuals are identified by lower case letters and the firm for whom they work by upper case letters. If the same letter is used to identify both an individual and a firm, then it means that the individual is the sole owner of the firm. In order to match up the resource flow scheme with the information flow scheme, it is necessary to identify which particular individual controls which plant. In Fig. 7.1 this is done visually. Individuals and plants that occupy the same position in the figure are assumed to be related, in the sense that the plant is controlled by the individual concerned. For example, if the right-hand diagram were superimposed on the left-hand diagram, then individual a (the owner of firm A) would overlay plant 1, and this is taken to indicate that he or she controls it. Individuals who do not control any plant are positioned in the information flow diagram so that they would not overlay any plant in the resource flow diagram.

The scheme also identifies the social relations which exist between the individuals who are involved in the process of information exchange. The lower case letters (denoting the individual located at the plant) are followed by a roman numeral, indicating the social group to which the individual belongs, or a string of numerals in the case of multiple membership of groups. An ordinary roman numeral indicates a fully integrated group in which every member trusts every other member not to default. A roman numeral followed by a plus or minus indicates a subgroup; a minus indicates a low-status subgroup and a plus indicates a high-status élite. The members of the high-status group have a reputation with the members of the low-status group (and with each other), which means that they are trusted by everyone in the group, whereas the members of the low-status group are not trusted by the élite of the group. Members of a high-status élite are not trusted by anyone outside the group to which they belong.

The central issue to be explored in the information flow diagram is the accuracy of the information exchanged. Accurate and undistorted flows of information will be characteristic of intra-firm flows created through the internalization of markets. It will also be a feature of information exchange between parties who trust each other because they belong to a well-defined social group. A situation of undistorted information flows is indicated by attaching a second arrowhead to a line of information flow. This means that the sender will supply information which is as accurate as possible, either because the two parties are part of the same firm or because they trust one another. If information flows are neither intra-firm nor intra-group, then information may be unreliable and co-ordination will suffer as a result.

INTEGRATION AND INTERMEDIATION

The main value of these conventions is that they facilitate a detailed comparison of alternative sets of contractual arrangements which may underpin a given set of physical resource transactions. Not all possible arrangements can be compared, however, because there are just too many of them. This section follows an informal step-wise approach which investigates a sequence of arrangements, each of which has the potential to improve upon its predecessor.

The starting-point is a critique of the contractual arrangements portrayed on the right-hand side of Fig. 7.1. The diagram assumes that co-ordination depends upon information flows between people from different social groups (I and II) who do not display moral trust in one another. If the costs of using the price mechanism are substantial due to market imperfections, then internalization theory suggests that the natural response will be vertical integration.

Integration can be effected either forwards or backwards. The downstream producers are more vulnerable than the upstream producers in the sense that they combine two complementary inputs, so that a shortage of either one could seriously disrupt production. The upstream producers, on the other hand, each face two sources of demand for their product, so that if one declines there may well be scope to expand supplies to the other. It therefore seems reasonable to assume that, on balance, backward integration is more likely than forward integration in this case.

There is a difficulty, however, in that both the downstream firms cannot acquire outright ownership of both upstream firms. If one of them did succeed in acquiring both, then this firm would be able to hold the other firm to ransom by threatening to cut off its supplies. If, on the other hand, they each acquired one of the firms, then each would be able to hold the other to ransom. Thus the left-hand diagram in Fig. 7.2 illustrates a scenario in which the owners of firms C and D, who belong to social group II, form a partnership to jointly take control of firms A and B. The information flows between the four individuals now take place under common ownership and are thus reliable.

If c and d do not belong to the same social group, however, then such a partnership will not be viable. In this case nothing short of full integration will do. In principle, any one of the four firms could take the initiative to do this. Nevertheless, it is more useful to introduce a fifth player, e, whose firm E would take over the other four. Individual e then intermediates between a, b, c, and d, who become employee managers of their plants, reporting to a headquarters run by e. What is important here is to illustrate that gains from internalization can be reaped by an agent who is not directly involved in the actual process of physical product flow. This is illustrated in the right-hand diagram of Fig. 7.2.

This internalization-based solution to the problem of market imperfections may be contrasted with the network arrangement which would be possible if all the independent owners were members of the same social group. Such a situation is illustrated in the left-hand diagram of Fig. 7.3. All the lines now carry double arrows. Everyone trusts everyone else and coordination proceeds smoothly: everyone compromises over price and no one ever defaults.

Although the case of the overseas Chinese in South East Asia provides examples of such network arrangements (Redding 1990), such harmony between buyers and sellers is somewhat unusual because buyers and sellers typically belong to different social groups. In the absence of such social homogeneity, what is required to sustain the network of trust is a

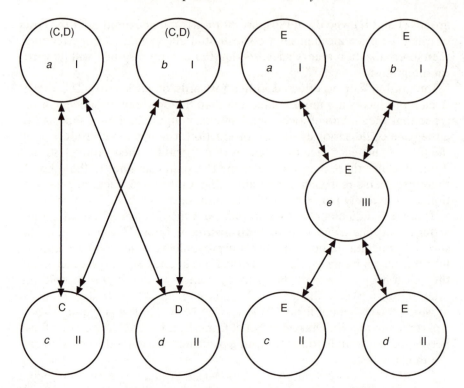

Fig. 7.2. Two internalization-based solutions to market imperfections

middleman who belongs to two or more social groups. Such dual membership creates a chain of trust linking pairs of producers who could not otherwise trust each other. This is the role played by the middleman, *e*, in the
middle diagram of Fig. 7.3.

Middlemen typically engage in trade continuously, whilst the customers
and suppliers with whom they trade often do so only intermittently Thus
middlemen tend to acquire a reputation which others lack. They become a
social élite, in the sense that they are trusted by others, and by each other,
but do not necessarily trust those with whom they trade. Such a situation is
illustrated in the right-hand diagram of Fig. 7.3, where the social groups I
and II have each been split into two subgroups, one comprising a reputable
élite and the other comprising the rest of the group. The middleman, *e*,
belongs to the élites of both I and II, and is therefore trusted by buyers and
sellers alike.

Comparing the left-hand and right-hand diagrams in Fig. 7.3 highlights
the significance of intermediation so far as networks are concerned. It shows

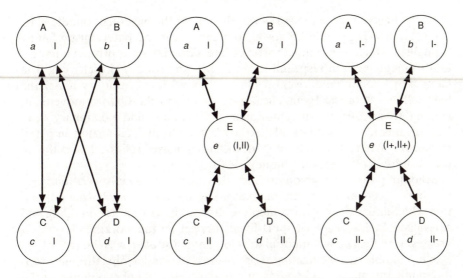

Fig. 7.3. Intermediation based on dual group membership and élite status

that a reputable intermediator can successfully overcome the problems of social segmentation without himself needing to trust any of the people with whom he deals. All that is required is his membership of an élite and that this be recognized by both the groups concerned.

The other point to re-emphasize is that the channelling of information through the intermediator does not necessarily require the channelling of the product through the intermediator's hands as well. In some cases the intermediator does indeed handle the product (as with most retail outlets), but in other cases, such as the merchant houses described in the example below, they do not.

BRITAIN'S NINETEENTH-CENTURY INTERNATIONAL BUSINESS NETWORKS

It was suggested earlier that investment in social institutions would reduce the cost of networking relative to other forms of co-ordination. Late Victorian Britain invested heavily in social institutions of the kind listed in Table 7.3, and these institutions provided the basis for international business networks which linked together the activities of independent firms. Thus, although they were not specifically tailored to the promotion of imperial development, these institutions indirectly served the cause of international business by creating a climate in which long-distance clusters of inter-firm networks could flourish.

At the heart of these networks was the family, the bastion of middle-class respectability. It provided a social foundation for the paternalistic family capitalism which was characteristic of late Victorian enterprise. An important ritual element in respectable family life was Sunday churchgoing. The Church of England underwent a spiritual revival in mid-century, under the twin influences of the Evangelical movement and the Oxford movement, leading to an upsurge in emotional commitment and missionary zeal. Indeed, missionary activity played a major role in legitimizing imperial expansion. Where trade developed, the missionaries followed, and this in turn fostered colonization (Stanley 1990).

Schooling was also high on the Victorian agenda. Compulsory attendance was introduced, and new schools built to accommodate a growing population. The Sunday School movement, reinforced by city church-building and revivalism, had a major (if short-lived) impact on the working classes. Of greatest significance for imperial development, however, was the role of the public schools in inculcating the virtues of leadership through self-discipline. Intense social bonding at school created the phenomenon of the 'old school tie'—an allegiance formed in youth which could be exploited for business purposes throughout a person's career (Jones 1993: 44–5). The school, the church, and the family all provided links between those in the colonies and those at home, allowing business transactions to proceed in a high-trust atmosphere even though the parties concerned were thousands of miles apart.

The role of the armed forces should not be overlooked either. Many explorers and business adventurers had a military background and could use these connections to raise capital when suitable opportunities arose, so that the military represented a significant group among the shareholders in imperial enterprises (Davis and Huttenback 1988: 162–82). The armed forces themselves were glamorised by their part in the rituals of imperialism. Whig historians placed the military successes of the early nineteenth century into a broader context of national progress. Parallels were drawn between the economic and social progress under Queen Victoria and the national revival under Queen Elizabeth three centuries earlier.

This sense of continuity with the past was not, however, purely subjective. Cain and Hopkins (1993) have formally charted the significant continuity of the British élite during this time. In late Victorian Britain this élite intermediated across a powerful international network which channelled capital raised in London into a vast number of business opportunities overseas.

Through the course of the nineteenth century, it was the service sector of the British economy in general, and the financial service sector in particular, which exerted an increasing influence on the shape of Britain's economic development (Rubinstein 1993). Despite the wealth generated in the north of England by the rapid growth of industrial production during the first half of the nineteenth century, important elements of the landed aristocracy succeeded in reconsolidating their dominant economic status through the development of financial and mercantile activities grouped around the south-east of the country. In transferring the basis of its power from the ownership of land to the control of finance, this aristocratic élite succeeded in creating, in Cain and Hopkins's terminology, a regime of 'Gentlemanly Capitalism' which dominated the subsequent pattern of Britain's international economic relations. As these writers explain, the members of this group exhibited a strong degree of cultural homogeneity, providing an ideal terrain in which to germinate interpersonal business linkages.

High finance, like high farming, called for leadership from 'opinion-makers' and trust from associates and dependants. A gentleman possessed the qualities needed to inspire confidence; and because his word was his bond, transactions were both informal and efficient. Shared values, nurtured by a common education and religion, provided a blueprint for social and business behaviour. The country house led to the counting house; the public school fed the service sector; the London club supported the City. Gentlemanly enterprise was strongly personal, and was sustained by a social network which, in turn, was held together by the leisure needed to cultivate it (Cain and Hopkins 1993: 36).

Augmenting these indigenous social networks were a variety of continental elements attracted to London as the commercial centre of the world. By the latter half of the nineteenth century, the networks fostered within the City had become sufficiently dispersed internationally to be considered as representing a cosmopolitan bourgeoisie (Jones 1987).

Together with their role of financing and facilitating international commodity trade, these mercantile groups also began to engage in international investment, notably through the promotion of so-called free-standing companies. According to Wilkins (1988: 261), during the period under consideration the free-standing company was probably the most typical mode of British direct investment abroad and was the form in which much investment previously considered as portfolio in nature was actually transferred.

Free-standing companies were joint-stock companies, registered in Britain (usually in London, but occasionally in Scotland) and with capital denominated in sterling, but which were designed to finance investment in a productive venture overseas (Casson 1994). They were free-standing in the sense that they were not developed in relation to any parallel operation within Britain itself, unlike the overseas subsidiaries of a conventional multinational corporation. Both the range of countries and the economic activities in which they were involved varied widely; with respect to the latter, Wilkins points out that free-standing companies were to be found in agriculture, timber, cattle raising, mining, oil production, manufacturing, transportation, public utilities, banking, land mortgages, and land development.

The central actor in the formation of a free-standing company was the promoter. Promoters were individuals with connections abroad, or the staff of City institutions such as merchant banks, or what Chapman (1985) has termed 'investment groups'. One merchant bank which helped to promote a cluster of free-standing companies in the mining industry was Rothschilds, which was instrumental in the formation of a mining engineering consultancy company called the Exploration Company. During the 1890s, the officers of the Exploration Company promoted many new mining concerns that were formed to exploit the growing number of mineral discoveries which became viable following the development of deep-mine technology (Turrell and van Helten 1986). Thus, during the late nineteenth century many of the operations which made up the international mining industry took the form of intermediated networks rather than integrated multinational corporations.

The clustering of individual free-standing companies around a particular merchant house created a set of inter-firm linkages that afforded scope economies in marketing and in the use of information regarding the level of reserves. In fact, clustering was a phenomenon which represented a hallmark of free-standing companies. The recurrence of the same providers of legal and accounting services in the promotion of the companies, for example, is a feature that provides important empirical evidence of the networking tendency displayed by this form of international economic coordination. Wilkins has noted, for example, that certain firms of solicitors (such as Ashurst's, Linklater's, and Freshfield's) were used frequently for the purposes of establishing free-standing companies. The services of a select group of accountants were utilized both for verifying accounts and auditing overseas operations in a quasi-management role. Mining engineering companies, such as Bewick, Moreing & Co., and John Taylor and Sons, provided many of the extractive-based free-standing companies with engineering and management services (Wilkins 1988: 266).

The board of directors of free-standing companies often included the representatives of indigenous firms from the industry in question. This gave investors confidence in the enterprise being promoted, and allowed domestic entrepreneurs the opportunity to 'go abroad' without relocating their own enterprises. Thus another clustering of firms tended to revolve around individuals with links to particular industries.

Thus an important function of the free-standing company is that it provided an alternative for British-based firms to international vertical integration. As such, it provided a means of international integration through a mixture of contractual arrangements, but one which featured recurring groups of connected individuals, rather than the impersonal links of the market process or the administrative hierarchies of the corporate firm.

Using the conventions set out in the previous two sections, Fig. 7.4 shows the role of the promoter, e, based in a London financial institution, E, as an

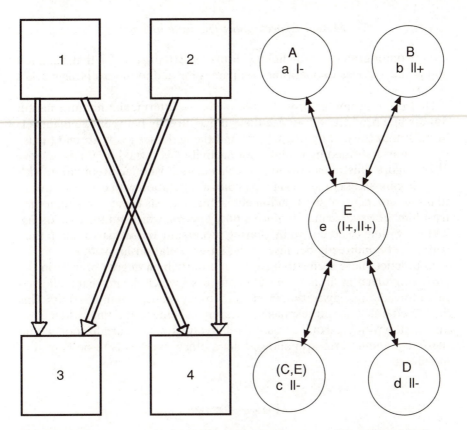

Fig. 7.4. Stylized representation of late nineteenth-century international business network

Notes
1. Capital equipment factory in Midlands or North of England owned by Co. A.
2. Professional practice of consulting engineers, solicitors, accountants, etc., owned by Co. B.
3. South African mine owned jointly by Co. C and Co. E.
4. Latin American plantation owned by Co. D.

a British industrialist.
b Senior partner in professional practice.
c Colonial expatriate.
d British-educated member of local social élite.
e Promoter, e.g. partner in London-based financial institution.

A British manufacturing firm producing capital equipment.
B Professional partnership of accountants, etc.
C Free-standing firm operating a mine in South Africa, part owned by London-based financial institution, E.
D Free-standing firm operating a plantation in Latin America.
E London-based financial institution engaged in company promotions.

I–   New middle class formed by entrepreneurial craftsmen and their descendants.
II– Poorer gentlemen who socialized with élite gentlemen at English public school.
I+, II+ Wealthy élite drawn from both middle and upper classes including aristocratic financiers, assimilated immigrants, and 'self-made' men.

intermediating mechanism linking firms in Britain (A, B) that supplied goods and services to operating companies located in the overseas market (C, D).

Hence the promoter provides the means of intermediating information flows, while product and service flows move directly between the plants (1, 2) in Britain (owned by firms A, B) and the activities (3, 4) abroad (activity 3 is jointly owned by C and E and activity 4 is owned by D).

The figure illustrates how individuals c and d, who lack reputation with a and b, gain access to them via e, who has a reputation with everyone owing to his membership of the London élite. Since e trusts c and d less than they trust him, however, e may require equity control, which (in the case of Fig. 7.4) c is willing to accede to by sharing ownership. Individuals a and b then trust c and d indirectly because of the latter's relationship with e.

In practice there seems to have been a fairly high degree of trust in the parties involved in firms C and D in any case, which meant that e allowed them considerable discretion in the day-to-day management of affairs. This facilitated efficient and responsive local management at a time when communication with head office was still relatively slow. Decentralization within the free-standing firm also allowed head office overheads to be kept to a minimum.

CONCLUSION

This chapter has attempted to explore how the existence of interpersonal networks which straddled national boundaries provided the basis for international business networks during the nineteenth century. The development of these networks involved the creation of a large number of independent free-standing companies which were floated in the UK but which actually operated in countries abroad. The setting-up, financing, and provisioning of these free-standing companies relied upon the ability of key actors in Britain to play the role of intermediator, and thus to co-ordinate independent firms abroad with the appropriate economic agents in the metropolitan country. These intermediators were able to perform this function because they held influential positions in a range of the social networks which were a hallmark of Britain's, and especially London's, nineteenth-century economic structure.

During the twentieth century, these networks increasingly gave way to the internalized managerial structures of the industry-specific multinational corporations. To date, the general failure of such networks to hold sway after 1914 has been attributed by US business historians to the functional shortcomings of this specific institutional form—especially its inability to transfer adequate managerial know-how (Wilkins 1988; Chandler 1990). On the contrary, the analysis of this chapter leads us to suggest that the explanation for their general demise needs to be sought in the changing international social relations which arose in the wake of World War I, rather than as a result of any purely functional shortcomings stemming from this particular organizational form.

In concluding, it is clear that the example of Britain's international inter-firm networks represents only one of many instances of the business network phenomenon, and that this institutional form has experienced a resurgence over recent years. In contrast to many of the more contemporary examples of inter-firm business networks which are discussed in this book, those described above tended to be founded upon social institutions and networks which already existed, such as the family and Britain's school system. Of the more recent examples, it has tended to be the existence of ongoing inter-firm relations which themselves have facilitated interpersonal relationships. Upon these interpersonal relationships many new instances of inter-firm networks have been founded. As in the past, however, they rely for their efficacy upon the existence of bonds of moral trust between the participants.

Clearly, the specific social circumstances of networks will vary over space and time, and their sociological implications can usefully be studied on a case-by-case basis. What this chapter has attempted to do is to illustrate that there are general economic principles which allow networks to be understood purely as an efficient institutional response to the problem of co-ordination. Whilst one implication of this analysis is that economists are no longer able to proceed on the assumption that economic transactions can be studied as if social relations between the participants do not matter, the basic analytical framework of economic theory remains well equipped to provide a rigorous explanation of the network phenomenon.

REFERENCES

Aoki, M. 1988. *Information, Incentives, and Bargaining in the Japanese Economy.* Cambridge: Cambridge University Press.

Cain, P. J., and Hopkins, A. G. 1993. *British Imperialism: Innovation and Expansion 1688–1914.* London: Longman.

Casson, M. C. 1990. *Enterprise and Competitiveness: A Systems View of International Business.* Oxford: Clarendon Press.

——1991. *Economics of Business Culture: Game Theory, Transaction Costs and Economic Performance.* Oxford: Clarendon Press.

——1992. 'Internalization Theory and Beyond'. In Buckley, P. J. (ed.). *New Directions in International Business Research: Priorities for the 1990s.* 4–27. Aldershot: Edward Elgar.

——1994. 'Institutional Diversity in Overseas Enterprise: Explaining the Free-Standing Company'. *Business History*. 36 (4): 95–108.

Chandler, A. D. 1990. *Scale and Scope: The Dynamics of Industrial Capitalism*. Cambridge, Mass.

Chapman, S. D. 1985. 'British-Based Investment Groups before 1914'. *Economic History Review*. 2nd series. 38: 230–51.

Davis, L. E., and Huttenback, R. A. 1988. *Mammon and the Pursuit of Empire: The Economics of British Imperialism*. Cambridge: Cambridge University Press.

Jones, C. A. 1987. *International Business in the Nineteenth Century: The Rise and Fall of a Cosmopolitan Bourgeoisie*. Brighton: Wheatsheaf Books.

Jones, G. 1993. 'British Multinational Banking Strategies over Time'. In Cox, H., Clegg, J., and Ietto-Gillies, G. (eds.). *The Growth of Global Business*. 38–61. London: Routledge.

Ouchi, W. 1981. *Theory Z: How American Business Can Meet the Japanese Challenge*. Reading, Mass.: Addison-Wesley.

Redding, S. G. 1990. *The Spirit of Chinese Capitalism*. Berlin: De Gruyter.

Rubinstein, W. D. 1993. *Capitalism, Culture and Decline in Britain, 1750–1990*. London: Routledge.

Stanley, B. 1990. *Bible and the Flag: Protestant Missions and British Imperialism in the Nineteenth and Twentieth Centuries*. Leicester: Apollos.

Turrell, R. V., and van Helten, J.-J. 1986. 'The Rothschilds, the Exploration Company and Mining Finance'. *Business History*. 28: 181–205.

Wilkins, M. 1988. 'The Free-standing Company, 1870–1914: An Important Type of British Foreign Direct Investment'. *Economic History Review*. 2nd series. 41: 259–82.

IV

INFORMATION
FLOWS:
The Role of Catalysts

8

Co-ordinating Multi-Firm Innovative Processes: *Entrepreneur as Catalyst in Small-Firm Networks*

ANDREA LIPPARINI AND MAURIZIO SOBRERO

INTRODUCTION

The relationship between firm size and innovation has traditionally generated a vivid debate in the literature. Earlier studies, primarily rooted in economics, were based on the assumption that the increasing costs and complexity of research activities favoured larger firms at the expense of smaller ones (Comanor 1967; Kamien and Schwartz 1975; Mansfield 1963). However, more recent contributions have challenged this perspective both within (Acs and Audretsch 1990) and outside (Tushman and Anderson 1986) the economic tradition. Small and medium-sized firms not only actively contribute to the innovation process, but they frequently represent the natural source of variation required to challenge the structural inertia of larger firms and to foster economic growth.

In particular, small and medium-sized firms seem to be successfully overcoming size constraints by exploiting localized economies. On the one hand, by clustering in geographically limited areas they co-determine complex networks of complementary activities (Miller and Cote 1987; Pyke *et al.* 1990; Ratti 1991; Saxenian 1991), thus generating strong mutual dependence with the external environment (Brüderl and Schüssler 1990; Hannan and Carroll 1992; Pfeffer and Salancik 1978). On the other hand, the set of relationships built up over time indicates the use of alternative organizational forms which go beyond localization effects (Larson 1991, 1992; Lorenzoni and Ornati 1988). The more small and medium-sized firms rely on external relations for the organization of manufacturing, distribution, and even of

Support for this research was provided by MURST 40% 'The Firms between Networks and Districts'. We wish to thank the participants to the workshop, 'Forms of Inter-Organizational Networks: Structures and Processes', European Science Foundation, Berlin, 6–7 September 1993, an anonymous reviewer, and Howard Aldrich for their comments and suggestions. We are particularly grateful to Mark Ebers for his thoughtful critiques which helped us to substantially improve our original ideas. The usual disclaimer applies.

development activities, the more their relational capabilities emerge as key elements for understanding both the sources and dynamics of inter-firm networks.

In this work, we focus on some, possible, explanatory elements for the governance and the co-ordination of small firm networks starting from their relationship activities. We examine relationships between manufacturers and suppliers in two industrial networks in the context of the development of new products, and we explore the role played by entrepreneurs *vis-à-vis* professional management in fostering innovative activities through these external relationships. We suggest that entrepreneurs are an important source of co-ordination within the network, acting both as information catalysts and as promoters of more complex and articulate types of relationships.

Previous studies have primarily focused on the division of labour in manufacturing activities, highlighting the advantages of more flexible and deverticalized production systems (see e.g. Piore and Sabel 1984). It was claimed that global scale effects were achieved through the fragmentation of the whole process in locally efficient units, operating at lower, minimum efficient, scale levels and moving, incrementally, along the path of innovation by means of small, minor improvements. The limitation on overall size of the individual units was also presented as being a system level mechanism for absorbing exogenous shocks. Our research differs from these traditional analyses of industrial networks in two ways. First, we do not confine our attention to manufacturing activities. Rather, we focus on upstream activities, on the development of new products, in order to investigate the extent of the contribution made by external relationships. Second, we examine the type of innovation carried out in more detail. Existing studies stress the incremental nature of innovative systems based on small firm networks. However, we have found that taking a more in-depth perspective on the type of innovative activities will reveal the significant presence of more complex and articulated types of innovation.

By focusing on entrepreneurs, and their role within the networks examined, we have also expanded their traditional role as technical innovators to that of co-ordinators of complementary activities. The Schumpeterian view of entrepreneurs as independent individuals able to exploit original ideas through a set of distinctive abilities loses its explanatory power within inter-firm networks. Rather, in these institutional contexts, because they are embedded within the local community, entrepreneurs appear as mechanisms of co-ordination. Their propensity to innovate and their skill in 'gluing together' a set of legally distinct, but complementary, abilities make entrepreneurs a central driving force within the network. We explore these ideas by comparing the extent and type of external relationships in firms managed by the original founder and firms managed by professional managers.

In our study, the emphasis placed on entrepreneurs is intended to divert attention from technology as the primary catalyst within inter-firm networks. While, certainly, they are extremely important for increasing the effectiveness and efficiency of co-ordination (see e.g. Chapter 10), technological solutions are not the only means of facilitating the emergence and the governance of inter-firm relations, especially within localized networks. By focusing on individual firms, we have also tried to concentrate on non-institutional boundary spanning roles. Government agencies (Tripsas *et al.* 1993), industry associations, and research centres (see e.g. Chapter 9) act by mandate to facilitate the emergence of inter-firm relations, while we have explored the role, and motivations, of individuals belonging to the business community.

The chapter is organized as follows: we begin by discussing the existing theoretical and empirical literature on industrial networks, first by focusing on the development of innovation and, secondly, by outlining the entrepreneurs' role in the network. In both cases we develop testable propositions regarding both the extent, and the type, of innovation-related activities which might be fostered or hindered within small firm networks and the key role played by entrepreneurs in these processes. In the next section, we present the empirical study performed to test these propositions. First, we discuss the operationalization of the theoretical constructs. Then, we describe the design of the research and the sample used, and offer some data. Lastly, we present the results of the analysis. In the final section, we discuss these results and offer some concluding remarks with the aim of stimulating further research both on inter-firm relations in the context of the development of innovation, and on the role of entrepreneurs as catalysts in networks of small and medium-sized firms.

THEORETICAL FRAMEWORK

Innovation and Small Firm Networks

The first person to be interested in the analysis of sets of small and medium-sized firms within circumscribed geographical areas was Alfred Marshall (1920). The English economist identified industrial districts as localized industrial communities, characterized by numerous small, technologically advanced firms, involved in specific, but complementary, activities. By specializing in distinct activities along the production chain, the firms in the district were able to overcome disadvantages of scale and to challenge larger competitors. More recent research (Becattini 1987; Pyke *et al.* 1990) has confirmed Marshall's intuitions about the advantages of such industrial districts, and described them as a combination of efficiency, typical of more mechanistic production structures, and of flexibility, typical of more organic structures.

The 'flexible specialization' models extended Marshall's theory from an economic perspective and assigned a prominent role, for understanding the dynamics of districts, to technology (Brusco 1982; Piore and Sabel 1984). These analyses attributed the rise of comparatively small Italian firms in international markets to the emergence of manufacturing technologies (CNC, CAD, CAM), which are characterized by lower costs and which operate at lower, minimum efficient, scale levels. Operationally distinct units, acting similarly to the separate departments of larger integrated structures, were observed to be linked and co-ordinated by a central firm, both specialized in the final part of the manufacturing process, namely the assembly process, and responsible for the distribution and marketing of the final product. Thus, the division of labour was achieved not within a multiple unit company, but rather through the interaction of several specialized, distinct firms.

The main advantage of the system described above is related to the ability to adapt more quickly to changes in markets, both in terms of changes in customers' preferences and in terms of upward or downward shifts in the demand curve. In the first case, the high degree of specialization facilitates the production of a wider variety of products and quicker response to particular needs. In the second case, the effects of exogenous shocks in demand are spread across multiple units, thus decreasing the risks for the whole system. All the actors constantly refine their knowledge and expertise, and the overall result is that improvements are continuously introduced, which determines a consistent pattern of incremental innovations.

However, this rather static view of the industrial district implicitly confines learning processes to the district itself and emphasizes system level dynamics at the expense of individual actions and choices. Yet, districts and networks of small and medium-sized firms can also be analysed as dynamic constellations of mutually adjusting firms (Best 1990). They are dynamic because responses to new challenges and opportunities require a continuous redefinition of the external boundaries of the districts. Adjustments are mutual because individual initiatives intersect with others and serve to modify production capabilities and opportunities in each firm. Higher levels of efficiency, leading to cost advantages, cease to be the only source of competitive advantage. Rather, innovation-based processes become more radical both in their means and their ends, and external relationships are extensively exploited to achieve these ends.

External partners in the network are considered as the owners of distinct, but complementary, knowledge assets (von Hippel 1990). Ideas and creativity can therefore be collected from outside the firm and can increase its ability not only to react to change, but also to promote it. By co-operating with external actors, firms in the network increase their ability to redefine their field of action and to reorganize their knowledge base (Nonaka 1994).

For example, suppliers may become sources of knowledge, instead of either mere providers of inputs or outside sources used to increase manufacturing flexibility (Piore and Sabel 1984). They may also contribute to extending the manufacturers' knowledge base and communication channels beyond their existing boundaries (Pennings and Harianto 1992).

Empirical results (Lipparini and Sobrero 1992, 1993; Rothwell and Dogson 1991) support this perspective, showing that more articulate and structural use of suppliers may enable small and medium-sized enterprises (SMEs) to overcome the constraints of size. Further support is also found in other research which highlights the importance of external links for a firm's survival (Fichman and Levinthal 1991; Venkatraman 1990), for its growth (Jarillo 1988; Lorenzoni 1990; Lorenzoni and Ornati 1988; Rothwell and Dogson 1991), and for entrepreneurial performance (Aldrich and Zimmer 1986; Birley 1985; Larson 1991, 1992). The above has led us to formulate the following proposition:

Proposition 1: Inter-firm relations for the development of innovation within small firm networks are not limited to cost reduction and incremental changes, but rather encompass more radical and complex changes.

The Role of Entrepreneurs

So far we have adopted a more traditional approach and focused on system level characteristics which affect the dynamics of networks. However, the attention paid to the overarching structural conditions has served to underline the role played by individual actors. Recent contributions to this argument have stressed the structural differences at the level of actors as being an indirect source of co-ordination within the networks (Fruin 1992; Håkansson 1989). Size differences between the focal firm (Lorenzoni and Baden-Fuller 1993) and its external links have been presented as a reason for the allocation of bargaining power among the parties and as an indirect source of co-ordination. Stick-and-carrot policies are, indeed, substituted by long-term relationships, but manufacturers clearly play a dominant role in the relationships and benefit from a more fragmented and highly competitive supply-side (Imai *et al.* 1985).

Asymmetries in bargaining power and resource endowments are, however, not wholly satisfactory as explanations for the different abilities found in managing and organizing a dispersed set of external relationships within small firm networks. On the one hand, they are based on premises that are founded on a set of assumptions which, it has frequently been argued, cannot be generalized to different economic systems (see e.g. Granovetter 1985; Harrison 1991). On the other hand, empirical observations offer evidence for close relationships even in the absence of size differences between the actors (Lipparini and Sobrero 1994).

Perhaps more convincingly, this approach suggests that the *actors* are as important as the *relationships* they depend upon. While characteristics specific to any one context might favour certain organizational forms rather than others, they are necessary, but not sufficient, conditions for the emergence and co-ordination of that network. Hence, governing mechanisms should also be sought at the level of actors (Dubois and Håkansson offer a similar view in Chapter 2).

Since Schumpeter's seminal work (1936), entrepreneurs have been allocated a central role in economic development. They have been seen as the engine which draws new ideas and new business visions along behind it, matching inventions, through exploitation, to innovation (Roberts 1988). If one broadens the Schumpeterian view, entrepreneurs are, more generally, those who put resources, labour, materials, and other assets into what are often new combinations (Norman 1977). Within small firm networks, the process of founding a new firm is particularly instructive for understanding the entrepreneur's role. In this context, firms usually start up as spin-offs from a limited number of 'incubator' organizations. During their previous working experience, entrepreneurs will not only have acquired considerable knowledge about the complex technical needs embedded in their products, but they will also have developed a personal network made up of other producers, potential clients, and innovative suppliers operating in the area.

Having worked in a large organization, they will have developed the ability to identify 'who' can do 'what', such as the supplier who could provide complex parts or sub-assembly groups. Very often the firm's founder and its potential suppliers already know each other well, having worked together at the same company (Saxenian 1991). Prior personal relationships reduce the level of uncertainty and enhance inter-firm co-operation. Entrepreneurs end up relying on a large number of 'innovative poles', orchestrated thanks to their reputation developed in previous relationships.

When compared with local entrepreneurs, professional managers within small firm networks, although they might well play an active role in the business community, may not be as deeply embedded in the wider social structure. As a result of earlier socialization processes entrepreneurs often have stronger and longer-lasting social ties within their communities, which will foster mutual understanding and trust and, by adopting a 'learning by co-operating' logic, they will be able to profit from any early sharing of critical information as well as from a continuous flow of technical and managerial suggestions.

From the outset entrepreneurs systematically turn to former business connections for information, resources, and support when taking an idea to the market. Personal networks are transformed into stable configurations of inter-organizational exchange (Larson and Starr 1993), where relationships are used, selectively, to trade knowledge as much, if not more, than to trade physical assets (Schrader 1991; von Hippel 1987). Key resources are therefore identified by using social exchange relationships (Starr and MacMillan 1990) and entrepreneurs emerge as the principal actors, able to create, manage, and recombine a set of external relationships (Lorenzoni and Lipparini 1999). We would, therefore, expect that:

Proposition 2: Entrepreneurs in small firm networks tend to rely more on external relationships for the development of innovation than do professional managers.

Turning to external resources seems to be an alternative that is planned for in order to overcome disadvantages of size. Pooling and gathering new ideas can draw small and medium-sized firms into partnership with more 'privileged' partners in a long-term commitment where the relationship dimension may prevail over the transactional one. The emergence of entrepreneurs as catalysts in innovation processes within small firm networks, therefore, raises further questions about the nature of innovation itself.

Several studies on the personality traits of entrepreneurs (Keirsey and Bates 1978; McClelland 1961; Roberts 1988) have portrayed these individuals as being able to translate a high need for achievement into economic development. Entrepreneurs thrive on situations where they can get personal satisfaction by taking the responsibility for success or failure. As the more innovative projects are characterized by greater uncertainty and, consequently, by higher risks, entrepreneurs will tend to pursue radical projects and avoid more incremental, or risk-free, situations because any certainty of the outcome is unchallenging in terms of personal achievement (McClelland 1961).

Risk-aversion asymmetries have also been used to explain managerial behaviour when decision-taking between sets of alternatives which differ, in the level of uncertainty, within the well-known principal-agent framework (Jensen and Meckling 1976). Managers are expected to prefer more conservative actions, with a short-term perspective that favours efficiency. Their defence of the status quo which guarantees a lower, albeit more certain, pay-off, also precludes investment decisions in favour of riskier options which may only bear fruit in the long term. A professional manager would, therefore, be expected to adopt the more incremental types of innovations rather than the more radical ones.

Within small firm networks, the founders' relationships favour the establishment of trust and personal commitment, which stimulates greater participation by external resources in the innovation process. When entrepreneurs are more inclined towards riskier projects, their partners too will also be involved in more demanding innovative projects. Accordingly, both because of their lower level of aversion to risk and because of their greater reliance on external sources as a means of overcoming structural disadvantages, not only will entrepreneurs gather innovative contributions from external partners but, also, these contributions will probably be more complex and articulated. We would, therefore, expect that:

Proposition 3: Inter-firm relations for the development of innovation within small firm networks are used to a greater extent to achieve radical and complex changes than incremental ones when entrepreneurs, rather than professional managers, are leading the firm.

EMPIRICAL STUDY

Constructs Operationalization

Out of all the different types of inter-firm relationships we chose to focus on the supplier–manufacturer relationship. The focus could, on the one hand, fall on the role of supplier relationships in building strengths in manufacturing (Cusumano and Takeishi 1991; Lamming 1989; Nishiguchi 1987). The emphasis, here, is on the improvements made in the production process owing to suppliers' involvement in quality control practices and to better integration of all parties in the production plan. On the other hand, one might tackle the roles that suppliers are called upon to play in the development of new products (Clark and Fujimoto 1991; Håkansson 1987, 1989; Imai *et al.* 1985). The work presented here shares a common concern with the second set of studies regarding the role of suppliers' involvement in influencing innovative processes and extends this analysis to small firm networks in order to improve our understanding of their dynamics and processes.

The sheer number of external sources, however, does not necessarily contradict the statement that a firm's success is based upon internal knowledge, and suppliers are used simply to incrementally improve a product developed internally. Hence, the type of contribution a supplier makes needs to be assessed, and defined, more accurately.

There seems to be general agreement about the concept of radical innovation (Abernathy and Clark 1985; Rothwell *et al.* 1974). A completely new product satisfying an emerged need (i.e. Sony's first portable cassette player: the Walkman) or satisfying existing needs in a new way (i.e. the portable CD player) would fit into this category. Suppliers who participate in the development of such products could be classified as making a radical contribution. However, if the focus of the effort is on the reduction of production costs or on marginal improvements to well-accepted products (i.e. a new version of a laptop with a greater capacity hard disk), the suppliers' contribution could be classified as incremental (Myers and Marquis 1969).

However, these typologies still leave room for different types of product changes, especially when we are dealing with assembled products resulting

Table 8.1. Suppliers' contribution to the innovative process: options, variables, and typologies

Options	Typology of contribution
Realization of a radically new product	Radical
Significant improvements of an existing product involving major changes in the component/ sub-systems used	Architectural
Re-engineering of an existing product, involving a redesign of components'/sub-systems' interfaces	Architectural
Marginal improvements of an existing product	Incremental
Internal costs reduction	Incremental

from the interaction of different sub-systems. Take, for example, top-loading domestic washing machines. Smaller size apartments and demographic changes encouraged the development of more compact models (Sobrero 1994). While the core concept of the product remained unchanged, this size reduction required substantial re-engineering efforts. This type of innovation could be termed architectural (Henderson and Clark 1990).

We propose to distinguish suppliers' contributions according to whether they are involved in the design and engineering of a completely new product (*radical*), or in the re-engineering and reconfiguration of an existing device where substantial effort must be devoted to the changes in the interfaces among the different components (*architectural*) or, lastly, in the substitution or fine-tuning of simple components for cost reduction (*incremental*). Table 8.1 illustrates this classification.[1]

To investigate the role of entrepreneurs as catalysts and co-ordinators of innovative activity we departed from the traditional approaches described in the literature. Organization theorists treat the entrepreneurial nature of the firm as a specific stage in the long-term evolution of its organizational form (Aldrich and Mueller 1982). Thus, the earlier phases of activities tend to be considered as entrepreneurial and are usually associated with less structured and more creative environments (Van de Ven *et al*. 1984).

In the analysis of small firm networks, however, reliance on age differences in the observed set as an operationalization of entrepreneurship might not be appropriate. Although no quantitative study has, to our knowledge, examined the evolution of organizational forms within small firm networks, qualitative evidence suggests some important differences. First,

[1] What we are interested in by now is more to stress the need for careful consideration of the content and the role of the activities rather than their labelling. This is why we decided to use a well-known, accepted terminology to operationalize the type of innovation being pursued rather than to advance another taxonomy of innovation, something which is beyond the scope of this chapter. The reader should therefore feel free to disagree with our choice and apply his/her own frameworks, as long as the articulation of the content of the activities remains the same.

growth processes do not seem to lead to higher concentration at the level of systems, at the expense of weaker and smaller competitors (Russo 1985). Rather, growth occurs by means of the expansion of the entire system through the niche specialization of its actors. Secondly, original founders are less likely to follow entrepreneurial models based on the early exploitation of the initial revolutionary phases and subsequent incapacity to lead the firms within more routinized phases.

Furthermore, our approach also differs with respect to the unit of analysis adopted. The use of indicators of entrepreneurship such as age, for example, might be appropriate when trying to assess some characteristics at the level of the firm. However, here we explore the impact of the entrepreneur's actions and choices on the firm. Our focus is on the role played by the individual actors. Thus, we decided to see whether the manufacturer firms were managed by their founder or by professional management. We recognize that this choice might overestimate the role and power of single individuals within the organizations. More detailed analysis of internal decision-making processes could perhaps clarify this. But, given the limited size of the firms studied and the charismatic role of entrepreneurs, we feel confident that the comparison of entrepreneurs with professional managers is capable of discerning influences at the level of the individual.

Sample Description and Research Methodology

We investigated entrepreneurship and innovation in two industries whose characteristics of firm size, geographical concentration, and division of labour fit the definition of industrial districts: packing and packaging machinery (hereafter PPM) and fluid power machinery and equipment (hereafter FPME).[2] Their critical factors for success lie in the production process where flexibility and technological innovation, obtained through the reorganization of procurement flows and the use of modular components, are of utmost importance.

In both cases, the product is a system of interactive components and subsystems, all highly interdependent. Each one of the major components of the machine is itself a system, made up of a set of interacting and interlocking parts. The nature of the product is that of a closed system characterized by critical configurations and engineering of the linkages between the sub-units, involving the combination of different technologies. The quality of the interaction between the parts is just as important as the quality of the individual pieces.

The machinery for packing and packaging drug pills is a good example of the products involved in this study. The blistering machine, made up of numerous independent groups, is a line where the powder mixture for the

---

[2] The SIC codes are respectively 3565 and 3592.

pill is the input, and a package, containing a varying number of pills ready to be delivered, is the output. In between these two instances, several complex operations, from the correct balance of the dose to sterilization of the wrapping material, are performed in a sequence of fine-tuned and completely automated steps.

We concentrated our analysis on the two industries for the following reasons:

- the relevance, at both the national and international level, of Italian producers. The supply side is composed of a few large-sector leading firms and many small firms which can adapt their products extremely rapidly to the changing needs of clients and allow for a level of product and service customization which cannot be matched by foreign competitors;[3]
- the geographical and productive concentration of the firms, both in the northern regions of Emilia Romagna and Lombardy;[4]
- the dense network of relationships among small firms which allows them to rely on different degrees, or forms, of competence;
- the existence of diffused and efficient sets of suppliers which have long been active in supplying other industries and which have recently been affected by re-qualification and rationalization processes.

Data Collection and Descriptive Statistics

Archival data on the firms operating in PPM and FPME industries were collected through industry associations and governmental agencies. Since we were interested in manufacturing activities, we excluded those units active only in assembling, engineering, consulting, and distribution from the sample. Each firm was then contacted by phone and the names of the CEO and of the manager in charge of new product development were requested. Given the limited average size, in response to the latter request, we were almost always referred to the manufacturing manager.

A three-part questionnaire was then sent to each firm contacted.[5] The first two parts, on the genesis of the firm, its general data, and the current product portfolio were addressed to the CEO. The third section, on the role of suppliers in the new product development process, was addressed to the technical manager. Respondents were asked to indicate how many of their suppliers were actively involved in the development of new products and to categorize them according to the type of activity performed.

---

[3] With regard to the first sector examined, Italy is the leader, while for the second sector it is fifth in the ratings of major global producers (ASSOFLUID, various years, CO.PA.MA., various years).

[4] Eighty per cent of national PPM producers are located in the cities and hinterland of Bologna and Milan, while 60% of the FPME producers are located in the provinces of Milan, Varese, Modena, Reggio Emilia, and Bologna.

[5] A copy of the questionnaire is available from the authors upon request.

Table 8.2. The final sample: descriptive statistics

Variable	PPM				FMPE				
	Min.	Max.	Mean	Std. dev.[a]	Min.	Max.	Mean	Std. dev.	Min.
Sales ($m.)	1	58	11	13	0.65	46	10	11	0.65
Employee	8	184	36	36	7	177	39	40	7
Exports (%)	4	94	39	30	0	85	30	24	0
Age	2	149	19	21	2	50	19	10	2
Founder	0	1	0.79	0.40	0	1	0.75	0.43	0
Suppliers	7	1,250	206	254	10	676	129	134	7

Note: [a] standard deviation.

After a first test on a smaller sample of 20 firms, the questionnaire was mailed, in Autumn 1991, to 110 firms in the PPM industry and to 130 in the FPME industry. One month after posting, telephone calls were made to encourage a response.

Data were checked by phone whenever values were either missing or in conflict with answers given in other parts of the questionnaire. In addition, several on-site interviews with respondents were arranged. The interviews lasted from one to two hours and focused on a more detailed discussion of the information reported and on a more precise definition of firms' activities. In July 1992, the collection phase ended with 53 questionnaires for the PPM industry and 44 questionnaires for the FPME industry.[6] Table 8.2 gives some statistics relating to the larger sample.

Net sales are slightly higher in the PPM industry (mean value about US$ 11m.), than in the FPME industry (US$ 10m.). In both cases, however, the limited size of the companies examined is clear from the average number of employees: 36 in the PPM industry and 39 in the FPME industry. The fact that this is a structural characteristic is confirmed by the average age of the firm—the number of years from its foundation—which is about 19 years in both industries. Hence, the small size of these firms cannot be seen as a temporary characteristic owing to the firm being at an early stage of its development. Moreover, in 77 per cent of the cases, the founder still manages the company. The firms in the sample are, as expected, well represented in foreign markets. On average, exports represent 33 per cent of

---

[6] During our interviews and the data collection phase we decided to exclude any firm with fewer than 6 employees from the analysis. The cut-off point was determined from the observation that firms below that limit were either consultancies or engineering companies which had passed through previous checks or simply represented a legal construct under which one or more craftsmen organized their specialized activity. Secondly, the class of from 6 to 200 employees well represents—at least in a European setting—the set of SMEs we were interested in and it has been used before in previous studies and statistical classification.

their annual sales, with a slightly higher value in the PPM industry, where the average is 39 per cent.

Thus, in terms of their characteristics, firms in both industries show several similarities, which reflect the similarities noted at the industry level that were discussed above. However, perhaps surprisingly, there are also close similarities between these industries when we look at their suppliers: indeed, there seems to be an exceptionally high, almost inflated number of them. On average, a firm in the PPM industry deals with 206 suppliers and one in the FPME industry has 129 suppliers, with an overall average of 177. At first, we could hardly believe these figures, but further investigation not only confirmed them, but also revealed an even more articulated situation than that which had initially emerged. Together with very inefficient rationalization of the supply side, exemplified by the frequent lack of any purchasing management, there is strong, and long-lasting, complementarity in the development of new products which represents the main source of competitive advantage for these firms. It is therefore to this specific aspect that we turned our attention in the statistical analysis.

Regression Analysis

To investigate the relationship between suppliers' involvement in new product development activities, the presence of the founder, and the type of innovation generally undertaken by suppliers, we performed a multiple regression analysis on the following model:

$$\text{PERINSUP} = f\left(\text{SECTOR, FOUNDER, LSALES, ARCH, INCR}\right)$$

where PERINSUP indicates the percentage of suppliers involved in the development of new products, and is calculated as the ratio of the number of suppliers involved to the total number of suppliers, as reported in the questionnaire. Percentages were used to check for differences in size between firms. FOUNDER is a dummy variable, equal to 1 when the founder is still leading the firm, and zero when there is professional management. LSALES is the natural log of 1991 firm sales in US dollars and is used as a control variable for firm's size.[7] SECTOR is a dummy variable, equal to zero if the firm is in the PPM industry, and to 1 if it is in the FPME industry.

The other two variables, ARCH and INCR, are two dummy variables used to express the dominant typology of the suppliers' contribution to the development of new products. ARCH is set equal to 1 if the majority of the innovative suppliers are involved in 'reengineering of an existing product, involving a redesign of component/sub-system interfaces' or 'significant improvements in an existing product involving major changes in the

---

[7] Figures were originally collected in Italian lira and then converted at the average 1991 exchange rate.

Table 8.3. Regression analysis: Pearson correlation matrix

	PERINSUP	SECTOR	FOUNDER	LSALES	ARCHDUM	INCRDUM
SECTOR	−0.06	—	—	—	—	—
FOUNDER	0.17	−0.05	—	—	—	—
LSALES	0.04	−0.01	−0.11	—	—	—
ARCHDUM	0.21	0.10	0.08	0.06	—	—
INCRDUM	−0.01	0.03	−0.24	0.08	−0.59	—
Mean	20.33	0.45	0.77	1.82	0.29	0.46
St. dev.[a]	23.21	0.50	0.42	1.07	0.46	0.50

Note: [a] standard deviation.

components/sub-systems used' and zero in other situations; INCR is set equal to 1 if the majority of the innovative suppliers are involved in 'marginal improvements in an existing product' or in 'internal cost reduction'. Our reference group fits the third possible case, where the majority of suppliers are involved in the 'realization of a radically new product', and the estimate of the intercept should be interpreted accordingly.

First, we estimated the baseline model, where the percentage of innovative suppliers was regressed against the two control variables (the industry dummy and the size variable). We then included the FOUNDER dummy and the ARCH and INCR dummies.[8] The impact of sets of predictors on the outcome was then examined with the aid of the increment-to-R^2 test. The increment-to-R^2 test is a test of the impact of the inclusion of a set of predictors on the outcome variable. If the increase in R^2 is sufficiently large, we can conclude that the predictors have added to the model, and, when taken together, have an effect on the outcome variable.[9] Residual analysis was performed on the final model to detect whether there were influential points and to check the normality assumptions of residuals distribution. We did not find evidence of any such potential sources of bias in the estimates. Table 8.3 shows the correlation matrix and the relevant statistics for the outcome and the predictors, while the two models and the corresponding tests are reported in Table 8.4.

In both models, the results clearly show that in our sample, the size effect

---

[8] The order of inclusion of the independent variables was altered but the results did not prove to be sensitive to the order in which the variables were taken.

[9] The formula we employ to make this determination is the following:

$$\frac{\Delta R^2}{\Delta df} \times \frac{dffull}{1 - R^2_{full}} = F_{\Delta df, dffull}$$

ΔR^2 and Δdf are simply the differences between the full model (the model including the set of predictors in question) and the reduced model (the model excluding the set of predictors in question) in R^2 and the degrees of freedom. The R^2 (full model) and the df (full model) pertain to the model including the set of predictors being investigated. The result is distributed as an F-test with (df, df full model) degrees of freedom. This will allow us to determine if we can reject the null hypothesis, that the impact of the predictors on the outcome variable is not different from zero.

Table 8.4. Suppliers' involvement in new product development

Variables	Model 1[a]	Model 2[a]
Intercept	20.08[b]	3.12
	(5.24)	(8.10)
SECTOR	–2.76	–4.33
	(4.79)	(4.68)
LSALES	0.83	0.34
	(2.23)	(2.18)
FOUNDER		10.80[c]
		(5.68)
ARCHDUM		17.41[b]
		(6.42)
INCRDUM		11.11
		(5.98)
n	96	96
R^2 model	0.005	0.107[c]
Increment-to-R^2 test[d]		3.41[e]

Notes: [a] standard errors in parenthesis.
[b] $p < 0.01$.
[c] $p < 0.10$.
[d] see footnote 9.
[e] $p < 0.05$.

does not influence the dynamics of buyer–supplier relations. Although it is consistently positive, the estimated coefficient for the natural log of the firm's sales is never statistically significant and it is relatively low—the estimated standardized coefficient for Model 2 is 0.02. Moreover, although the sample was a cross-section, there is no evidence of an 'industry effect', given that the estimated coefficient of the dummy SECTOR is not statistically different from zero in either of the two models. The use of a dummy variable to reveal an industry effect could be criticized on the grounds that it entails the implicit assumption that the slope coefficients are the same in both cases. The implication here would be that firm size is an explanatory variable for differences in the percentage of suppliers involved in new product development for one industry but not for the other. This reasoning could easily be extended to all the other dummies too. Thus, to rule this possibility out we computed increment-to-R^2 tests on all the interactions between each of the dummy variables and the size variable, using Model 2 as the baseline model. From the results reported in Table 8.5, we concluded that industry and size were not significant explanatory variables either directly or through interactions.

However, both the importance of the presence of the founder and the

Table 8.5. Testing for the presence of interactions (differences in slope) between firm size and all the dummies

Interaction	Increment-to-R-square test	df1, df2	Significance level
Size by Sector	0.4	1, 89	>0.10
Size by Founder	0.2	1, 89	>0.10
Size by Architectural	0.7	1, 89	>0.10
Size by Incremental	0.1	1, 89	>0.10
All together	0.4	3, 86	>0.10

Note: baseline model is Model 2 in Table 8.4.

typology of the suppliers' contribution emerge clearly from the results. First, each of the estimated coefficients is statistically different from zero. Secondly, taken together, they enhance the explanatory power of the baseline model (increment-to-R^2 test = 3.41, p < 0.05).

On average, when the founder, and not professional management, leads the firm, the percentage of suppliers directly involved in any new product development (NPD) activity is 11 points higher. As expected, the percentage of suppliers involved in *incremental* types of contribution is, on average, higher—14 per cent—than the percentage of suppliers involved in *radical* types of contribution—3 per cent. However, the *architectural* types of contribution emerge, clearly, as being the most relevant type of contribution made—average 20 per cent. The magnitude of the involvement of external actors in such a strategic activity is surprising for two reasons. First, this indicates an industrial reality which is characterized by an extremely high degree of involvement of external actors in complex activities, which require managerial skills not usually associated with small and medium-sized firms. Secondly, despite evidence to the contrary from other research, recombining the existing knowledge base through re-engineering emerges here as a widely adopted practice and one in which suppliers are key actors.

DISCUSSION AND CONCLUSIONS

In this paper, we have examined two aspects of network dynamics: the type and content of the relationships among the actors and the role played by some of these actors. In constructing our theoretical framework, we have presented some of the special characteristics of small firm networks and we discussed their implications for inter-firm relations and entrepreneurial activity. On the one hand, the deliberate use of external firms in the design phase and the construction of a set of relationships brings innovative skills into the firm which can be exploited in order to gain sustainable competitive advantage. On the other hand, entrepreneurs, who can rely on personal networks and embeddedness in the competitive arena, are able to identify possible sources of knowledge and act as orchestrators of inter-firm linkages. As co-ordinators of such innovative ties, they have access to, and embody, a wide range of diverse skills for the realization of more complex typologies of innovation (i.e. architectural and radical). In this way, small entrepreneurial firms can overcome size disadvantages and bypass the organizational filters encountered by more integrated organizations.

In the empirical analysis, conducted on a sample of 97 firms in two Italian industrial districts we found the following:

1. Although *incremental* contributions certainly exist and are relevant, more complex relationships, largely focused on joint design and development, emerge as the dominant patterns in buyer–supplier interaction. While suppliers are clearly involved in increasing internal efficiency, and achieving the fragmentation of the value chain typical of industrial districts, our results point to a more complex set of interactions where suppliers are mainly called upon to actively contribute their own ideas and solutions to the development of new products, and are less and less the blind recipients and executors of manufacturer-designed OEMs.

2. When the founder is still leading and managing the business, more suppliers are involved in the development of new products. Entrepreneurs often seek new combinations among inter-firm ties with external actors, relying upon such linkages to transfer and combine their organizationally embedded learning capability.

3. The suppliers' role in actively developing new products is even more important when the founder is still leading the business. When the type of activities performed in the relationships is studied, the different roles played by entrepreneurs emerge. Entrepreneurs act as catalysts of the innovative skills located outside the firm, co-ordinate the information flows which are generated by interaction with external sources by using different governance mechanisms.

Empirical analysis has confirmed the need for more in-depth investigation of the type of relationships that exist within small firm networks and of the role of individual actors as catalysts. Moreover, by switching the analysis from the level of the system to that of the individual firm, we suggested that, in order to fully understand the emergence and the governance mechanisms of such complex sets of relations, more attention should be paid to those characteristics of firms which seem to have been lost in the district analysis: that is, the direct appreciation of the entrepreneurial content of business activities. The use of more restricted units of analysis in future research would help to reveal further details of these processes. Focusing attention on a lower number of firms and collecting data at the project level would seem to offer a promising line of enquiry (see Chapter 2 for an example of such a more detailed perspective).

While other mechanisms discussed in this book (i.e. technology, institutional actors) might function as a source of co-ordination, we have proposed that a broader recognition of the relational capacities and skills of networked organizations could help to better understand the processes of network formation and performance. On the one hand, a finer distinction of the type of relationships would help to separate out different sets and cliques within the network, and to examine whether their individual contingencies are reflected in asymmetries in the forms of governance used. On the other hand, differences in relational capacities and skills could be investigated in terms of being a source of competitive advantage.

REFERENCES

Abernathy, W. J., and Clark, K. B. 1985. 'Innovation: Mapping the Winds of Creative Destruction'. *Research Policy*. 14: 3–22.

Acs, Z. J., and Audretsch, D. B. 1990. *Innovation and Small Firms*. Cambridge, Mass.: MIT Press.

Aldrich, H. E., and Mueller, S. 1982. 'The Evolution of Organizational Forms: Technology, Coordination, and Control'. *Research in Organizational Behavior*. 4: 33–87.

——and Zimmer, C. 1986. 'Entrepreneurship through Social Network'. In Sexton, D. L., and Smilor, R. W. (eds.). *The Art and Science of Entrepreneurship*. 2–23. Cambridge, Mass.: Ballinger.

ASSOFLUID (various years). Statistics.

Becattini, G. (ed.) 1987. *Mercato e forze locali: il distretto industriale*. Bologna: Il Mulino.

Best, M. 1990. *The New Competition: Institutions of Industrial Restructuring*. Cambridge, Mass.: Harvard University Press.

Birley, S. 1985. 'The Role of Networks in the Entrepreneurial Process'. *Frontiers of Entrepreneurship Research*. Wellesley, Mass.: Babson College.

Brüderl, J., and Schüssler, R. 1990. 'Organizational Mortality: The Liability of Newness and Adolescence'. *Administrative Science Quarterly*. 35: 530–47.

Brusco, S. 1982. 'The Emilian Model: Productive Decentralisation and Social Integration'. *Cambridge Journal of Economics*. 6: 167–84.

Clark, K. B., and Fujimoto, T. 1991. *Product Development Performance: Strategy, Organization, and Management in the World Auto Industry*. Boston, Mass.: Harvard Business School Press.

Comanor, W. 1967. 'Market Structure, Product Differentiation and Industrial Research'. *Quarterly Journal of Economics*. 81: 639–57.

CO.PA.MA. (various years). Statistics.

Cusumano, M., and Takeishi, A. 1991. 'Supplier Relations and Management: A Study of Japanese, Japanese-Transplant, and U.S. Auto Plants'. *Strategic Management Journal*. 12: 563–88.

Fichman, M., and Levinthal, D. A. 1991. 'Honeymoons and the Liability of Adolescence: A New Perspective on Duration Dependence in Social and Organizational Relationships'. *Academy of Management Review*. 16: 442–68.

Fruin, M. W. 1992. *The Japanese Enterprise System*. New York: Oxford University Press.

Granovetter, M. 1985. 'Economic Action and Social Structure: The Problem of Embeddedness'. *American Journal of Sociology*. 91: 481–510.

Håkansson, H. (ed.) 1987. *Industrial Technological Development. A Network Approach*. London: Croom Helm.

——1989. *Corporate Technological Behaviour: Co-operation and Networks*. London: Routledge.

Hannan, M. T., and Carroll, G. R. 1992. *Dynamics of Organizational Populations: Density, Legitimation and Competition*. New York: Oxford University Press.

Harrison, B. 1991. 'Industrial Districts: Old Wine in New Bottles'. *Regional Development*. 26: 469–83.

Henderson, R. M., and Clark, K. B. 1990. 'Architectural Innovation: The Reconfiguration of Existing Product Technologies and the Failure of Established Firms'. *Administrative Science Quarterly*. 35: 9–30.

Imai, K., Nonaka, I., and Takeuchi, H. 1985. 'Managing the New Product Development Process: How Japanese Learn and Unlearn'. In Clark, K. B., Hayes, R. H., and Lorenz, C. (eds.). *The Uneasy Alliance: Managing the Productivity-Technology Dilemma*. 337–76. Boston, Mass.: Harvard Business School Press.

Jarillo, C. J. 1988. 'On Strategic Networks'. *Strategic Management Journal*. 9: 31–41.

Jensen, M. C., and Meckling, W. H. 1976. 'Theory of the Firm: Managerial Behavior, Agency Costs, and Ownership Structure'. *Journal of Financial Economics*. 3: 305–60.

Kamien, M. I., and Schwartz, N. L. 1975. 'Market Structure and Innovation: A Survey'. *The Journal of Economic Literature*. 13: 1–37.

Keirsey, D., and Bates, M. 1978. *Please Understand Me: An Essay on Temperament Style*. Del Mar, Calif.: Prometheus Nemesis Books.

Lamming, R. 1989. 'The Causes and Effects of Structural Change in the European Automotive Components Industry'. MIT International Motor Vehicle Program, working paper.

Larson, A. 1991. 'Partner Networks: Leveraging External Ties to Improve Entrepreneurial Performance'. *Journal of Business Venturing*. 6: 173–88.

——1992. 'Network Dyads in Entrepreneurial Settings: A Study of the Governance of Exchange Relationships'. *Administrative Science Quarterly*. 37: 76–104.

——and Starr, J. A. 1993. 'A Network Model of Organization Formation'. *Entrepreneurship Theory and Practice*. 17: 5–15.

Lipparini, A., and Sobrero, M. 1992. 'Relazioni verticali tra imprese e processi innovativi: alcune verifiche intersettoriali'. *Economia e Politica Industriale*. 74–6: 185–223.

———— 1993. 'Innovation and Small Firms: The Role of Suppliers in Two Industrial Networks'. International Symposium on Logistics. Nottingham, 6–7 July.

————1994. 'The Glue and the Pieces: Entrepreneurship and Innovation in Small Firm Networks'. *Journal of Business Venturing*. 9: 125–40.

Lorenzoni, G. 1990. *L'architettura di sviluppo delle imprese minori: costellazioni e piccoli gruppi*. Bologna: Il Mulino.

————and Baden-Fuller, C. 1995. 'Creating a Strategic Center to Manage a Web of Partners'. *California Management Review*. vol. 37, no. 3: 146–63.

————and Lipparini, A. 1999. 'The Leveraging of Interfirm Relationships as a Distinctive Organizational Capability: A Longitudinal Study'. *Strategic Management Journal*. 20 (forthcoming).

————and Ornati, O. 1988. 'Constellations of Firms and New Ventures'. *Journal of Business Venturing*. 3: 41–57.

McClelland, D. C. 1961. *The Achieving Society*. Princeton, NJ: D. Van Nostrand Co.

Mansfield, E. 1963. 'Size of Firm, Market Stucture and Innovation'. *The Journal of Political Economy*. 6: 83–108.

Marshall, A. 1920. *Principles of Economics*. London: Macmillan.

Miller, R., and Cote, M. 1987. *Growing the Next Silicon Valley: A Guide for Successful Regional Planning*. Lexington, Mass.: Lexington Books.

Myers, S., and Marquis, D. G. 1969. 'Successful Industrial Innovation'. National Science Foundation, Washington, DC. NSF 69-17.

Nishiguchi, T. 1987. 'Competing Systems of Automotive Components Supply: An Examination of the Japanese Clustered Control Model and the Alps Structure'. International Motor Vehicle Program, MIT, working paper.

Nonaka, I. 1994. 'A Dynamic Theory of Organizational Knowledge Creation'. *Organization Science*. 3: 14–37.

Norman, R. 1977. *Management for Growth*. Chichester: John Wiley and Sons.

Pennings, J. M., and Harianto, F. 1992. 'Technological Networking and Innovation Implementation'. *Organization Science*. 3: 356–82.

Pfeffer, J., and Salancik, G. R. 1978. 'The External Control of Organizations: A Resource Dependence Perspective'. New York: Harper and Row.

Piore, M., and Sabel, C. 1984. *The Second Industrial Divide*. New York: Basic Books.

Pyke, F., Becattini, G., and Sengenberger, W. (eds.) 1990. *Industrial Districts and Inter-firm Co-operation in Italy*. Geneva: International Institute for Labour Studies.

Ratti, R. 1991. 'Small and Medium-Size Enterprises, Local Synergies and Spatial Cycles of Innovation'. In Camagni, R. (ed.). *Innovation Networks: Spatial Perspectives*. 71–88. London: Belhaven Press.

Roberts, E. B. 1988. 'The Personality and Motivation of Technological Entrepreneurs'. MIT Sloan School of Management, working paper no. 2078–88.

Rothwell, R., and Dogson, M. 1991. 'External Linkages and Innovation in Small and Medium-Sized Enterprises'. *R&D Management*. 21: 125–37.

————Freeman, C., Horlsey, A., Jervis, V. T. P., Robertson, A. B., and Townsend, J. 1974. 'SAPPHO Updated—Project SAPPHO Phase II'. *Research Policy*. 3: 258–91.

Russo, M. 1985. 'Technical Change and the Industrial District: The Role of Inter-Firm Relations in the Growth and Transformation of Ceramic Tile Production in Italy'. *Research Policy*. 14: 329–43.

Saxenian, A. 1991. 'The Origin and Dynamics of Production Networks in Silicon Valley'. *Research Policy*. 20: 423–37.

Schrader, S. 1991. 'Informal Technology Transfer between Firms: Cooperation through Information Trading'. *Research Policy*. 20: 153–70.

Schumpeter, J. A. 1936. *The Theory of Economic Development*. Cambridge, Mass.: Harvard University Press.

Sobrero, M. 1994. 'The European Home Appliance Industry: History, Structure and Technology 1945–1992'. Alfred P. Sloan School of Management, Massachusetts Institute of Technology, working paper.

Starr, J., and MacMillan, I. 1990. 'Resource Cooptation via Social Contracting: Resource Acquisition Strategies for New Ventures'. *Strategic Management Journal*. 11: 79–92.

Tripsas, M., Schrader, S., and Sobrero, M. 1993. 'Discouraging Opportunistic Behavior in R&D Consortia: A New Role for the Government'. Alfred P. Sloan School of Management, Massachussets Institute of Technology, working paper no. 3622–93/BPS.

Tushman, L. M., and Anderson, P. 1986. 'Technological Discontinuities and Organizational Environments'. *Administrative Science Quarterly*. 31: 439–65.

Van de Ven, A. H., Hudson, R., and Schroeder, D. M. 1984. 'Designing New Business Startups: Entrepreneurial, Organizational, and Ecological Considerations'. *Journal of Management*. 10: 87–107.

Venkatraman, S. 1990. 'Liabilities of Newness, Transaction Set, and New Venture Development'. Snider Entrepreneurial Center. The Wharton School of the University of Pennsylvania, working paper series.

von Hippel, E. 1987. 'Cooperation between Rivals: Informal Know-how Trading'. *Research Policy*. 16: 291–302.

——1990. 'Task Partitioning: An Innovation Process Variable'. *Research Policy*. 19: 407–18.

9

Learning through Intermediaries: *The Case of Inter-Firm Research Collaborations*

SUSANNE LÜTZ

INTRODUCTION

The notion of network-like institutional arrangements, of multilateral forms of collaboration between a number of economic actors, has received increasing attention by researchers in the fields of management and business theory, organization theory, or economic sociology (for the most recent synopses of the field, see e.g. the special issue of *Research Policy* on 'Networks of Innovation', 20 (5), October 1991; Axelsson and Easton 1992; Nohria and Eccles 1992; Sydow 1992; Powell 1990; Powell and Smith-Doerr 1994). Inter-firm networks, for example, research collaborations, strategic alliances, or technological partnerships, are perceived as a major source of a firm's innovation capacity and competitive strength. Conversely, industry's lack of interest or ability to engage in inter-firm co-operative arrangements is repeatedly presented as a powerful explanation of nations' difficulties in regaining the productive edge (Dertouzos 1989: 94).

The popularity of the network concept may be traced back to the structural qualities collaborative forms of interaction are seen to possess, thereby allowing specific norms, informal mechanisms, and innovation outputs to follow. Inter-organizational networks are composed of autonomous, but interdependent actors who have different, but mutually contingent, interests (Mayntz 1991: 13). Network members usually exchange resources of different types (e.g. money or information), the modalities of this exchange being objects of bargaining between the collaboration partners (for this element of negotiation in horizontal forms of co-ordination, see Mayntz 1991; Scharpf 1993*b*). Being engaged in bargaining and the exchange of resources, network members interact recurrently and mostly over a longer

In writing this chapter, I am indebted to Uwe Schimank and James March for helpful comments. Moreover, I benefited immensely from the feedback of the members of the network of network researchers, developed around the Workshop on Inter-Organizational Networks, namely Geoff Easton, Andreas Mehlhorn and, especially, Mark Ebers.

time period. Thus, network relationships are neither spontaneously co-ordinated by price mechanisms, like markets, nor authoritatively set by administrative fiat, like hierarchical forms of organization; however, multi-lateral forms of collaboration combine elements of flexibility and stability in a unique way (Powell 1990).

It is this special character of network structures, allowing collaboration partners to develop informal rules and modes of interaction, which may finally foster innovativeness. Thus the success of multilateral co-operation consists in the network members, engaged in repeated, sequential forms of interaction, obeying the rule of *reciprocity* in their exchange relations—only those actors willing to give something will receive something in return (Gouldner 1960). Since this norm of reciprocity effectively controls free-riding behaviour, actors will engage in a sequence of mutually beneficial transactions, in which partners evolve a common understanding of mutual commitments, and will end up *trusting* one another. Trust in the goodwill of other parties can thus be considered as the 'cumulative product of repeated past interactions' in which actors get to know each other fairly well (Smith-Ring and Van de Ven 1994: 110; for this process-based understanding of trust, see also Zucker 1986; as well as Ring, Chapter 5 this volume). Reci-procity and trust, as the main governing mechanisms of multilateral col-laboration, can be sources of innovation. Since they offer the opportunity to benefit from the knowledge of one's collaboration partner, network members have the chance to change their ways of 'building, supplementing and organizing knowledge and routines around their activities and within their cultures' (Dodgson 1993: 377). In other words, networks promise to be institutional arrangements enabling their members to *learn* (Bradach and Eccles 1989; Lundvall 1990; Håkansson 1989; Johanson and Mattson 1987; Kogut *et al.* 1993; Powell and Brantley 1992; Powell and Smith-Doerr 1994).

Nevertheless, it is a special and very demanding type of learning, which could be the consequence of multilateral collaboration between trusting actors; in the 'organizational learning' literature, this form of learning is usually referred to as *higher-level* or *double-loop* learning (Fiol and Lyles 1985; Argyris and Schön 1978). By openly exchanging complementary knowledge, actors are stimulated to give up well-known rules of procedure and to explore alternative problem-solving strategies. Learning of this kind does not only focus on specific activities, but involves the modification of the prevailing assumptions and underlying models of the actors' behaviour; their, up to this point, well-established organizational frame of reference tends to be restructured. Since actors are inspired to experiment with new and probably alternative technological paths, innovations of a far-reaching, 'radical' character (Dosi 1982) may result from multilateral collaboration networks.

Although multilateral networks seem to be quite promising institutional arrangements, in terms of their governing mechanisms and their expected outputs of innovation, this co-operation phenomenon seems to be far from ubiquitous in the world of inter-firm relationships. By looking at research co-operations for example, we have to face the empirical fact that firms usually favour internal over external R&D.[1] Especially in those technological fields considered as core technologies of strategic importance for one's long-term success, firms are very unenthusiastic towards external co-operation (Bullinger 1990: 34). The main reason for this relative reluctance of companies to get involved in external research collaborations are the risks and costs connected with them (see Chapter 6). Collaboration with competitors, for instance, always implies the danger that previously established internal know-how could leak to the rival company, stimulating it to practise opportunistic behaviour.[2] Even if firms do not have to be afraid of losing strategic knowledge, as in supplier–user relationships for example, it might simply be the partner's incompetence which could turn the collaboration into a costly endeavour.

In other words, despite the fact that multilateral networks are institutional arrangements likely to promote innovativeness and industrial success, they often entail costs and risks, turning them into only second-best solutions from the companies' point of view. This is the reason why the frequently cited 'trusting inter-firm relationships' are very unlikely to exist. Conversely, it is often secrecy and distrust which govern the relationships between competing firms. Even if partners engage in collaborations, as in the supplier–user case, existing power asymmetries may prevent one partner from benefiting from the collaboration. Since the needs of the dominating actor guide the collaboration, costs and benefits are unequally distributed.

It is therefore not surprising that a less demanding type of learning can be expected to emerge when co-operation is lacking or bilateral transactions are practised: since actors mostly rely on their own or tend to determine the innovation output of their partners, knowledge acquisition and transmission will proceed within a constant, well-known framework of performance. Within this *lower-level* or *single-loop* learning model, organizations are simply adapting to changes in their environment by readjusting their action strategies through repetition and routine within their own set

[1] Basically, German companies are spending less than 10% of their internal R&D budget on external collaboration activities (Häusler 1989: 74). Based on an extensive empirical study of R&D collaborations in Germany industry, Täger (1988: 18) reports that 96% of the companies in his survey conducted their research predominantly in-house, 36% used external R&D contracts, and 26% co-operated with other companies (multiple answers were possible).

[2] In spite of recent attempts by a number of economic analysts to demonstrate that leakages accompanying informal know-how trading are very much in the companies' interests (Hippel 1987; Schrader 1991).

of rules (Fiol and Lyles 1985: 807–8; Argyris and Schön 1978). Consequently, learning of this, probably very common, type is supposed to exploit existing technological trajectories, thereby producing innovations of an incremental character.

Multilateral networks undoubtedly seem to be promising arrangements for their participants; but given that companies are frequently quite reluctant to engage in collective activities of this kind, the question as to how and under which conditions they are nevertheless capable of doing so appears to be crucial. For this reason, this chapter, on the basis of a case study analysis, will shift attention to the process of network formation. In particular, the chapter will analyse the factors which enabled a group of either bilaterally connected or uncoupled firms to transform themselves into a multilateral network, allowing a higher-level kind of learning to occur. The analysis will show that this requires, first, unlearning the norms and rules characterizing the actors' former relationships (for the notion of unlearning, see Hedberg 1981; Nystrom and Starbuck 1984; Johnson 1992; Argyris 1993). The concept of unlearning refers to a form of cognitive reorientation, a redefinition of one's interaction situation. Paradoxically, the importance of unlearning is due to successful learning processes: since organizations encase learning processes and their results in programmes and standard operating procedures, executed routinely, actors often generate habits of thought and practice which render experimentation with alternative problem-solving strategies less attractive (March 1991: 71).[3] In the present case, actors had to unlearn rules, like secrecy, distrust, and inequality, hitherto preventing higher-level learning processes from evolving. It is argued that learning of this kind could only occur because network participants were able to establish new rules and norms of collaboration—reciprocity and trust were governing inter-firm relationships from that time on. Moreover, this paper specifies certain preconditions which foster unlearning and learning: *inter alia*, the intervention by intermediaries, changing the flow of information within the net, as well as a positive-sum-game task and a common professional culture, and facilitating the establishment of collaboration within the group. The analysis is based on the results of a case study of a successful multilateral research collaboration which could only emerge as a result of the above-mentioned contingencies and processes. Attention is drawn to the fact that it may be fruitful not only to distinguish different processes of network formation but also different stages of network-building.

---

[3] Successful learning processes might finally result in a competency trap—a favourable performance with an inferior procedure leads an organization to accumulate more experience in this procedure, thereby keeping experience with a superior procedure inadequate rather than rewarding to use (Levitt and March 1988: 322). In order to keep themselves innovative, organizations have to balance this dilemma between exploitation and exploration (March 1991).

THE EARLY STAGE: SUSTAINING BILATERAL RELATIONSHIPS

The case study this chapter will be based upon, refers to a multilateral research collaboration, conducted as part of the German government programme on production technologies, sponsored by the Federal Ministry for Research and Technology. The project 'Adhesion as a Production Technology' represents an example of a quite demanding and, at the same time, successful, multilateral network, both in terms of innovation and its level of collaboration.[4] Technologically, the research group was able to prove that an alternative manufacturing technology (i.e. adhesive bonding) could be employed in those areas of industrial production where a historically grown, that is institutionalized, technology (i.e. welding) had previously dominated. A lack of basic knowledge (concerning a scientifically sound understanding of adhesion, as well as general construction rules), but also uncertainty with respect to the application in repetitive processes of mass production, characterized the research at the onset of the project. Multilateral research successfully demonstrated the technical feasibility of adhesion as a mass production technology, established a sound body of chemical and physical knowledge, and substantiated pilot applications under actual working conditions. Thus it seems justified to qualify this technological output as a radical innovation, opening up the chance to switch from an established technological trajectory to a promising new one.

In terms of co-operation, a constellation of actors evolved who had never collaborated before: the research group consisted of twenty participants, among them scientific institutes (IFaM, Fraunhofer-Institut für Angewandte Materialforschung, and LWF, Laboratorium für Werkstoff- und Fügetechnik at Paderborn University) doing basic research and providing testing facilities. Two steel producers (Hoesch and Thyssen) provided the materials to be connected, and eight adhesive producers individually developed a great number of adhesives; a user's perspective was introduced by two automobile producers (Volkswagen (VW) and Audi), who firstly specified their requirements regarding the adhesive products, and finally tested them.

It should be stressed that this kind of actor constellation was genuinely new because different types of interdependency were connected for the first time: horizontally, a large group of competitors worked together, primarily adhesive producers, but also steel suppliers. Vertically, adhesive and steel suppliers collaborated with customers from the automobile industry. Scientific institutes, however, played a crucial role in this setting of actors: since they conducted tests on the products of each participating firm, they were linked to each industrial partner. One particular consequence of this was that scientific partners acted as brokers between competing adhesive producers. In this way, the arrangement differed slightly, but decisively, from a

---

[4] For an extended description of this case, see Lütz (1993); Häusler *et al.* (1994).

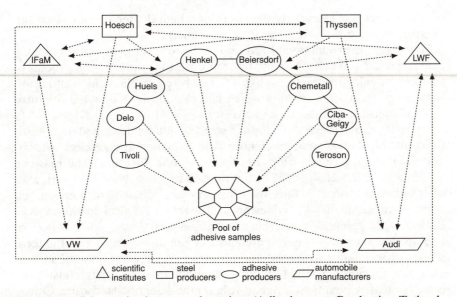

Fig. 9.1. Participants in the research project, 'Adhesion as a Production Technology'

purely segmented division of labour. Although each of the competitors developed an adhesive of his own, they were nevertheless linked to each other via the scientific intermediaries: the institutes tested the adhesives and gave accounts of their specific properties to each project member. By informing each competing producer about the 'state of the art' of adhesive technology among the group of rivals, institutes created a state of almost complete information—each competitor came to know about his rival's capacities to fulfil the requirements of the users from the automobile industry. The special intermediary role scientific partners played within the group, was one of the main factors which made the process of network formation successful in the end.

Linked by scientific intermediaries, a research group evolved, transcending well beyond the scope of conventional R&D projects. For the first time, this actor constellation allowed the combination of different types of know-how, which, by being synthesized, rendered a paradigm shift possible: fundamental knowledge concerning the principles of adhesion could be combined with applied know-how about the use of adhesives in actual production processes. At the same time, knowledge from several disciplines, such as chemical and engineering know-how, was linked. Forms of collaboration included a common definition of goals and plans of work, a jointly agreed division of labour, a joint use of testing facilities, and an interactive evaluation of necessary adaptations in the research process. Although R&D was mainly conducted in separate company labs, the technological outcome of the project was essentially the result of a high degree of joint decision-making, of successful multilateral co-ordination.

However, the production of radical innovations through multilateral co-ordination did not constitute the first step, but the very end of a process of network-building, characterized by efforts to re-establish old, well-known patterns of (non-)co-operation which had previously dominated the institutional landscape of the adhesive sector.

Up to the early 1980s, the adhesive sector could be described as an institutionally highly fragmented scientific field. Fragmentation concerned, first and foremost, the relationships between scientific disciplines and between activities at different stages of the innovation process: there were a number of scientific institutes dealing with the problem of adhesive bonding, but none of these dealt with adhesion exclusively. Chemical institutes conducted basic research concerning the principles of the composition of adhesives, and engineering-oriented institutes, mainly focusing on the technology of welding, only considered problems of adhesive bonding in connection with other available joining technologies. These latter institutes, none the less, played the dominant role on the scientific landscape. Consequently, addressing problems of adhesive bonding technologies regularly meant working in the shadow of other paradigms, especially the welding paradigm.

This restricted type of innovation activities was reinforced by the dominant structure of inter-organizational co-operation in the adhesives sector. Adhesives producers did not prastise any form of co-operation. However, the dominant collaborative arrangements were close bilateral relationships, mostly linking engineering institutes and users as well as suppliers and users of adhesives. These relations were mostly in the form of short-term contractual research with very clear requirements, specified by the customer and contractually fixed. In that way, the usual type of bilateral collaboration in the adhesive sector might well be characterized as a form of 'relational contracting' (Williamson 1979: 238; 1985: 74–8), governing the research and development activities of industrial and scientific actors.

Owing to this lack of collaborative arrangements within competing adhesive producers, it is not very surprising that the climate between them was characterized by secrecy and distrust. The only, albeit usual, place for them to meet was in the vestibule of the car producers (see interview in Lütz 1993: 124; translation by the author). As suppliers of the car industry, they were predominantly competing for the orders of their customer; this lack of communication within the adhesive supplier group was the reason why the client was able to put them under competitive pressure—since each supplier was eager to strengthen his relation with the customer, it was mostly the user's needs that governed the research activities of his suppliers. In this way, not only secrecy and distrust, but also a feeling of inequality characterized the informal relationships between actors of the adhesive sector.

The dominance of bilaterally structured relationships, characterized by power dependencies between supplier and user firms, was the reason why innovation activities in this sector could only lead to *incremental* progress along the existing technological trajectory. Adhesive producers either relied on their own competences or had to follow the instructions of potential customer firms. Owing to this underlying pattern of innovation strategies, there was very little autonomy to experiment with new ways of problem-solving. Suppliers mostly had to concentrate on their market interests and to intensify their relations with customers, in order to strengthen their position *vis-à-vis* competitors. The acquisition and transmission of knowledge proceeded within a well-known and also quite narrow framework, only allowing for 'lower-level' learning processes to emerge.

It is understandable that a sectoral innovation strategy, with the aim of establishing a viable alternative to the dominating production technology, seemed unlikely to be organized within an institutional setting composed of multiple relationships of bilateral character. But paradoxically, the main reason why industrial actors were willing to establish a multilateral network as a new form of institutional arrangement was that each of them hoped to sustain or to build up a traditional one.

From the viewpoint of competing adhesive producers, the wider use of adhesive bonding technologies meant an opportunity to diversify into a promising and attractive market. The participation of a major user turned out to be of importance in order to receive information about the required performance specifications and on the market potential of the new product. Moreover, faced with the prospect that an attractive customer would collaborate with one or several competitors, thereby defining future technological trajectories, each of the adhesive producers had to be interested in defending or opening up new market shares. Especially for those competitors who already served as suppliers of the car industry, it was virtually impossible not to join the project once their customer expected them to do so.

The relationship between the supplier group could therefore still be described as a competitive one: their main incentive for project participation was the perspective of being selected as one of the future business partners of the car industry. Therefore collaboration with rivals had to appear as a zero-sum game. Each adhesive manufacturer tried to maximize his own gain or to minimize losses *vis-à-vis* his competitors. Symptomatic of this competitive orientation were several efforts to prevent competing adhesive producers from collaborating closely with the car producer. In the early phase of project constitution, for instance, one of those adhesive producers who was already a supplier of Audi, was eager to establish a closed-shop type of project together with his customer, one of the steel suppliers (Hoesch), and one of the research institutes (LWF). When the actors had to negotiate the definitive type of collaboration structure, the group of existing adhesive suppliers, trying to defend their market shares against the newcomers in the field of adhesives, were seeking to form a sub-project together with the user firms.

As competition was still the rule governing the suppliers' relationships, their expectations towards each other were based on incomplete information about knowledge base and learning capacities. In the suppliers' view, status differences were due to varying market shares or to different size and equipment of the respective R&D departments. Large corporations were expected to employ about twenty scientists and engineers to work on a project, while the representatives of smaller firms were seen to be relatively unskilled and often incompetent. Shaped by earlier experiences of non-collaboration, their new relationship was also governed by prejudice, secrecy, and distrust.

Given this lack of solidarity within the supplier group, the position of the car industry as an influential user of adhesives was strengthened. The general reason for car manufacturers to participate was that they were interested in solving a demanding technological problem, which was of potential relevance for the whole car industry. With the growing importance of lightweight construction, adhesives were seen as an intriguing possible technological solution. At the same time, however, the users pursued quite individual interests in this project; they were interested in an innovation of a highly specific character, which would completely fulfil their requirements. By collaborating with a large group of actual or potential adhesive suppliers, the car manufacturers found themselves in a position of structural power, enabling them to pursue a *divide et impera*—strategy. Since the customers were able to control the information flows within the group of competing firms, they could use the suppliers' state of incomplete information about the individual performance of each competitor, in order to put each of them under pressure to optimize his products. By controlling a bunch of bilaterally structured relationships, customers could choose between a set of alternatives (for this relational definition of power, see Emerson 1962), thereby determining the market survival of each adhesive product. Although the users did not from the beginning of the project recognize all the advantages which a collaboration with a set of suppliers—instead of a closed shop—could provide, they later took the chance of using the project as an opportunity structure to put all adhesive producers under competitive pressure: to intensify the race for the product best fitting their individual specifications, representatives of the car producers requested that only those adhesives be optimized during the second phase of the project which came closest to their requirements. A firm, whose product was not selected, would have been excluded from further competition.

It seems obvious that under these given circumstances a higher-level type of learning did not and could not develop: as long as incomplete information between the competing firms led to an atmosphere of distrust and as long as it was the customer's needs governing the research activities of the different actors, only incremental steps forward along the existing technological path could be expected.

INTERMEDIATION AND COLLABORATION

It was mentioned before that the structure of this newly created multilateral network differed in one important respect from the traditional type of multiple, bilaterally connected relationships: the intermediary role of scientific institutes. According to the work schedule of the group, each of the adhesive producers was to develop an adhesive of its own, the properties of which would be examined by one of the institutes. This institute would then inform the project members about its tests, revealing the specific characteristics of the products but keeping the formula details secret. Since each supplier was motivated to present his best efforts with regard to his actual or potential customer from the car industry, a rather clear picture of the state of the art in the technology of adhesives could develop. Owing to the reports issued by the institutes, each competitor developed an estimation of his individual performance, as well as of the capacities of his group members to fulfil the requirements of the car producers. For the first time in the adhesive sector, a state of complete information about the technological potential of rivals was created.

There were two main reasons why scientific partners could step into the role of informational brokers between industrial actors. First, the technological task this group intended to solve required that basic knowledge had to be generated, concerning, for example, the composition of adhesives or their applicability to steel sheets, thereby enabling the producers to optimize their products step by step. Since this technological undertaking was much more demanding than the usual problems dealt with in bilateral research collaborations, different types of knowledge had to be gathered and synthesized.

Furthermore, the model of financing collaborative research projects in the governmental programme on production technologies implied that the state, together with the pool of industrial partners, covered the research costs of scientific institutes. The consequence was that one company alone was neither able to determine the research tasks of the scientific partners nor to be sure to be the only one to profit from their work. Since it was the pool of industrial firms that partly covered the institutes' costs, it was also the group of firms, to which the scientific actors felt committed. This financial arrangement laid the basis for the relative autonomy of the scientific actors within the network—being not too closely linked to single firms but to the whole group of industrial partners, their research output had the character of a club-good (Buchanan 1965).

By informing each partner about the testing results, a rather unexpected definition of the situation emerged: none of the firms taking part in the project provided a product even approximately fulfilling the specifications of the car industry. For the adhesive producers in particular, this information altered their situation fundamentally. Based on this changed flow of information within the network, a switch to a cognitive reorientation, to a new definition of the interaction situation, was possible: the information that none of the participating firms possessed a marketable product, made it feasible to define the group's work as pre-competitive. Competing for the orders of the manufacturer was no longer the dominating rule of the game. If no one was able to fulfil the user's requirements by now, it was no use hoping to gain competitive advantages and to maximize the individual gain within a perceived zero-sum game. Given the fact that all participants in the project were collectively worse off than expected, the relative benefits of possible gains from co-operation increased. Exchanging information about how to improve one's own adhesive in order to fulfil the users' requirements could increase the chance of developing a marketable product. Therefore, trying to become collectively better off at this early stage of the innovation process could at the same time mean becoming individually better off in the future. Grounded on a revised perception of the group's status quo, collaboration between suppliers could now be regarded as a positive-sum game.[5]

Within this new frame of reference, competing actors were able to unlearn well-established rules and to change their expectations towards each other: results from testing the adhesives revealed, for example, that the knowledge among the project members differed less than had been expected with regard to the firms' varying market shares or the different size and equipment of their R&D departments. Actors noticed that 'in general, only two people are engaged in a project and that the quality of technical developments depends on the qualifications of these employees' (interview, translation by the author). In this way, the experience served to minimize status differences between representatives of the adhesive producers and predisposed their future behaviour within the project context. The former competitive relationship among the suppliers' representatives was reinterpreted in terms of sportsman-like competition between a team of equally qualified, technical experts. Their common professional culture became the dominating link between the researchers, allowing them to partially drop their roles as representatives of competitors.

However, a cognitive reorientation within the suppliers' group alone

[5] The pre-competitive character of the interaction situation was also the reason why the contract of this collaboration did not play a crucial role as an instrument of regulation. The project members saw no relevance in the contract for guiding their activities and referred to this contractual agreement merely as a 'marriage contract' arranging for workable exit conditions. 'If you really intend to collaborate, you are simply not allowed to use the contract in order to put your partners under pressure' (Lütz 1993: 169, translation by the author).

would not have rendered the project successful—as long as the car customers were sticking to their old habits and trying to put their customers under competitive pressure, their newly found positive-sum-game definition of interaction was still in danger. In order to allow a higher-level type of learning to occur, the car producers had to unlearn, too.

THE FINAL STAGE: LEARNING WITHIN A MULTILATERAL SETTING

Indeed, the car producers did not share the suppliers' perception at first. By issuing their 'pyramid proposal', they tried to intensify the race for the products that fitted their specifications best; only those adhesives coming closest to these requirements were to be optimized during the next phase of research. Intending to select step by step those alternatives best fulfilling their own needs, the car producers tried to re-establish old forms of dependency relationships, of power asymmetries. Old habits, forms of standard operating procedures (March and Simon 1958) were governing the users' behaviour, thereby preventing the whole group from reaching a higher learning standard.

Each adhesive producer, knowing that neither he himself nor one of the other suppliers was able to fulfil the users' requirements by now, was facing the very likely perspective of being excluded from further collaboration. Based on the common perception that no one in the suppliers' group was able to gain a competitive advantage, the supplier representatives could practise collective resistance more easily. In several meetings parallel to the project meetings, the so-called 'adhesives group' agreed to take concerted action and was able to reject the procedure requested by the automobile firms.

For the first time, adhesive suppliers were the winners in a power struggle with their customers. This interaction effect could only evolve owing to a state of complete information within the group of competitors. Since the users no longer possessed a lead of information about the suppliers' performances, they could not put them under competitive pressure. Furthermore, a coalition of producers now replaced several atomized firms, thereby simply reducing the number of the users' alternatives (for this strategy of balancing power relationships, see Emerson 1972).

Not surprisingly, then, this conflict caused the car producers to revise their definition of interest towards collaboration. Rather than insisting on products developed to fulfil their actual needs, the customers now attempted to use the research project to work on technical problems of common interest and of an uncertain nature. Along with this cognitive reorientation, the car producers also emphasized the pre-competitive character of the common research. The consequence was that the producers' expectations towards their suppliers shifted from their actual performance to the question: what in the future could be expected from them beyond the ordinary? In other words, it was the suppliers' learning potential, their capacity to conform to the users' needs at a later stage of research and development which had now to be proved. In this way, they were allowed to concentrate on the mid- or long-term output of their common research instead of the short-term output. Research could now be done in a more autonomous way than in the former type of bilaterally structured power-dependency relationships.

As a result of unlearning processes, leading to the project's revised objectives, not only the suppliers' representatives, but also the members of the user corporations were able to partially drop their roles as representatives of certain institutions within the group and to present themselves predominantly as technical experts.[6] This shared professional identity enabled the group members to develop a 'common language'. For the first time in the adhesive sector, technicians belonging to different disciplines were discussing problems of adhesive bonding; chemists from the supplier firms and chemical research institutes on the one hand and engineers from the car and steel manufacturers as well as from the engineering research institutes on the other hand were thus able to synthesize complementary knowledge in order to solve their demanding technological problem.

During the sequence of this interdisciplinary discourse, research partners cultivated new rules of the game: since information could now be exchanged quite openly, a give-and-take philosophy of interaction was now welcomed, implying that not every member of the group shared in the exchange of information equally. According to this norm of reciprocity, only those group members willing to pass on information received information (for the role of reciprocity in exchange relationships, see Blau 1964). At the same time, free-riding behaviour could easily be identified and immediately punished: one project member, being perceived as the potential 'black sheep' within the exchange circle, was to an increasing extent excluded from communication. Since that norm of reciprocity allowed opportunism to be punished and at the same time rewarded faithful behaviour, co-operation partners were stimulated to engage in an increasingly open and finally trusting exchange of information. Each actor was now willing to share his knowledge, because he could be sure of receiving novel information in the future. Within this sequence of mutually beneficial transactions, the collaboration partners developed a relationship of *trust*, allowing them to discuss technical problems without giving the whole show away.[7]

---

[6] One of the project members stated in an interview that most participants behaved in a 'two-faced' way in the last stage of the project—in specific situations performing as a representative of the firm and in other situations primarily as a chemical engineer (Häusler *et al.* 1994).

[7] Peter Smith Ring classifies this kind of relationship as 'resilient trust'—the confidence in the goodwill of others is based on the sequence of repeated past interactions in which norms

Trustful multilateral collaboration was ultimately the reason why actors ended up at a higher-level standard of learning. First, all of them were now ready to share their know-how. The result of this was that, for the first time, knowledge of different disciplines as well as different stages of the innovation process was combined: chemical and engineering know-how as well as knowledge of a basic and an applied character was synthesized. And secondly, different types of information could be combined in a new and different way; since all participants eventually shared a pre-competitive definition of their situation of interaction, the technological goals were, in the end, only loosely coupled with actual market needs. As neither competitors nor the powerful car customers fell back into old habits and followed old learning paths, a more experimental form of improving one's own competences occurred instead. Prevailing assumptions of problem-solving strategies were modified; alternative ways to solutions were explored. In the end, participants referred to their research collaboration as a 'programme of continuing education' (Häusler *et al.* 1994). For this reason, the cornerstone for a far-reaching, radical type of innovation was set up.

CONCLUSION

The empirical analysis revealed the multilateral network between different economic organizations as an efficient institutional arrangement, finally enabling its participants to produce a radical innovation. Governed by norms like reciprocity and trust, all actors were in the end willing to engage in an open exchange of information, allowing the whole group to achieve a higher-level learning standard. Although multilateral collaboration obviously can be a beneficial arrangement for those who participate, it is, however, often questionable whether institutional arrangements of this type will always work. With regard to this, the chapter also disclosed important obstacles to as well as preconditions for successful multilateral co-operation.

First, habits, in the form of standard operating procedures (March and Simon 1958) participants had practised previously, turned out to be one of the most important barriers to collaboration. When actors are engaged for a long time in a particular form of relationship with each other, it is not very surprising that these structures will frame their cognitive orientations towards one another; in this case, the participating actors formerly either had forms of dependency relationships or practised no collaboration at all. The consequence was, that, if a flow of information did take place between

and sanctions are established, thereby endogenously safeguarding faithful behaviour. This type of relation differs especially from modes of relational contracting where formal arrangements like contracts and credible commitments should protect partners from opportunism (see Chapters 5 and 6).

them, it was unilaterally directed, that is, framed by the needs of the more powerful partners. Being used to this type of communication, they carried on in this manner, although newly created structures of multilateral collaboration provided the chance to open up new channels of communication. Obviously it is useless to establish a new type of institutional setting which would provide its members with learning opportunities, if these are captured by old action orientations, thus preventing the realization of new possibilities. In other words—networks do not only have to be established, but one also has to make them work!

This case study emphasized that informational brokers can play a crucial role in overcoming these cognitive obstacles to multilateral co-operation. By breaking up channels of information that have evolved historically and replacing them with an open multilateral exchange, intermediaries helped to transform actors' expectations towards each other, finally leading to a trustful, mutually beneficial, learning relationship.[8] Furthermore, one should keep in mind that intermediaries were only able to play this role because of the institutional framework in which this research project was embedded: owing to the financial rules being fixed in the governmental programme, scientific partners were committed to the collectivity of industrial partners and not to single firms. Since the pool of firms was covering the institutes' costs, all of them were entitled to receive information about testing results, and thereby on the group's state of the art. By switching the direction of information flows, this brokerage function served to change the type of interaction within the network.

Probably the most important lesson this case might teach network researchers is the observation that networks are obviously capable of changing their face. Even if the network structure, that is, the number of participating actors, does not change, actors might alter their orientation towards each other during the course of interaction. A remodelled flow of information within the network might finally enable them to change their interests towards the collaboration. Therefore, network interaction seems to differ from the game-theoretical notions of infinitely repeated games or simple chains of exchange relationships. Since actors are able to cognitively switch during the process of interaction to revise their interests regarding the collaboration's output, the modalities of exchange, the rules of the game, are also transformed: in the present case a zero-sum-game definition of the interaction situation could be transformed into a positive-sum-game perspective. It is exactly this capacity to restructure rules of interaction which the higher-level-learning potential of network partners can exploit.[9]

---

[8] See especially Chapter 7 by Casson and Cox, who emphasize the role of intermediators as engineers of trust in network-like arrangements.

[9] This type of learning shares some characteristics with the 'Learning by Monitoring' model Charles Sabel has identified: common to both concepts is the idea that actors are able to reinterpret the modalities of their interaction during the sequence of their transactions. In Sabel's

Once these actors have revised their expectations and interests towards each other, the step to restructuring existing cognitive models of knowledge acquisition and transmission is not very far. Thus, this case once more underlines the need to look at process patterns of network relationships (see also Chapter 5); by investigating the micropolitics of network interaction, different mechanisms and stages of network formation should be marked—in general: long-term studies revealing the life cycles of networks are called for.

REFERENCES

Argyris, C. 1993. *Knowledge for Action*. San Francisco: Jossey-Bass Publ.
——and Schön, D. A. 1978. *Organizational Learning: A Theory of Action Perspective*. Reading, Mass.: Addison-Wesley.
Axellsson, B., and Easton, G. (eds.) 1992. *Industrial Networks: A New View of Reality*. London: Routledge.
Berger, J., Zelditch, M. Jr., and Anderson, B. (eds.) 1972. *Sociological Theories in Progress*. ii. New York: Houghton Mifflin.
Blau, P. M. 1964. *Exchange and Power in Social Life*. New York: Wiley and Sons.
Bradach, J. L., and Eccles, R. G. 1989. 'Price, Authority and Trust: From Ideal Types to Plural Forms'. *Annual Review of Sociology*. 15: 97–118.
Buchanan, J. M. 1965. 'An Economic Theory of Clubs'. *Economica*. 32: 1–14.
Bullinger, H.-J. 1990. 'Integrierte Produktentwicklung XV. Produktionsmittelhersteller und Zulieferer müssen weiterentwickeln. Eine Kooperation kann eigene F&E-Kapazitäten für die Schlüsseltechnologien freimachen'. *Handelsblatt*. 6 November: 20.
Dertouzos, M. L. 1989. *Made in America. Regaining the Productive Edge*. Cambridge, Mass.: MIT Press.
Dodgson, M. 1993. 'Organizational Learning: A Review of some Literatures'. *Organization Studies*. 14: 375–94.
Dosi, G. 1982. 'Technological Paradigms and Technological Trajectories'. *Research Policy*. 11: 147–62.
Emerson, R. M. 1962. 'Power-Dependence-Relations'. *American Sociological Review*. 27: 31–41.
——1972. 'Exchange Theory, Part II: Exchange Relations and Network Structures'. In Berger, J., Zelditch, M. Jr., and Anderson, B. (eds.). *Sociological Theories in Progress*. 2: 58–88. New York: Houghton Mifflin.
Fiol, C. M., and Lyles, M. A. 1985. 'Organizational Learning'. *Academy of Management Review*. 10: 803–13.

view, these endogenous learning processes can be stimulated by an institutional framework, i.e. a specific system of production or by public intervention in the sequence of interactions, thereby transforming discrete exchanges into continuing discourses (Sabel 1994).

Gouldner, A. W. 1960. 'The Norm of Reciprocity: A Preliminary Statement'. *American Sociological Review*. 25: 161–78.

Grabher, G. (ed.) 1993. *The Embedded Firm. On the Socioeconomics of Industrial Networks*. London: Routledge.

Håkansson, H. 1989. *Corporate Technological Behavior. Co-operation and Networks*. London: Routledge.

Häusler, J. 1989. 'Industrieforschung in der Forschungslandschaft der Bundesrepublik: Ein Datenbericht'. MPIFG Discussion Paper 89/1, Max-Planck-Institut für Gesellschaftsforschung, Köln.

——Hohn, H.-W., and Lütz, S. 1994. 'Contingencies of Innovative Networks: A Case Study of Successful Interfirm R&D Collaboration'. *Research Policy*. 23: 47–66.

Hedberg, B. 1981. 'How organizations learn and unlearn'. In Nystrom, P. C., and Starbuck, W. H. 1981 (eds.). *Handbook of Organizational Design*. 1: 3–27. New York: Oxford University Press.

Hippel, E. von 1987. 'Cooperation between Rivals: Informal Know-How Trading'. *Research Policy*. 16: 291–302.

Johanson, J., and Mattson, L.-G. 1987. 'Interorganizational Relations in Industrial Systems: A Network Approach compared with the Transaction-Cost Approach'. *International Studies of Management and Organization*. 17: 34–49.

Johnson, B. 1992. 'Institutional Learning'. In Lundvall 1992: 23–45.

Kogut, B., Shan, W., and Walker, G. 1993. 'Knowledge in the Network and the Network as Knowledge: The Structuring of New Industries'. In Grabher 1993: 67–95.

Levitt, B., and March, J. G. 1988. 'Organizational Learning'. *Annual Review of Sociology*. 14: 319–40.

Lundvall, B.-A. 1990. 'Explaining Inter-Firm Cooperation and Innovation: Limits of the Transaction Cost Approach'. Paper presented at the workshop 'Networks. On The Socio-Economics of Inter-Firm Cooperation' at the Social Science Centre Berlin, 11–13 June 1990.

——(ed.) 1992. *National Systems of Innovation*. London: Pinter.

Lütz, S. 1993. *Die Steuerung industrieller Forschungskooperation. Funktionsweise und Erfolgsbedingungen des staatlichen Förderinstrumentes Verbundforschung*. Frankfurt am Main: Campus.

March, J. G. 1991. 'Exploration and Exploitation in Organizational Learning'. *Organization Science*. 2: 71–88.

——and Simon, H. A. 1958. *Organizations*. New York: Wiley and Sons.

Mayntz, R. 1991. 'Modernization and the Logic of Interorganizational Networks'. MPIFG Discussion Paper 91/8. Max-Planck-Institut für Gesellschaftsforschung Köln.

Nohria, N., and Eccles, R. G. (eds.) 1992. *Networks and Organizations: Structure, Form and Action*. Boston, Mass.: Harvard Business School Press.

Nystrom, P. C., and Starbuck, W. H. (eds.) 1981. *Handbook of Organizational Design*. i. New York: Oxford University Press.

————1984. 'To Avoid Organizational Crises, Unlearn'. *Organizational Dynamics*. 13: 53–65.

Powell, W. W. 1990. 'Neither Market nor Hierarchy: Network Forms of Organization'. *Research in Organizational Behavior*. 12: 295–336.

——and Brantley, P. 1992. 'Competitive Cooperation in Biotechnology: Learning through Networks?' In Nohria and Eccles 1992: 366–95.

——and Smith-Doerr, L. 1994. 'Networks and Economic Life'. In Smelser and Swedberg 1994: 368–402.

Sabel, C. F. 1994. 'Learning by Monitoring: The Institutions of Economic Development'. In Smelser and Swedberg 1994: 137–65.

Scharpf, F. W. (ed.) 1993*a*. *Games in Hierarchies and Networks: Analytical and Empirical Approaches to the Study of Governance Institutions*. Frankfurt am Main: Campus.

——1993*b*. 'Coordination in Hierarchies and Networks'. In Scharpf, F. W. 1993*a*: 125–67.

Schrader, S. 1991. 'Informal Technology Transfer between Firms: Cooperation through Information Trading'. *Research Policy*. 20: 153–70.

Smelser, N. J., and Swedberg, R. (eds.) 1994. *The Handbook of Economic Sociology*. New York: Princeton University Press.

Smith-Ring, P., and Van de Ven, A. H. 1994. 'Developmental Processes of Cooperative Interorganizational Relationships'. *Academy of Management Review*. 19: 90–118

Sydow, J. 1992. *Strategische Netzwerke. Evolution und Organisation*. Wiesbaden: Gabler.

Täger, U. C. 1988. 'Technologie- und wettbewerbspolitische Wirkungen von Forschungs- und Entwicklungs (FuE-) Kooperationen—Eine empirische Darstellung und Analyse'. Abschlußbericht, IFO-Institut für Wirtschaftsforschung. München.

Williamson, O. E. 1979. 'Transaction-Cost-Economics: The Governance of Contractual Relations'. *Journal of Law and Economics*. 22: 233–62.

——1985. *The Economic Institutions of Capitalism: Firms, Markets, Relational Contracting*. New York: Free Press.

Zucker, L. G. 1986. 'Production of Trust: Institutional Sources of Economic Structure, 1840–1920'. *Research in Organizational Behavior*. 8: 53–111.

10

Mixed Mode Operation of Electronic Markets and Hierarchies

CHRISTOPHER P. HOLLAND AND †GEOFF LOCKETT

ABSTRACT

The impact of inter-organizational systems (IOSs) on network structures is analysed from a managerial perspective. The research problem is to explain the role of IOSs in the context of other variables such as asset specificity which have also been shown to partly determine the formation and change of network structures. One attempt at this problem is to apply transaction cost economics. In its simplest form this type of analysis suggests a move towards electronic markets rather than electronic hierarchies. However, this is not supported by empirical evidence from the subject disciplines of industrial marketing, manufacturing strategy, and by certain organization theory research which highlights the importance of integrated supply chains co-ordinated through hierarchical links. Although electronic markets have been involved in some industries such as travel and grocery, there is clearly a move towards electronic hierarchies, particularly in manufacturing, which have been termed virtual organizations, or vertical integration without ownership. In this chapter it is argued that by considering asset specificity, market complexity, and co-ordination strategy from an individual firm perspective, different forms of business relationships and network structures can be predicted and explained. This represents a broader application of transaction cost economics which includes issues of quality and exogenous changes in markets. The basic premise of electronic markets is that IOSs affect the relative cost structures of markets and hierarchies. This analysis is questioned and an alternative explanation is offered, namely that information technology makes all network structures more efficient and effective. In addition to the well-known market, hybrid, and hierarchy concepts, a mixed mode operation which combines a market element and a hierarchy element simultaneously is identifiable. It is argued that although the mixed mode is a concept independent of information technology, in practice it would be very difficult to manage using only manual systems.

Economic forces are an important factor in determining changes in network structures but economic variables are tempered by individual firm strategies which are reflected by choices in the way that IOSs are implemented and in how competition is managed with trading partners. Rather than a general move towards electronic markets or electronic hierarchies, the mixed mode theory predicts that organizations will evolve mixed mode network structures. The balance between the market and hierarchy elements in these structures will be contingent upon changes in market complexity, asset specificity, and the specific strategy. The mixed mode theory demonstrates that there is no longer a dichotomy between market or hierarchy style structures because they can co-exist. For example, an organization may choose to adopt the market mechanism but implement it through a limited number of trading partners. This can be conceptualized by (limited) market competition within a hierarchical set of supplier relationships and would manifest itself as competition within an integrated supply chain. Several hypotheses are offered concerning the relationships between IOSs, asset specificity, co-ordination strategy, market complexity, business relationships, and network structures.

INTRODUCTION

The importance of networks consisting of organizations and business relationships is well documented in the management literature (e.g. Aldrich and Whetten 1981; Mahoney 1992; Kanter 1989; and Jarillo 1988). Previous research has been very diverse but includes the nature of business relationships (Bensaou and Venkatraman 1996), competitive strategy formulation (Harrigan 1986), structure (Ghoshal and Bartlett 1990) and the processes of change (Ebers 1992). In this chapter the effect of Inter-Organizational Information Systems on network structure is considered. Of particular interest are the mechanisms by which exogenous economic and market variables are mediated by individual firm strategies to influence business relationships and hence market structures.

Historically it can be seen that organizations have adopted a wide range of vertical integration strategies to effect the manufacture, distribution, and retail of products. Total vertical integration is one extreme of a continuum of possible structures, and some large organizations are now questioning the logic of controlling all aspects of production and distribution and are exploring other more flexible forms of industrial organization (e.g. Benetton and IBM), in order to be able to react quickly and effectively to market changes (*The Economist* 1993). These questions have been explored from many different perspectives, economic, strategic, organizational, and regulatory. Recently the same subject area has become the focus of interest for information systems (IS) researchers exploring the role and influence of modern computerized information systems based on high speed computer networks and utilizing powerful software and cheap computing power.

RESEARCH PROBLEM

The widespread implementation of electronic data interchange (EDI) systems, and latterly more complex inter-organizational (information) systems (IOSs), has already had dramatic effects in some industries (see e.g. Johnston and Vitale 1988; Short and Venkatraman 1992; and Clemons and Row 1992*b*). However, there is considerable disagreement over the long-term effects. The dominant theory of electronic markets does not appear to be supported by recent evidence (Johnston and Lawrence 1988; Bakos and Brynjolfsson 1993; Freeland and Ashby 1987) which suggests that manufacturing organizations are actually *reducing* their supplier base rather than using information technology to manage a larger portfolio of product suppliers. The question of interest here is the pattern of interactions between organizations (whether or not supported by some form of electronic link) rather than the EDI network itself which has also been studied as a separate entity (e.g. Wang and Seidmann 1995; Reimers 1996). The theme of organizational networks can be expanded to include other aspects of the network, such as market characteristics, types of relationships (legal aspects, role of trust, intensity, level of integration), and strategic intent of individual organizations (e.g. co-operative versus competitive strategies). In marketing and economics these wider concerns can be termed the study of network structure and governance structure respectively. If the topic is treated as an applied management/IS one, the research problem can be stated as a question: what are the factors and mechanisms of change driving network structures and how do inter-organizational information systems affect this process?

In the next section the different approaches to this problem are considered before proposing a model for the explanation and prediction of different network structures, given particular economic and market variables, and the potential exploitation of IOSs.

IMPACT OF INFORMATION SYSTEMS ON NETWORK STRUCTURES

Information systems research is spread across different subject disciplines (see e.g. Swanson and Ramiller 1993 for an analysis of IS research themes which concludes that IS research is topically diverse and is based on different reference disciplines). This is evident from the most influential IS theories, for example Nolan's stage theory based on evolution (e.g. Gibson

and Nolan 1974; Nolan 1979), competitive advantage theory based on strategy models (e.g. Johnston and Vitale 1988), IS design centred on systems
thinking (e.g. Checkland 1981), and electronic markets grounded in transaction cost economics (e.g. Malone *et al.* 1989). The approach taken here is
therefore one of identifying relevant theory on business relationships and
network structure from economics, strategy, organizational behaviour, and
marketing, and analysing the likely changes to occur as information systems
are introduced. A discussion of the different approaches to the research
question and theories on the evolution of market structures, as well as the
impact of electronic communication technologies introduces this chapter.
These have been organized according to subject area and an outline of each
theory is presented. The objectives are to identify relevant theory, common
themes, and differences across subject areas, and to determine the key variables from the competing theories and synthesize the results into a comprehensive model.

ECONOMIC THEORY

The dominant theory on the structure of markets as electronic trading
becomes the norm is Malone's electronic market theory (Malone *et al.* 1987;
Malone and Rockart 1992). It is based on transaction cost economics, especially those ideas propounded by Williamson (1991) on the relative costs of
markets, hybrids, and hierarchies for different economic conditions. The
outline of Malone's theory is summarized in Table 10.1.

Malone argues that although electronic links will make both markets and
hierarchies more effective and efficient, the overall advantage will shift
towards markets because the relatively high co-ordination costs of markets
will be reduced substantially and production costs, relative to hierarchical
structures, will remain low. The logic of this model is very simple and compelling. However, it does not appear to be fully supported in practice. For
example, recent research in information systems suggests that many of the
benefits of hierarchies can be gained by organizational integration, achieved
using inter-organizational information systems (e.g. Johnston and Lawrence
1988; Holland *et al.* 1992), but close integration cannot be termed a market-

Table 10.1. Malone's model of transaction costs in
markets and hierarchies

Cost type/ network structure	Production costs	Co-ordination costs
Market	Low	High
Hierarchy	High	Low

style system. Although Malone acknowledges the importance of asset specificity in influencing network structure, in particular the advantage of hierarchies over markets in co-ordinating economic activity between companies with high levels of asset-specific investments, this aspect of the model is not dealt with in any great detail, except to maintain that IOSs will be used to reduce asset specificity wherever possible.

The other dimension considered to be of importance is that of product description complexity (and hence data complexity). Here a similar assertion is put forward, namely that IOSs will reduce the logistical difficulties in exchanging complex product descriptions as the capabilities of the technology are increased. In order to gain a better understanding of how transaction cost economics can be applied to IOSs it is worthwhile returning to the seminal work of Williamson (1991).

A critical element of Williamson's work is the importance of asset specificity in determining appropriate governance structures. The definition of asset specificity, given by Williamson, reads as follows: 'Asset specificity has reference to the degree to which an asset can be redeployed to alternative uses and by alternative users without sacrifice of productive value'.

Williamson (1991) describes six types of asset specificity: site specificity, which refers to the geographic location of plant and machinery; physical asset specificity, such as specialized production technology; human asset specificity; brand-name capital; dedicated assets, such as production capacity reserved for a particular individual company or group of companies; and temporal specificity, which refers to time dependency.[1]

If the link between asset specificity and governance structures is accepted (that is, an increase in asset specificity leads to an increase in interdependencies between organizations which is more economically managed in a hierarchy rather than a market), then the question of interest becomes: what effects will information systems have on asset specificity? This is unclear at this stage but two separate theories have emerged. Malone *et al.* (1989) argue that advanced technologies such as computer-aided design and manufacture (CAD/CAM) will make manufacturing plants more flexible, thereby reducing the level of asset specificity. Hart and Estrin (1991) offer a different interpretation based on their research in the semiconductor industry and suggest the IOSs can be used to increase asset specificity. IOSs are therefore clearly an important variable but one that is not well understood.

Another application of transaction cost economics is to apply it to EDI networks (Ebers 1992; Reimers 1996). These studies assume that the technology is an important cost in itself. In this paper the importance of the

---

[1] Other definitions also exist for asset specificity, for example Walker and Poppo (1991) defined it with respect to the uniqueness of a company's investment in technical labour skills and manufacturing equipment for a particular product. This is consistent with Williamson (1991) but represents a narrower view of the concept.

technology is assumed to be small compared with the actual business relationships. The analysis is therefore focused on the patterns of interaction between organizations rather than the growth and evolution of the electronic networks themselves. The EDI network itself is not considered to be of direct importance *per se* in determining *network structure.*

In accordance with economic theory which posits the relationship between asset specificity and governance structure, Harrigan (1986) proposed a contingency theory in which successful firms are those which match appropriate vertical integration strategies to their competitive environments. Similarly Stuckey and White (1993) offer frameworks to assist in the choice of vertical integration strategy. Although none of these authors specifically consider the role of information systems, they identify the importance of *strategic choice* in the determination of governance structures, and show that there is not a simple deterministic relationship between external economic variables and governance structures.

In summary, economic theory provides important theoretical insights into the relationship between economic variables and governance structures but does not adequately incorporate the role of IOSs or strategic choice in determining governance structures. It is also questionable whether the conceptualization of governance structures as a continuum between market and hierarchy, with intermediate forms being labelled hybrid, is adequate in representing the diversity of business relationships in practice. Mahoney (1992) expands Williamson's hybrid concept by specifying a more detailed scheme of governance structures, but retains the notion of a continuum between market and hierarchy, in which intermediate forms are averages of market and hierarchy, to describe such a scheme. Asset specificity, legal ownership, and contractual arrangements are important variables, but only partially explain the evolution and performance of governance structures.

STRATEGY

An assumption in the economic models is that variables such as asset specificity, external change, and network structures drive individual organizations' activities. This ignores the role of strategic choice and the proactive involvement of individual managers—the strategic processes by which external economic conditions are related to the formation of network structures. Organizations do not therefore respond in some simple predictable manner to external economic and market variables but can instead be proactive and seek out opportunities, change markets, set up or sever business relationships, enter into new markets, or leave existing ones. Of course existing economic variables place constraints on what is possible, but they do not determine the course of future action.

In the IT literature, particularly that which considers competitive advantage, there are many examples of individual firms dramatically affecting their own competitive positions and hence the industries in which they compete through some form of strategic action. For example, Ives and Learmonth (1984) cite examples of IT being used as a competitive weapon in the airline and drug industries. Similarly Johnston and Vitale (1988) argue that it is possible for individual firms to achieve a sustainable competitive advantage from the innovative use of IOSs. On supply chains, Johnston and Lawrence (1988) and Konsynski and McFarlan (1990) both observe the emergence of new types of structures which utilize IOSs to co-ordinate economic activity between organizations. These examples are not claimed to be representative, but are given purely as illustrations of what is possible. Even the more conservative claims about the business potential of IT by authors such as Earl (1989) and Keen (1991) accept the dramatic impact of IT coupled with strategic intent, when employed strategically to improve on an organization's competitive position. A firm's strategy in co-ordinating economic activity with trading partners, co-ordination strategy, is therefore considered to be a significant variable in the evolution of business relationships and network structures.

INDUSTRIAL MARKETING

Industrial markets consist of trade between organizations, whereas retail markets consist of trade between individual consumers and retailing organizations. One of the differences between the two markets lies in the level of interdependency between separate organizations, which is much greater in industrial markets than that which exists between an individual consumer and a retailer. Turnbull (1986) argues that long-term stable relationships are the norm in industrial markets and that their business relationships are characterized by mutual adaptation and change. One influential approach to industrial markets is the interaction model (Håkansson and Wootz 1979; Cunningham 1987, 1990), which emphasizes the processes of interaction between separate organizations normally occurring across a wide range of business functions and over long periods of time. These references are part of a wider body of knowledge that is relevant to the research problem. It signals that organizations may choose to use IOSs to support close relationships, and hence improve their management, rather than use the new technology to fragment individual business relationships when moving to a market system. Of course not all industrial markets are stable in terms of trading partners; financial and commodity markets, for example, are characterized by fluidity between buyers and sellers. These are simple markets in the sense that individual parties do not rely on other individuals but rather behave autonomously in response to the collective action of the whole market. The problem, from an industrial marketing view, is whether

EDI/IOSs reinforce/accentuate existing types of business relationship and patterns of interaction, or change the economics of network structures to make rapid switching of suppliers both possible and desirable in terms of business performance. This problem has also been considered by Cunningham and Culligan (1989) who observed two contradictory effects of EDI on business relationships: the cementation of business relationships in the initial stages of EDI implementation and the plausible long-term outcome of electronic markets. The thrust of industrial marketing theory is that stable, integrative relationships cannot be easily replaced with a larger number of electronic market relationships. In industrial markets, relative stability appears to be maintained by the existence of close ties, while at the same time competition still takes place through the changing or severing of existing relationships and by the formation of new relationships.

ORGANIZATIONAL BEHAVIOUR

Recent research on inter-organizational relationships from an organizational behaviour perspective has identified a theme that is common to strategy and marketing, namely the importance of long-term relationships based on co-operation and trust (e.g. Kanter 1988; Harrigan and Newmann 1990). This is important because it suggests that organizations choose to work closely with other organizations for mutual benefit and that co-operation can lead to better overall economic performance (see also Chapter 7). The importance of legal contracts in these relationships is secondary to that of trust, indicating that it appears to be possible to manage transactions which can only be partially defined in advance without recourse to the power of fiat enjoyed by divisions under common ownership. Trust seems to enable a different type of network structure (see Chapter 5).

THEORETICAL SYNTHESIS AND PROPOSED RESEARCH FRAMEWORK

The above theories are the main ones that have been applied to the impact of information technology on the formation of network structures. The phenomena have, however, not yet been adequately explained. Each subject area makes an important contribution to the research problem but with differences in emphasis. Transaction cost economics provides a theoretical framework for the analysis of business relationships and identifies the relationship between asset specificity and network structure. However, economic theory is narrow in its emphasis on legal ownership and contractual arrangements. It also presents a rather mechanistic, predictive model of network structure and largely ignores strategy and the role of trust in explaining the functioning of business relationships. One of the most plausible and applicable theoretical approaches to market structures is the concept of networks developed in industrial marketing. It provides a framework which captures both the structural changes occurring in the network of organizations and also the processes of evolution at an individual business relationship level. The theories outlined above suggest several possible approaches but within each subject area research into the effects of information systems on network structures is rare. The aim of the approach taken here is to identify the key variables and their interrelationships based on a synthesis of the different theoretical approaches. Under the aspect of our research question, network structures are the focus of interest. What are the factors which influence and/or determine their formation? According to economic theory, asset specificity is clearly an important variable in determining network structures. Similarly, economic and marketing theory both identify different types of markets, albeit from different perspectives. From an economic viewpoint, Williamson (1991) notes the difference between those markets which require autonomous adaptation and those which require co-ordinated adaptation between organizations for a global optimal outcome. In industrial marketing theory, the need for a co-ordinated response to many external changes in markets is implicitly recognized in network theory. To capture the type and scale of external market changes and to distinguish between fundamentally different types of products (e.g. commodity finance services and specialized engineering products) and customers (e.g. retail versus industrial markets) the variable market complexity is used. Both strategy and marketing research demonstrate that managers can be proactive in their choices regarding the co-ordination of individual business relationships and larger market networks. The variable co-ordination strategy is therefore included in the model to represent the processes by which external changes are monitored, analysed, and acted upon.

It can be seen from the review of competing theories on network structures and IOSs that market networks exhibit complex phenomena which are difficult to analyse and understand. The analyses from different subject areas have resulted in diverse but often complementary findings. Based on this literature and earlier research carried out by the authors, a framework is proposed which allows us to assess the effects of IOSs and network structures through the application of the theoretical constructs of asset specificity, market complexity, and co-ordination strategy. The possible interrelationships between the constructs are depicted in Fig. 10.1.

The logic of the research framework is that given a particular market complexity, separate firms organize their activities with trading partners in an interactive exchange process to design, manufacture, distribute, and retail a certain product. Asset-specific investments arise from the action of individual firms, which, in turn, develop co-ordination strategies to manage (a)

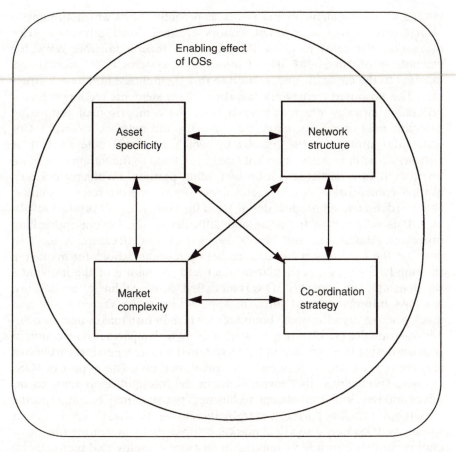

Fig. 10.1. Research framework

market complexity and (b) asset-specific investments. Inter-organizational systems are used to support the shared business processes and may therefore be used to support both market and hierarchy elements in a relationship. An IOS, for example, may be used to integrate a logistics system of a retailer into those of its suppliers. This supports the hierarchical, stable element of the relationship. In parallel, an IOS may be used to monitor the performance of suppliers and employ this information to encourage them to support the market element of the relationship by providing information on subsequent competitive tendering amongst the suppliers.

Co-ordination strategy is taken as the focal point of the framework. It is proposed that strategic choices made by individual firms and networks of organizations represent the mechanisms by which economic and market variables are related to network structures. That is, organizations are not viewed as passive elements but rather as proactive units which attempt to *change and influence* external factors to their own advantage. Co-ordination strategies manifest themselves in several tangible ways, for example in organizations' use of information systems both internal and external to the company and, related to this, their choice of network structure. The proposed framework has three main elements feeding into co-ordination strategy which are taken from the comparison of competing theories: asset specificity, market complexity, and network structure. Co-ordination strategy is the *process* by which managers determine their network structures. Asset specificity can be defined as the uniqueness of an investment to a particular group of trading partners (Williamson 1991). Market complexity is operationalized by considering the rates of market change (demand and product design) and the complexity of product attributes. It is reflected in the scale and difficulty of the buying and selling processes (Håkansson and Wootz 1979). Network structure is used to describe the legal ownership pattern between organizations for managing the supply chain of a particular product and the nature of the individual relationships. The impact of IOSs is modelled as an enabling effect because it allows information and software applications to be shared easily and quickly across organizational boundaries, which in turn makes new co-ordination strategies possible (e.g. to work closely with a partner on a common product design through shared CAD systems) and new network structures feasible (e.g. electronic financial and travel markets). The impact of IOSs on asset specificity is that investments in the information systems themselves and the associated change to business practices may become specific to particular trading partners, thereby increasing the overall level of asset specificity. IOSs may also affect market complexity by increasing the information content of products, making them more complex, and indirectly by making it possible to launch new products very quickly, which can increase the rates of change in a market due to suppliers' behaviour.

DISCUSSION

The proposed framework suggests a more complicated set of influences on network structures than has otherwise been reported. IOSs do not directly affect the evolution of either markets or hierarchies; this is instead determined by the three connecting factors, asset specificity, market complexity, and network structure. However, IOSs can affect all three of these determining factors by enabling a much greater flexibility of outcome both in the short and longer terms. IOSs allow market forces to act much more efficiently and therefore improve electronic markets. They also allow complex hierarchies to be developed far more economically in situations where there exists a high level of market complexity and/or asset specificity. One result of this is the emergence of integrated supply chains in industrial markets.

In the past, hierarchical structures have been extremely difficult to change. This has, however, been made simpler by information systems, making electronic hierarchies not only feasible but enabling them to be constructed in the first place. These ideas have been formulated in a general proposition that is intended to direct future data collection and theory building.

GENERAL PROPOSITION

It is proposed that in practice the outcome of employing IOSs will be a *mixed mode operation* in which elements of both the market and the hierarchy form are evident *simultaneously*. Although it is accepted that the occurrence of pure forms of market and hierarchy are not excluded, it is asserted that these would be exceptional. The strategy of employing a mixed mode network structure is not only an attempt to gain the benefits of both markets and hierarchies; it also implies, more fundamentally, that there is no simple average or continuum existing between market and hierarchy, but rather that elements of both are implemented at the same time, the precise balance being determined by managerial choice and contingent on external market and economic variables. The polarization to markets and hierarchies will therefore not occur. The mixed mode hypothesis encompasses aspects of Malone *et al.* (1987, 1989), Malone and Rockart (1992), Clemons and Row (1992*a*), and Powell (1990).

The general proposition is that by employing IOSs organizations will move towards mixed mode network structures which contain market and hierarchy elements simultaneously. This idea is developed in a series of hypotheses concerning the relationships between what are considered to be the key variables. These are: asset specificity, market complexity, the enabling force of IOSs, co-ordination strategy and network structure.

The logic of the proposed framework is that, given existing levels of asset specificity and market complexity, organizations will implement IOSs through a process of strategic choice in order to manage particular co-ordination mechanisms with trading partners, which in turn define the overall network structure of organizations and business relationships. By including strategic choice, it can be seen that under similar market and economic conditions different organizations may choose different strategies. Organizations are therefore not seen as passive elements in an economic system. One of the assumptions made is that the cost of the IOS itself is small in comparison to the cost of initiating, maintaining, and developing business relationships.[2] The economic and market terms therefore refer to the business relationship as a whole and to the network of organizations

---

[2] This assumption is reasonable given that simple personal-computer-based EDI systems, which allow the exchange of data, cost approximately $2,000 and larger mainframe systems often have a built-in EDI/IOS capability, making the cost to connect the internal system to a supplier or customer marginal.

connected by such relationships, rather than to the computer systems. The mixed mode proposition can be stated formally as a hypothesis.

H1: The mixed mode network structures which combine elements of hierarchy and network structure simultaneously will become the norm for managing economic activity in industrial markets.

Null: Organizations will choose to operate simple markets, hybrids, or hierarchies for the co-ordination of economic activity in business markets.

This hypothesis contends that IOSs enable organizations to gain the benefits of hierarchical and market structures. The rationale for adopting a mixed mode strategy is to attempt to gain a competitive advantage by achieving superior performance over rivals through a co-ordinated approach to external changes, whilst retaining an element of market competition to encourage cost reduction and innovation in stable, long-term relationships. The evidence from research supports the view that managers are striving to achieve competitive advantage, often through co-operative relationships with suppliers and customers or through strategic alliances with organizations in other industries (e.g. Johnston and Vitale 1988; Holland and Lockett 1993; Kanter 1988). There is, however, very little evidence to support the contention that individual organizations are motivated to set up open business relationships, other than the theoretical arguments based on transaction cost economics (e.g. Malone and Rockart 1992).

There are several direct implications which follow from the mixed mode hypothesis which are principally concerned with forms of competition. There will be a tendency for firms not to employ the polar forms of network structure but rather to use mixed mode network structures. A market system implemented using hierarchical links can be thought of as a 'hierarchy within a market'. Similarly a hierarchical system which encapsulates market competition can be thought of as a 'market within a hierarchy'. The mixed mode hypothesis is advanced in the next section.

HYPOTHESES CONCERNING INTER-ORGANIZATIONAL INFORMATION SYSTEMS AND NETWORK STRUCTURES

The general mixed mode proposition formalized in H1 is plausible and preliminary research findings appear to support it, for example, the case vignette, presented in this paper and in earlier research by the authors (Holland and Lockett 1993). In order to complement the mixed mode hypothesis and to develop a research agenda, a series of more detailed hypotheses concerning the interactions between the theoretical constructs is proposed. This represents the next stage of theory development (Eisenhardt 1989).

The objectives of developing more detailed hypotheses are to improve the validity of the theoretical constructs asset specificity, market complexity, network structure, co-ordination strategy, and IOS, and to formalize relationships between them. This requires an explanation of how and why these variables are related and how they affect each other. It also demands methods and techniques for measuring their values so that the hypotheses can be tested. The hypotheses are concerned with network structures, that is, the arrangement of separate organizations connected together by business relationships and the nature of the individual relationships which constitute the overall network.

H2: In industrial markets, which typically have significant levels of market complexity and asset specificity, the proportion of the hierarchy element to the market element in network structures will increase. This represents an increase in the level of organizational integration between separate companies. IOSs will reflect the relative importance of the hierarchy and market elements by supporting closely integrated relationships for the hierarchy element and by supporting pricing mechanisms and monitoring performance systems for the market element of the relationship.

Null: In industrial markets the proportion of the hierarchy element to the market element will remain the same or decrease. The level of organizational and IS integration between separate companies will remain constant or decrease, leading to no change or more fragmented business relationships.

This hypothesis can be tested by two sub-hypotheses.

H2A: The number of suppliers and customers will decrease.
Null: The number of suppliers and customers will stay the same or increase.

H2B: IOS growth will occur directly from an increase in the intensity of business relationships (rather than through an increase in the number of participants). This will be reflected in a wider range of IOS applications, in shared data, in increased volumes of transactions, and the use of shared software between fairly small numbers of trading partners.

Null: IOS growth will occur by an increase in the number of trading partners, which may also be accompanied by an increase in the intensity of business relationships.

There is already preliminary evidence which supports this hypothesis from the academic literature (Bakos and Brynjolfsson 1993; Holland 1993) and the business literature (Treece *et al*. 1995). The argument is that, given finite organizational and IS resources, companies have a choice of how to use the enhanced capabilities offered by information systems. Rather than a simple move towards markets, organizations appear to be developing more intensive integrated relationships to manage high levels of market complexity and asset specificity, whilst retaining a small market element of competition. This strategy must lead to fewer suppliers and customers because individual relationships will use more resources. This results in increased concentration of economic activity in industrial markets and in reduced levels of open competition. To support and enable close organizational integration, companies will have to share software and data in order to be able to manage the increased interdependencies between themselves.

By conceptualizing industrial markets as networks of organizational nodes connected by business relationships, properties of structure, stability, and dynamic changes over time can be considered. Based on H2, the concept of extending the hierarchy element of a relationship between two organizations to multiple stages of a supply chain, coupled with the ability to share data quickly and easily between organizations, it is likely that supply chain systems will evolve into more integrated units based around shared information systems.

> H3: The dominant economic structure in an electronic trading environment will be market supply chains consisting of integrated groups of organizations involved in the design, manufacture, marketing, and distribution of a product.
> Null: Market-style structures will evolve in which business relationships are based on market transactions employing IOSs to trade with many suppliers and many customers in a particular product.

Research into the textiles industry (Holland 1995) and the semiconductor industry (Hart and Estrin 1991) provides empirical evidence that competition is taking place between integrated supply chains rather than between separate organizations.

> H3A: The rate of change towards integrated supply chains is proportional to the levels of asset specificity, product market complexity, and interdependency, mediated by individual firm strategy.
> Null: The rate of change towards integrated supply chains is not proportional to the levels of asset specificity, product market complexity, and interdependency, mediated by individual firm strategy.

A key concept in dynamic changes in economic structure towards supply chains is the rate of change because it indicates the likely time-scales of transition from traditional (non-EDI) trading to full electronic support of business relationships. This is important for individual firm strategy and also for regulatory bodies interested in influencing competition through legal policy. Nevertheless it appears to be extremely difficult to collect data to test this type of hypothesis. Holland (1993) used an organization's internal IT systems to collect data over a period of five years on the number and intensity of supplier relationships measured by the expenditure with each supplier on an annual basis. The results indicated a clear trend towards fewer suppliers.

H3B: Information systems will develop along the supply chain. That is, organizations at each stage of the supply chain will use common systems.
Null: Information systems will evolve separately within each organization.

A trend within organizations has been towards integrated information systems to ensure effective business performance, supported by the sharing of common data and software between separate business functions and between different geographic sites. One rationale for these integrated systems is that they enable company-wide strategies to be implemented. These, in turn, avoid local optimization efficiencies within say a function, division, or profit centre that can be suboptimal for the organization as a whole. A key concept in integrated systems is the use of common data. This hypothesis extends the logic of integrated information systems within organizations to common systems within a supply chain. The benefits of just-in-time, quick response and fast product development cycles will drive the implementation of common systems between all companies involved in the design, production, and marketing of a product.

H4: Competition will take place *within* supply chains as outlined in the mixed mode hypothesis (H1) and *between* supply chains.
Null: Competition will take place between separate organizations.

It is asserted that the forms of competition will change. As organizations become part of larger supply chain structures, the previous form of competition between customer and supplier will become more inappropriate due to the existing extensive interdependencies. A more co-ordinated approach will therefore be necessary.[3] The mixed mode hypothesis is that market competition will be retained but contained inside hierarchical style relationships. This has already been extensively discussed. The other form of competition that will become more important will be that between supply chains. Although consisting of legally separate organizations, supply chains will behave as single entities. The focus of competition will therefore shift away from multiple levels of competition between separate organizations at each stage of the supply chain to competition between supply chain entities. This has several ramifications. First, suppliers may be inhibited from selling to a competing supply chain. Secondly, in buying a product a

---

[3] Co-operation and mutual adaptation between customers and suppliers is not a new idea, but it is the extent to which this will take place that is different, so much so that it will not be possible to distinguish between the behaviour of companies involved in a common supply chain and different divisions belonging to the same company.

consumer or business organization will consider the network or organizations behind the selling organization as of equal importance to the actual selling organization.

> H5: Competing supply chains will clump into larger units in order to reduce new product development and other marketing costs, as well as to reduce the level of competition in specific product markets.
> Null: Competing supply chains will remain separate or fragment into electronic markets.

This is probably the most contentious of the proposed hypotheses. It is, however, based on the premise that, if possible, most organizations attempt to reduce the levels of competition in their markets and also try to minimize risk. These strategies are in response to higher research and development and capital investment costs, especially in high technology industries, as well as an attempt to improve profits in low margin industries, such as textile fibres.

The purpose of the paper has been to develop a theoretical argument on the formation of network structures and, in particular, to develop the concept of mixed mode competition, in which elements of market and hierarchy are simultaneously present in network structures. The hypotheses are intended as a framework to guide empirical research. However, given the novelty of the mixed mode theory, a case vignette is presented to illustrate how mixed mode co-ordination works in practice between a retailing organization and its suppliers. The case vignette is not intended to test the hypotheses comprehensively but is given to illustrate the mixed mode concept.

CASE VIGNETTE OF FASHION STORES

Fashion Stores is a large UK-based retailing organization which sells a wide range of fashion garments for men, women, and children. It also has an international presence with a small number of prestige stores in large cities overseas. The case vignette is structured around the theoretical constructs from the research framework.

Market Complexity

Fashion markets change very quickly because of fashion trends which demand new product designs and different colours. New product designs are launched at least twice per year, and this is likely to increase as fashions appear to be changing faster. Within a product life cycle there may also be significant fluctuations in demand volumes for a particular design and also significant variations in demand for particular colours.

Asset Specificity

Asset specificity arising from investments in machinery is quite low because investments in computerized design systems and distribution systems could be transferred to different suppliers fairly easily. However, the integration of business processes and systems has been undertaken in the context of sharing knowledge and expertise of retail markets and manufacturing processes. The collaboration between Fashion Stores and its suppliers has resulted in sophisticated quick-response systems to cater for fluctuations in demand for particular garments and colours, and shared computer-aided-design systems which shorten the time taken from the concept design of a product to its full-scale production. Since the shared business processes of logistics and new product design would take time and effort to transfer to new suppliers, the overall level of asset specificity of the business relationship is judged to be medium to high.

Co-ordination Strategy

The co-ordination strategy is to work closely with a small number of first-tier suppliers (ten suppliers account for over 80 per cent of product volumes) and to develop shared information systems and business processes which support a quick response to market changes and encourage innovation in new product design. At the start of every fashion season, each supplier is invited to tender for a particular range of products. This does not exclude them from bidding for other product ranges if they think that they can offer a superior set of designs and production facilities than their competitors. In this way competition between suppliers is encouraged. However, there is also continuity of supply relationships. Individual suppliers are maintained over long periods of time through the award of annual contracts coupled with close monitoring of the performance of suppliers in every aspect of the business relationship.

Inter-Organizational Systems

There are three main groups of IOS: computer-aided-design systems shared between Fashion Stores and some of its leading suppliers; shared logistics systems with all of its suppliers; and a shared colour system which supports the exchange of dye information with suppliers. The CAD systems are designed to shorten product life cycles by reducing the time it takes to move from a concept design to full production and retail sale of a product. The shared logistics system is designed to increase the manufacturing and distribution efficiency between suppliers and the retail stores, and, in particular, to cope with volume fluctuations within a product life cycle. The shared colour system gives colour flexibility by allowing a part of the production

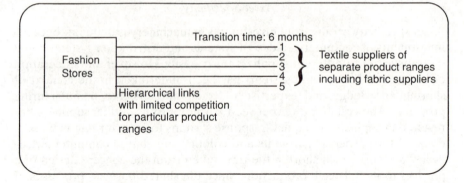

Fig. 10.2. Mixed mode network structure

to be made in grey cloth so that it can be dyed at the last possible moment when colour demand information is available.

Network Structure

The resulting network structure is a classic mixed mode operation of a market system which is conducted through a set of hierarchical relationships. Market competition over designs, production agreements, and prices takes place through a small number of relationships which closely resemble hierarchies in the way that information is shared and economic activity is organized. The principal role of the IOSs is to support the smooth operation of the design and delivery of products. However, only once the IOSs are established and the hierarchy element of the relationships is in place, do they provide a source of easily accessible data on the performance of suppliers in activities such as delivery times, accuracy of orders, number of quality control failures, and adherence to agreed volumes. This performance data supports the market element of the relationship and allows Fashion Stores to work with a small number of suppliers connected by hierarchical style relationships and still retain a market element of competition through performance monitoring and limited competition within the hierarchical relationships. A schematic diagram of the relationship with suppliers is shown in Fig. 10.2.

CONCLUSIONS

In industrial markets IOSs are being used to implement mixed mode network structures to co-ordinate economic activity between separately owned organizations. The determining factors of network structure are market complexity, asset specificity, and co-ordination strategy. In general, high levels of market complexity demand specialized investments by companies at all stages of the supply chain so that high levels of asset specificity follow. Co-ordination strategies vary, but high market complexity and high asset specificity are best managed by hierarchical style structures. Conversely, in relatively simple markets, where extremely low levels of asset specificity exist, more market-style structures are evolving.

Asset specificity arises from co-ordination strategies, designed to manage market complexity, and the generally high levels of interdependency between organizations involved in the design, manufacture, and marketing of a product in an industrial market. Rather than use IOSs to decrease the level of asset specificity and deal with larger numbers of suppliers, organizations are implementing IOSs that *increase* the level of asset specificity, either as part of an explicit strategy to tie in customers, or as a result of improving the co-ordination of hierarchical style business relationships. This phenomenon of increasing the level of asset specificity intentionally as part of a business strategy will make it more difficult to sever business relationships in the future. The net result from these strategies is increased organizational and information technology integration across organizational boundaries, accompanied by a pay-off in terms of improved responsiveness to market changes, shorter product development life-cycles and better product quality. The evidence to support these ideas are the emergence of integrated supply chains and a reduction in the number of suppliers used by many manufacturing companies. There is also a move to electronic markets, but only in markets where autonomous adaptation by individual organizations is sufficient, for example in some financial markets.

The mixed mode network structure hypothesis is based on the assumption that IOSs make all network structures more effective and efficient. The proposition implicit in electronic markets theory that IOSs change the economics of network structures, thereby making only market-style network structures significantly more attractive to organizations, is not supported. It is proposed here that competition is evolving into mixed mode business relationships in which elements of both hierarchy and market co-exist. The precise form of the mixed mode used is dependent on the need to co-ordinate decisions throughout the supply chain between separate organizations. Future network structures will therefore be determined through choices in co-ordination strategy, depending on the existing and historical market complexity, asset specificity, and network structure. The existence of mixed mode operations arising from the inherent flexibility of information systems requires a different interpretation of markets versus hierarchies because it seems that they can co-exist. The co-existence of market and hierarchy elements simultaneously is therefore a development on the electronic markets and a move to the middle theories of Malone, and Clemons and Row respectively. The direction of future research has been outlined in the form of several hypotheses which are designed to test the general proposition of mixed mode network structures. It is asserted, for example, that the rate of change towards integrated supply chains is proportional to the levels of asset specificity and market complexity, and that these economic and market variables will be mediated by individual firm strategy. Mixed mode theory offers a new method of conceptualizing the developments and changes in co-ordination strategies and network structures of industrial markets, and provides a different interpretation to the classical electronic markets and hierarchies debate.

REFERENCES

Aldrich, H., and Whetten, D. A. 1981. 'Organization-Sets, Action-Sets, and Networks: Making the Most of Simplicity'. In Nystrom, P. C., and Starbuck, W. H. (eds.). *Handbook of Organizational Design*. 385–408. London: Oxford University Press.

Bakos, J. Y., and Brynjolfsson, E. 1993. 'Why Information Technology Hasn't Increased the Optimal Number of Suppliers'. In Nunamaker, J. F., and Sprague, R. H. (eds.). *Proceedings of the Hawaii International Conference on System Sciences*. iv: 799–808.

Benjamin, R. I., de Long, D. W., and Scott, M. S. 1990. 'Electronic Data Interchange: How Much Competitive Advantage?' 23 (1) (February): 29–40.

Bensaou, M., and Venkatraman, N. 1996. 'Inter-Organization Relationships and Information Technology: A Conceptual Synthesis and a Research Framework'. *European Journal of Information Systems*. 5 (2): 84–91.

Blois, K. J. 1972. 'Vertical Quasi-Integration'. *Journal of Industrial Economics*. 20: 253–72.

Checkland, P. 1981. *Systems Thinking, Systems Practice*. Chichester: John Wiley and Sons.

Clemons, E. K., and Row, M. C. 1992a. 'Information Technology and Industrial Co-operation'. In Nunamaker, J. F., and Sprague, R. H. (eds.). *Proceeding of the Hawaii International Conference on System Sciences*. iv: 644–53.

——— 1992b. 'Rosenbluth International Alliance: Information Technology and the Global Virtual Corporation'. In Nunamaker, J. F., and Sprague, R. H. (eds.). *Proceedings of the Hawaii International Conference of System Sciences*. iv: 678–85.

Cunningham, M. T. 1990. 'Survival and Growth Strategies in New Technology Markets: A Study of the Electronic Data Interchange Industry'. In Fiocca, R., and Snehota, I. (eds.). 'Research Developments in International Industrial Marketing and Purchasing'. Proceedings of the 6th IMP Conference. i: 346–72.

—— and Ford, D. 1993. 'Technology, Networks and Purchasing Strategy'. In Sharma, D. D. (ed.). *Advances in International Marketing*. v: 205–19. Greenwich and London: JAI Press.

Earl, M. J. 1989. *Management Strategies for Information Technology*. London: Prentice Hall.

Ebers, M. 1992. 'Transaction Scale and Scope: How Organizations Get Hooked On Interorganizational Systems'. Paper prepared for the ESF Planning Workshop, 'Modes of International Integration of European Management and Organization'. Milan, 11–12 June.

Eisenhardt, K. M. 1989. 'Building Theories from Case Study Research'. *Academy of Management Review*. 14: 532–50.

European Community 1992. *TEDIS, Implementing EDI: An Evaluation of 12 Pilot Projects*. Commission of the European Communities. xiii: 180–92: 34.

Freeland, J. R., and Ashby, H. L. 1987. 'An Exploratory Study of Just-In-Time Purchasing in Japan and the United States'. Presented at the Joint Meeting of The Institute of Management Sciences and Operations Research Society of America. New Orleans, May.

Ghoshal, S., and Bartlett, C. A. 1990. 'The Multinational Corporation as an Interoganizational Network'. *Academy of Management Review*. 15 (4): 603–25.

Gibson, C. F., and Nolan, R. L. 1974. 'Managing the Four Stages of EDP Growth'. *Harvard Business Review*. 52: 76–88.

Håkansson, H., and Wootz, B. 1979. 'A Framework of Industrial Buying and Selling'. *Industrial Marketing Management*. 8: 28–39.

Harrigan, K. R. 1986. 'Matching Vertical Integration Strategies to Competitive Conditions'. *Strategic Management Journal*. 7: 535–55.

——and Newmann, W. H. 1990. 'Bases of Interorganization Co-operation: Propensity, Power, Persistence'. *Journal of Management Studies*. 27: 417–34.

Hart, P., and Estrin, D. 1991. 'Inter-Organization Networks, Computer Integration, and Shifts in Interdependence: The Case of the Semiconductor Industry'. *ACM Transactions on Information Systems*. 9: 370–98.

Holland, C. P. 1993. 'The Evolution of Electronic Hierarchies in Business Markets'. 9th International Marketing and Purchasing Conference, Bath, 23–5 September.

——1995. 'Co-operative Supply Chain Management: The Impact of Inter-Organisational Information Systems'. *Journal of Strategic Information Systems*. 4: 117–33.

——and Lockett, A. G. 1993. 'Forms of Association in Business Markets: The Impact of Inter-Organisational Information Systems'. In Sharma, D. D. (ed.). *Advances in International Marketing*. Selected Proceedings of the 7th IMP Conference, 1991. v: 125–43. Greenwich: JAI Press.

————and Blackman, I. D. 1992. 'Planning for Electronic Data Interchange'. *Strategic Management Journal*. 13: 539–50.

————Richard, J. M., and Blackman, I. D. 1993. 'Motorola Cash Management: The Evolution of a Global System'. *Hawaii International Conference on System Sciences*. Koloa, Hawaii: IEEE Computer Society Press, 5–8 January.

Hopper, M. D. 1990. 'Rattling SABRE—New Ways to Compete on Information'. *Harvard Business Review*. 68: 118–25.

Ives, B., and Learmonth, G. P. 1984. 'The Information System as Competitive Weapon'. *Communications of the ACM*. December.

Jarillo, J. C. 1988. 'On Strategic Networks'. *Strategic Management Journal*. 9: 31–41.

Johnston, H. R., and Lawrence, P. R. 1988. 'Beyond Vertical Integration, the Rise of the Value-Addng Partnership'. *Harvard Business Review*. 66: 94–101.

——and Vitale, M. R. 1988. 'Creating Competitive Advantage With Interorganizational Information Systems'. *MIS Quarterly*. 12: 153–65.

Kanter, R. M. 1988. 'Becoming PALs: Pooling, Allying and Linking across Companies'. In Kanter 1989.

——1989. *When Giants Learn to Dance*. London: Unwin Hyman Ltd.

Keen, P. G. W. 1991. *Shaping the Future, Business Design Through Information Technology*. Cambridge, Mass.: Harvard Business School Press.

Konsynski, B. R., and McFarlan, F. W. 1990. 'Information Partnerships—Shared Data, Shared Scale'. *Harvard Business Review*. 68: 114–20.

Mahoney, J. T. 1992. 'The Choice of Organizational Form: Vertical Financial Ownership versus other Methods of Vertical Integration'. *Strategic Management Journal*. 13 (8) (November): 559–84.

Malone, T. W., and Rockart, J. F. 1992. 'Information Technology and the New Organization'. In Nunamaker, J. F., and Sprague, R. H. (eds.). *Proceedings of the Hawaii International Conference on System Sciences*. iv: 636–43.

——Yates, J., and Benjamin, R. I. 1987. 'Electronic Markets and Electronic Hierarchies'. *Communications of the ACM*. 30: 484–97.

————1989. 'The Logic of Electronic Markets'. *Harvard Business Review*. 67: 166–70.

Meier, J., and Sprague, R. H. 1991. 'The Evolution of Interoganizational Systems'. *Journal of Information Technology*. 6: 184–91.

Nolan, R. L. 1979. 'Managing the Crises in Data Processing'. *Harvard Business Review*. 57: 115–26.

Powell, W. W. 1990. 'Neither Market Nor Hierarchy'. In Staw, B. M., and Cummings, L. L. (eds.). *Research in Organizational Behaviour*. 12: 295–336. Greenwich: JAI Press.

Reimers, K. 1996. 'The Non-Market Preconditions of Electronic Markets: Implications for their Evolution and Applicability'. *European Journal of Information Systems*. 5 (2): 75–83.

Short, J. E., and Venkatraman, N. 1992. 'Beyond Business Process Redesign: Redefining Baxter's Business Network'. *Sloan Management Review*. 34: 7–22.

Stuckey, J., and White, D. 1993. 'When and When Not to Vertically Integrate'. *Sloan Management Review*. 34: 71–83.

Swanson, E. B., and Ramiller, N. C. 1993. 'Information Systems Research Thematics: Submissions to a New Journal'. *Information Systems Research*. 4: 299–330.

The Economist 1993. 'The Fall of Big Business'. *The Economist*. 327: 13–14.

Treece, J. B., Kerwin, K., and Dawley, H. 1995. 'Ford 2000'. *Business Week*, International Edition, 3402–732: 36–44.

Turnbull, P. W. 1986. 'Tri-Partite Interaction: The Role of Sales Subsidiaries in International Marketing'. In Turnbull, P. W., and Paliwoda, S. J. (eds.). *Research in International Marketing*. 193–212. London: Croom Helm.

Walker, G., and Poppo, L. 1991. 'Profit Centres, Single-Source Suppliers, and Transaction Costs'. *Administrative Science Quarterly*. 36: 66–87.

Wang, E. T., and Seidmann, A. 1995. 'Electronic Data Interchange: Competitive Externalities and Strategic Implementation Policies'. *Management Science*. 41 (3) (March): 401–18.

Williamson, O. E. 1991. 'Comparative Economic Organization: The Analysis of Discrete Structural Alternatives'. *Administrative Science Quarterly*. 36: 269–96.

Wrigley, C. D. 1991. 'Research on EDI: Present and Future'. The 4th International Electronic Data Interchange Conference, Bled. Slovenia, Yugoslavia, 10–11 June.

Yin, R. K. 1981. 'The Case Study Crisis, Some Answers'. *Administrative Science Quarterly*. 26: 58–65.

V

CONCLUSION

11

The Forms, Costs, and Development Dynamics of Inter-Organizational Networking

MARK EBERS AND ANNA GRANDORI

In this concluding chapter we outline some specific implications for organizational theory and practice that may be derived from the chapters assembled in this volume. At the same time, we take this opportunity to point out what we believe to be some important issues for the further development of the field of inter-organizational network analysis. With regard to theoretical implications, we begin by returning to an issue discussed in the Introduction, namely the conceptualization and characterization of inter-organizational networks. A summary of the general explanatory argument for the formation of inter-organizational networks, as suggested by the chapters of this volume, follows. We then move on to discuss what we perceive to be two important yet under-researched areas in the study of inter-organizational networking, namely the possible costs and dynamics of networking. We end this concluding chapter by highlighting a number of practical implications that may be derived from the research reported in this book.

The field of network research is characterized by a high degree of theoretical and conceptual heterogeneity. The chapters of this volume to some extent reflect this heterogeneity. Nevertheless, despite their obvious differences, the chapters also share some important commonalities and implications that are worthwhile pointing out. In this section, we wish to concentrate on some conclusions that straddle the boundaries of different theories applied to the study of inter-organizational networks. The conclusions might therefore be of relevance for researchers irrespective of their particular theoretical orientation.

A RELATIONAL PERSPECTIVE ON NETWORK FORMATIONS

When analysing the formation of inter-organizational networks, the chapters of this volume all highlight the importance of studying the nature of the ties that link organizations. This does not come as a surprise, of course, because establishing and exploiting ties is what networking is all about. However, the chapters of this volume seem to suggest clearly distinguishing two levels of ties that may link organizations: ties at an institutional level, usually conceptualized as organizational forms, and ties at a more micro-analytic, transactional level. With regard to the former, the chapters seem to indicate the potential fruitfulness of a more fine-grained conceptualization of organizational forms of networking; with regard to the latter, the chapters suggest that they may be conducive to explaining network formations. In the following, we discuss both points subsequently.

Conceptualizing Network Formations in Relational Terms

In inter-firm network research, there has been a dominant tendency to conceptualize networks as a distinct type of organizing economic exchange, to be added to the two traditional forms of markets and hierarchies (Thompson *et al.* 1991). This way of conceiving inter-organizational networks seems to be shared by the two main alternative views and definitions of networks that have been rival perspectives in other respects. A first view, often rooted in transaction cost economics, interprets networks as an intermediate or hybrid organizational form in which some features of both markets and hierarchies are present. This perspective tends to suggest a fairly wide definition of networks. It includes any intermediate form between a market and an integrated firm: from bilateral to trilateral to multilateral governance, and from formal to informal agreements (Bradach and Eccles 1989; Osborn and Baughn 1990; McKechnie 1994; Chapter 7, this volume). A second view, diffused in the studies on networks in many areas of business administration, considers inter-firm networking as a 'third' organizational form with its own distinctive features, different from those of markets and hierarchies. In contrast to the first perspective, it tends to define networks more narrowly. This is due to the fact that its proponents try to identify organizational traits of networking that are neither typical of markets nor of hierarchies. Such traits are said to include peer group joint decision-making, reciprocal, preferential, mutually supportive actions, trust, and informal, extra-contractual agreements (Håkansson and Snehota 1995; Powell 1990; Chapter 5, this volume).

Both views, however, seem to offer a rather limited view of the variety of network forms that can be found in practice and are described in network research. This may be due to the fact that both lack a more fine-grained analysis of the mechanisms by which the activities of organizations within networks are co-ordinated, be they distinctive for networks or not. One way of trying to achieve such a refinement in the conceptualization (and subsequently explanation) of different forms of inter-organizational networking would be to focus on the relationships or ties among firms, specifically on the resource, information, and activity flows or interdependencies, and to analyse how these are governed. The studies that appeared in this book (as well as other EMOT papers on networks) show that a wide variety of co-ordination mechanisms are employed within networking arrangements. They include at least the following:

- direct mutual adjustment among two or more parties through joint decision-making on a parity basis and without explicit contractual protections and certifications (Dalum 1993; Schrader 1991; Chapter 2, this volume);
- adjustment and co-ordination supported by third parties without authority, in a transversal intermediating and mediating role similar to that played by liaison and integration roles in internal organization (Chapters 7 and 9, this volume; McEvily and Zaheer 1995);
- delegation, in various degrees, of co-ordination and control tasks to central authorities and structures (e.g. through information pooling and central planning, inspection and supervision, operational policy and decision-making); this delegation can be both informal, as realized in some local networks of firms (Chapter 3, this volume; Lorenzoni and Ornati 1988; Lorenzoni and Baden-Fuller 1995), or more formal, as in authority- or agency-based contractual forms such as franchising networks (Chapter 8, this volume; Rubin 1978; Pilotti and Pozzana 1990);
- the institutionalization of inter-firm systems of rules and procedures, be it formally (through their incorporation into contracts), or informally (through shared social norms and routines); these shared rules and procedures seem to perform an important regulatory function at the intermediate level between the external public law system and the internal rule systems of firms (Brusco 1982; Chapters 5 and 7, this volume; Stinchcombe 1990);
- the use of bilateral or multilateral systems of guarantee and safeguarding via incentives and resource commitments (e.g. hostages, pawns, securities), rather than via supervision, defined both in contractual or extra-contractual ways (de Laat 1996; Williamson 1983);
- the creation of incentive architectures through dividing, in various combinations, the 'bundle of property rights' among different firms (e.g. the rights to buy and sell assets or shares, rights to residual rewards, rights to decide upon resource uses, and rights to monitor and control); these incentive architectures are capable of generating co-operative behaviour in otherwise hazardous activity links (Jensen and Meckling 1976; Daems 1983; Grandori 1995).

Focusing on co-ordination mechanisms, we could develop a somewhat different and more fine-grained conceptualization of networks and various forms of networking, as compared with those anchored to the two extreme ideal types of markets and hierarchical firms (Alter and Hage 1993; Grandori and Soda 1995). Moreover, this conceptualization can be theoretically fruitful. This is because it allows us to draw on the extensive pool of knowledge that has been accumulated in the organizational literature with regard to the antecedents and consequences of various co-ordination mechanisms. Let us discuss these potential benefits in turn.

First, the proposed differentiation could enable us to describe and distinguish more precisely from an organizational point of view a variety of forms of networking that heretofore have been regarded as distinct on the basis of practice or law. Take, for example, the divergent and not always precisely defined forms of joint ventures. We could distinguish those joint ventures that involve only a sharing of rights over rewards (as is often the case in joint venture contracts for regulating joint participation in international auctions) from those ventures that involve shared ownership of assets (as in some joint technological development projects); and we could further refine these and other conceptualizations of joint venture forms by specifying how decision and control rights are distributed among the partners, and which forms of managerial co-ordination are employed.

Secondly, this conceptual exercise seems to be useful especially if we are interested in the assessment and prediction of which forms of networking may produce which results under which circumstances. On a theoretical and more general basis, we know reasonably well how to predict the successful application of specific co-ordination mechanisms, at least along dimensions such as those employed for constructing the above list of co-ordination mechanisms. They include, for example, the degree of centralization of decision-making and control, degree of centralization of property rights, degree of formalization, degree of routinization and institutionalization of co-ordination. Furthermore, there is considerable organizational research that spells out the conditions for the effective application of various co-ordination mechanisms. It is known, for example, when the use of authority and arbitration is likely to be more or less effective than peer group or negotiated co-ordination; when governance through rules and routines is more attractive than any system of governance based on case-by-case decision-making; when formalization of contracts and/or private agreements supports informal understandings; and it is known when the nature of activities and interdependencies requires governance through the design of incentives and the reallocation of property rights. This general organizational knowledge could be usefully applied to the analysis and design of inter-organizational relationships if the structures and processes of networking were defined in an appropriate theory-based fashion.

Thirdly, the development of a conceptualization of network forms on the basis of inter-firm co-ordination mechanisms can also help us understand the antecedents and predictors of the emergence of inter-organizational networks. A core research question in this respect can be: which configurations of flows of resources, expectations, and information can be effectively governed by what configurations of co-ordination mechanisms? With regard to their conceptualization, the analytic elements of this question have received unequal attention up until now. As to co-ordination mechanisms, some types have been better operationalized and used more extensively in empirical research than others. Namely, co-ordination mechanisms based on concerted decision-making and control have been operationalized and disaggregated in a more fine-grained way than the mechanisms that are based on the design of property rights and incentives. A consolidated view of ownership as a trait seems to prevail in network studies. In this view, ownership can either be present or absent; operationalizations thus are restricted to discrete binary terms (e.g. equity or non-equity alliances, unilateral or shared ownership). More differentiated treatments of ownership could contribute to more refined analyses. As to the types of interdependence generated by the flows of resources, expectations, and information, it seems that a major effort is required that aims at modelling what the salient configurations might be. Such efforts might fruitfully draw on some of the relevant dimensions that have been specified and widely used in earlier network research, for example:

- the direction and intensity of resource flows (Alter and Hage 1993);
- technology and the economies of scale, scope, and learning (Cantwell forthcoming);
- the complexity of information and the specificity of resources (Colombo forthcoming); and
- the levels of risk involved and the capacity of actors to predict their transaction partners' propensity towards opportunism (Nooteboom 1996).

Explaining Network Formations in Relational Terms

As was just outlined, the literature on inter-organizational networking, with some notable exceptions (Aldrich and Whetten 1981; Håkansson and Snehota 1995), has often tended to conceptualize the ties linking organizations at the rather aggregate level of organizational forms. Some research, often anchored in strategic management, then sought to explain these organizational forms of networking and their various outcomes by referring to the characteristics, intentions, aspirations, or situation of participating actors and organizations (e.g. Contractor and Lorange 1988; Jarillo 1993). Other researchers, often applying transaction cost or resource dependence theory, focused instead on attributes of the resource linkages among organizations when seeking to explain different forms of networking (e.g. Alter and Hage 1993; Larson 1992; Pisano 1989). The chapters of the present volume often tend to combine both lines of reasoning. They seek to explain the forms of inter-organizational networking not by the characteristics of the individual organizations and their members alone but also by what goes on *between* the organizations, that is, by characteristics of some lower-level ties among organizations. Since the latter aspect was somewhat less comprehensively developed in the individual chapters, we shall concentrate on it in what follows.

Although individual chapters only focused on one or two kinds of lower-level ties, taken together they in different ways suggest and indeed demonstrate that researchers and practitioners might better understand the formation of inter-organizational networks if they analyse three kinds of ties that exist between organizations:

(1) the *flows of resources and activity links* that lead to interdependencies among organizations, which in particular conditions might best be managed through specific forms of inter-organizational networking;

(2) the *flows of mutual expectations* among organizational actors that influence actors' perceptions of the opportunities and risks of collaboration and thus significantly shape the organization of the emerging inter-organizational network; and

(3) the *information flows* that influence the actors' perceptions and guide their decisions and actions with regard to the form and content of inter-organizational networking.

The chapters suggest that characteristics of these lower-level ties among organizations can help to explain which aggregate-level ties, namely different organizational forms of an inter-organizational networking, organizations will realize. One important benefit of this approach is that it applies a truly relational perspective, in which lower-level inter-organizational ties or relations are used to explain higher-level ones. This seems quite appropriate for network studies. Moreover, as was indicated in the preceding section, the more micro-level perspective allows us to systematically relate network research to that earlier organizational literature which has taught us a lot about, for example, the organizational implications of resource interdependencies, informational complexity, and uncertainty.

However, we should note that none of the three kinds of inter-organizational ties that are highlighted in this book is entirely new to the field. Earlier studies have focused on the role of resource interdependencies, trust, and catalysts for networking. We are quick to add that this book has offered neither a complete nor a systematic test of whether these three kinds of ties indeed represent important building blocks for a theory of inter-organizational network formation. Yet the chapters did point out in respect of each of the three kinds of ties, specific properties or conditions that might lead to and shape the formation of inter-organizational networks. A more complete analysis of the role of these ties for networking, however, would also require the identification of features of the ties that might prevent the formation of lasting inter-organizational relationships. Moreover, this book has little to say about the possible significance of other kinds of micro-level ties.

Despite these reservations, we believe that this volume as a whole does underscore the importance of considering the three kinds of ties when analysing the formation of inter-organizational relationships. This claim receives support from the evidence presented in the individual chapters. Perhaps paradoxically at first sight, a further credit to this claim might be derived from the fact that the chapters are so different. They are grounded in different theoretical research traditions, are based on studies of different forms of networking, at different points in time, in different industries and settings. However, at their conceptual core they nevertheless centre on the three above-mentioned kinds of ties.

This observation leads us to two conclusions, one with regard to theory and one substantive. First, despite their important differences, the theories applied to the analysis of inter-organizational networking seem in some respects to be more in agreement and more congruent than the theoretical debates often convey. This should encourage debate across theoretical boundaries. Secondly, the flows of resources and activities, expectations and information among organizations apparently represent important dimensions of, and seem to play a prominent role for, the structuring and functioning of inter-organizational networks. Of course, the core concepts of resource and activity links, mutual expectations and information flows are all too general and need further refinement and specification. Yet the chapters of this volume seem to indicate that these concepts might be fit to take on the role of beacons in the sea of network analysis, pointing out useful avenues along which future research could fruitfully travel and develop.

As the Introduction and this volume as a whole have outlined, the literature on inter-organizational networking has identified a number of important predictors both of the emergence of inter-organizational networks and of different institutional forms of networking. Despite considerable achievements, a number of open issues nevertheless remain to be tackled by research (see Kanter and Eccles 1992; Nohria 1992; Parkhe 1993; Salancik 1995). In the following, we shall draw attention to and discuss two such issues, which in our view have not so far received the attention they deserve, namely specific costs of networking and network dynamics.

THE COSTS OF NETWORKING

A heretofore neglected yet important area of research concerns the analysis of the specific costs that come with inter-organizational networking. Research has revealed a lot about the reasons and motives that firms may have for engaging in inter-organizational networking. As outlined in the Preface to this volume, the literature particularly stresses the advantages that specific forms of networking may possess over other solutions, for example vertical integration or arm's-length market relationships (Jarillo

1993; Lorenzoni and Baden-Fuller 1995; Miles and Snow 1986; Ohmae 1989). Yet networking clearly also comes at a cost. Some of these costs have been noted in the literature. Transaction costs of networking have received considerable attention (Hennart 1991; Kogut 1988a); in addition the 'costs' induced by the potential erosion of competitive position that firms may experience in many forms of networking have also been addressed (Jarillo 1993; Porter and Fuller 1986). Nevertheless, more comprehensive analyses of the internal governance costs of networking are still lacking. In a comparative analysis of the efficiency of networking, these should be adequately considered and compared to the advantages that can be achieved through inter-organizational networking. In addition, the obvious but highly neglected costs of networking in terms of negative externalities should be included in analyses as well as the possible positive side-effects of networking on third parties. It seems to us that without such analyses, the appraisal of different forms of networking remains incomplete. We thus stress the need for more studies that inform us about the far-reaching intended and unintended consequences of networking practices both for those actors involved and for third parties.

Internal Costs of Networking

The internal costs of inter-organizational networking are those costs that the parties to a network have to bear for establishing, maintaining, and managing their inter-organizational relationships. In a rather general way, we can regard these costs as transaction costs, such as information costs, bargaining costs, the costs of safeguarding against possible opportunistic behaviour by networking partners, or conflict resolution costs. In line with transaction cost theorizing, most research to date has focused on the transaction costs that are induced by investments in specific assets and/or by conditions of uncertainty. Other cost categories, however, that are not related to coping with (possible) opportunistic partner behaviour and/or uncertainty, have largely escaped our attention.

First, as Ring (1994) points out, establishing an inter-organizational networking relationship may involve some hidden, longer-term 'costs' of contracting. For example, when firms rely on outside attorneys to negotiate a contract intended to govern their inter-organizational relations, managers to some extent forgo an opportunity to explore face to face their networking partners' intentions, abilities, and interpretations of the deal. This may produce information deficits that in the course of the trading relationship can then impede learning, effective collaboration, and can lead to costly conflict. Secondly, when designing their relationship, transaction partners not only incur costs in order to deal with (possible) detrimental conditions, such as uncertainty and potential partner opportunism, but also to try to increase the benefits from their inter-organizational relationship. Let us give some pertinent examples: networking partners may invest in new com-puter systems in order to reduce reaction times and stocks; they may mutu-ally adjust their reporting systems in order to reduce conflict and improve the quality of their joint decision-making; they may accommodate their operating standards and procedures for more efficient linking of their activ-ities; they may hire new personnel specifically for managing the partner interfaces; or alliance partners may invest in personnel development pro-grammes in order to bridge their cultural differences and to communicate more effectively. All these activities, and others besides, incur costs that should be taken into account and contrasted with the benefits achieved when evaluating the relative advantage of alternative forms of networking.

Why is it that researchers so far have devoted only very little attention to the costs that are generally associated with the management of net-working relationships? This neglect may be for at least two reasons. First, a large part of research on inter-organizational networking is based on a transaction cost perspective. While this theory has a lot to say about possi-ble market failures, its analyses of the internal workings of organizations and associated costs are less well developed (see, however, Masten *et al.* 1991). Moreover, transaction cost theory does not analyse possible trans-action benefits (and the costs for achieving them) because it compares gov-ernance costs for a *given* transaction thus holding constant the value of a transaction for the parties (Dietrich 1993; Zajac and Olsen 1993). Secondly, the literature is largely silent on the management tools that firms may employ for managing their inter-organizational networking relationships. These tools include, for example, planning systems, budgets, negotiation and bargaining, accounting and reporting, programmes, or inter-organizational information systems. When the management tools and management activ-ities are not discussed, the associated costs will also go unrecognized.

External Costs of Networking

Joint ventures, consortia, franchising, and inter-firm associations may be favourable for the firms involved, but detrimental to those not party to the networking arrangement. Possible negative consequences for other firms or for consumers, that is the negative externalities of networking, are often due to the increases in concentration and collusion that are effected by inter-organizational networking. A striking example of negative externalities of inter-organizational networking may be that of the coalitions that con-struction and engineering firms form through consortia or joint venture contracts in order to win bidding auctions for job assignment (Soda and Usai 1996). Such contracts are usually signed among firms that entertain tight informal links and have co-operated in the past. Through this recip-rocal co-operative process, the firms involved create strong entry barriers for potential competitors. A further consequence of this anti-competitive behaviour is that efficiency considerations are less likely to decide the bidding process. As a result, the cost–benefit ratios for clients and consumers are likely to decrease.

Of course, networks may also have positive effects for third parties or the efficiency of an economic system as a whole. Such positive network externalities can be achieved, for example, if pooling resources allows the players to reach minimum economies of scale, stabilizes economic environmental conditions, and thus allows for more informed investment decisions, reduces the risk of mis-investment through joint strategizing (Bower and Rhenman 1985), or creates technological spillovers (Peters and Becker 1998).

Again, the relative neglect of possible positive and negative externalities of inter-organizational networking by earlier research may stem from the particular theoretical perspectives that have inspired pertinent research. Research in management and organization has focused mainly on the advantages of networking for a set of interdependent firms. This literature has thus tended to cast alliances in the positive light of a shift from competition to co-operation. Moreover, the organizational focus of these approaches has led them to consider only the firms involved, and thus to overlook the possible effects outside the focal system of actors. Whereas orthodox economics, applying a systems view and being sensitive towards general welfare issues, has often tended to view networks rather sceptically as departures from the ideal state of perfect competition. This literature has thus played down the possible gains in cost efficiency that networking can generate for the economic system.

Clearly, therefore, we need a more balanced evaluation of network forms and pertinent economic regulation (Jorde and Teece 1989). To this end, we need tools that help us estimate and compare the various external costs of networking and the welfare benefits of co-ordinated action by competitors. This surely is a challenging and difficult task, especially because the various categories of network costs and benefits pertain to different actors. Therefore simple trade-off models that 'balance' costs and benefits in additive terms would not be appropriate. Game-theoretic or negotiation-analytic models could perhaps offer fruitful alternatives for tackling these issues.

THE SIGNIFICANCE OF NETWORK DYNAMICS AND DEVELOPMENTS

As with the literature on organizations, that on inter-organizational networking is dominated by comparative static analyses.[1] Calls and specific

---

[1] Inter-organizational network studies that highlight developmental and process issues are relatively rare. While some useful conceptual frameworks have been suggested (D'Aunno and Zuckerman 1987; Dwyer *et al.* 1987; Ring and Van de Ven 1994), empirical research is still largely lacking (see, however, Gadde and Mattsson 1987; Gulati 1995; Van de Ven and Walker 1984).

suggestions for complementing this research by longitudinal, process-oriented studies abound (Abbott 1990; Kimberly 1976; Monge 1990; Parkhe 1993; Van de Ven and Huber 1990; Van de Ven and Poole 1995). Therefore, we do not need to reiterate here the potential merits and general possibilities of longitudinal analyses and process studies. Rather, in the following we would like to address two specific, less often examined questions: for which inherent reasons and for which issues does longitudinal research on inter-organizational networking seem particularly necessary and important? We shall argue that there are more powerful reasons for dynamic analyses of the formation and transformation of networks over time in the case of inter-organizational networking than of individual organizations.

In a nutshell, our argument goes as follows (Ebers 1999). Inter-organizational networking is subject to dynamic evolution because over time the forms, outcomes, and actors' evaluations of inter-organizational networking change due to inherent development processes. The dynamics driving these development processes originate, we submit, in the specific outcomes of networking. These outcomes change over time the (pre-)conditions for networking. Through processes of revaluation, learning, and adaptation, they may thus lead to adjustments, and sometimes the termination, of the originally implemented ties and forms of inter-organizational networking. The development dynamic thus has the structure of a feedback loop. Below we shall present specific reasons for why we suspect that these feedback loops and the resulting development dynamics play a significant role in inter-organizational networking. We conclude that the forms of inter-organizational networking should be considered as inherently dynamic, as opposed to static, forms. Finally, we outline some implications for research.

At least for some forms of inter-organizational networking, the instability of organizational forms has been confirmed empirically. A number of studies have found for joint ventures that between 25 and 50 per cent of those studied were unstable, that is, significantly changed their ownership structures (see the summary by Kogut 1988*a*). The studies explained this instability either in terms of some sort of negative outcome of the relationships, for example, inter-partner conflict or bad joint venture performance, or in terms of problematic initial set-up conditions, for example, a high degree of partner rivalry or declining industry conditions (Kogut 1989). Instability of network forms in this view is thus chiefly the result of a process of weeding out ill-designed solutions that from their inception were doomed to fail.

Two further explanations may, however, also play a role. They both trace back the relative instability of forms of networking to the often temporary character of such arrangements. First, some networking relationships are explicitly chosen as temporary arrangements for achieving specific ends, for example, the development of a specific product component. Upon achieving their goals, the networking partners dissolve the inter-organizational arrangement (Harrigan 1985). Secondly, firms sometimes deliberately use a network form of organizing as a stepping-stone towards a future solution, that is, as an intermediary form of organizing. Corning Inc., for example, included its medical diagnostics business in a joint venture with Ciba-Geigy in order to be able to more profitably and more easily spin off this business in the long run. By forming a joint venture, rather than spin off the business immediately, Corning had more opportunity to convince Ciba-Geigy as the potential (and eventual) buyer of the value of the business. Furthermore, Corning's employees through the joint venture had a better opportunity of keeping their jobs and had a smoother transition to a new employer than otherwise; in this way, Corning could dodge internal labour unrest for the pertinent division and the company as a whole (Nanda and Bartlett 1990).

In addition to these circumstances, we argue, the instability of inter-organizational relationships that one can observe might to some extent also be traced back to the 'natural' evolution of originally well-designed and 'healthy' networking arrangements that their creators had intended to last for some extended period of time. We thus wish to draw attention to the possibility that the forms of networking may typically change and develop due to some inherent evolutionary forces. As mentioned above, we characterize these evolutionary forces as outcome-driven feedback loops.

What are the possible outcomes of inter-organizational networking that may in turn change the (pre-)conditions for networking and thus drive the evolution of inter-organizational networking relationships? Again, it seems useful to classify these outcomes according to the core concepts applied throughout this volume. Accordingly, we shall highlight in the following some outcomes that are related to changes in organizational actors' resource base, changes in the actors' information base, and changes in the actors' expectations of their network partners' behaviour and actions.

Changes in Actors' Resource Base

Inter-organizational networking relationships are often explicitly created to exploit differences in the resource bases of partners (Contractor and Lorange 1988; Geringer 1988; Hill and Hellriegel 1994). In international joint ventures for foreign market entry, to use a familiar example, one of the partners might possess an attractive product but lacks local market know-how or access to distribution channels. A local firm might in turn be able to provide these latter resources but would like to be able to offer to its customers an additional attractive product that it cannot supply on its own. While in the beginning, given specific conditions (see Hennart 1991; Kogut 1988*a*), a joint venture might be comparatively the best organizational form for the provision of the foreign product to the local market, the scales may turn over the course of the relationship. For example, the foreign partner may learn the ropes of the local market. After some time, this partner may have acquired the contacts and skills and may have earned the reputation to be able to successfully penetrate the foreign market without the help of a local partner company. Likewise, the local partner in the course of the relationship may acquire product-related know-how that enables the company to produce and market a competing product. By exploiting the differences among their original resource endowments and achieving their individual goals for the joint venture, the joint venture partners may thus set in motion a dynamic that lays the foundation for and indeed produces the termination of their relationship. This is due to the fact that as an outcome of the joint venture both partners reduce the diversity of their resource bases and thus gradually destroy the foundations on which their relationship rests. Such development processes have been reported, for example, not only for international joint ventures but also for product development and production joint ventures (Beamish and Inkpen 1995; Duerr 1992; Earl 1992; Kogut 1988*b*).

Changes in Actors' Information Base

When dealing with their networking partners, actors will gradually gain better information about, for example, their partners' competencies, capabilities, intentions, needs, and limits. Clearly, the kind of change that better information induces with regard to a given networking relationship will vary, other things being equal, with the type and content of information. A number of studies provide pertinent evidence. Dubois and Håkansson, for example, have pointed out in this volume that with better knowledge of their partners' resources and capabilities, it becomes easier for firms to detect more (and less) effective or efficient activity links, to restructure their relationships accordingly, and to learn about opportunities for forging new ties. Luetz (this volume) has outlined in considerable detail how new pieces of information on competitors' capabilities that emerged in the networking relationship changed the game structure for the participants. This in turn significantly altered the forms in which actors interacted in the technology development project towards greater and more intensive collaboration. Earl (1992) likewise describes for three alliances in the Australian automotive industry, how growing experience with one another led the companies to change over time the contents and the forms of their original relationships. The longitudinal study by Gulati (1995) underscores in a different way the important role that changes in actors' information base play in the formation of inter-organizational relationships. His research reveals that firms with a history of past alliances ally with each other more repeatedly than firms with no such history, though at diminishing rates. Gulati moreover found an inverted U-shaped relationship between the time that had elapsed since the last alliance between two firms and the likelihood of their forming a new alliance. Parkhe (1991) suggests that growing familiarity with regard to communication style, core values, or other cultural traits may lubricate social interaction among the managers of alliance partners and foster mutual adaptation and learning; whereas the discovery of greater goal differences and cultural diversity among partners may lead to the premature termination of a relationship. In sum, this research demonstrates that, due to the interactions of networking partners, their information bases are likely to change over the course of a relationship, something which then often has repercussions for the structuring and functioning of this inter-organizational relationship.

Changes in Actors' Expectations

As was just outlined, over time network partners gain additional information on their partners' abilities, motives, and actions. Sometimes, as Earl (1992) notes, organizations may deliberately take on limited commitments in order to test their partners' reliability and intentions; at other times organizations wait and see whether their expectations about partner behaviour were accurate or not. As a result of novel information and revised (or confirmed) expectations among actors, the structuring and functioning of a particular networking relationship will gradually change. The process model of the formation of entrepreneurial networks proposed by Larson (1992), and her case studies, provide more detailed descriptions of the relevant processes.

With regard to trust among networking partners, for example, the perceived outcomes of trusting behaviour towards another party (favourable or unfavourable) will influence actors' expectations for the next interaction with that party. Depending on the perceived outcomes, actors' growing experience with one another can thus either lead to an increase in mutual trust or result in the build-up of distrust among partners. As a result of their changing perceptions and expectations of their partners' trustworthiness, firms will adapt the contents and/or the form of their inter-organizational relationships. Ring (Chapter 5) has outlined the formal and informal processes as well as some conditions in which trust among partners may develop (see also Mayer *et al.* 1995). As de Laat (Chapter 6) has argued, trust among partners may be fostered over time, for example by credible commitments that are perceived to be reciprocated. Whereas the continued application of the instruments of classical contracting and conscious monitoring are likely to induce distrust and possibly opportunistic behaviour (Chapter 6, this volume; Van de Ven and Walker 1984; Williamson 1993). When trust increases, joint action is more likely, as the study by Zaheer and Venkatraman (1995) has shown. Henceforth, the partners may also be ready to take on more risky joint projects together without changing the agreed governance structure; or they may (informally) agree not to invoke and use the more formal measures and procedures originally devised for governing their relationship. In their day-to-day working relationship they may, for example, rely less than before on formally agreed *ex ante* or *ex post* safeguards intended to deter partner opportunism (Ring and Van de Ven 1994). Instead, partners may turn to more informal means of co-ordination and co-operation, as the case described by Luetz (Chapter 9) illustrates.

From the above observations we conclude that inter-organizational networking may display some important inherent development dynamics that need to be recognized and studied by research. We suggested that these inherent dynamics originate in changes in actors' resource bases, their information bases, and expectations that are the very outcomes of an unfolding inter-organizational relationship. As a result of these dynamics and the associated feedback processes, the different forms of inter-organizational networking, for inherent reasons, may be less stable forms of organizing business transactions than, say, the different forms of organizing an individual firm. We do not wish to convey, however, that the forms of inter-organizational networking always have to change in response to the evolutionary forces noted above. It might well sometimes be the case that partners do *not* adapt the structures and practices of their networking arrangement, although specific outcomes of networking have changed the partners' needs, evaluations, and the relative advantage of alternative forms of networking. That is, as individual organizations, inter-organizational relationships may well be subject to organizational inertia. Nevertheless, without a sense of the dynamic evolution of inter-organizational networking, a case of inertia, particularly the outcomes of the networking relationship, may not be well understood. Notwithstanding the possibility of organizational inertia, the proposed development dynamics of inter-organizational networking thus seem a worthwhile area of study.

Beyond a renewed call for more longitudinal studies, the inherent dynamics and potential generic instability of different forms of inter-organizational networking also have implications for comparative static research. For one thing, research should reconsider the measures of success and performance that are used. In view of the dynamics outlined above, it would clearly be misleading in quite a few cases to use the longevity of an organizational arrangement as an indicator of success. Furthermore, if the forms of inter-organizational networking change over time, the point in time at which success is assessed becomes crucial. Take, for example, the above mentioned Corning–Ciba-Geigy case. Of course, Corning had not announced its intentions of eventually spinning off the division when it formed the joint venture with Ciba-Geigy. Had a researcher therefore measured (by whichever indicators) the success of the Corning–Ciba joint venture before Ciba-Geigy took full control, he or she would most likely have captured only part of the relevant goals and would have underrated the degree of Corning's goal achievement. Or the example of the research collaboration described by Luetz (Chapter 9) could have been declared a complete failure (as it was by some of the participants) after it had become clear that none of the partners had possessed the necessary know-how and true research collaboration was not (yet) in sight. In the long run, however, the project did deliver. One important reason why the results of cross-sectional studies may be misleading in such cases, is that these studies typically assume that all adjustment processes have been completed by the time of the research. It is therefore not only the point in time at which success or failure are measured which is crucial for obtaining sound results. The time perspective is also of relevance with regard to the organizational forms of networking that research intends to explain. If organizational decision-makers, for example, design structures for some expected future conditions, correlations of present conditions and present solutions will neither reflect the quality of the decision nor do they seem appropriate for testing theoretical propositions. The same holds true in cases of (inter-)organizational inertia. Researchers should therefore be careful to design cross-sectional studies which take into account these temporal aspects. This is surely a formidable, yet also a much needed and potentially rewarding task.

IMPLICATIONS FOR PRACTICE

This volume certainly is more research- than practice-oriented in character. Nevertheless, the papers do provide several important insights for the practical management of inter-organizational networking relationships. Three practical conclusions will be highlighted in the following: these pertain to the rationales for inter-organizational networking, partner choice decisions, and the design of inter-organizational relationships.

Obviously, there have to be clear gains from collaboration before firms will decide to form a networking relationship rather than rely on their own strengths or arm's-length market relations. These gains, as the papers have shown, can come from different sources. Dubois and Håkansson (Chapter 2), for example, have stressed how firms may exploit scale and scope economies by streamlining their inter-organizational ties. Easton and Araujo (Chapter 3) have pointed out that through networking organizations can attain the flexibility to successfully cope with heterogeneous demand over time. The informational benefits associated with information technological links among companies are emphasized by Holland and Lockett (Chapter 10). Finally, the case described by Luetz (Chapter 9) exemplifies how a network can be used by weaker partners (in her case the car suppliers) to collude and thus enhance bargaining power *vis-à-vis* major industry players.

From the research presented in this volume we may also derive insights for supporting partner-choice decisions for networking. Several papers have pointed to important dimensions of partner fit. While Dubois and Håkansson would call for a strategic match of the partners, the research by Luetz emphasizes the significance of a cognitive match. The benefits of a cultural match are nicely illustrated by Casson and Cox with reference to the example of late Victorian English institutions. However, the papers also point out that it would clearly be too one-sided a view if one interpreted partner fit as choosing partners almost identical to oneself. While in some cases partnering among organizations of similar orientations, strategies, and capabilities may be beneficial, in other cases partner variety and diversity may be crucial for success. For example, as the chapters by Dubois and Håkansson, Lipparini and Sobrero, as well as Luetz illustrate, partner diversity may be particularly important when network formation aims at learning and innovation.

In line with earlier literature, several chapters of this volume stress that successful networking depends significantly on choosing trustworthy partners. Establishing *ex ante* the trustworthiness of potential partners, however, seems no less difficult than selecting the right 'match' of partners. Nevertheless, some authors have offered potentially helpful clues. Ring has identified and described the relevant formal and informal processes in which trustworthiness can be probed (and possibly established). The chapters by Casson and Cox as well as by Lipparini and Sobrero highlight a more indirect approach. They point out that a potential partner's social embeddedness and background may provide important information for inferring partners' possible interests and trustworthiness.

With regard to the design of inter-organizational networking relationships, the research emphasized that it is too limited a view to focus only on price, authority, and trust when devising governance mechanisms for inter-organizational relationships. Rather, networking can take many forms because, as we have outlined above, a wider variety of co-ordination mechanisms are available and may be employed to allow and support effective and efficient collaboration among networking partners. Network design on this view would thus entail the choice of appropriate co-ordination mechanisms for the collaborative execution of particular tasks. Although comprehensive modelling and research is still lacking, the chapters of this volume suggest that the design of networking relationships depends, among other things, on characteristics of the resource flows, information processes, and expectations among collaborators.

While some pertinent co-ordination mechanisms, such as inter-organizational information systems or joint decision-making, are well known and widely recognized, others are perhaps less obvious. With regard to the latter, several chapters stressed the possible importance of the co-ordinating roles that intermediaries may play within the formation of inter-organizational networks. Compared to other forms, intermediaries represent a more indirect means of inter-organizational co-ordination. As several chapters showed, in some cases direct co-ordination may fail or falter because it may be too difficult, too costly, or too risky to deal directly with particular exchange partners. Firms can then nevertheless engage in such deals if they use third parties that act as interlocutors, catalysts, or brokers. With regard to this theme, Casson and Cox highlight why and how trusted brokers may foster the establishment of inter-organizational ties. Luetz shows that trusted brokers may also be important catalysts for conflict resolution. And Lipparini and Sobrero describe how partnering with firms assuming entrepreneurial and leadership roles may nurture more radical innovation. The use of intermediaries, in various respects, thus represents an important design option for networking relationships.

The chapters of this volume also imply that the design of inter-organizational networking relationships should be recognized as an ongoing task. Despite the costs involved, it should not be regarded as completed after an initial contract and relationship structure have been devised. Several chapters showed that due to inherent development dynamics alone, not to mention possible external shocks, inter-organizational networking relationships undergo changes over time that require a revaluation and possibly redesign even of good relationships. De Laat (Chapter 6), for example, reminds us to carefully consider the development dynamics that might be set in motion by overly careful, risk-averting network design decisions. Ring (Chapter 5) conversely argues that investments into sense-making, understanding, and committing can pay off in the long run, because through these processes economic actors build (and later benefit from) trust in their networking relationships. By a careful consideration of these and other development dynamics that have been outlined above, networking partners can appraise the possible development of their inter-organizational relations over time. In this way, they can perhaps improve the quality of their design and policy decisions, may be in a better position to make timely adjustments, and may thus profit more from their inter-organizational networking activities.

The above thoughts seem to suggest that networking relationships are not a standard organizational solution that is devised according to the current circumstances, implemented, and then simply administered. Rather, such forms of organizing require permanent management attention and action. These requirements should, however, not only be viewed as a cost factor. Certainly there can be considerable costs involved, as we have tried to argue in this conclusion. Yet managers and their organizations should be aware that these costs are incurred in order to reap the full benefits of networking. Managers have to be ready to regularly analyse, appraise, and possibly revalue existing inter-organizational ties and networking relationships; otherwise important benefits of these forms of organizing—namely improved responsiveness and flexibility, more rapid and effective decision-making, and enhanced learning and innovation—cannot be achieved. However, while several chapters have outlined these and other specific outcomes of networking, we are still far from being able to offer sufficiently precise and comprehensive guidelines for the design and management of inter-organizational networks. Our knowledge of the relationships between the nature of inter-organizational ties, forms of networking, and the outcomes of networking under various contextual conditions is still not sufficiently developed. However, in our view this volume, together with the growing body of research on which it builds, has presented some evidence that suggests it might be fruitful and worthwhile for both organizational theory and practice to try and improve this state of affairs.

REFERENCES

Abbott, A. 1990. 'A Primer on Sequence Methods'. *Organization Science*. 1: 375–92.

Aldrich, H., and Whetten, D. A. 1981. 'Organization-Sets, Action-Sets, and Networks: Making the Most of Simplicity'. In Nystrom, P. C., and Starbuck, W. H. (eds.). *Handbook of Organizational Design*. I: 385–408. Oxford: Oxford University Press.

Alter, C., and Hage, J. 1993. *Organizations Working Together*. Newbury Park, Calif.: Sage.

Beamish, P. W., and Inkpen, A. C. 1995. 'Keeping International Joint Ventures Stable and Profitable'. *Long Range Planning*. 28 (3): 26–36.

Bower, L., and Rhenman, E. A. 1985. 'Benevolent Cartels'. *Harvard Business Review*. 63: 124–32.

Bradach, J., and Eccles, R. 1989. 'Markets versus Hierarchies: From Ideal Types to Plural Forms'. *Annual Review of Sociology*. 15: 97–118.

Brusco, S. 1982. 'The Emilian Model: Productive Decentralization and Social Integration'. *Cambridge Journal of Economics*. 6: 167–84.

Colombo, M. G. (ed.) 1998. *The Changing Boundaries of the Firm. Explaining Evolving Inter-Firm Relations*. London: Routledge.

Contractor, F. J., and Lorange, P. (eds.) 1988. *Cooperative Strategies in International Business*. Lexington, Mass.: Lexington Books.

D'Aunno, T. A., and Zuckerman, H. S. 1987. 'A Life-Cycle Model of Organizational Federations: The Case of Hospitals'. *Academy of Management Review*. 12: 534–45.

Daems, H. 1983. 'The Determinants of Hierarchical Organization of Industry'. In Francis, A., Turk, J., and Willman, P. (eds.). *Power, Efficiency and Institutions*: 35–53. London: Heinemann.

Dalum, B. 1993. 'North Jutland—A "Technology District" in Radiocommunications Technology?' Paper presented at the European Science Foundation EMOT Conference: 'Coping with Complexity and Diversity of Assets: Adapting to Strategic Change'. 1–2 October 1993, Strasbourg.

de Laat, P. 1996. 'Dangerous Liaisons: Sharing Knowledge within R&D Alliances'. Paper presented at the European Science Foundation EMOT Conference: 'Inter-Firm Networks: Outcomes and Policy Implications'. 6–8 September 1996, Modena.

Dietrich, M. 1993. 'Transaction Costs . . . and Revenues'. In Pitelis, C. (ed.). *Transaction Costs, Markets and Hierachies*: 166–87. Oxford: Blackwell.

Duerr, M. S. 1992. 'New United Manufacturing Inc. at Midlife: Experience of the Joint Venture'. *Research in International Business and International Relations*. 5: 193–214.

Dwyer, R. F., Schurr, P. H., and Oh, S. 1987. 'Developing Buyer-Seller Relationships'. *Journal of Marketing*. 51: 11–27.

Earl, P. E. 1992. 'The Evolution of Cooperative Strategies: Three Automotive Industry Case Studies'. *Human Systems Management*. 11: 89–100.

Ebers, M. 1999. 'The Dynamics of Inter-Organizational Relationships'. *Research in the Sociology of Organizations*. 17 (forthcoming).

Gadde, L.-E., and Mattsson, L.-G. 1987. 'Stability and Change in Network Relationships'. *International Journal of Research in Marketing*. 4: 29–41.

Geringer, J. M. 1988. *Joint Venture Partner Selection: Strategies for Developed Countries*. Westport, Conn.: Quorum Books.

Grandori, A. 1997. 'An Organizational Assessment of Inter-Firm Coordination Modes'. *Organization Studies*. 18: 897–925.

——and Soda, G. 1995. 'Inter-Firm Networks: Antecedents, Mechanisms, and Forms'. *Organization Studies*. 16: 183–214.

Gulati, R. 1995. 'Social Structure and Alliance Formation Patterns: A Longitudinal Analysis'. *Administrative Science Quarterly*. 40: 619–52.

Håkansson, H., and Snehota, I. 1995. *Business Networks*. London: Routledge.

Harrigan, K. R. 1985. *Strategies for Joint Ventures*. Lexington, Mass.: Lexington Books.

Hennart, J. F. 1991. 'The Transaction Costs Theory of Joint Ventures'. *Management Science*. 37: 483–97.

Hill, R. C., and Hellriegel, D. 1994. 'Critical Contingencies in Joint Venture Management: Some Lessons from Managers'. *Organization Science*. 5: 594–607.

Jarillo, J. C. 1993. *Strategic Networks: Creating the Borderless Organization*. Oxford: Butterworth-Heinemann.

Jensen, M. C., and Meckling, W. H. 1976. 'Theory of the Firm: Managerial Behavior, Agency Costs and Ownership Structure'. *Journal of Financial Economics*. 3: 305–60.

Jorde, T. M., and Teece, D. 1989. 'Competition and Cooperation: Striking the Right Balance'. *California Management Review*. 32 (Spring): 25–37.

Kanter, R. M., and Eccles, R. G. 1992. 'Making Network Research Relevant to Practice'. In Nohria, N., and Eccles, R. G. (eds.). *Networks and Organizations: Structure, Form, and Action*: 521–27. Boston, Mass.: Harvard Business School Press.

Kimberly, J. R. 1976. 'Issues in the Design of Longitudinal Organizational Research'. *Sociological Methods and Research*. 4: 321–47.

Kogut, B. 1988*a*. 'Joint Ventures: Theoretical and Empirical Perspectives'. *Strategic Management Journal*. 9: 319–32.

——1988*b*. 'A Study of the Life Cycle of Joint Ventures'. In Contractor and Lorange 1988: 169–85.

——1989. 'The Stability of Joint Ventures: Reciprocity and Competitive Rivalry'. *Journal of Industrial Economics*. 38: 183–98.

Larson, A. 1992. 'Network Dyads in Entrepreneurial Settings: A Study of the Governance of Exchange Relationships'. *Administrative Science Quarterly*. 37: 76–104.

Lorenzoni, G., and Baden-Fuller, C. 1995. 'Creating a Strategic Center to Manage a Web of Partners'. *California Management Review*. 37 (Spring): 146–63.

——and Ornati, O. A. 1988. 'Constellations of Firms and New Ventures'. *Journal of Business Venturing*. 3: 41–57.

McEvily, W. J. Jr., and Zaheer, A. 1995. 'The Moderating Effects of Mediators: Exploring the Role of Third Parties in Inter-Organizational Networks'. Paper presented at the European Science Foundation EMOT Conference: 'Industry Structure and Inter-Organizational Networks'. 1–2 December 1995, Geneva.

MacKechnie, G. 1994. 'A Typology of Organizational Network Designs'. Paper presented at the European Science Foundation EMOT Conference: 'Assessing Inter-Organizational Networks'. 3–4 February 1994, Jouy-en-Josas.

Masten, S. E., Meehan, J. W., and Snyder, E. A. 1991. 'The Cost of Organization'. *The Journal of Law, Economics, and Organization*. 7: 10–25.

Mayer, R. C., Davis, J. H., and Schoorman, F. D. 1995. 'An Integrative Model of Organizational Trust'. *Academy of Management Review*. 20: 709–34.

Miles, R. E., and Snow, C. C. 1986. 'Organizations: New Concepts for New Forms'. *California Management Review*. 28 (Spring): 62–73.

Monge, P. R. 1990. 'Theoretical and Analytical Issues in Studying Organizational Processes'. *Organization Science*. 1: 406–30.

Nanda, A., and Bartlett, C. A. 1990. 'Corning Incorporated: A Network of Alliances'. *Harvard Business School Case Study* (no. 9-391-102). Boston, Mass.: The President and Fellows of Harvard College.

Nohria, N. 1992. 'Is a Network Perspective a Useful Way of Studying Organizations?' In Nohria, N., and Eccles, R. G. (eds.). *Networks and Organizations: Structure, Form, and Action*: 1–22. Boston, Mass.: Harvard Business School Press.

Nooteboom, B. (1996) 'Trust, Opportunism and Governance: A Process and Control Model'. *Organization Studies*. 17: 985–1010.

Ohmae, K. 1989. 'The Global Logic of Strategic Alliances'. *Harvard Business Review*. 67 (March–April): 143–54.

Oliver, C. 1990. 'Determinants of Interorganizational Relationships: Integration and Future Directions'. *Academy of Management Review*. 15: 241–65.

Osborn, R. N., and Baughn, C. C. 1990. 'Forms of Interorganizational Governance for Multinational Alliances'. *Academy of Management Journal*. 33: 503–19.

Parkhe, A. 1991. 'Interfirm Diversity, Organizational Learning, and Longevity in Global Strategic Alliances'. *Journal of International Business Studies*. 22: 579–601.

——1993. ' "Messy" Research, Methodological Predispositions, and Theory Development in International Joint Ventures'. *Academy of Management Review*. 18: 227–68.

Peters, J., and Becker, W. 1998. 'Vertical Corporate Networks in the German Automotive Industry: Structure, Efficiency, and R&D Spill-Overs'. *International Studies of Management & Organization*. 27(4): 158–85.

Pilotti, L., and Pozzana, P. (eds.) 1990. 'I contratti di franchising: organizzazione e controllo di rete'. CESCOM Bocconi, EGEA, Milano.

Pisano, G. P. 1989. 'Using Equity Participation to Support Exchange: Evidence from the Biotechnology Industry'. *Journal of Law, Economics, and Organization*. 5: 109–26.

Porter, M. E., and Fuller, M. B. 1986. 'Coalitions and Global Strategy'. In Porter, M. E. (ed.). *Competition in Global Industries*: 315–44. Boston, Mass.: Harvard Business School Press.

Powell, W. W. 1990. 'Neither Market nor Hierarchy: Network Forms of Organization'. *Research in Organizational Behavior*. 12: 295–336.

Ring, P. S. 1994. *The Hidden Costs of Contract*. Paper presented at the Annual Meeting of the Strategic Management Society. 20–3 September, Jouy-en-Josas.

—— and Van de Ven, A. H. 1994. 'Developmental Processes of Cooperative Interorganizational Relationships'. *Academy of Management Review*. 19: 90–118.

Rubin, P. H. 1978. 'The Theory of the Firm and the Structure of the Franchise Contract'. *Journal of Law and Economics*. 21: 223–33.

Salancik, G. R. 1995. 'WANTED: A Good Network Theory of Organization'. *Administrative Science Quarterly*. 40: 345–9.

Schrader, S. 1991. 'Informal Technology Transfer between Firms: Cooperation through Information Trading'. *Research Policy*. 20: 153–70.

Soda G., and Usai A. 1996. 'Institutional Embeddedness and Interorganizational Networks in the Italian Construction Industry'. Paper presented at the European Science Foundation EMOT Conference: 'Industry Structure and Interorganizational Networks'. 1–2 December 1995, Geneva.

Stinchcombe, A. L. 1990. *Information and Organizations*. Berkeley, Calif.: University of California Press.

Thompson, G. J., Frances, J., Levacic, R., and Mitchell, J. (eds.) 1991. *Markets, Hierarchies and Networks: The Coordination of Social Life*. London: Sage.

Van de Ven, A. H., and Huber, G. P. 1990. 'Longitudinal Field Research Methods for Studying Processes of Organizational Change'. *Organization Science*. 1: 213–19.

—— and Poole, M. S. 1995. 'Explaining Development and Change in Organizations'. *Academy of Management Review*. 20: 510–40.

—— and Walker, G. 1984. 'The Dynamics of Interorganizational Coordination'. *Administrative Science Quarterly*. 29: 598–621.

Williamson, O. E. 1983. 'Credible Commitments: Using Hostages to Support Exchange'. *American Economic Review*. 73: 519–40.

—— 'Calculativeness, Trust, and Economic Organization'. *Journal of Law and Economics*. 36: 453–86.

Zaheer, A., and Venkatraman, N. 1995. 'Relational Governance as an Interorganizational Strategy: An Empirical Test of the Role of Trust in Economic Exchange'. *Strategic Management Journal*. 16: 373–92.

Zajac, E. J., and Olsen, C. P. 1993. 'From Transaction Cost to Transactional Value Analysis: Implications for the Study of Interorganizational Strategies'. *Journal of Management Studies*. 30: 131–45.

INDEX

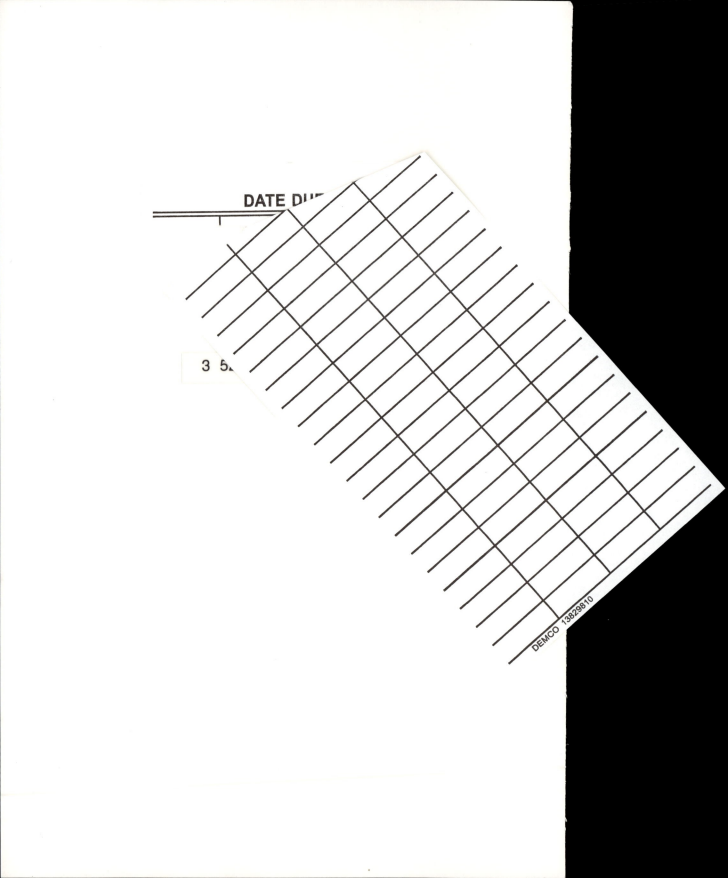

DATE DUE

3 5

DEMCO 13829810